Christmas, 1997

W9-ANF-537

The Tiger in the House

Carl Van Vechten

DOVER PUBLICATIONS, INC.
New York

Published in Canada by General Publishing Company, Ltd., 30 Lesmill Road, Don Mills, Toronto, Ontario.

Published in the United Kingdom by Constable and Company, Ltd., 3 The Lanchesters, 162–164 Fulham Palace Road, London W6 9ER.

Bibliographical Note

This Dover edition, first published in 1996, is an unaltered and unabridged republication of the third edition of the work as published by Alfred A. Knopf, Inc., New York, in 1936 (first edition: Knopf, 1920).

Library of Congress Cataloging-in-Publication Data

Van Vechten, Carl, 1880–1964.
    The tiger in the house / Carl Van Vechten.
        p.   cm.
    Originally published: 3rd ed. New York : Knopf, 1936.
    Includes bibliographical references (p.   ) and index.
    ISBN 0-486-29129-4 (pbk.)
    1. Cats—Miscellanea.   I. Title.
SF445.5.V36   1996
599.74″428—dc20   95-45906
                                                                                  CIP

Manufactured in the United States of America
Dover Publications, Inc., 31 East 2nd Street, Mineola, N.Y. 11501

FOR EDNA KENTON
AND FEATHERS

> " *How lucky to be a cat*
> *Free to accept or — refuse*
> *What is offered!* "

> *"Dieu a fait le chat pour donner à*
> *l'homme le plaisir de caresser le tigre."*
> MÉRY

An Introduction to the Third Edition

Since the publication of "The Tiger in the House" in 1920, several other books about cats have been issued. My own anthology of cat stories, "Lords of the Housetops," appeared in 1921, Richard Miller's anthology, "Just Cats" (Doubleday, Doran) in 1934, and "Puss in Books" (Geoffrey Bles; London) edited by Elizabeth Drew and Michael Joseph, in 1932. There is some duplication of material in these anthologies—"The Cat," by Mary E. Wilkins Freeman, is included in all three of them—but each volume presents a few discoveries of the compiler. The Drew-Joseph book is particularly fortunate in the inclusion of Ethel Coburn Mayne's fine story, "The Man of the House."

In 1930 Michael Joseph issued a volume called "Cat's Company," devoted to the habits and adventures of the author's own cats, and a most charming narrative it is. The illustrations, which also please me enormously, were drawn by the German artist, B. F. Dolbin. Algernon Blackwood's "Dudley and Gilderoy," the history of a cat and a parrot (Ernest Benn; London; 1929) is delightful reading and Svend Fleuron's "Kittens" (Knopf; 1922) might be regarded as the superlative of cat fiction. In my Foreword to this novel I wrote: "Grey Puss and her kittens are observed in their relations with nature. Their relations with man are recorded from their point of view rather than his. This is the new note in this authentic cat story, authentic, at least, within the limitations the author has set himself. In much of the previous fiction involving the cat, puss has been handled quite in the manner of a Ouida duchess; 'Kittens' is the feline 'Esther Waters.' "

Introduction tó the Third Edition

"The Cat in Verse," compiled by Carolyn Wells and Louella D. Everett (Little, Brown and Co.; 1935) is a more elaborate, if less selective, poetical anthology in this department than had hitherto appeared. Many of the more celebrated poems about cats are included, but there are also many new ones. M. Old-field Howey's "The Cat in the Mysteries of Religion and Magic" (Rider and Co.; n.d.) is more unusual. Typical chapter headings are Vampire Cats, The Cat as Phallic Symbol, The Cat in Chaldean and Egyptian Magism, Christ and the Cat, and The Cat in Heraldry. There are thirty-five such chapters, each with its special bibliography, and the work is profusely illustrated. I would say that every one of these books is essential to any well-selected library of books about cats.

I would also like to recommend Zhenya Gay's "Town Cats," a book of drawings (Knopf; 1932). Some of the best cat pictures I remember seeing are to be found in this book. Miss Gay has been catholic in her choice of subjects, ranging from haughty Persians and sleek Siamese to rowdy alley cats. Foujita, the Japanese artist, issued a portfolio of cat-drawings too: "The Book of Cats," with text by Michael Joseph (Covici Friede; 1930). If you admire Foujita's sketches of women you will assuredly prefer his cats. The stylized and decorative felines of the French painter Jacques Nam have become popular since "The Tiger" was originally published and I cannot resist awarding honourable mention to the American Louis Bouché's painting of a cat with a ball of yarn and to the Mexican Adolfo Best-Maugard's white cat on a cushion, which hangs in my Victorian room. The sweet face of the pussy in this painting has always reminded me of Tallulah Bankhead.

Certainly I have devoted sufficient space in these pages to Steinlen's cats, but when I was writing this book I was not familiar with two lithographs in colour by this artist, L'Hiver and L'Eté, his masterpieces in this category. I think I should

viii

miss these, were they taken from me, more than anything else I possess.

In 1927 Sergei Lifar danced in "The Cat," music by Henri Sauget, produced by Sergei de Diaghileff and the Russian Ballet. Amy Lowell's "To Winky," which appeared in "Pictures of the Floating World"; 1919, stamps her as a felinophile. How did I come to omit all mention of May Sinclair? When, on her losing a cat to which she was devoted, W. L. George sent her an orange kitten, she returned the gift at once with the explanation: "I cannot bear to have another cat. I lost my first one twenty years ago and my grief was so prolonged that I vowed I would never have another. I have just lost my second and last." A little later when Miss Sinclair visited New York she wrote me, a stranger to her, to inquire if she might call upon me to see my cats. She spent an afternoon with Scheherazade in my Nineteenth Street garret and apparently had a happy time. This cat enjoyed a pleasant habit of sleeping in a great yellow salad bowl, curled up with her tail protruding over the brim. If she were placed in this bowl at almost any time it usually pleased her to relax and fall asleep. Ellen Glasgow still refers admiringly to this "bowl of cat."

It wouldn't be difficult to ramble on in this vein. . . . Fannie Hurst told me that after a lecture on some literary subject before a college group, when she called for questions, one girl rose and demanded, "How many cats has Carl Van Vechten got?" . . . In a restaurant at Formia where I stopped for lunch, driving from Naples to Rome in 1934, I saw a tremendous cat fight, really the most formidable encounter between savage animals I have ever witnessed. A waiter separated the combatants with a considerable display of sadism. There should be some mention of the strange, seven-pound Abyssinian cat who turned up at a cat show in New York in 1935. Ena was described as wearing a ruddy brown undercoat ticked with dark brown and a dark stripe down the spine; the head long

Introduction to the Third Edition

and pointed, the ears standing straight up, and the eyes, which now seemed yellow and now green, brilliant. Ena was friendly. On page 245 of the volume which follows, in reference to the dedication of "Blind Alley" there is mention of a "creature named Russet." Actually, I have discovered, this was the first Mrs. George. I might add that those who want a more complete history of Feathers, with an account of her touching end, will find it in my book, "Sacred and Profane Memories."

Sixteen years older now than I was in 1920, on re-reading "The Tiger" I pause dumfounded before the amount of erudition displayed and vastly admire the evidences of research. If, in these days, I were required to write a book about the U.S.S.R. or Swing Music, I believe I should undertake the task of assembling my material with far less thoroughness. On the other hand I stand in not a little awe of this younger and apparently more studious self!

CARL VAN VECHTEN

June 11, 1936
New York

CONTENTS

ILLUSTRATIONS

Illustrations

The Tiger in the House

Chapter One: By Way of Correcting a Popular Prejudice

Whenever the subject comes up, and it may be said, speaking with moderation, that it comes up forty times a day, some one invariably declares, " No, I don't like cats, I like dogs." The cognate dichotomous remark, which is equally popular, prevalent, and banal, is " No, I don't like Dickens, I like Thackeray." As James Branch Cabell has conveniently pointed out for all time, " to the philosophical mind it would seem equally sensible to decline to participate in a game of billiards on the ground that one was fond of herring." Nevertheless both controversies continue to rage and careless thinkers continue to force Dickens and the cat into categories. The dog-lovers, in the opposition sense (for it is really possible to care for both dogs and cats, just as it is possible to read " Pendennis " and " Bleak House " with equal delight), say of the soft puss that he is sly and deceitful, thieving and ungrateful, fickle and cruel, a friend to home and not to man. From this inconsiderate, and unconsidered, opinion the derogatory and catachrestic adjective " catty " has been derived, an adjective which when used in its ordinarily accepted sense I find particularly abhorrent, for who should be described as catty unless it be some gracious and graceful female, dignified and reserved, redolent of beauty and charm and the mystery of love? The cat-lovers on their side, so ardent, indeed, that in France they have earned the sobriquet of *félinophiles enragés*, have not been guiltless. Affectionate, intelligent, faithful, tried and true are some of the adjectives they lavish indiscriminately on their darling pets. It would seem, indeed, after reading some of the books, that cats spend their nine lives caring for the sick, saving children from burning buildings, and helping Mrs. Jellyby make small-clothes for the heathen in Africa.

The cat himself might have settled the question long ago, had settling such matters been a part of the cat's purpose in life. You cannot reasonably expect a near relative of the king of beasts (whom he much more closely resembles, by the way, than a Japanese spaniel resembles a Newfoundland dog), an animal who has been a god, a companion of sorceresses at the Witches' Sabbath, a beast who is royal in Siam, who in Japan is called "the tiger who eats from the hand," the adored of Mohammed, Laura's rival with Petrarch, the friend of Richelieu's idle moments, the favourite of poet and prelate, to view the stupidity of humankind in regard to him with anything warmer than disdain. The cat, indeed, makes no advances. He cares for the hearth and often he condescends to display affection to human friends, just as he has been known to entertain a vast liking for horses, parrots, and tortoises, but even in the most heated of such relationships he preserves a proper independence. He stays where he likes to stay; he goes where he wants to go. He gives his affection where it pleases him to give it (when, also, it might be added) and he withholds it from those whom he deems unworthy of it. In other words with a cat you stand on much the same footing that you stand with a fine and dignified friend; if you forfeit his respect and confidence the relationship suffers. The cat, it is well to remember, remains the friend of man because it pleases him to do so and not because he must. Resourceful, brave, intelligent (the brain of a kitten is comparatively larger than that of a child), the cat is in no sense a dependent and can revert to the wild state with less readjustment of values than any other domestic animal. Therefore he is easily enabled to determine his own end and purpose and to lead his own life. "I love in the cat," said Chateaubriand to M. de Marcellus, "that inde-

By Way of Correcting a Popular Prejudice

pendent and almost ungrateful temper which prevents him from attaching himself to any one; the indifference with which he passes from the *salon* to the housetop. When you caress him, he stretches himself out and arches his back, indeed, but that is caused by physical pleasure, not, as in the case of the dog, by a silly satisfaction in loving and being faithful to a master who returns thanks in kicks. The cat lives alone, has no need of society, does not obey except when he likes, pretends to sleep that he may see the more clearly, and scratches everything he can scratch. Buffon has belied the cat; I am labouring at his rehabilitation and I hope to make of him a tolerably good sort of animal, as times go." [1]

Without some such guide to the nature of the most interesting of animals it is impossible to approach the subject from any angle whatever. But with these few facts in mind I must at once beg to insist upon a paradox. Stated simply the case is this: each individual cat differs in as many ways as possible from each other individual cat. Any unprejudiced observer, interested enough in cats to inspire their devotion, will have found this out for himself if he has ever become acquainted with several cats at one time. Doubtless there are seraph cats and demon cats as well but the characters of most pussies lie somewhere between these intense blacks and whites. Cats differ so much, indeed, that some of them even lack the most generally distributed feline characteristics. It can be said of cats in general, however, that they are all independent, most of them amorous (their love habits, inspired by the hardiest desires, are often supremely cruel [2]), and mystic. On this last point there is little reason for doubt. Cats have gnosis to a degree that is granted to few bishops as I shall attempt to show in a later chapter. As for their independence

[1] " Chateaubriand et son temps," by the Comte de Marcellus; 1859.

[2] The theory of the American Shakers that the functions of sex " belong to a state of nature and are inconsistent with a state of grace " is not held by the cat.

it is simply the aristocratic quality of being natural. Cats do not force their attentions upon others and they do not care to have attentions forced upon them. But when a cat is hungry or wishes to go out of doors or has amorous desires he plainly declares his feelings. " Why not? " asks Colette's Kiki-la-Doucette. "Why not? People do." [3] These are reminiscences, inheritances, of the wild life which the cat has never lost and never will lose. For in keeping with his royal brother, the lion, he also has a strong racial instinct which survives to be awakened when it is called. He has a longer memory than Monna Lisa.

Yet in the degree in which they react to these instincts individual cats differ, and these differences are accentuated by treatment and by breeding, for cats inherit many traits, and although it almost seems unscientific to say so, there is strong evidence to the effect that they inherit acquired characteristics. You will find it stated in some of the books that a cat who has been deprived of her tail will occasionally produce tailless kittens.

Many observers have recorded the eccentricities and idiosyncrasies of cats. Wynter [4] speaks of a cat of his who selected blotting paper on which to sit or lie. Meredith Janvier's Major Pussman contracted tuberculosis from sleeping on a hot radiator. Clara Rossiter [5] describes a puss whose favourite occupation was to pull all the pins out of a cushion and lay them out on the table, " and when the last was taken out, looking up into our faces with the most comical expression and making us understand she wanted them replaced. However many times we stuck the pins in she would pull them out." This cat also took pleasure in devouring flowers, which she removed from the vases. The Reverend J. G. Wood tells us of a tom cat who was such an aristocrat

[3] " Sept Dialogues de Bêtes."
[4] " Fruit Between the Leaves."
[5] "Anecdotes of Pets": " North British Advertiser " (Edinburgh) ; 1874.

that " nothing would induce him — not even milk when he was hungry — to put his head into the kitchen, or to enter the house by the servants' door." Wynter had a cat who rose suddenly one day and sprang up the chimney, a fire burning in the grate all the while. A couple of hundred years earlier the writer would have been burned for relating this incident. This cat would eat pickles and liked brandy and water. Lindsay [6] mentions a cat with a fondness for porter and Jerome K. Jerome [7] writes of another who drank from a leaky beer-tap until she was intoxicated. In a letter to Samuel Butler, dated December 24, 1879, Miss Savage remarks, " My cat has taken to mulled port and rum punch. Poor old dear! he is all the better for it. Dr. W. B. Richardson says that the lower animals always refuse alcoholic drinks, and gives that as a reason why humans should do so too."

It is the popular belief that cats have an inherent dislike for water and in general they are catabaptists, but my Ariel had no aversion to water; indeed, this orange Persian puss was accustomed to leap voluntarily into my warm morning tub and she particularly liked to sit in the wash-hand-bowl under the open faucet. Artault de Vevey [8] also had a cat, Isoline, who took baths, jumping into the full tub. " Cats are popularly supposed to dislike wet," writes Olive Thorne Miller, " but I have seen two of them in a steady rain conduct an interview with all the gravity and deliberation for which these affairs are celebrated." There are innumerable recorded examples of cats swimming rivers to return to their old homes and St. George Mivart tells us of a cat who plunged into a swiftly running stream and rescued her three drowning kittens, bearing them one by one to the shore. A writer in " Chambers's Journal " [9] recalls a dejected black cat who com-

[6] " Mind in the Lower Animals."
[7] " Novel Notes," P. 151.
[8] Artault de Vevey: " Des Actes Raisonnés chez le Chat ": " Bulletin de l'Institut Général Psychologique," Année III, No. 1; P. 13–14; Paris; 1903.
[9] " Chambers's Journal "; October 9, 1880, P. 646.

mitted suicide by drowning! Fishing cats seem to be a commonplace. Lane [10] quotes the "Plymouth Journal" in regard to a cat who was accustomed to dive for fish and Ross [11] writes of a Mr. Moody, near Newcastle-upon-Tyne who had a cat who caught minnows, eels, and pilchards in this manner. There is likewise the evidence of a celebrated Egyptian fresco in the British Museum which depicts a cat acting as a retriever, shows us a gentle puss leaping into the Nile from a boat in order to fetch and carry the slaughtered duck back into the boat, an incident that G. A. Henty has woven into his tale for boys, "The Cat of Bubastes." [12] Certain cats of today find it natural to retrieve. My Ariel would run after a catnip mouse and bring it to me, as often as I would throw it.

[10] C. H. Lane: "Rabbits, Cats and Cavies." P. 239. The cat was named Puddles. "He used to go out a-fishin' with me every night," relates the fisherman. "On cold nights he would sit on my lap while I was a-fishin', and poke his head out every now and then, or else I would wrap him up in a sail and make him lay quiet. He'd lay down on me while I was asleep, and if anybody came, he'd swear a good un, and have the face off on 'em if they went to touch me, and he'd never touch a fish, not even a little teeny pout, if you didn't give it to 'im. I was obliged to take him out a-fishin' or else he'd stand an' yowl and marr till I went back and ketched him by the poll and shied him into the boat, and then he was quite happy. When it was fine he used to stick up at the bow of the boat and sit a-watchin' the dogs (dog-fish). The dogs used to come along by the thousands at a time, and when they was thick all about, he would dive in and fetch 'em out, jammed in his mouth as fast as may be, just as if they was a parcel of rats, and he didn't tremble with the cold half as much as a Newfoundland dog who was used to it. He looked terrible wild about the head when he came out of the water with a dog-fish. I larnt him the water myself. One day, when he was a kitten, I took him down to the sea to wash and brush the fleas out of him and in a week he could swim after a feather or a cork."

[11] C. H. Ross: "The Book of Cats."

[12] To the black cat, who has it in mind to move, the chinchilla cat gives the following advice in Jerome K. Jerome's "Novel Notes," P. 147: "Try and get yourself slightly wet. Why people should prefer a wet cat to a dry one I have never been able to understand; but that a wet cat is practically sure of being taken in and gushed over, while a dry cat is liable to have the garden hose turned upon it, is an undoubted fact. Also, if you can possibly manage it, and it is offered you, eat a bit of dry bread. The human race is always stirred to its deepest depths by the sight of a cat eating a bit of dry bread."

6

By Way of Correcting a Popular Prejudice

" When visiting a friend in Patagonia," W. H. Hudson records in " The Book of a Naturalist," " I was greatly astonished one day on going out with a gun to shoot something followed by the dogs to find a black cat in their company, and to see her when I fired my first shot actually dashing off before the dogs to retrieve the bird! "

One person observes that cats are always gentle and polite, that they eat their food daintily and never greedily, but I have watched otherwise good-mannered felines who could gobble and growl over their food with as much greediness and ill-manneredness as any dog. In the mere matter of the selection of food cats vary as much as people. There are imperious, haughty, aristocratic cats who insist on being fed esoteric dishes in a certain fixed spot, by certain people. Other cats resemble Lafcadio Hearn's little red kitten who " ate beefsteak and cockroaches, caterpillars and fish, chicken and butterflies, mosquito hawks and roast mutton, hash and tumblebugs, beetles and pigs' feet, crabs and spiders, moths and poached eggs, oysters and earthworms, ham and mice, rats and rice pudding,— until its belly became a realization of Noah's Ark." [13]

Cats are exceedingly nervous and they are not as a rule to be trusted in railroad trains, for the slightest sound or movement is likely to awaken terror and fast moving objects usually inspire them with the keenest sense of fright. But Avery Hopwood's orange tabby Persian, Abélard,[14] takes

[13] " The Little Red Kitten," in " Fantastics," P. 33.

[14] " Fulbert . . . now deeply troubled and revengeful, determined to inflict that punishment and indignity on Abélard, which, in its accomplishment, shocked even that ruder civilization to horror and reprisal." From " The Story of Abélard and Héloïse."

Raoul Gineste has treated the subject in a poem which begins:

> *On a fait couper matou,*
> *Pour cause de propreté,*
> *Et par esprit de bonté;*
> *L'amour l'aurait rendu fou.*

The Tiger in the House

motor rides with him, sitting sagely on the front seat without a leash. When the car stops he leaps out and walks about, ready to get back again when a start is agreed upon. Theodore Hammeker, a flyer on the French front and in Palestine during the late war, took his black cat, Brutus, with him on his flights. The R-34, the first dirigible to cross the Atlantic from England to America, carried the tabby cat, Jazz, as the only animal passenger. And I am acquainted with a eupeptic

> *Son maître, bardé de lard,*
> *Bourgeois stupide et cruel,*
> *A trouvé spirituel*
> *De l'appeler Abélard.*

In "Les Chats" (P. 74) Moncrif quotes Isaac de Benserade's poem, inspired by the castration of a cat belonging to Madame Deshoulières:

> *Je ne dis mot et je fais bonne mine*
> *Et mauvais jeu depuis le triste jour*
> *Qu'on me rendit inhabile à l'amour*
> *Des Chats galans, moi la fleur la plus fine.*
> *Ainsi se plaint Moricaut et rumine*
> *Contre la main qui lui fit un tel tour;*
> *Il est glacière, au lieu qu'il étoit four;*
> *Il s'occupoit, maintenant il badine,*
> *C'étoit un brave, et ce n'est plus qu'un sot,*
> *Dans la gouttière il tourne autour du pot,*
> *Et de bon coeur son Serrail en enrage;*
> *Pour les plaisirs il avoit un talent,*
> *Que l'on lui change au plus beau de son âge:*
> *Le triste état qu'un état indolent!*

Catulle Mendès writes: "*Rue Mansard, j'eus un chat, à qui l'on donna le nom d'un personnage de la Walkyrie. Mime était beau comme un amour. C'était un matou d'un noir superbe; mais il répandait une odeur formidable et ne se faisait pas faute de lacérer mes rideaux. On fut bien obligé de le confier à un homme de l'art, qui nous le ramena dans un état absolu de neutralité. A dater de ce jour, Mime s'enfonça dans une tristesse plus noire que lui-même. Nous habitions au cinquième étage. Mime avait coutume, à certains moments de la journée, de faire un petit tour sur la corniche de zinc qui régnait au long de la façade intérieure, sous nos fenêtres. Un matin, je le vis — ou je crus le voir — s'élancer volontairement de cette corniche dans la rue. En tombant, il rencontra un réverbère contre lequel il se cassa les reins. Je vous affirme que je garde l'impression que Mime s'est suicidé.*"

8

By Way of Correcting a Popular Prejudice

altered tom silver Persian who even goes to the movies on the shoulder of his mistress!

Cats are popularly supposed again to prefer places to people and there are literally thousands of recorded examples of cats who have surmounted every kind of physical obstacle in order to return to old homes from which they had been removed. It would be as easy to give as long a list of cats who move regularly with their families every year or so. A further list could be compiled of cats who move of their own accord, often from homes in which they are treated with every mark of respect and in which they are surrounded with every comfort and luxury. To those who feel that the recipient of attentions should be grateful no matter in what form they come, this strange conduct of cats will seem inexplicable, but I am sure that some of my readers will understand that it is possible to desire something which has nothing to do with luxury or comfort. Occasionally, indeed, you will even find people who are willing to leave rich homes for the pleasures of adventure.

> *The Cat's winged yearnings journey,*
> *Unrestrained, o'er Time and Space,*

muses Hiddigeigei, the Tom Cat, and cats with longings in their souls invariably satisfy these longings, so far as they are able. Carefully bred, tenderly nurtured Persian pussies have been known to leave the silks and satins of the drawing-room for the free life of the rooftop and companionship with extremely ill-bred, low-spoken, short-haired felines. Spousebreach has been known to result. Other cats have left luxurious homes to take up a broader existence in a green grocer's shop, where the hunting is better and there is less petting. The reverse often happens. A cat leaves a life of poverty to enter into a life of luxury. On the whole, however, I would say that cats pattern their lives more on that of May Yohe than on that of Cinderella. . . . To return to our text it is undoubtedly true that there are perverse cats just as there are perverse people, who insist on residing in a certain spot. But these cats have a good instinctive reason for this obstinacy as I shall show later.

Some cats make fond and zealous mothers, taking every care of their young, hiding them from danger, washing and feeding them, and teaching them to play. Alice's Dinah,[15] whose method of washing her babies was to hold the poor things down by their ears with one paw, and with the other paw rub their faces all over, was an excellent mother. Some cats have such a strong instinct for motherhood that if their offspring is taken away from them they suckle babies,[16] leverets,[17] and even rats. Other cats have been known to neglect or even to kill their young. One stolid young queen, probably having read Maupassant's " Inutile Beauté," drowned her babies in a water butt; another, refusing to suckle her kittens or, indeed, to go near them at all, was shut up with them in a shed, whereupon she promptly put out their little lives with blows from her strong hind feet. When she was released she walked out purring, evidently in a high state of relief and contentment.

Cleanliness in the cat world is usually a virtue put above godliness. Puss spends more time washing than débutantes do changing their clothes and her attention to Gulliverian hydraulics and other demands of nature is fastidious to a degree. In the Cat State, Clarence Day, jr., quaintly observes, the plumber, the manicurist, and the soap-maker would occupy the highest social positions; preachers and lawyers, the lowest. Nevertheless Siamese and Russian short-haired blue cats have an odour, and I have seen cats of whatever colour, of whatever breed, dirtier than any other animal could possibly be. A kitten once lived with me, a kitten in every respect super-intelligent, who refused to systematize his toilet operations. He

---

[15] " Through the Looking Glass ": Chapter I.
[16] W. Lauder Lindsay: " Mind in the Lower Animals."
[17] Gilbert White: " The Natural History of Selborne."

was a most amusing, adorably impudent, tailless kitten who followed me on the street one night in Paris. He walked closely behind me for a quarter of a mile and when I put him — he was very tiny — into my pocket he assented to the arrangement by purring loudly. But when together we ascended the steps of an omnibus, the conductor waved his hand grandly with the admonition, "*Pas de bêtes!*" So, with puss in my pocket, I walked to my hotel. This cat had a delectable habit of springing on my shoulder in the dark when I returned home at night. Rubbing himself against my cheek he purred like the kettle-drums in Berlioz's *Requiem*. He was not impressed by the art of Franz von Stuck and invariably, until I no longer fastened it up, he succeeded in wresting an engraving of *Salome* from the wall, although it was pinned very high and no article of furniture underneath offered assistance in the operation. This puss also had a mania for breaking dishes, and there was no leaving tea-things around in his presence. Like all cats he could alight on a full table of such knick-knacks without upsetting anything, but once landed he delighted in disturbing the equilibrium of the porcelain with his nimble and roguish paw. These qualities did not alienate my affections, quite the contrary. We quarreled irrevocably over another matter about which puss (as cats always are) was inexorable and paramount. He refused to learn the uses of a box of sand;[18] nor

[18] Claudine's Fanchette was irreproachable in this respect. Colette Willy observed her one day and set down her observations with such truth and good humour that I cannot resist the temptation to quote the passage from "Claudine à Paris" (P. 19): "*Fanchette, heureuse fille, a pris gaîment l'internat. Elle a, sans protestation, accepté, pour y déposer ses petites horreurs, un plat de sciure dissimulé dans ma ruelle, et je m'amuse, penchée, à suivre sur sa physionomie de chatte les phases d'une opération importante. Fanchette se lave les pattes de derrière, soigneuse, entre les doigts. Figure sage et qui ne dit rien. Arrêt brusque dans le washing: figure sérieuse et vague souci. Changement soudain de pose; elle s'assied sur son séant. Yeux froids et quasi sévères. Elle se lève, fait trois pas et se rassied. Puis, décision irrévocable, on saute du lit, on court à son plat, on gratte . . . et rien du tout. L'air indifférent reparaît. Mais pas longtemps. Les sourcils angoissés se rapprochent; elle regratte fièvreusement la sciure, piétine, cherche la bonne place et pendant trois*

would a sheet of paper or sawdust tempt him. Not even " Le Temps " or " Le Journal " with the revues of Catulle Mendès. . . .

There is no one thing that cats are supposed to care more for than heat, and it is true that a cat will seek a hearth, a cozy wood fire, or the companionship of a kitchen stove, but it is perfectly possible for a cat to exist in the cold. When it was discovered that the extremely frigid temperature of the great cold-storage plants was not sufficiently bitter to exterminate the sturdy rats and mice some one proposed the introduction of cats. The first felines carried into these bleak quarters did not thrive. Some of them, indeed, perished, but a few survived and, after a winter or two, grew an astonishing coat of fur, as thick as that of a beaver. The kittens born in this ice-like temperature were hardy little beasts, and it is said that now the cold-storage cats would pant and languish with nervous exhaustion were they exposed to a New York July day.

There is a feud between the cat and the dog, but this dislike is superficial and can, in most instances, be easily set aside. It is, to be sure, instinctive. Kittens with their eyes scarcely open have been known to spit at a dog. But cats who live with dogs usually do so with dignity and ease; in many cases a deep affection springs up between the two. When Flecknoe's miserable old gentlewoman in his " Enigmatical Characters " (1658) speaks of letting her prayer book fall into the dripping pan and the cat and dog quarreling over it and at last agreeing to pray on it she becomes in a sense symbolical. You may likewise remember that Old Mother Hubbard went to the hatter's to buy her dog a hat, " but when she came back he was feeding the cat."

minutes, l'oeil fixe et sorti, semble songer âprement. Car elle est volontiers un peu constipée. Enfin, lentement, on se relève et, avec des précautions minutieuses, on recouvre le cadavre, de l'air pénétré qui convient à cette funèbre opération. Petit grattement superfétatoire autour du plat, et sans transition, cabriole déhanchée et diabolique, prélude à une danse de chèvre, le pas de la délivrance. Alors, je ris et je crie: 'Mélie, viens changer, vite, le plat de la chatte!'"

By Way of Correcting a Popular Prejudice

Mademoiselle Antoinette Thérèse Deshoulières wrote a remarkable heroic tragedy, after the manner of Corneille, the subject of which is the passion of Madame Deshoulières's cat, Grisette, for Cochon, the dog of the Duc de Vivonne, brother to Madame de Montespan. The play is called *La Mort de Cochon* and all the ram-cats of Madame Deshoulières's household and the neighbourhood have gathered on a convenient rooftop to rejoice at the news conveyed by the title, and to express the hope that one of them may win the paw of the perverse Grisette. That young lady, however, gives herself whole-heartedly to grief. In vain the Chorus of Cats cries:

> *Redonnez-vous à votre espèce,*
> *Votre destin sera plus doux.*

Grisette replies:

> *Je dois à Cochon ma tendresse.*
> *Dussiez-vous être encor mille fois plus jaloux,*
> *Vous verrez à quel point pour lui je m'intéresse.*

The Chorus cries:

> *Ah cruelle chatte, arrêtez!*

But she does not relent and disappears from the rooftop to make way for Eros, the god in the car, who holds out the following hope:

> *Tendres matous, laissez-la-faire:*
> *Votre infortune finira;*
> *J'en jure par mon arc, j'en jure par ma mère,*
> *La constance est une chimère*
> *Dont Grisette se lassera.*

Through the convenient pen of Madame Deshoulières, Grisette and Cochon had previously penned a long correspondence. It is perhaps the first literary friendship between a dog and a cat but by no means the last. Indeed a cat prefers, in

13

most cases, a dog for a companion rather than another cat. A mother cat will suckle puppies and she has been known to suckle rats. For rats and cats, too, can become friends, as Théophile Gautier discovered when his dynasties of white rats and white cats were contemporaries.[19]

" Respect of slumber," writes S. B. Wister,[20] " is a most curious characteristic of cats and I have often wondered if it is the same instinct which is said to prevent lions and tigers from attacking sleeping prey." This is all very well, but have cats respect for slumber? Some of them have. My Feathers has not. She wants her breakfast at a certain hour in the morning; if the door of my bedroom is closed she gives little cries outside. If it is open she enters, puts her forepaws on the edge of my bed close to my face and licks my cheek. If I brush her away, in a few moments she is nibbling my toes. I put an end to this and very shortly she is marching up and down, using me as a highroad. She is equally persistent if I am taking a nap. On such occasions she often climbs high on my breast and sleeps with me, but when she awakes she digs her claws into my chest and stretches, quite as if I didn't exist. This alternate protrusion of the forepaws, with toes separated, as if pushing against and sucking their mother's teats, is a favourite gesture of cats when they are pleased.

Cats make a radical distinction, naturally enough, between their relations with human beings and their relations with other cats. An anonymous writer quoted by Moncrif,[21] has put this beautifully in his description of the lovely Menine of Madame de Lesdiguieres who was

Chatte pour tout le monde, et pour les chats, tigresse.

Cats are extremely sensitive and nervous; their pulses register

[19] W. H. Hudson relates the story of a remarkable friendship between a cat and a rat in " The Book of a Naturalist."

[20] " Cats and their affections "; " Temple Bar "; Vol. 107, P. 84.

[21] " Les Chats "; P. 89.

160 throbs a minute. A good-natured kitten may be worried into becoming a bad-natured cat, or the bad characteristics of a cat may sometimes be softened by tender treatment. I know of an instance in which a guest handled a kitten about three months old rather roughly. When released the kitten fled to safety; she was not accustomed to suffering such indignities and she resented them. Familiarity always breeds contempt in a cat. However, once the guest had taken his departure she resumed her old-time offhand manner and was as playful as possible. A year elapsed before the offending guest again appeared in the circle, a year during which the kitten had grown into cathood, but the moment the young man entered the door she disappeared under a bed and could not be induced to come out until he had left. Cats have long memories. Jessie Pickens had a very remarkable brown tabby Persian who snarled and growled and spit at everybody except her mistress. She would indeed suffer no one but Jessie to come near her at all, but for Jessie she had an excessive fondness and had even crossed the Atlantic in her cabin seventeen times. Her fear of strangers was due to an accident which occurred when she was a kitten. Willy, really a great admirer of cats and at that time the husband of Colette, than whom no one has written more delicately and sensitively about these little rogues in fur, was calling one day. He picked the kitten up to play with her and tossed her up towards the ceiling, catching her as she dropped, but a sudden twist and puss slipped through his fingers, falling to the floor. With a cry of terror she fled from the room and it was only after two days that she was discovered hiding behind some trunks in the garret. She never permitted a stranger to touch her again. Another cat fell into a well. He managed to keep from drowning by climbing to a small rock and in time he was rescued, but thereafter he was completely insane; he never regained interest in life nor seemed to have the slightest consciousness of what was going on about

him. Lindsay [22] has culled another example from the " Animal World." This cat was frightened by a peacock; a sort of terror-mania developed, agoraphobia, perhaps, involving an utter loss of self-possession, followed by a permanent timidity that permitted the animal to feed only in his master's presence.

Whether they inherit these traits or whether their manners and habits are encouraged or embarrassed by treatment, the fact remains that there are all kinds of cats, cross and gentle, cruel and tender, savage and tame. The curious thing is that several kittens by the same mother brought up together in the same house will exhibit many differences. Gautier describes three kittens of the same litter: " Enjolras was solemn, pretentious, aldermanic from his cradle; even theatrical at times in his vast assumption of dignity. Gavroche was a born Bohemian, enamoured of low company, and of the careless comedies of life. Their sister Eponine — best loved of the three — was a delicate, fastidious little creature with an exquisite sense of propriety, and of the refinements of social intercourse. Enjolras was a glutton, caring for nothing so much as his dinner. Gavroche, more generous, would bring in from the streets gaunt and ragged cats, who devoured in a scurry of fright the food laid aside for him. I was often tempted to remonstrate, and to say to this little scamp, ' A nice lot of friends you do pick up ! ' But I refrained. After all, it was an amiable weakness. He might have eaten his dinner himself."

Madame Michelet [23] thinks that colouring may have something to do with temperament. Black cats, according to this *femme savante,* have passionate and sombre characters. The blondes are amiable and facile, with a certain submerged smiling melancholy. Those between the two extremes, neither blonde nor brunette, have equable temperaments. These

[22] " Mind in the Lower Animals "; Vol. II, P. 186.
[23] " Les Chats."

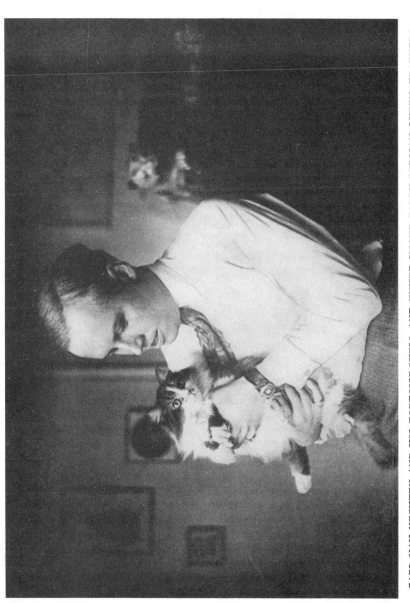

CARL VAN VECHTEN AND HIS TORTOISE-SHELL AND WHITE SMOKE TABBY PERSIAN QUEEN, FEATHERS

From a photograph by Harriet V. Furness

THE CAT SOMETIMES MAKES STRANGE FRIENDS

From a drawing by Grandville in Les Métamorphoses du Jour

THIS BROWN TABBY SHORT-HAIRED CAT IS NAMED MARY GARDEN

From a copyright photograph by Harriet V. Furness

THE CAT AND THE FROG

From a drawing by Steinlen in Des Chats

MRS. CHANNING POLLOCK'S OSIRIS RESENTS AN INVASION

From a photograph by Paul Thompson

CHAMPION KING WINTER

From a copyright photograph by Harriet V. Furness

"GATHER KITTENS WHILE YOU MAY"

From a copyright photograph by Harriet V. Furness

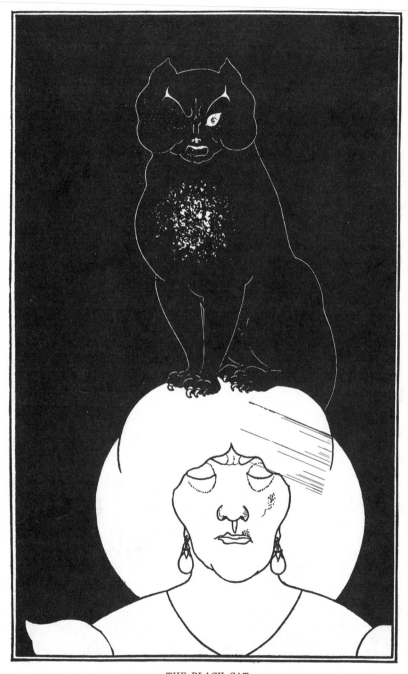

THE BLACK CAT
*From a drawing by Aubrey Beardsley to illustrate Poe's story, published in a large paper
edition of Tales of Mystery and Wonder, by Stone and Kimball; Chicago; 1895*

By Way of Correcting a Popular Prejudice

classifications of Madame Michelet will be considered rather fantastic by any one who has known cats of different colours.

But Diderot's " *il y a chat et chat* " is certainly just. Some cats are cold and haughty, imperious and ironic. Other cats are so frank, so persistent in demanding affection, that they almost lack mystery. There are cats who will climb on any one and purr with delight. Catnip is vodka and whisky to most cats, but Feathers merely sniffs at it and walks away. There are all varieties and kinds and sorts of cats; there are long and short-haired cats, and Mexican cats without any hair; there are strange Australian cats with long pointed noses; there are Angora and Persian and Siamese cats, and Manx cats without any tails; there are blue, black, and white cats; there are tortoise-shells and creams; there are orange and silver and chinchilla cats; there are combinations of all these colours; my Feathers is a tortoise-shell and white smoke tabby queen, with seven toes on each front paw! Seven or six-toed cats are by no means rare. Even in regard to the freaks of catdom there are variations: in spite of much popular opinion to the contrary white cats are not always deaf, tortoise-shells are not always females, and orange tabbies are not always males.

Some pussies' coats are yellow; some amber streaked with dark;
No member of the feline race but has a special mark.
This one has feet with hoarfrost tipped; that one has tail that curls;
Another's inky hide is striped; another's decked with pearls.

Cats loom in the mind's eye, indeed, with the heroes of history and the characters of fiction: Zola's roving Angora, worsted in a street fight, and Edward Peple's roving Angora who does up an alley cat and returns home tired and happy; Baudelaire's occult cat; Lafcadio Hearn's tortoise-shell, Tama, who played with her dead kittens in dreams, cooing to them, catching for them small shadowy things; Corporal Bunting's devilishly grim, brindled, bandit cat, Jacobina; Madame Joli-

The Tiger in the House

cœur's cuddlesome, Shah de Perse, whose " rare little cat tan-
trums were but as sun-spots on the effulgence of his otherwise
constant amiability "; Mr. Tarkington's Gipsy, " half broncho
and half Malay pirate "; snarling, green-eyed, grey Lady
Jane, who follows Mr. Krook about in " Bleak House "; the
pious papal cats of Leo XII, Gregory XV, and Pius IX; [24]
the playful kitten companions of Richelieu; [25] the oyster-eating
Hodge of Dr. Johnson, the bane of Boswell; Edward Lear's
Old Foss; " that troublesome old rip," Hector G. Yelverton,

[24] When Pius IX sat down to dine, his cat came in with the soup, mounted a
chair opposite him, and dumbly and decorously looked on until the pontiff had
finished his meal. Then he received his own at his master's hands and took
leave until the same hour next day. The demise of puss alarmed the Pope's
household, lest he should be painfully affected by the loss of his old table companion, but His Holiness " did not seem to care a bit more about it than he had
cared for the death of his secretary, the Cardinal Antonelli."

[25] The fondness of Richelieu for kittens has been generally taken for granted
and is stated as a fact in most of the books about cats. Champfleury, however,
questions the matter in a footnote: " It is surprising that Moncrif, who, notwithstanding the jesting tone of his book, made extensive researches on the subject of cats, has not said a word about Richelieu's passion for those animals.
Can it be that this peculiarity, attributed to a great political personage, is a
legend misapplied? ' Everybody knows,' says Moncrif, ' that one of the greatest
ministers France ever possessed, M. Colbert, always had a number of kittens
playing about that same cabinet in which so many institutions, both useful and
honourable to the nation, had their origin.' "

Alexandre Landrin (" Le Chat," p. 93) writes, " With Richelieu the taste for
cats was a mania; when he rose in the morning and when he went to bed at night
he was always surrounded by a dozen of them with which he played, delighting
to watch them jump and gambol. He had one of his chambers fitted up as a
cattery, which was entrusted to overseers, the names of whom are known.
Abel and Teyssandier came, morning and evening, to feed the cats with *patés*
fashioned of the white meat of chicken. At his death Richelieu left a pension
for his cats and to Abel and Teyssandier so that they might continue to care
for their charges. When he died Richelieu left fourteen cats of which the names
were: Mounard le Fougueux, Soumise, Serpolet, Gazette, Ludovic le Cruel, Mimie
Piaillon, Felimare, Lucifer, Lodoïska, Rubis sur l'Ongle, Pyrame, Thisbé, Racan,
and Perruque. These last two received their names from the fact that they were
born in the wig of Racan, the academician."

Gaston Percheron (" Le Chat," p. 19) writes, " History records that Richelieu
with one hand caressed a family of cats which played on his knees, while with
the other he signed the order for the execution of Cinq-Mars."

18

By Way of Correcting a Popular Prejudice

" with no more principle than an injun "; Mr. Garnett's in-domitable queen, of whom has been written:

And all the Toms, though never so bold,
Quailed at the martial Marigold.

The esoteric procession continues to pass in front of me: Scheffel's philosophical and lyrical Tom Cat, Hiddigeigei, of sable coat and majestic tail; Hamilcar,[26] the cat of Sylvestre Bonnard, who combined in his personality the formidable aspect of a Tartar chief with the heavy grace of an odalisque; John F. Runciman's Felix-Mendelssohn-Bartholdy-Shedlock-Runciman-Felinis, who spit at hansoms at the age of six months and later attempted to play the viola-alta by trailing the bow across the floor, and his Minnie who used to put dogs to rout and died of eating needles; the charming Kallikrates of W. L. George's " Blind Alley "; Tieck's prodigiously de-lightful Hinze; Alexandre Dumas's clairvoyant Mysouff, who once ate a 500 franc breakfast; the terrible one-eyed Pluto of Poe's story and the one-eyed Wotan, Kraft's cat in " Maurice Guest "; Mr. Warner's sage Calvin and Mark Twain's Tom Quartz, who objected to quartz mining; Agnes Repplier's Agrippina and Lux; John Silence's psychic cat, Smoke, who loved to rub up against the legs of spirits; the gamine cat, Fanchette, of the adorable Claudine; Dr. Nicola's eschatological cat, Apollyon, who was privy to the mysteries of cartomancy; Dickens's Williamina (first named William); Southey's Rumpel, " the Most Noble the Archduke Rumpel-stiltzchen, Marcus Macbum, Earl Tomlefnagne, Baron Rati-cide, Waowhler and Scratch "; Chateaubriand's greyish red Micetto, the gift of a Pope; Tom Hood's Tabitha Longclaws

[26] Hamilcar was Anatole France's own cat. After his death he was succeeded by a cat named Pascal by France's cook, who had overheard a luncheon con-versation about the French philosopher. Pascal was a stray cat who wandered in from the streets, liked the " city of books," and decided to remain. He al-ways maintained his independence, and sometimes went away for a week at a time.

19

The Tiger in the House

Tiddleywink and her three kittens, Pepperpot, Scratchaway, and Sootikins; the black cat of Fray Inocencio called Timoteo, a name " bestowed upon him for the reason that this is a name well suited to a cat, and also in derisive reprobation of that schismatic monophysite of Egypt, who in the fifth century usurped the Patriarchate, and was known popularly as ' Timothy the Cat.' "; later this puss was called Susurro,[27] which in Spanish signifies Purrer; Sandy Jenkins's hoodoo cat, Mesmerizer; Théophile Gautier's Madame Théophile, who delighted in perfumes and music, India shawls lifted from boxes of sandalwood, and faint aromatic odours of the East; Victor Hugo's Chanoine and Sir Walter Scott's Hinse; Pierre Loti's Moumoutte Blanche and Moumoutte Chinoise; the wicked Rutterkin of ways mephitic; and Rosamund Marriot Watson's Egyptian cat desired by Arsinoë:

> *A little lion, small and dainty sweet*
> *(For such there be!)*
> *With sea-grey eyes and softly stepping feet.*

On strings the solemn march:

> *Les chats prudents, les chats silencieux,*
> *Promènant leur beauté, leur grâce et leur mystère,*

" furred serpents," " green-eyed Venuses," the " house-animal," the " fireside sphinx," " rat-eater," " mouse-enemy," the " panther of the hearth," " cats . . . of titles obsolete or yet in use, Tom, Tybert, Roger, Rutterkin, or Puss,"

> *Calumnious cats, who circulate faux pas,*
> *And reputations maul with murderous claws;*
> *Shrill cats, whom fierce domestic brawls delight,*
> *Cross cats, who nothing want but teeth to bite,*
> *Starch cats of puritanic aspect sad,*
> *And learned cats who talk their husbands mad;*

*   *   *   *   *

[27] Asura, the ancient Aryan name for deity, signifies the breather.

By Way of Correcting a Popular Prejudice

Uncleanly cats who never pare their nails,
Cat-gossips, full of Canterbury tales;
Cat-grandams, vex'd with asthmas and catarrhs,
And superstitious cats, who curse their stars.

Chapter Two: Treating of Traits

Now that I have, perhaps, convinced the reader that cats have character, it is time to assert with equal positiveness that cats have characteristics. No cat-lover would be willing to deny this, for the characteristics of the cat are what make her generally beloved. Many of these traits are born of feral habits, hundreds and even thousands of years old. The dog is an animal who in the wild state travels in packs; he follows his leader in hunting expeditions. In the domestic state he transfers this allegiance from his leader to his master, for man is literally the master of the dog, as he is of the horse and the ass, and as he has been of the maid-servant. The cat on the other hand, in the wild state hunted and lived alone; he retains the independent habits of such a condition. Observe, for instance, a dog eating: if a man or another dog approaches him he will growl. He has a racial memory of fighting for the best food and it is his instinct to bolt it down before it can be taken away from him. A cat, ordinarily (there are exceptions, as I have previously pointed out), displays no such trepidation. Accustomed as a wild animal to eating alone in tranquillity, as a domestic he usually eats slowly and with decorum, having no instinctive fear that his food will be stolen.

Similarly a cat's regard for his person is acutely traceable to a memory of life in the forest and plain. A cat does not chase his prey as a dog does; he can run swiftly for a short distance, but running is not his specialty. He lies in wait for his quarry and pounces upon it suddenly. Now some of the animals of which the cat is most fond for food, notably the mouse, have a keener sense of smell than their enemy; it is therefore essential for the good mouser to be devoid of odour. Consequently he washes and rewashes his fur and trims his whiskers to the last speck. " The love of dress is very marked in this attractive animal," writes Champfleury; " he is proud of the lustre of his coat, and cannot endure that a hair of it shall lie the wrong way. When the cat has eaten, he passes his tongue several times over both sides of his jaws, and his whiskers, in order to clean them thoroughly; he keeps his coat clean with a prickly tongue which fulfills the office of a curry-comb; but as, notwithstanding its suppleness, it is difficult for the cat to reach the upper part of his head with the tongue; he makes use of his paw, moistened with saliva, to polish that portion." Hippolyte Taine has written a charming description of the operation:

> *His tongue is sponge, and brush, and towel, and curry-comb,*
> *Well he knows what work it can be made to do,*
> *Poor little wash-rag, smaller than my thumb.*
>
> *His nose touches his back, touches his hind paws too,*
> *Every patch of fur is raked, and scraped, and smoothed;*
> *What more has Goethe done, what more could Voltaire do?*

A similar instinct induces the cat to bury his offal, an instinct which leads him to do a deal of scratching in the domestic pan.

Louis Robinson [1] has expressed an interesting and credible theory to the effect that even the cat's colouring and the habit of hissing or spitting are protective mimicry. The most aggressive enemy of the cat in the wild state is the eagle. Now it is known that all animals (save perhaps the cat!) fear snakes. Tabby markings are the most common coloration in felines. If you observe a tabby cat rolled up asleep with his head in the centre of the coil you may note that he bears a very fair resemblance to a coiled serpent, quite enough resemblance to deceive an eagle in the air. Again, suppose a cat has

---

[1] " Wild Traits in Tame Animals."

concealed her kittens in a hollow tree. At the approach of an
enemy they begin to spit, and this spitting sounds very much
like the hissing of a snake. No fox will stick his nose into the
dark hollow of a tree from which hisses are ejected.

The cat is an anarchist, while the dog is a socialist. He is
an aristocratic, tyrannical anarchist, at that.

> *So Tiberius might have sat,*
> *Had Tiberius been a cat,*

wrote Matthew Arnold in a moment of wise inspiration. He
prefers delicate textures, rich foods, and the best of everything.[2] " It is necessary to say that if the cat holds a big
place in the household it is not alone by his graces of spoiled
child, his loving calineries, and the seductive abandon of his
lovely indolence; more than anything it is because he demands
so much. His personality is strong, his awakenings and his
wishes impatient. He refuses to wait. Under his supple
grace his gesture is one of insistence and command. You defend yourself in vain, he is master and you yield." Thus has
written Madame Michelet,[3] of whom her husband, the good
Jules, once retorted to her boast that she had owned a hundred
cats, " Rather a hundred cats have owned you! " A writer in
the " Spectator " [4] describes a typical cat: " We have seen
a tabby with a black muzzle who, for cold, calculated, and yet

---

[2] " It is odd that cats show an intense dislike to anything destined or set apart
for them. Mentu had a basket of his own, and a cushion made by a fond mistress, but to put him into it was to make him bound out like an india-rubber ball.
He liked to occupy proper chairs and sofas, or even proper hearthrugs. In the
same way, the well-bred cat has an inconvenient but aesthetic preference for
eating its food in pleasant places, even as we consume chilly tea and dusty
bread and butter in a summer glade. A plate is distasteful to a cat, a newspaper still worse; they like to eat sticky pieces of meat sitting on a cushioned
chair or a nice Persian rug. Yet if these were dedicated to this use they would
remove elsewhere. Hence the controversy is interminable." Margaret Benson
in " The Soul of a Cat."

[3] " Les Chats," p. 17.

[4] " The Cat as Unconscious Humorist " in " The Spectator ": August 2, 1890.

perfectly well-bred insolence, could have given points to a spiteful dowager duchess whose daughter-in-law ' wasn't one of us, you know.' The heartless and deliberate rudeness of that cat's behaviour on occasion would, had she been a man, have unquestionably justified shooting at sight. The courtiers in the most slavish palace in the East would have rebelled had they received the treatment she meted out daily to those who waited on her hand and foot. After a devoted admirer had hunted breathless and bare-headed over a large garden, and under a blazing July sun, lest puss should lose her dinner, and had at last brought her into the dining-room in his arms, that cat, instead of showing gratitude, and instead of running with pleasure to the plate prepared for her, has been known to sit bolt upright at the other end of the room, regarding the whole table with a look of undisguised contempt, her eyes superciliously half-shut and a tiny speck of red tongue protruding between her teeth. If the thing had not been so exceedingly well done it would have been simply vulgar; as it was it amounted to the most exasperating form of genteel brutality imaginable. The company having been at last thoroughly stared out of countenance and put down by this monstrous exhibition of intentional rudeness, the cat in question slowly rose to her feet, and digging her claws well into the carpet, stretched and balanced herself, while yawning at the same time with lazy self-satisfaction. After this she proceeded by the most circuitous route obtainable to the plate put before her, evidently intending it to be clearly understood that she held its presence under the side-board to be due in some way or other to her own skill and forethought, and that she in no sense regarded herself as beholden to any other person." The cat is the only animal that lives with man on terms of equality, nay superiority. He willingly domesticates himself but on his own conditions and never gives up his complete liberty no matter how closely he is confined. He preserves his independence in this unequal struggle even at the cost of his life. A common tom cat, living on the domestic hearth, on the best of footings with the family, visits the rooftops and the fences, becomes a leading figure at prize-fights, negotiates his *amours* on a lavish scale, and otherwise conducts himself when he is away from the house exactly as he would in the incult state. Indeed, when he is thrown on his own resources, as frequently happens both in town and country, he is perfectly capable of taking care of himself and adjusts himself to the new conditions without a moment's hesitation. This characteristic is admirably illustrated in a story by Charles G. D. Roberts,[5] a story founded on a true incident. A dog in a similar predicament would be entirely helpless; the dog, indeed, in submitting to slavery, has entirely lost the power to take care of himself when occasion arises.

It has amused Mr. Booth Tarkington, and his readers will share this jocund emotion, to paint a picture of such a cat,[6] a prodigious lanky beast who has forsaken the comforts of the fireside and the affections of a little girl for the pleasures of wild life and the chase. He had been a roly-poly, pepper-and-salt kitten, named Gipsy, a name to which in his subsequent career he gave real meaning. Early in youth he began to dissipate and was wont to join rowdy alley cats in their midnight maraudings. His taste for a fast life increased with age and one night, carrying the evening beefsteak with him, he joined the underworld.

" His extraordinary size, his daring, and his utter lack of sympathy soon made him the leader — and, at the same time, the terror — of all the loose-lived cats in a wide neighbourhood. He contracted no friendships and had no confidents. He seldom slept in the same place twice in succession, and though he was wanted by the police, he was not found. In appearance he did not lack distinction of an ominous sort; the slow, rhythmic, perfectly controlled mechanism of his

[5] " How a cat played Robinson Crusoe " in " Neighbours Unknown," p. 175.
[6] " Penrod and Sam," Chapter XII.

tail, as he impressively walked abroad, was incomparably sinister. This stately and dangerous walk of his, his long, vibrant whiskers, his scars, his yellow eye, so ice-cold, so fire-hot, haughty as the eye of Satan, gave him the deadly air of a mousquetaire duelist. His soul was in that walk and in that eye; it could be read — the soul of a bravo of fortune, living on his wits and his valour, asking no favours and granting no quarter. Intolerant, proud, sullen, yet watchful and constantly planning — purely a militarist, believing in slaughter as in religion, and confident that art, science, poetry, and the good of the world were happily advanced thereby — Gipsy had become, though technically not a wild cat, undoubtedly the most untamed cat at large in the civilized world."

The cat whose portrait Mr. Tarkington has painted in these few brilliant strokes, discovers the back-bone of a three-pound white-fish lying within a few inches of the nose of Penrod's old dog, Duke, and Duke awakens to the terrifying spectacle of the cat, bearing the fishbone in his horrid jaws. "Out from one side of his head, and mingling with his whiskers, projected the long, spiked spine of the big fish; down from the other side of that ferocious head dangled the fish's tail, and from above the remarkable effect thus produced shot the intolerable glare of two yellow eyes. To the gaze of Duke, still blurred by slumber, this monstrosity was all of one piece — the bone seemed a living part of it." Duke gave a shriek of terror and the massacre began. Gipsy, too, sounded his war-cry, "the subterranean diapason of a demoniac bass viol." Then, "never releasing the fishbone for an instant, he laid back his ears in a chilling way, beginning to shrink into himself like a concertina, but rising amidships so high that he appeared to be giving an imitation of that peaceful beast, the dromedary. Such was not his purpose, however, for having attained his greatest possible altitude, he partially sat down and elevated his right arm after the manner of a semaphore. This semaphore arm remained rigid for a second, threatening;

then it vibrated with inconceivable rapidity, feinting. But it was the treacherous left that did the work. Seemingly this left gave Duke three lightning little pats upon the left ear, but the change in his voice indicated that these were no love-taps. He yelled, ' help! ' and ' bloody murder! ' . . . Gipsy possessed a vocabulary for cat-swearing certainly second to none out of Italy, and probably equal to the best there." Presently, this time with his right paw, he drew blood from Duke's nose, but on the approach of Penrod he saw fit to retire, not out of fear, Mr. Tarkington explains, but probably because he could not spit without dropping the fishbone, and, " as all cats of the slightest pretensions to technique perfectly understand, this can neither be well done nor produce the best effects unless the mouth be opened to its utmost capacity so as to expose the beginnings of the alimentary canal."

Gipsy should not be regarded as a curious exception in the feline world. The cat, indeed, is the only animal without visible means of support who still manages to find a living in the city. I do not mean to say that all cats do. Both in the city and in the country cats without homes, and even cats with homes, are largely at the mercy of a great many enemies, both aggressive and accidental. The wicked small boy, the automobile, the dog, the tram-car, the rabbit-trap, all quickly put an end to many superfluous pussies' lives, but it is equally certain that the number of apparently unprovided-for cats who live wild lives in both city and country is very large indeed. Some of the males become enormous, fat and sleek, living on the contents of stray ashcans, occasionally stealing better food through an open window, catching mice in warehouses and sparrows in parks. Even the females manage somehow not only to care for themselves but also to bring up families.[7]

[7] The cat's ability to leap and climb gives him a marked advantage both in hunting and escaping from his enemies. It is a curious fact, however, that cats who climb to considerable heights frequently refuse to descend from more modest ones. A cat in a tree, whither he has fled from a dog, or in a second storey window, yowling piteously, is no uncommon sight. Sometimes the rescue

Treating of Traits

Water alone is sometimes difficult or impossible to procure, but cats can do without water for several days, the blood automatically thickening. One very hot August Sunday afternoon walking up Fifth Avenue I observed a large orange tabby tom rubbing himself against a hydrant and mewing. I stopped to speak with him, as is my custom with cats, when an Irish policeman approached. " I believe he wants a drink," suggested this very intelligent officer. " He's noticed that water sometimes comes from that hydrant." " I think you are right," I replied. " Let's get him one." Now a cat will not take an excursion merely because a man wants a walking companion. Walking is a human habit into which dogs readily fall but it is a distasteful form of exercise to a cat unless he has a purpose in view. I have never known a cat with a purpose in view to refuse a walk. This case was no exception. The orange tabby was a complete stranger to both the policeman and myself and yet when we suggested a little drink he walked peaceably a little way behind us as we strolled down Fifth Avenue. " I think Page and Shaw's is open," said the policeman. Now Page and Shaw's was three blocks below the hydrant and yet that cat followed at our heels. When we arrived at the shop I asked Tom to sit down for a moment; the policeman went in and presently emerged with a paper cup full of water. Tom drank every bit of this and then asked for more. He had another cup. Then, having no further use for us, without a word or gesture he trotted off.

An ingenious friend of Louis Robinson suggested to him that cats may look upon man as " a kind of locomotive tree, pleasant to rub against, the lower limbs of which afford a comfortable seat, and from whose upper branches occasionally

of such a cat becomes an international matter. It has even been found expedient, on occasion, to call out the fire department. It should be remembered that a fall from any considerable height is a serious matter for a cat. In spite of the popular superstition that he always lights on his feet, he is quite likely to break his spine.

drop tid-bits of mutton and other luscious fruit." [8]   There is
a good deal to be said for this theory.   However cats have
been known to give a more complete affection.   Most cats
are ready with very friendly morning greetings but there is
even a certain reserve in these attentions, a reserve which increases as the day lengthens.   There is none of the excessive
cataglottism indulged in by canines.   Cats only give affection
where it is deserved, except sometimes through sheer perversity when they annoy an ailurophobe with their attentions.
Return good for evil is not in the cat's book of rules.   To a
person deserving of their friendship, however, they occasionally pour out a really deep and beautiful affection.   This is
slow in growing and may be easily interrupted.   Cats will not
tolerate rough handling, beating, or teasing.   They dislike
exceedingly to be laughed at.   A seeker of a cat's affection
must therefore proceed with care; in time he may receive some
of the benefits due him, but, if he offends his cat friend, the
work of the past is all undone.   Cats seldom make mistakes
and they never make the same mistake twice.   How stupid
a cat must think a human being who is constantly repeating the
same errors!   A cat can be duped but once in his life [9] as

[8] The following curious description of the cat from Edward Topsell's "History
of Four-footed Beasts" (1658) is interesting enough to quote: "It is needless
to spend any time over her loving nature to man, how she flattereth by rubbing
her skin against one's legs, how she whurleth with her voice, having as many
tunes as turnes, for she hath one voice to beg and to complain, another to testify
her delight and pleasure, another among her own kind by flattering, by hissing,
by puffing, by spitting, in so much that some have thought that they have a
peculiar intelligible language among themselves. Therefore how she playeth,
leapeth, looketh, catcheth, tosseth with her foot, riseth up to strings held over her
head, sometimes creeping, sometimes lying on the back, playing with foot, appre-
hending greedily anything save the hand of a man, with divers such gestical
actions, it is needless to stand upon; in so much as Collins was wont to say, that
being free from his studies and more urgent weighty affairs, he was not ashamed
to play and sport himself with his cat, and verily it may be called an idle man's
pastime."

[9] An incident described by Louis de Grammont is typical of the cat's instinct in
this respect: A friend of mine occupied a house in which gas was used for
cooking. He had a cat which at the period of which I write was the mother of

there is plenty of proverbial evidence to prove. The celebrated affair of the cat and the chestnuts is the only historic or fabulous occasion on which the cat has been fooled.

Cats can be, most of them are, very cruel, but I think that George J. Romanes's [10] assumption that they torture mice simply for torture's sake is wholly unjustifiable. Occasionally this may be true. The Reverend J. G. Wood's remarkable cat, Pret, had a habit of carrying his trembling and terrified mouse quite alive to the very top of the five-storey house in which she resided and then dropping it down the well in the centre of the circular staircase and watching results with eager eyes from between the banisters.[11] But the fact remains that if a cat is going to keep himself in any kind of hunting condition a certain amount of practice is necessary and practice on a live animal is better practice than practice with a ball or a piece of paper with which the kitten takes his first lessons in pouncing on prey.[12] Some mother cats, indeed, have been known to keep hunting preserves of slightly wounded animals, released

two half-grown kittens. At dinner these cats, very badly bred, had the habit of jumping on the table and helping themselves to such morsels as they could secure. One day at luncheon the cats were on the table as usual when the servant brought in the cutlets. At the same instant there was an explosion. Upon inquiry it was discovered that the cook had been careless and that there had been a slight explosion of gas. No one was injured and everybody took his place again at the table except the cats who, thoroughly frightened, had disappeared. They did not come back, indeed, for several days. When they finally returned their fear was gone and they resumed their former habits. But some weeks later, when the maid again brought cutlets to the table, they fled at once. They had connected the explosion with the appearance of cutlets!

[10] " Animal Intelligence."

[11] " Glimpses into Petland," p. 30.

[12] Madame Michelet is not of the opinion that all of the play of the kitten is an apprenticeship for the chase ("Les Chats," p. 48): "A world of ideas, of images awake first in him, which are not images of prey. That will come to him, but later. The first attraction for him, as for a baby, is the thing that moves. It seems that this life of objects deceives their immobility. Both follow these movements with an eye at first uncertain, but soon they are captivated. The infant wishes to seize the ball suspended to the cradle and the kitten in the evening pursues his shadow. Tigrine showed a very lively taste for these silhouettes, which assumed in her eyes more reality than the object itself."

on occasion for their kittens to play with. This instinct, too, accounts for the seemingly needless slaughter indulged in by some cat-hunters, who kill and bring in eight or ten times as much game as they consume. It may also be true that some cats carry the love of hunting far beyond necessity; there is reason to suppose, indeed, that some cats love hunting as much as Theodore Roosevelt loved it, and why, in the name of all that is just, should they not love it? There are those who protest against the killing of wild life by cats who see no evil in leading tame lambs and calves to the slaughter, who enjoy eating lobsters that have been boiled alive, who wear on their hats aigrettes torn from the breasts of live nesting birds, who send cows on long sickening ocean journeys crowded so closely together that they can scarcely lie down, or pack chickens in crates so tightly that they cannot move. People who go fox-hunting three times a week in the season object to a cat torturing a mouse.[13] Even owners of factories employing child labour and dramatic critics have told me that cats are cruel. Now a cat, like a man, is a carnivorous animal; he is even more so than a man, for a healthy cat must have animal food while a healthy man (*vide* Bernard Shaw) may subsist entirely on fruits and nuts. He is therefore following a natural instinct in killing birds and mice and he is keeping himself in training when he subjects his captures to a certain amount of torture. " But cats resemble tigers? They are tigers in miniature? Well,— and very pretty miniatures they are," writes Leigh Hunt. " And what has the tiger himself done, that he has not a right to eat his dinner, as well as Jones? . . . Deprive Jones of his dinner for a day or two and see what a state he will be in." Of course, one may bell the cat, which simply means to tie a loud sounding bell around puss's neck. Then as he runs or springs the bell warns the bird to fly away. Unfortunately for the success of this expedient an

---

[13] But they see no harm in teaching dogs to hunt. The crime of the cat is that he does his own hunting instead of man's.

intelligent cat who is also an obstinate hunter will soon learn to hold the bell under his chin in such a manner that it will not ring.

Cats, of course, are determined fighters, but these fights are like the romantic combats of chivalry, or the brabbles of the *apaches* of modern Paris: they are broils over the female of the species. For the cat is a great lover. The amount of amorous instinct in a healthy full-grown tom can scarcely be overestimated. And any attempt at holding this instinct in check, short of castration, is usually frustrated. As Remy de Gourmont has pointed out, chastity is a quixotic ideal towards which only man in the animal kingdom strives. It is impossible even to keep a silky Angora, whose ancestors have all been housebred, sequestered for any length of time unless he has become a neuter. Any one who tries it will be delighted, after a week or so, to let tom have his own way.[14] But it has become the general custom, except for those who keep kings for breeding purposes, to alter these toms, so that they grow into large, affectionate, and lazy animals, who sleep a good deal, eat a good deal, and are generally picturesque but not very active. These altered toms are generally the favourites as pets. Personally I am more interested in cats who retain their natural fervour.

The females fight occasionally, especially in the protection of their young, and when they are calling [15] (so their period of heat is poetically and literally described, for it is marked by little amorous coos, almost like the tender sighs of an eighteenth century lover), with an effrontery born of desire, they bite the males in the throat, usually with satisfactory re-

[14] In the Middle Ages it was the custom to attach cats outside the windows of remarried widows in reference to the lubricity of the animal. The cat is opposed to marriage. She will accept one lover, two lovers, three lovers, as many slaves as possible, but never a tyrant.

[15] The vocabulary of the professional cat-breeder is generally poetic. When a female cat is sent to a male the event is called a " visit " and the male's act is called " signing."

sults. The males are formidable fighters both with their own species and with other animals. They do not usually fight dogs unless they are driven into corners but cats have been known to gratuitously attack dogs. Their sharp claws and their supple joints, kept constantly in condition by applying the claws to a tree or a chair or a table or a rug and pulling and stretching, are very effective in warfare, an effectiveness that is increased by powerful jaws and sharp teeth. It is the habit of the cat when fighting to lie on his back, if possible, thus bringing all his best talents into full play and protecting his spine, his most vulnerable spot. When a cat attacks a dog he usually jumps on the dog's back and is able to cling and at the same time tear at the beast's head and eyes. Nature, ironic, as usual, allows the eagle this procedure with the cat. Cats frequently emerge unscathed from the most bloody frays, save for a torn ear or a scarred tail, for the skin of the feline is so loose that it can be pulled almost half way around the body without tearing and the lateral movements of the head, while not as extensive as those of the owl, are nevertheless considerable.

When the cat is fighting or in danger, he usually emits the most blood-curdling yowls; why, is a mystery, for these are not calls for assistance as the animal fighting in the wild state is usually alone and in no case can he depend on receiving help from others of his kind. These yowls may very well be battle cries, like the fife and drum corps of the army, to keep up the morale! When a cat is beaten or mistreated, however, he never cries, although he may growl or spit.

" Cats dread death terribly," writes Andrew Lang. " I had a nefarious old cat, Gyp, who used to open the cupboard door and eat any biscuits accessible. Gyp had a stroke of paralysis, and believed he was going to die. He was in a fright: Mr. Horace Hutchinson observed him and said that this cat justly entertained the most Calvinistic apprehensions of his future reward. Gyp was nursed back into health, as was proved when we found him on the roof of an outhouse with a cold chicken in his possession. Nothing could be more human."

The cat has been called a thief. To be sure, he has no respect whatever for other people's property, although he can be taught to keep off a dinner-table while he is being watched. It is easier to teach a cat not to do things than to do them. When he is left alone, however, it is best to lock up the fish and the cream. There are proverbs to this effect and they have the ring of truth. Ariel used to hide spools, keys, pens, pencils, and scissors under rugs. She saw no more reason why she should not make such booty her own than the early settlers of America saw any reason why they should not convert aboriginal property to their uses. These early settlers looked upon the Indians as inferiors who had no rights, and the cat looks upon man in the same way.

But Walt Whitman was wrong when he said of the animals, " not one is demented with the mania of owning things." As far as their own property is concerned cats have a very definite sense of property rights, rights, however, which they protect themselves; they never call in the police or the militia. Evidence of this trait is very easy to collect. All cats understand it thoroughly, so thoroughly, indeed, that only a very hungry or a very daring cat will attempt to slink through an open door into the home of another cat. In case he does so he proceeds warily and if he goes very far there is usually a scrimmage. A scene of this kind is frequently very comic. The master of the hearth crouches very low watching every move of the intruder while his hair begins to bristle. The stranger enters obliquely and appears to be unconscious of the presence of the cat who belongs in the house. Usually a few warning spits and passes of the paw from the insulted householder terrify the interloper into taking his departure. Occasionally, however, cats with charitable instincts bring in stray animals to share their food. I have already mentioned

The Tiger in the House

Gautier's Enjolras. I have been told of a tramp cat, fed once at a farm-house, who returned the next day with twenty-nine of his friends! But such interest in outsiders is rare in felines; they have been accustomed to rule over their solitary hunting ground in the wild state and the instinct survives.

Persian cats share it. Not long ago I brought home a little orange kitten as gentle and sweet as possible, a little model of quaint dignity and grace. The annoyance and anger of my Feathers, the established queen of the household, showed itself immediately with sundry growls and spits. A dog will almost always exhibit signs of jealousy in the presence of a newcomer, but this emotion was downright rage. Rage that any one should dare attempt to usurp a part of her life, share her food, sit on her cushions, slink into her places in the sun. So, with that persistent patience which is as effective as inquisitional methods, Feathers set about converting me to the idea that the thing was impossible. For three days she made the kitten's life a grievous burden. Did the kitten try to sleep, Feathers bit his tail; was he awake, Feathers would stare at him disconcertingly, then with a bound over his back light on the other side, a terrifying procedure punctuated with a growl and a spit, calculated to send chills down stouter spines. She followed the kitten from room to room, never permitting him peace or quiet or any assurance of a foothold in the apartment. More than this, Feathers altered completely in her relations with me. Ordinarily a gentle cat, during the kitten's brief sojourn she never permitted me to pick her up or to become familiar with her in any way. She bit, she scratched, she arched her back, and she bristled her hairs. Indeed I never went near her during those three days without being spit at. Savage home life is something I do not crave; I bowed to the inevitable and bore the orange kitten away. Immediately Feathers became all smiles and caresses, a changed and de-lighted being.[16]

[16] Cats often consider certain chairs as their property and they will allow

Treating of Traits

This quality in cats, this incessant potentiality of a return to feral conditions, is very puzzling to those who have no feeling for or understanding of these animals. It is usually called "bad temper" and out of it has grown the legend that "you cannot trust cats." As a matter of fact no animal is so sure to react in certain ways to certain phenomena as the cat.[17] He is fond of his home and its surroundings, regards them with pride and delight. How would you, reader, care to have a stranger (of either sex) suddenly foisted on you to share your bed and board? Do you think it unreasonable for a cat to protest against so great an attack on personal liberty? You would not like it; neither does the cat. But the cat being more independent, more assertive, more liberty loving, than that sneaking cowardly animal called man, refuses absolutely to tolerate encroachments on his individuality. A man quite conceivably would put up with the inconvenience; in fact, often does.

This dual personality, with its lights and shades, is in a great measure an explanation of the formidable power of fascination the cat possesses. There is always the possibility of a reversion to the wild state. The sight of a fly or a cockroach, a rat or a mouse, another cat or dog, will make a wild beast out of a tame animal in a quarter of a second. Moreover, if Fate and Nature so rule, it is entirely possible for the cat to live either existence for extended periods of time. And it must always be remembered that a cat's relations with man, whom he usually regards with a certain amused contempt, are on an entirely different plane from his relations with cats or any other animals.

neither dogs nor human beings to occupy them. I have observed a cat, in a household which he ruled, make the round of the drawing-room, driving each occupant out of his chair. His method was a simple one. He weighed twelve pounds and he insinuated himself between the person seated and the back of the chair.

[17] A well-treated cat will never scratch a friend, except accidentally in play, or under the nervous strain of a supreme insult, and a friend will never insult a cat.

37

The Tiger in the House

The cat's love for places has been exaggerated by unintelligent persons, who are constantly making remarks about an animal that even the most intelligent of us does not begin to understand. This love of home is regarded as a highly moral and generally satisfactory trait in man, especially when it takes the general form of patriotism. But somehow it is entirely different for a cat to love his home; once he does so he is regarded with horror by the populace. The question, like that of the relative merits of cats and dogs, has become an international one and is invariably introduced as a subtopic in any lay conversation about cats. "But the home," Madame Michelet [18] points out, "is often an assemblage of objects which belong to your habits, which are even you, yourself. . . . The cat is essentially conservative in his habits. However it is less to the walls of the house that he clings than to a certain arrangement of objects, of furniture, which bear more than the house itself the trace of personality. So our actual life, our facility of locomotion, the varied circumstances and the inconstant tastes which render us today so fluid, are highly antipathetic to the cat." A poet in " The Spectator " has it:

> *You hold your race traditions fast,*
> *While others toil, you simply live,*
> *And based upon a stable past,*
> *Remain a sound conservative.*

The cat thinks what has been will be. As he waits for his prey he waits for his master. He learns all the ways of escape from danger in his house, finds his favourite chair to sleep in, his familiar nook to lurk in; he does not relinquish these sureties without a certain objection. Indeed in a case where a cat has not formed an attachment for any member of the family it seems absurd to ask him to give up these advantages. The cat becomes attached to his master when that one caresses him, feeds him, and loves him. But when he is largely ig-

[18] " Les Chats," p. 79.

38

nored he becomes more attached to the house itself than he does to its inmates. . . . Above all else it must be remembered that the cat loves order.

In "A Story Teller's Holiday," George Moore tells how, wandering about the ruins of Dublin after the Irish rebellion, he discovered a broken wall to which a mantelpiece still clung. "A plaintive miaw reached me, and a beautiful black Persian cat appeared by the fireplace. A cat is almost articulate, and Tom asked me to explain the meaning of all this ruin. He has found his old fireplace, I said, and tried to entice him; but, though pleased to see me, he would not be persuaded to leave what remained of the hearth on which he had spent so many pleasant hours, and pondering on his faithfulness and his beauty I continued my search among the ruins, meeting cats everywhere, all seeking their lost homes among the ashes and all unable to comprehend the misfortune that had befallen them. It is true that the cats suffer vaguely, but suffering is not less because it is vague, and it seemed to me that in the early ages of the world, shall we say twenty thousand years before Pompeii and Herculaneum, men groped and suffered blindly amid incomprehensible earthquakes seeking their lost homes, just like the cats in Henry Street. We are part and parcel of the same original substance, I said, and then my thoughts breaking off suddenly, I began to rejoice in Nature's unexpectedness and fecundity. She is never commonplace in her stories, we have only to go to her to be original, I muttered, as I returned through the silent streets. I could have imagined everything else, the wall-paper, the overmantel, and the French clock, but not the cats seeking for their lost hearths, nor is it likely that Turgenieff could, Balzac still less."

But some cats have no aversion to moving. Some cats, indeed, move of their own accord as did Guy Wetmore Carryl's capricious Zut, described further along in this volume. Andrew Lang felt that there was a mystic free-masonry, a sort of Rosicrucian brotherhood among cats, so strange are their move-

ments, so inexplicable. It is possible that boredom is sometimes a motive for a peregrination. " Monotony," writes
Lindsay,[19] " as a factor of mental derangement in the lower
animals, is closely associated with, and usually inseparable
from, solitude and captivity. Other animals dislike monotonous lives and occupations as much as man does; they suffer
as much as he from want of novelty and variety; they have the
same desire for amusement; there is equal necessity in the case
of many of them for relaxation on the one hand and pleasant
excitement on the other. Sameness has a similar depressing
influence on them as on man, whether this sameness be of scene,
surroundings, air, or food." Persian cats, doomed usually to
pass their lives in city apartments, go, of course, from one to
the other without apparent discomfort or unhappiness. Occasionally a cat with a grand passion for a man will hunt him
out. Pennant records that when the Earl of Southampton,
the friend and companion of the Earl of Sussex in his fatal
insurrection, was confined to the Tower of London, he was
surprised by a visit from his favourite cat, who, it is said,
obtained access to the Earl by descending the chimney of his
apartment.

" Animals are such friends; they ask no questions, they pass
no criticisms," wrote the unenlightened George Eliot somewhere or other. This is certainly not true of cats. An ordinary kitten will ask more questions than any five year old boy.
He is the most catechismal of animals, with the possible exception of the monkey. Curiosity, indeed, is a predominant cat
trait and a cat's first duty on entering a new domain is to ex-
plore every square inch of it. He not only examines every
corner of the house he lives in but investigates the country for
miles around. Lane [20] thinks this is the reason he can find
his way back home when he has been carried away. Once
this initiative ceremony is completed, the cat, in most in-

[19] " Mind in the Lower Animals "; Vol. II, p. 247.
[20] C. H. Lane: " Rabbits, Cats and Cavies."

stances, expresses his satisfaction by turning round and round and finally settling down to sleep. There is a superstition to the effect that if you butter or grease a cat's feet after taking him to a new home he will not run away, and Ernest Thompson Seton has introduced a reference to it in his story, " The Slum Cat." [21] The basis of the superstition is the fact that a cat will wash himself directly you put grease on his paws and that almost always after washing, a cat will fall asleep and that if you can get a cat to sleep in a place it is pretty safe to say that he will be satisfied to remain there. Curiosity, of course, is an instinct taken over from the wild state, in which exploration was dangerous but necessary and it has been ingeniously explained that a cat circles round and round before lying down because he dimly remembers that he is treading a lair out of the tall grass. Curiosity in a cat, however, goes further than mere protective instinct. No box, no package, no paper bag ever enters my door that Feathers does not examine it, and this is no rare quality but one which is generally distributed. Any new box, any open drawer serves as a new place to nap in. Cats, however, can seldom be induced to eat from the hand, and then only with great reluctance, hesitation, and delicacy, so exactly are curiosity and caution balanced in the feline mind. They also sniff at objects, but one smell is enough. They do not return for reassurance. There are those who assert that the sense of smell in a cat is not highly developed.[22] I think myself that it is largely super-

---

[21] " Animal Heroes."

[22] But cats are frequently intoxicated by the odour of valerian and they adore the fragrance of flowers. Sometimes even they express delight over the artifices of Houbigant, Coty, and Bichara. In this they differ from dogs, as W. H. Hudson has pointed out ("The Great Dog-Superstition" in "The Book of a Naturalist") : "The pampered lap-dog in the midst of his comforts has one great thorn in his side, one perpetual misery to endure, in the perfumes which please his mistress. He too is a little Venetian in his way, but his way is not hers. The camphor-wood chest in her room is an offence to him, the case of glass-stoppered scents an abomination. All fragrant flowers are as asafoetida to his exquisite nostrils and his face is turned aside in very ill-concealed disgust from

seded by a highly charged electrical nervous system and by the senses of sight, hearing, and touch.[23] Madame Michelet [24] decided that the sense of smell in a kitten was more highly developed than in the grown cat. She was able to awaken kittens by putting milk under their noses. The same experiment with older cats did not prove successful.

It has long been a favourite contention of mine that nothing is more ephemeral than science; no books are sooner ready for the garret or the waste-basket than serious books. When a serious book has an artistic value, such as a book by Nietzsche, for instance, the case is altered, but the ordinary professor's or scientist's profound discoveries are absolutely worthless in a few years. They serve, indeed, only to indicate the quaint fluctuations, the ebb and flow, of human thought. The first to admit this is the scientist himself, who tells you that you must work only along the lines of the " latest discoveries." Now these latest discoveries are usually ideas that have been filched from some philosopher, black magician, or monk who lived in the neolithic age. The mediaeval grimoires are probably unworked gold mines of " new thought." Freud is foreshadowed in eighteenth century philosophy; even Christian Science is not new. You can find the germ of almost every science or philosophy in Aristotle, Paracelsus, or Mesmer. Alchemists were familiar with laws which scientists have recently rediscovered. Aristeus, the philosophical alchemist, is said to have delivered to his disciples what he termed the golden key of the Great Work, which had the power of rendering all metals diaphanous. Yet I have never heard Aristeus

the sandal-wood box or fan. It is warm and soft on her lap, but an incurable grief to be so near her pocket-handkerchief, saturated with nasty white-rose or lavender. If she must perfume herself with flowery essences he would prefer an essential oil expressed from the gorgeous *Rafflesia Arnoldi* of the Bornean forest, or even from the humble carrion-flower which blossoms nearer home."

[23] Cats have an especial fondness for certain textures. They like paper or something rough that tears with a noise.

[24] " Les Chats," p. 202.

described as the inventor of the X Ray. There are few today who would attempt to duplicate the engineering feats of the Egyptians.

Men who devote their lives to science usually have no sense of humour. They are often asses. A. G. Mayer, according to John Burroughs, has proved conclusively that the promethea moth has no colour sense. The male of this moth has blackish wings and the female reddish brown. Mayer caused the two sexes to change colours; he glued the wings of the male to the female and vice versa and found that they mated just the same! Well, Professor Mayer could have arrived at the same brilliant conclusion if he had painted a yellow tom cat black and a cream queen green. There is a certain little reason by which a female can distinguish a male but no scientist would ever think of that. Serious scientific works, therefore, may be regarded as generally negligible, in the first place because it is impossible to approximate truth by rushing blindly in one direction, closing out all distracting sights and sounds, no matter how strongly they bear on the subject, in the second place because there is no such thing as truth. Any mystic philosopher can *feel* more than a scientist can ever learn.

There have been sects of somatists who do not believe that the cat is endowed with a soul. But this discussion has gone out of fashion because man is no longer very much interested in the soul. It is now the part of smart scientific conversation to talk more about the brain. During the nineteenth century many scientists, psychologists, natural historians, zoologists, and the like, have devoted their entire time to the consideration of the problem as to whether or no animals think. Darwin, of course, for the sake of his evolutionary theory, warmly espoused the cause of thinking brutes, and Romanes and others have followed him in this direction. Other men of more or less importance have disagreed and talk about " instinct," etc. A whole literature of neglected and contradictory books has grown up on the subject and I imagine anything written before the hour of midnight of the morning on which you are reading these pages would be considered entirely worthless in any self-respecting professor's class-room. *" Il n'y a pas un de ces livres qui n'en démente un autre,"* remarks the supremely sagacious Sylvestre Bonnard, *" en sorte que, quand on les connaît tous, on ne sait que penser."* Elsewhere I have given a short bibliography of the subject and you may take a melancholy pleasure in perusing some of the arguments pro and con. The worthy John Burroughs [25] informs us that when he hears an animal laugh he will believe in his reason. Man, he says, can be reached through his mind, an animal only through his senses. The whole secret of the training of wild animals is to form new habits in them. Any army captain will inform Mr. Burroughs that this is the whole secret of training men. There are others who will contradict Mr. Burroughs. " There is really nothing so primitive, even so animal as reason," writes Havelock Ellis.[26] " It may plausibly, however unsoundly, be maintained that it is by his emotions, not by his reason, that man differs most from the beasts. ' My cat,' says Unamuno, who takes this view in his new book, ' Del sentimiento tragico de la vida,' ' never laughs or cries; he is always reasoning.' "

Mr. Burroughs also decided that animals cannot think because they have no language and that you cannot think without language. But have they not? The vocal language of cats is extraordinarily complete as I shall show in a later chapter. This is complemented by a gesture language which can, of course, only be completely understood by other cats. There is, for instance, the language of the tail. The cat with a tail raised high like a banner is a satisfied, contented, healthy, and proud cat. A tail carried horizontally indicates stealth or terror. A tail curled under the body is a signal of fear.

[25] " The Animal Mind "; " The Atlantic Monthly "; November 1910; Vol. 106, p. 622.
[26] " Impressions and Comments," p. 233.

Treating of Traits

The cat waves his tail from side to side when he is dissatisfied, annoyed, or angry; in rage he extends it with the fur distended. He lashes it as a preparation for battle and he twitches it when he is amused or pleased. And cats sometimes use their tails, as women use boas or muffs, as a means of keeping warm.

The variety of ways in which a cat uses his paw is even greater. Lindsay [27] gives us a catalogue: " The cat not infrequently uses its paw to touch or tap its master's shoulder when it desires to attract his notice ('Animal World'). A pet cat sitting at a carriage window, when anything passing takes her fancy, ' puts her paw on my chest,' says her mistress, ' and makes a pretty little noise, as though asking me if I had seen it also.' Another laid her paw on the lips of a lady who had a distressing cough every time she coughed, in evidence possibly of pity, possibly in order to the physical suppression of the cough by the closure of the aperture by which alone it could find vent (Wood).[28] A third cat touched with her paw the lips of those who whistled a tune, ' as if pleased with the sound ' (Wood). Cats ' cuff ' each other or their young — that is, they give blows, and so punish or administer rebuke to some unruly or troublesome kitten — with their paws. They also warm their paws before a fire and use them for shading the face either from the fire or the sun ('Animal World'). We are told of a cat frequently patting the nose of a companion horse. It is well known that our domestic cats are in the habit of washing their faces by means of their paws, by which means also they brush and clean their foreheads and eyes. The cat uses its forepaw too in touching or testing objects — to ascertain, for instance, their hardness or other qualities ('Percy Anecdotes '), or to measure the quantity or discover the level of the fluids certain vessels may contain. Thus a cat, ' when wishing to drink water from a jug,' used its paw to ' ascertain if it was full enough ' ('Animal World').

[27] "Mind in the Lower Animals," Vol. 1, p. 416.
[28] "Man and Beast: Here and Hereafter," p. 370.

The Tiger in the House

It takes milk from a narrow milk-pot by inserting its paw, curling it for removal when saturated with milk, and then licking it (Wood). In a Birmingham burglary case, heard at the Warwick Assizes in March 1877, ' the prosecutor deposed that he was awakened by his cat patting his face, puss having discovered the burglars rummaging his bedroom.' ('Inverness Courier,' March 29, 1877)." It might be added that the cat frequently scratches to attract attention. It would also be possible to enumerate countless ways in which the cat uses his head, his eyes, and even his fur for purposes of conversation.

Professor Edward L. Thorndike undertook to make some exceedingly ingenious and involved experiments with cats and other animals and he has written a book [29] about them. His experiments with cats were made with " puzzle boxes." Cats which had been starved for a considerable period were shut in boxes over which food was placed. Now there were numerous more or less complicated ways of opening these boxes from within. The problem was to see how long it would take a cat to open his box and reach the food. From the results the professor drew his absolutely valueless conclusions. If the cats did not find the doctor's boxes adapertile this is no starting point on which to found a system of animal psychology. The experiment seems to me entirely analogous to that of putting a hungry and terrified Cherokee Indian into a Rolls-Royce and asking him, in a strange language, to run it if he wants his dinner.

One of the favourite arguments of the instinct-pushers educes the fact that cats, accustomed to bury dung in the wild state, will go through the motions of digging up earth on a marble or wooden floor, an instinctive memory of an act no longer necessary, and therefore unworthy of a being who thinks. Now this sort of thing can be knocked over by an idiot baby with one blue eye and one black one. Why, for instance, do you still shake hands? All reason for doing so,

[29] " Animal Intelligence: Experimental Studies."

the assurance that your friend and you carry no weapons, has passed away, and yet the stupid instinct survives. With the cat there is cause for the survival. Nature is well aware that he may be forced through circumstances or desire to again lead the wild life; when this happens he is prepared to conceal all evidence of his whereabouts from his enemies.

Other scientists in claiming inferiority for the beasts, bring forward as an argument that they always do the same things, make the same movements, that they neither invent nor progress. The bee constructs the same receptacle for honey, the spider weaves the same web, and the barn swallow builds the same nest. All individual liberty and spontaneity seem to have been refused them. They appear to obey mechanical rhythms which are transmitted through the centuries. But who can say that these rhythms are not superior moral laws and if the beasts do not progress it is because they sprang perfect into the world and do not need to, while man gropes, searches, changes, destroys, and reconstructs without being able to find anything stable in intelligence, any end to his desire, any harmony to his form? It is well to remember, O Christian reader, that it was man that God ejected from Paradise and not the animals. Besides it is preposterous and stupid to contend that animals have not freedom of thought, that they do not think, that they cannot solve individual problems.

Personally I am convinced that all these scientists, psychologists, etc., mean more or less the same thing; they are struggling more or less with the same idea, only they express it in dissimilar terms. One means instinct when he says intelligence and the other means intelligence when he says instinct. A very important system of philosophy, indeed, is based on the theory that animal instinct is of greater utility than intelligence and asks man to trust to it as much as possible. Women, I believe, are popularly supposed to be entirely guided by such principles.

To my mind there is no more doubt that animals think,

after their fashion, than there is that men as a rule do not think at all. Scientists make the mistake of observing too closely and of writing down what they think they have seen. Such matters should be discussed mystically with a certain aloofness. " I observe authors who speak concerning cats with a familiarity most distasteful," writes Andrew Lang.

Animals do not think after the manner of man; their thinking processes are quite different. There is a certain amount of truth in the theory that they think in abstractions, cold, heat, etc., but that they do not think of them afterwards *as* abstractions as human beings do. But I can see no particular advantage in remembering and discussing such matters. Robert Louis Stevenson once observed that animals never used verbs: " That is the only way in which their thinking differs from that of men."

However one point and one point only concerns us greatly here, that is the relative intelligence of the cat, who by many is considered inferior mentally to the dog and the horse. The intelligence of cats, has, I think, been greatly underestimated.[30] It can hardly be overestimated. " We cannot without becoming cats, perfectly understand the cat mind," writes St. George Mivart.[31] The cat as an individual thinks in entirely different directions from his human companions and therefore it is difficult to secure the right kind of evidence, especially as most of the professors judge an animal's intelligence by his susceptibility to discipline, in other words by his comparative ability to become the willing slave of man. In this kind of contest the dog and the horse naturally carry off all the honours. Because the cat refuses to bend under the yoke and accept this discipline I do not think he can be proved an unintelligent animal; quite the contrary. The cat is far too intelligent to be inveigled into any drudgery or mummery.

[30] I hope I have impressed the reader with the fact that all cats are not alike. I have seen cats as stupid as any tax-payer.
[31] " The Cat," p. 366.

Treating of Traits

Va, le secret de réussir,
C'est d'être adroit, non d'être utile,

is the advice of the lazy old cat in a fable of Florian. He compels his human friend to accept him on his own terms. A dog's acts are much more imitative and therefore more applicable to human reasoning. But T. Wesley Mills,[32] who studied both animals, writes, " The cat is far in advance of the dog in power to execute highly complex co-ordinated movements." And again, " In will-power and ability to maintain an independent existence the cat is superior to the dog."

Some acts of cats are entirely consonant with human intelligence. Cats have the power to draw inferences from observation. They easily learn to open doors; many of them learn to ring bells for admittance. Frequently they answer bells, knowing that they mean dinner or somebody's arrival. Feathers not only goes to the door when the bell rings but also when she hears the elevator ascending. She even runs to the telephone when it rings. These and other such accomplishments as retrieving the cat is not easily taught. If, however, she finds it convenient to acquire them she will do so. Artault de Vevey had a cat [33] who was fond of visiting friends on the fifth floor (de Vevey lived on the first). She would cry for admittance; if no one answered her she would scratch at the doorpanel; as a last resort she would pull the bell rope.

A writer in " The Spectator " [34] observed " a large male cat who in turn was watching sparrows feeding in a court-yard. When disturbed by the opening of a back-door the sparrows always flew to a beech-hedge near. The cat noted this, walked behind the hedge and waiting opposite the spot to which the birds generally flew, jumped into the middle of them when

[32] " The Cat and the Dog Compared "; McGill University; Papers from the Department of Physiology, 1896.
[33] This was the same Isoline who took baths.
[34] " The Cat as Wild Animal "; " The Spectator," September 12, 1896.

49

they were next disturbed. This was the result of deliberation and calculation. Another cat which was watching sparrows stepped behind a row of paving stones recently taken up as soon as it saw the writer approaching and secured one driven over its head. It saw the probability that the birds would be driven in its direction and it acted on its conclusions in a second." Wynter [35] relates an incident of a tom cat of Callendar who was seen bearing away a piece of beef in his jaws. The servant who followed him watched him lay the morsel down near a rat hole. Then he hid himself. Presently the rat came out and was dragging away the meat when the cat pounced upon him. Émile Achard's Matapon,[36] having killed all the mice in the house, took to killing field mice. This was difficult and unpleasant on rainy days but it was not long before he conceived the idea, and carried it out, of restocking the house. He brought field mice in alive and let them loose, thus establishing a new hunting preserve.

Lindsay [37] quotes the following example from the "Animal World": A certain cat and dog were confederates in a larder theft. The cat by its mewing called the dog when circumstances were favourable to their depredations. On one occasion when the dog was followed the cat was discovered mounted on a shelf, keeping the cover of a dish partly open with one foot and throwing down good things to the dog with the other! The Reverend J. G. Wood describes an old disabled tom cat who made a bargain with a younger and more active animal to catch mice for him, the apprentice being paid with bones and cats' meat. The compact was honourably carried out on both sides. Once, during an illness, Mrs. Siddons [38] fed her cat the richest cream, the finest parts of the

[35] " Fruit Between the Leaves."
[36] " The History of My Friends, or Home Life with Animals."
[37] " Mind in the Lower Animals "; Vol. I, p. 391.
[38] " Fruit Between the Leaves."

chicken. Thereafter he occasionally shammed lameness in order to get these delicacies.

Eugène Muller, in "Animaux Célèbres," furnishes us with another admirable example: A professor, who wished to demonstrate to his pupils the uses of a pneumatic machine, introduced a cat under the glass bell. The animal, of course, made frantic efforts to escape, but the glass held him a prisoner. " I am going to show you," said the professor, " how, as I pump, the air under the globe will become rarefied; the cat will breathe with more and more difficulty, and indeed would be asphyxiated if I pumped long enough, but we will conclude the experiment before that, and you will see that the moment the air re-enters the cat will immediately regain all his forces." It all happened exactly as he had described it. The professor pumped, and the cat fell panting, thinking, doubtless, that his last hour was upon him. But, the instant the professor ceased to pump, puss was himself once more. He was released and ran away, making a vow, no doubt, that he would not be caught again. In a few days, however, before another class, the good doctor had occasion to repeat the experiment. The cat was captured and placed under the bell and the professor began his explanation, " I am going to show you how, as I pump . . ." But the students observed a quite different phenomenon from that which was intended, for, as the professor pumped, the cat placed one of his paws over the opening through which the air was to be drawn away. And as often as the professor attempted to repeat the experiment he repeated his counter-gesture!

During the Crimean War, Col. Stuart Wortley's cat visited the doctor's hut to get a bayonet wound in the foot examined and bandaged. The colonel found her wounded after the battle of Malakoff and took her daily for a time to the regimental surgeon for treatment. But when he himself became ill she continued the visits of her own accord and sat quietly down for her usual treatment.[39] There are many recorded instances of cats bringing their kittens to their mistresses for treatment and cats have been known to give one another obstetrical assistance. In Madame Michelet's book, Mr. Frederick Harrison relates a touching incident of an old lady cat. She felt she was dying before her kittens were weaned. She could hardly walk but she disappeared one morning carrying a kitten and came back without it. Next day, quite exhausted, she took away her other two kittens and then died. She had carried each kitten to a separate cat, each of which was nourishing a family and accepted the new fosterling.

A cat will sit washing his face within two inches of a dog in the most frantic state of barking rage, if the dog be chained. He knows the dog cannot get away. Cats also have a habit of tantalizing dogs by lying on exposed window-sills, with paws temptingly depending just out of reach. You may also have observed for yourself how impertinent cats can be to dogs who are muzzled.

Any one who has lived on terms of comparative equality with a cat knows that he will show his intelligence fifty times a day. To be sure this intelligence is usually of the variety called selfish. Thereby the cat shows how much finer his intelligence is than that of the rest of the animal world. He is quite unwilling to perform feats of intelligence for which he can see no legitimate reason, or through which he is unable to derive any personal satisfaction. If he wants submaxillary massage he knows that he is pretty sure of getting it by leaping into some one's lap. If he does not want it he knows that the best way of avoiding it is to avoid the person who insists on lavishing it. A cat, it has been said, will only come when called if dinner is in the offing. This is very much my procedure. I refuse to make casual calls but often accept invitations to dinner.

In spite of his independence and his inadaptability to human

[39] "Mind in the Lower Animals," Vol. II, p. 374.

desires the cat can be made useful, which is perhaps fortunate as there are certain people who consider an animal worthless who cannot be made in some way to serve that superior being man. In England cats work for the government in offices, barracks, docks and workshops. There are at least two thousand felines so employed and they are all on the pay-roll, receiving a shilling a week. This is for food, for contrary to popular belief hungry cats do not make the best mousers. Benvenuto Cellini was right when he said, " Cats of good breed hunt better fat than lean." They serve to effectually rid these places of rodents. The National Printing Office of France employs a large staff of cats to guard the paper from rats and mice. Vienna has official cats and the Midland Railway in England has eight cats among its employees. Cats are kept in all the large United States Post Offices and in the military magazines. A writer in " The Spectator " [40] tells of the regret felt in a large London factory when the " best foundry cat " died. The sand moulds for making casts in the foundry are mixed with flour. Mice eat the flour and spoil the moulds. Cats are kept to kill the mice but they have to be taught not to walk on the moulds or to scratch them up. The cat who died was absolutely perfect in this respect. The number of mice a good cat-hunter can destroy goes quite beyond the probable. Lane [41] writes of walking with his cat Magpie into his stables when a mob of mice dashed across the room. Magpie leaped into the group and caught four simultaneously, two in her jaws and one under each forepaw ! Such prowess is not rare in a good mouser. Every retail and wholesale butcher-shop and green-grocer, every stationer, every restaurateur, must therefore have his cat or cats. In some groceries a cellar cat and a shop cat are kept. I have already mentioned the cold-storage cats. The cat also destroys a great number of insects, flies, cockroaches, grasshoppers and mosqui-

[40] " The Cat About Town "; " The Spectator "; Vol. 80, p. 197.
[41] C. H. Lane: " Rabbits, Cats and Cavies," p. 231.

The Tiger in the House

toes. During the late war the English government conscripted
500,000 cats, a few of which were sent to sea to test submarines
and the remainder to the trenches. Their warnings of the
approach of a cloud of gas, long before any soldier could
smell it, saved many lives. They also did a good deal towards
ridding the trenches of rats and mice, and probably served as
pets for many a doughboy.

The cat also is the one animal, save the mongoose, that is
not afraid of snakes and can battle successfully even with the
venomous varieties. J. R. Rengger, who has written of the
mammals of Paraguay,[42] declares that he has more than once
seen cats pursue and kill snakes, even rattle-snakes, on the
sandy, grassless plains of that land. " With their rare skill,"
he writes, " they would strike the snake with their paw, and
at the same time avoid its spring. If the snake coiled itself
they would not attack it directly, but would go round it till it
became tired of turning its head after them; then they would
strike another blow, and instantly turn aside. If the snake
started to run away, they would seize its tail, as if to play with
it. By virtue of these continued attacks they usually destroyed their enemy in less than an hour, but would never eat its
flesh." The subject has served in fiction but the man who
wrote the following description [43] was certainly writing something he had once observed: " Now, as the Dryad, curled
to a capital S, quivering and hissing, advanced for the last time
to the charge, it was bound to strike across the edge of the
sofa on which I lay, at the erect head of Stoffles, which vanished with a juggling celerity that would have dislocated the
collar-bone of any other animal in creation. From such an
exertion the snake recovered itself with an obvious effort,
quick beyond question, but not nearly quick enough. Before
I could well see that it had missed its aim, Stoffles had launched
out like a spring released, and, burying eight or ten claws in

[42] " Säugethiere von Paraguay."
[43] G. H. Powell: " The Blue Dryad " in " Animal Episodes."

54

the back of its enemy's head, pinned it down against the stiff cushion of the sofa. The tail of the agonized reptile flung wildly in the air and flapped on the arched back of the imperturbable tigress. The whiskered muzzle of Stoffles dropped quietly, and her teeth met once, twice, thrice, like the needle and hook of a sewing-machine, in the neck of the Blue Dryad; and when, after much deliberation, she let it go, the beast fell into a limp tangle on the floor." Moncrif [44] speaks of this special talent of cats. According to the Frenchman a certain promontory in the Island of Cyprus is known as the Cape of Cats. Formerly there was a monastery there and the promontory was infested with black and white snakes. The cats belonging to the monks spent happy days hunting serpents, but, when the bell rang, always returned to the monastery for their meals.

Lieutenant Colonel A. Buchanan, M. D. [45] is convinced that the Indian plagues are caused by rats and that they could be prevented if the natives could be prevailed upon to keep cats. [46] He produces statistics which seem to prove that the villages in which there were cats in each household were free from epidemics of cholera.

In the sixteenth century a German, one Christopher of Hapsburg, projected a plan for having poison gases in jars attached to the backs of cats disseminated in battle. Chris-

[44] Moncrif: "Les Chats," p. 59.

[45] "Cats as Plague Preventers": "British Medical Journal"; London; October 24, 1908; Vol. 2, p. 1231.

[46] Hindus, who believe in the doctrine of metempsychosis, have a valid objection to taking life. In Bombay there is a hospital for sick animals. Professor Monier Williams, who visited it, says, "The animals are well fed and well tended, though it certainly seemed to me that a great majority would be more mercifully provided for by the application of a loaded pistol to their heads. . . . It is even said that men are paid to sleep on dirty woollen beds in different parts of the building that the loathsome vermin with which they are infested may be supplied with their nightly need of human blood. These men are drugged so that they will not involuntarily kill the vermin in their sleep." E. P. Evans: "Evolutionary Ethics and Animal Psychology," p. 140.

topher was an officer of artillery and he presented his drawing, which was not accepted for practical use, to the Council of One and Twenty at Strassbourg. It still exists in the great library there. There is another story, certainly apocryphal, that the Persians, bearing pussies in their arms, once marched upon the Egyptians who, refusing to harm the sacred animal, were put to rout.

I have elsewhere related how occasionally cats bring rabbits home to their masters. They have served even stranger purposes. A physician told me of a lady whose milk came slowly after child-birth. He suggested the substitution of an animal at the nipple. It happened that the family cat had kittened the same night and the tiny mammal was substituted with complete success. Daughter and kitten therefore grew up as *soeurs de lait*. This cat acquired the pretty habit of lighting the Christmas tree, by pressing a button with her forepaw. She lived to the remarkable age of 28 but in her last year developed a cancer. The physician dressed and cared for the disease until Christmas eve when she lighted her last Christmas tree and immediately afterwards was chloroformed.

But it seems to me that the more useless a cat is the more he has earned his right to companionship. There are enough people " trying to make themselves useful " in this world without the added competition of cats. And those who care most for the cat certainly never think of him as a mouser or a snaker. A writer in " The Nation " has it: " To respect the cat is the beginning of the aesthetic sense. At a stage of culture when utility governs all of its judgments, mankind prefers the dog";[47]

---

[47] He continues: " To the cultivated mind the cat has the charm of completeness, the satisfaction which makes a sonnet more than an epic. . . . The ancients figured eternity as a serpent biting its own tail. There will yet arise a philosopher who will conceive the Absolute as a gigantic and self-satisfied cat, purring as it clasps in comfortable round its own perfection, and uttering as it purrs, that line of Edmund Spenser's about the Cosmos —'It loved itself because itself was fair.' A cat blinking at midnight among your papers and your books declares with more eloquence than any skull the vanity of knowledge and the use-

and a distinguished scholar at Oxford avowed to believe that men admired cats or dogs according as to whether they were Platonists or Aristotelians: " The visionary chooses a cat; the man of concrete a dog. Hamlet must have kept a cat. Platonists, or cat-lovers, include sailors, painters, poets, and pick-pockets. Aristotelians, or dog-lovers, include soldiers, foot-ball players, and burglars." Champfleury's dictum is that " refined and delicate natures understand the cat. Women, poets, and artists hold it in great esteem, for they recognize the exquisite delicacy of its nervous system; indeed, only coarse natures fail to discern the natural distinction of the animal." Madame Delphine Gay writes of the catlike man: " The catlike man is one upon whom no tricks can be played with success. He possesses none of the qualities of the doglike man but he enjoys all the advantages of those qualities. He is selfish, ungrateful, miserly, avaricious, dapper, persuasive, gifted with intelligence, cleverness, and the power of fascination. He possesses refined experience; he guesses what he does not know; he understands what is hidden from him. To this race belong great diplomats, successful gallants, in fact all the men whom women call perfidious."

The cat is admired for his independence, his courage, his prudence, his patience, his naturalness, and his wit. He is, as Madame Michelet reminds us, essentially a noble animal. There is no mixture in his blood. This is so true that you can tell any member of the family at a glance. Tiger, lion, and house-cat differ more in size than in appearance. The originality of the cat is to offer in himself an exquisite and harmless miniature of his wild brothers. He lives like a great lord and there is nothing vulgar about him. The delicacy of the animal is one of his fascinations. All of us have wondered how a cat can leap upon a table littered with

lessness of striving. . . . The cat enjoys the march of the seasons, spins through space with the stars, and shares in her quietism the inevitable life of the universe. In all our hurrying can we do more? "

breakable objects, alighting firmly without disturbing anything. Curiously enough, as Philip Gilbert Hamerton [48] has pointed out, this is not a proof of lady-like civilization in the cat but again evidence that she has retained her savage habits. " When she so carefully avoids the glasses on the dinnertable she is not thinking of her behaviour as a dependent of civilized man, but acting in obedience to hereditary habits of caution in the stealthy chase, which is the natural accomplishment of her species. She will stir no branch of a shrub lest her fated bird escape her, and her feet are noiseless that the mouse may not know of her coming." Mr. Hamerton has captured and crystallized another interesting trait of the cat when he says, " The cat always uses precisely the necessary force, other animals roughly employ what strength they happen to possess without reference to the small occasion. One day I watched a young cat playing with a daffodil. She sat on her hind-legs and patted the flower with her paws, first with one paw and then with the other, making the light yellow ball sway from side to side, yet not injuring a petal or a stamen. She took a delight, evidently, in the very delicacy of the exercise, whereas a dog or a horse has no enjoyment in his own movements, but acts strongly when he is strong, without calculating whether the force used may be in great part superfluous. This proportioning of the force to the need is well known to be one of the evidences of refined culture, both in manners and in the fine arts. If animals could speak as fabulists have feigned, the dog would be a blunt, outspoken, honest fellow, but the cat would have the rare talent of never saying a word too much. A hint of the same character is conveyed by the sheathing of the claws, and also by the contractability of the pupil of the eye. The hostile claws are invisible, and are not shown when they are not wanted, yet are ever sharp and ready. The eye has a narrow pupil in broad daylight, receiving no more sunshine than is agreeable, but it will

[48] " Chapters on Animals."

gradually expand as twilight falls, and clear vision needs a larger and larger surface. Some of these cat-qualities are very desirable in criticism. The claws of a critic ought to be very sharp, but not perpetually prominent, and the eye ought to see far into rather obscure objects without being dazzled by plain daylight.''

There are those who find themselves uninterested in the appearance and doings of full-grown felines who are unable to resist the fascinations of kittens. The kitten, indeed, is an irresistible bundle of animate fur, all nerves and tenderness, all play-actor, dashing madly against nothing, prancing down the garden walk with the affected arched back of a Rutterkin about to commit foul deeds, chasing his tail, making a vain attempt to capture and worry his own shadow, peering curiously at esoteric insects, or entranced and delighted with a viper, like Cowper's kitten,

> *Who, never having seen in field or house*
> *The like, sat still and silent as a mouse;*
> *Only projecting, with attention due,*
> *Her whisker'd face, she asked him, ' Who are you?'*

Where there are peacocks it is a pretty sight to see the kittens, amazed by the proud and spreading tail, dash and spring upon it and go whirling round while the furious bird attempts to throw the demons off. But it is enough to watch them lap the cream from a bowl on the breakfast table with the innocence of cherubs, or lie contented purring balls of warm fur in your lap or on your shoulder. Kittens, like Japanese and Negro babies, may lose some of their charm when they grow older, but as kittens they are paramount. And therefore, it is wise to follow the advice of Oliver Herford:

> *Gather kittens while you may,*
> *Time brings only sorrow;*
> *And the kittens of today*
> *Will be old cats tomorrow.*

Chapter Three: Ailurophobes and Other Cat-Haters

Some men there are love not a gaping pig;
Some that are mad if they behold a cat.

Shylock.

One is permitted to assume an attitude of placid indifference in the matter of elephants, cockatoos, H. G. Wells, Sweden, roast beef, Puccini, and even Mormonism, but in the matter of cats it seems necessary to take a firm stand. The cat himself insists upon this; he invariably inspires strong feelings. He is, indeed, the only animal who does. From his admirers he evokes an intense adoration which usually finds an outlet in exaggerated expression. It is practically impossible for a cat-lover to meet a stray feline on the street without stopping to pass the time of day with him. I can say for myself that it takes me considerably longer to traverse a street in which cats occur than it does a catless thoroughfare. But so magnetic an animal is bound to repel when he does not fascinate, and those who hate the cat hate him with a malignity which, I think, only snakes in the animal kingdom provoke to an equal degree. Puss has, indeed, been dubbed the " furred serpent." The association of the cat with witches and various superstitions is responsible for a good deal of this antipathy; there is also the aversion of those who love dogs and birds with unreasonable exclusions; finally it has pleased many small boys to make scientific investigation into the proverbial saying that a cat has nine lives. So the cat through the ages has been more cruelly and persistently mistreated than any other beast. This is, I suppose, natural, when we remember that in one

Ailurophobes and Other Cat-Haters

epoch he was regarded as a god and in another as an adjunct of sorcery; accordingly he has suffered martyrdom along with other gnostics.

There is even a disease for cat-haters, known as ailurophobia, in spite of the fact that *ailuros* (the waving ones) which the Greeks took aboard their ships to kill mice, are now thought to have been snowy-breasted martens.[1] Ailurophobia is a stronger feeling than hate; it is a most abject kind of fear. Strong men and women are seized with nausea, even faint, in the presence of a tiny kitten, sometimes even an *unseen* kitten. The simplest form of this complaint is asthmatic ailurophobia; in other words people who suffer from asthma or hay-fever find the disease aggravated by the presence of cats. The other form is more serious. I have a friend, otherwise seemingly sane, who exhibits symptoms of the most violent terror at the sight of a kitten four weeks old; an older cat will sometimes throw her into convulsions. This malady is not rare, nor is it limited to women. Scott writes of a gallant Highland chieftain who had been " seen to change into all the colours of his plaid "[2] when confronted with a cat. Probably the most celebrated ailurophobe in history was Napoleon. According to a popular legend, not long after the battle of Wagram and the second occupation of Vienna by the French, an aide-de-camp of the Corsican, who at the time occupied, together with his suite, the Palace of Schönbrunn, was proceeding to bed at an unusually late hour when, on passing the door of Napoleon's bedroom, he was surprised to hear a most singular noise and repeated calls for assistance from the Emperor. Opening the door hastily, and rushing into the room, he saw the greatest soldier of the age, half undressed, his countenance agitated, beaded drops of perspiration standing on his brow, making frequent and convulsive lunges with his sword through the tapestry that lined the walls, behind which a cat had secreted

[1] According to the researches of Professor Rolleston of Oxford.
[2] " Letters on Demonology and Witchcraft," p. 30.

61

herself. Madame Junot was aware of this weakness and is reported to have gained an important political advantage over the Little Corporal merely by mentioning a cat at the right moment. In one of his Spectator papers Addison tells how a lover won his lady from an ailurophobic rival with the assistance of a " purring piece of tortoise-shell." And Peggy Bacon has woven a diverting tale of an ailurophobic King and a felinophilistic Queen whose troubles were finally solved by the Court Physician, who brought them a thin, wiry, long-legged creature, with no tail at all, large ears like sails, a face like a lean isosceles triangle with the nose as a very sharp apex, eyes small and yellow like flat bone buttons, brown fur, short and coarse, and large floppy feet. It had a voice like a steam siren and its name was Rosamund. " The King and Queen were both devoted to it; she because it was a cat, he because it seemed anything but a cat." [3]

Dr. S. Weir Mitchell spent some time investigating the matter of ailurophobia, sending letters of query all over the world. He reported [4] that from one point of view the result was entirely unsatisfactory. The mass of evidence he accumulated gave him no clue to the cause of the ailment. It has sometimes been included with prenatal phenomena but without, it would seem, sufficient justification. Dr. Mitchell educes a theory that it is the odour which these ailurophobes detect when they ferret out hidden pussies but cats, house-cats at any rate, are practically devoid of odour to the ordinary nose. However it must be remembered that there are people who can sort handkerchiefs fresh from the laundry by smelling them. Nevertheless Dr. J. G. Wood's theory that ailurophobes sense hidden cats by their electricity seems more plausible.

Whatever the cause there are many recorded instances of persons suffering from ailurophobia exhibiting symptoms of distress in rooms which apparently contained no cats; later cats

[3] " The Queen's Cat " in " The True Philosopher."
[4] " Cat Fear "; " The Ladies' Home Journal "; March 1906.

Ailurophobes and Other Cat-Haters

would be discovered, hidden behind curtains or in closets. Dr. Mitchell furnishes us with an interesting example: " In my own family an uncle was the subject. My father, the late Professor John K. Mitchell, having placed a small cat in a closet with a saucer of cream, asked Mr. H. to come and look at some old books in which he would be interested. He sat down, but in a few minutes grew pale, shivered and said, ' There is a cat in the room.' Doctor Mitchell said, ' Look about you. There is no cat in the room. Do you hear one outside?' He said, ' No, but there is a cat.' He became faint and, complaining of nausea, went out and promptly recovered."

Rudyard Kipling once wrote an amusingly ironic story [5] about an ailurophobe, who, through seemingly mystic channels, was plagued with cats even as the Egyptians were plagued with locusts. Half the psychical societies in India appear to have been interested in the solution of the phenomenon but the explanation when it finally came was neither supernatural nor miraculous. The page in which Kipling describes the " sending " is very diverting: " When a man who hates cats wakes up in the morning and finds a little squirming kitten on his breast, or puts his hand into his ulster-pocket and finds a little half-dead kitten where his gloves should be, or opens his trunk and finds a vile kitten among his dress-shirts, or goes for a long ride with his mackintosh strapped on his saddle-bow and shakes a little squalling kitten from its folds when he opens it, or goes out to dinner and finds a little blind kitten under his chair, or stays at home and finds a writhing kitten under the quilt, or wriggling among his boots, or hanging, head downwards, in his tobacco-jar, or being mangled by his terrier in the veranda,— when such a man finds one kitten, neither more nor less, once a day in a place where no kitten rightly could or should be, he is naturally upset. When he dare not murder his daily trove because he believes it to be a

[5] " The Sending of Dana Da " in " In Black and White."

Manifestation, an Emissary, an Embodiment, and half a dozen other things all out of the regular course of nature, he is more than upset. He is actually distressed."

Ailurophobes, as a rule, do no harm to cats, although they are often quite willing to have others put them out of the way. They usually let cats alone and as cats like to be let alone they often manifest perverse attention towards ailurophobes, giving them marks of affection and honour. "I once had a large silver-ringed cat," writes Andrew Lang, "of unemotional temperament. But finding a lady, rather ailurophobic, in a low dress at dinner, Tippoo suddenly leaped up and alighted on her neck. He was never so friendly with non-ailurophobes."

No, it is not from people who fear cats that puss's greatest enemies are recruited. Perhaps unjust and stupid natural historians [6] have had something to do with the occasional disfavour in which domestic felines are held. Witness, for. example, what Buffon has to say about the tiger in the house: " The cat is a faithless domestic, and only kept through necessity to oppose to another domestic which incommodes us still more, and which we cannot drive away, for we pay no respect to those, who, being fond of all beasts, keep cats for amusement. Though these animals are gentle and frolicsome when young, yet they, even then, possess an innate cunning and perverse disposition, which age increases, and which education only serves to conceal. They are naturally inclined to theft and the best education only converts them into servile and flat-

[6] Those who have no feeling for cats regard them as ululant retromingent mammals. Thomas Pennant, perhaps, was one of these. Here is his description of the sphinx of the fireside: "It is an useful, but deceitful, domestic; active, neat, sedate, intent on its prey. When pleased it purres and moves its tail; when angry it spits, hisses, and strikes with its foot. When walking it draws in its claws: it drinks little: is fond of fish: it washes its face with its fore-foot (Linnaeus says at the approach of a storm): the female is remarkably salacious; a piteous, squalling, jarring lover. Its eyes shine in the night: its hair when rubbed in the dark emits fire; it is even proverbially tenacious of life: always lights on its feet: is fond of perfumes, *marum,* cat-mint, valerian, etc."

tering robbers; for they have the same address, subtlety, and inclination for mischief or rapine. Like all knaves, they know how to conceal their intentions; to watch, wait, and choose opportunities for seizing their prey; to fly from punishment, and to remain away until the danger is over, and they can return with safety. They readily conform to the habits of society, but never acquire its manners; for of attachment they have only the appearance, as may seem by the obliquity of their motions and the duplicity of their looks. They never look in the face those who treat them the best, and of whom they seem to be the most fond, but either through fear or falsehood, they approach him by windings to seek for those caresses they have no pleasure in, but only to flatter those from whom they receive them. Very different from that faithful animal the dog, whose sentiments are all directed to the person of his master, the cat appears only to feel for himself, to live conditionally, only to partake of society that he may abuse it, and by this disposition he has more affinity to man than the dog, who is all sincerity." Buffon somewhat redeems himself by his last sentence but the foregoing part of this diatribe is arrant nonsense. Far from averting their gaze, cats have a habit of staring at one by the hour; it is one of their most disconcerting tricks. But why waste time confuting Buffon? In that invaluable work of reference, "The Devil's Dictionary," I find that Ambrose Bierce remarks in his definition of " Zoology ": " Two of the science's most illustrious expounders were Buffon and Oliver Goldsmith, from both of whom we learn (' 1 ' Histoire générale des animaux ' and ' A History of Animated Nature ') that the domestic cow sheds its horns every two years." Bierce, himself, however, was no lover of cats. I do not think he cared for any kind of animal, certainly not for man. His definition of " Cat " in this same dictionary is " A soft indestructible automaton provided by nature to be kicked when things go wrong in the domestic circle." Noah Webster may be added to this infamous list. In his dictionary he inserted this gratuitous insult to "the stealthy-stepping cat": "The domestic cat is a deceitful animal and when enraged extremely spiteful." [7] Sir Walter Scott originally disliked cats; in his latter days he admitted: "The greatest advance of age which I have yet found is liking a cat, an animal which I detested, and becoming fond of a garden, an art which I despised." King Henry III of France, a weak and dissolute monarch, hated cats. So did Meyerbeer. M. Jusserand says of Ronsard, "He cannot hide the fact that he likes to sleep on the left side, that he hates cats, dislikes servants 'with slow hands,' believes in omens, adores physical exercises and gardening, and prefers, especially in summer, vegetables to meat." And Ronsard himself left evidence of his aversion in the following stanzas:

> *Homme ne vit, qui tant haïsse au monde*
> *Les chats que moi, d'une haine profonde.*
> *Je hai leurs yeux, leur front, et leur regard;*
> *Et les voyant je m'enfuis d'autre part.*[8]

Edmund Gosse has rendered these lines into English:

> *There is no man now living anywhere*
> *Who hates cats with a deeper hate than I;*
> *I hate their eyes, their heads, the way they stare,*
> *And when I see one come, I turn and fly.*[9]

Honoré Schœfer and Toussenel also hated cats. The latter once remarked that no man of taste could maintain sympathetic relations with an animal which was fond of asparagus.

Hilaire Belloc has very forcibly expressed his dislike of cats,

---

[7] Dr. Johnson, who really liked cats better than Boswells, was somewhat diffident about saying so. The definition in his dictionary is ambiguous: "A domestick animal that catches mice, commonly reckoned by naturalists the lowest order of the leonine species."

[8] From a long poem addressed to Remy Belleau, the poet, quoted in Graham R. Tomson's anthology, "Concerning Cats."

[9] "Gossip in a Library," p. 178.

but in spite of himself, admiration for the little animals sneaks in and out of his horrid lines:

"I do not like Them. It is no good asking me why, though I have plenty of reasons. I do not like Them. There would be no particular point in saying I do not like Them if it were not that so many people doted on Them, and when one hears Them praised, it goads one to expressing one's hatred and fear of Them.

"I know very well that They can do one harm and that They have occult powers. All the world has known that for a hundred thousand years, more or less, and every attempt has been made to propitiate Them. James I would drown Their mistress or burn her, but *They* were spared. Men would mummify Them in Egypt, and worship the mummies; men would carve Them in stone in Cyprus and Crete and Asia Minor, or (more remarkable still) artists, especially in the Western Empire, would leave Them out altogether, so much was Their influence dreaded. Well, I yield so far as not to print Their name, and only to call Them, 'They' but I hate Them and I am not afraid to say so.

"Their master protects Them. They have a charmed life. I have seen one thrown from a great height into a London street which when It reached it It walked quietly away with the dignity of the Lost World to which It belonged.

"They will drink beer. This is not a theory; I know it; I have seen it with my own eyes. They will eat special foods; They will even eat dry bread . . . but never upon any occasion will They eat anything that has been poisoned, so utterly lacking are They in simplicity and humility, and so abominably well filled with cunning by whatever demon first brought Their race into existence.

"All that They do is venomous, and all that They think is evil, and when I take mine away (as I mean to do next week — in a basket), I shall first read in a book of statistics what is the wickedest part of London, and I shall leave It there, for

The Tiger in the House

I know of no one even among my neighbours quite as vile as to deserve such a gift." [10]

Alphonse Daudet was afraid of cats; he told Georges Docquois the cause of this terror: " One evening we were at home, circled around the lamp. My father alone was absent and not expected to return that night. Indeed, we expected nobody. The peace of the fireside was complete and charming. Suddenly, in the next room, the piano began to play itself. As if under the gloved fingers of thick mittens, the notes cried feebly at intervals. . . . I was terrified. All of us were frightened. . . . After a moment of silence, the piano suggested lugubrious chromatic groans. It was as though souls were weeping in the drawing-room. What a sensation! Then the piano spoke no more, ceased to groan, but there was a fall on the carpet of something light and heavy at the same time, a muffled weight impossible to describe. . . . After another silence, a little cry. . . . It was the house-cat."

If cat-haters would only be content with hating no one would have any complaint to make, but poor puss has been persecuted as virulently as Christians in ancient Rome and Jews in modern Poland.

Cats both black and brave unnumbered
Have for naught been foully slain.

As he frequently jumped in and out of the windows of houses inhabited by witches he speedily became affiliated in the public mind with the pythoness herself and often shared her dread fate. These mediaeval hags did nothing to dispel this belief, for often in their confessions they inculpated cats. In a seventeenth century execution fourteen cats were shut in a cage with a woman who was roasted over a slow fire while the cats in misery and terror clawed her in their own death agonies. When Queen Elizabeth was crowned a feature of

[10] " On Them " in " On Nothing and Kindred Subjects "; Methuen and Co.; 1908.

the processon was a wicker pope, the interior of which was filled with live cats, who " squalled in a most hideous manner as soon as they felt the fire." The culmination of many a religious fête in Germany, France, and England consisted in pitching some wretched puss off a height or into a bonfire. In 1753 certain Frenchmen received a quittance of one hundred *sols parisis* for having furnished during three years all the cats necessary for the fires of the festival of St. John.

In Vosges, cats were burned on Shrove Tuesday; in Alsace they were tossed into the Easter bonfire. In the department of the Ardennes, cats were flung into the bonfires kindled on the first Sunday in Lent; sometimes, in a more graceful form of cruelty, they were hung over the fire from the end of a pole and roasted alive. " The cat, which represented the devil, could not suffer enough." In the midsummer fires formerly lighted in the Place de Grève at Paris it was the custom to burn a basket, barrel, or sack full of live cats which was hung from a tall mast in the midst of a bonfire. In 1648 Louis XIV, crowned with a wreath of roses and bearing roses in his hands, ignited this fire, danced before it, and partook of the banquet afterwards in the Hotel de Ville.[11]

Workmen in France were at one time accustomed before laying the last board in a floor to intern underneath it a living cat; this ceremony was supposed to carry good fortune to the inmates of the house. In demolishing old mansions in Paris the dried remains of pussies convulsed in suffering that they endured in dying are often found.

In the old remedies devised by hags and sorcerers there were cat ingredients: cats' brains, cats' eyes and cats' grease were called for in certain prescriptions. In an old collection called " The Young Angler's Delight " the following recipe for catching fish may be found: " Smother a cat to death; then bleed him, and having flea'd and paunched him, roast him on a spit without larding; keep the dripping to mix with the

---

[11] These examples are from Frazer's " The Golden Bough."

yolks of eggs and an equal quantity of oil of spikenard; mix these well together, and anoint your line, hook or bait therewith, and you will find them come to your content."

Small boys have long held it to be their prerogative to torment cats, tying cans or a string of exploding firecrackers to their tails, installing their paws in walnut shells, or sending them to navigate the horse-pond in a bowl. Booth Tarkington, who may be considered an authority on the adolescent period, writes, " The suffering of cats is a barometer of the nerve-pressure of boys, and it may be accepted as sufficiently established that Wednesday — after school-hours — is the worst time for cats. . . . Confirming the effect of Wednesday upon boys in general, it is probable that, if full statistics were available, they would show that cats dread Wednesdays, and that their fear is shared by other animals and would be shared, to an extent by windows, if windows possessed nervous systems. Nor must this probable apprehension on the part of cats and the like be thought mere superstition. Cats have superstitions, it is true, but certain actions inspired by the sight of a boy with a missile in his hand are better evidence of the workings of logic upon a practical nature than of faith in the supernatural." [12] Edwin Tenney Brewster [13] tells how boys in default of a proper football played their game through with two living cats bound together with a clothes line. " The public is sentimental," he observes. " It can't bear to have the little things killed. So it drops them into ash-barrels, where they die — in the course of time and not altogether comfortably. It tosses them into cess-pools, and happily the next rain sends water enough to drown them. Specially careful house-wives before consigning kittens to the waste heap have been known to make them into neat bundles, in paper boxes, tied with string. This kindly device protects the helpless creatures from stray dogs and allows them to smother or starve in quiet.

[12] " Penrod and Sam," p. 205.
[13] " The City of 4,000,000 cats "; " McClure's Magazine "; May 1912.

Ailurophobes and Other Cat-Haters

A short and easy method in tenement districts is simply to open the window and toss the kittens out. A four-story drop on to the brick pavement or area spikes is commonly a sufficient hint to an intelligent kitten not to return." Cats are thrown off church towers with blown bladders attached to their necks, killed by dogs, thrown into barrels with dogs to fight, kicked to death, drowned, turned alive into bakers' ovens [14] and stoves, thrown into lime, their heads crunched under heels, tied together by their tails and hung up. In Spain, in Gautier's day, it was the custom to deprive cats of their ears and their tails, giving them the appearance of "Japanese chimeras." [15] In Havana, I have been told, urchins enjoy a merry sport which entails the dipping of puss into a pail of kerosene and a subsequent ignition. Then the comet-like trail of howling fiery fur is released. In 1815, just before the departure of Napoleon for St. Helena, a wag perpetrated a joke in the city of Chester. Handbills were distributed which announced that the island was overrun with rats and that 16 shillings would be paid for every full-grown tom cat, 10s. for every full-grown female, 2s. 6d. for every kitten. On the day appointed the city was filled with men, women, and children carrying cats. A riot ensued and the cats escaped. Several hundred were killed and many others drowned while the remainder infested neighbouring houses and barns for many weeks afterwards. [16] In France puss is undoubtedly fre-

[14] In the early editions of "Marius the Epicurean" you may discover this paragraph: "It was then that the host's son bethought him of his own favourite animal, which had offended somehow, and had been forbidden the banquet,— 'I mean to shut you in the oven a while, little soft, white thing!' he had said, catching sight, as he passed an open doorway, of the great fire in the kitchen, itself festally adorned, where the feast was preparing; and had so finally forgotten it. And it was with a really natural laugh, for once, that, on opening the oven, he caught sight of the animal's grotesque appearance, as it lay there, half-burnt, just within the red-hot iron door." Mr. Pater removed this passage from later editions of this book.

[15] "Voyage en Espagne," p. 299.

[16] Phyfe: "5,000 Facts and Fancies."

71

quently eaten as rabbit. Of this custom I have found a
brief mention in a book, the name of the unworthy author
of which I will not further advertise. A French sailor is
speaking: "Sometimes we have rabbit stew. When my
sister was married we had rabbit stew. For weeks before-
hand we caught cats on the roads, in the fields, in the
barns. My brother caught cats and I caught cats, and my
father caught cats; we all caught cats. We caught forty cats,
perhaps fifty cats. Some were toms, some were females with
kittens inside them. Some were black and some were white
and some were yellow and some were tabbies. One cat
scratched a big gash in my brother's face and he bled. Then
we locked them in a room, my father and I. . . . My brother
was afraid after he had been scratched. . . . We went into
the room with cudgels and beat about us, beat the cats on
the head. For an hour we chased them round the room until
all the cats lay dead on the floor. How they did howl, and
screech, and fight, but we were a match for them. Then my
brother and my mother skinned the cats and made a magnificent rabbit stew for my sister's wedding." One of the adventures of that arch-rogue, Till Eulenspiegel, relates how
he sewed a cat in a hare's skin and sold the beast to some fur-
riers at Leipsig. Before dining on its carcass the merchants
wished to enjoy the pleasures of the hunt; so they loosed the
animal in the garden and set the dogs after it, but the hare
climbed a tree and begun to mew, whereupon, of course,
Till's merry prank was exposed and the cat was killed.

In order to test their superior theories on the subject of
education it will be remembered that the inimitable Bouvard
and Pécuchet experiment with a boy and a girl. These incorrigible children proceed at once, of course, to demolish the
theories. One of Victor's horrible exploits entails the torture of a cat. Hearing the screams of Marcel, the servant,
Bouvard and Pécuchet rush to the kitchen.

" 'Take him away! It's too much — it's too much!'

Ailurophobes and Other Cat-Haters

" The lid of the pot flew off like the bursting of a shell. A greyish mass bounded towards the ceiling, then wriggled about frantically, emitting fearful yowls.

" They recognized the cat, quite emaciated, with its hair gone, its tail like a piece of string, and its dilated eyes starting out of its head. They were as white as milk, vacant, so to speak, and yet glaring.

" The hideous animal continued its howling till it flung itself into the fireplace, disappeared, then rolled back in the middle of the cinders lifeless.

" It was Victor who had perpetrated this atrocity, and the two worthy men recoiled, pale with stupefaction and horror. To the reproaches which they addressed to him, he replied, ' Well ! since it's my own,' without ceremony and with an air of innocence, in the placidity of a satiated instinct."

In " The Brothers Karamazoff " Dostoievsky indicates the malignance of Smerdyakoff by telling us that in his childhood he " was very fond of hanging cats, and burying them with great ceremony. He used to dress up in a sheet as though it were a surplice and sang, and waved some object over the dead cat as though it were a censer." In an extremely bad book called " Nightshade " the malevolent Dr. Meisterlimmer flings a cat out of an open window into a courtyard. " It fell four storeys and broke its spine. He laughed in his own hearty fashion to see it dragging itself along on its front paws and wailing. . . ." [17]

At least one cat suffered for having religious convictions. George Borrow in " Wild Wales " [18] describes this poor animal left behind in Llangollen by a former vicar. Nearly all the inhabitants of the village were dissenters and they refused to harbour the beast, nay more they persecuted it. " O, there never was a cat so persecuted as that poor Church of England animal, and solely on account of the opinions which it

[17] "Nightshade," by Paul Gwynne; Constable and Co., London, 1910; p. 270.
[18] Chapter VII.

was supposed to have imbibed in the house of its late master, for I never could learn that the dissenters of the suburb, nor indeed of Llangollen in general, were in the habit of persecuting other cats; the cat was a Church of England cat, and that was enough: stone it, hang it, drown it! were the cries of almost everybody. If the workmen of the flannel factory, all of whom were Calvinistic Methodists, chanced to get a glimpse of it in the road from the windows of the building, they would sally forth in a body, and with sticks, stones, or for want of other weapons, with clots of horse-dung, of which there was always plenty on the road, would chase it up the high bank or perhaps over the Camlas — the inhabitants of a small street between our house and the factory leading from the road to the river, all of whom were dissenters, if they saw it moving about the perllan, into which their back windows looked, would shriek and hoot at it, and fling anything of no value, which came easily to hand at the head or body of the ecclesiastical cat." The reader will be glad to learn that Borrow took puss in hand, cured him of an eruptive disease, fed him until he was sleek, and when he left the neighbourhood gave him in charge to a young woman of " sound church principles." He subsequently learned that the cat " continued in peace and comfort till one morning it sprang suddenly from the hearth into the air, gave a mew and died."

On vivisection, although undoubtedly one of the perils of cat life, I have no intention of dwelling here, but it seems an apt point to speak of the infernal operations of Professor Mantegazza of Milan, whose " Physiology of Love " is more or less familiar to English readers. Professor Mantegazza has also written a " Physiology of Pain," for which he conducted experiments " with much delight and extreme patience for the space of a year." [19] There is no necessity of rehearsing the sickening details of this fiendish book but it may be stated that among other torments the Italian devised a ma-

[19] " Fisiologia del Dolore," p. 101.

chine, which indeed he dubbed a " tormentor " in which little animals which had first been " quilted with long thin nails "so that the slightest movement was agony, were wracked with added tortures, torn and twisted, crushed and lacerated, hour after hour. " In the august name of Science, animals have been subjected to burning, baking, freezing; saturation with inflammable oil and then setting on fire; starvation to death; skinning alive; larding the feet with nails; crushing and tormenting in every imaginable way. Human ingenuity has taxed itself to the utmost to devise some new torture, that one may observe what curious results may ensue." [20] There are those who defend cats in trouble. Octave Mirbeau describes such a one in his very harrowing story, " Le Gardien des Vaches " [21] in which a kitten is tortured but the torturer in turn meets his death. What, one wonders, would the author of " Le Jardin des Supplices " have written about Mantegazza?

There are further the bird-lovers, some of whom are so rabidly hysterical on the subject of cats that they would have them all destroyed.[22] About the mere sentimentalists who protest against the cruelty of the cat I have nothing to add to my remarks in the second chapter of this book. It is natural for a cat to kill birds; the cat is carnivorous and, like the Follies girls, he finds a bird particularly tasty. Some cats enjoy hunting for its own sake and kill many birds they do not eat. Persian cats, because of their value, are usually kept in semi-captivity and may therefore be ruled out of the discussion.

The majority of those who write against the cat as a bird-hunter give the question an economic twinge. This is an old dodge of reformers, a tried and true formula of the uplift, and it almost always is efficacious in stirring up a certain kind

[20] Albert Leffingwell, M. D.: "Vivisection in America" in Henry S. Salt's book, "Animals' Rights"; Macmillan and Co., New York, 1894.

[21] In the volume entitled "La Vache Tachetée," p. 40.

[22] In 1897 there was founded in Westphalia the Antikatzenverein, the avowed object of which was war against the cat.

of public interest. In this instance these gentlemen assert that the birds free the farm vegetation of grubs and that the cat in destroying the birds helps to destroy farm produce. This is all very well but I have never thought that the object of a scare-crow was to frighten cats and I have seen an entire cherry-tree denuded of its fruit in a morning by a flock of birds.[23] It is pleasant to remember that Mr. Darwin made a curious speculation as to how a scarcity of cats in a rural district would soon affect the neighbouring vegetation as the field animals and birds they prey on would, of course, proportionately increase and their greater numbers tell on vegetable life.

When Calvin, Charles Dudley Warner's exceptional cat, first brought in a bird, Mr. Warner told him that it was wrong, "and tried to convince him, while he was eating it, that he was doing wrong; for he is a reasonable cat, and understands pretty much everything except the binomial theorem and the time down the cycloidal arc. But with no effect. The killing of birds went on to my great regret and shame." However one day when he found the pea-pods empty and the strawberry bed raped of fruit Mr. Warner had a change of heart. He called Calvin and petted him. "I lavished upon him an enthusiastic fondness. I told him that he had no fault; that the one action that I had called a vice was an heroic exhibition of regard for my interests. I bade him go and do likewise continually. I now saw how much better instinct is than mere misguided reason. Calvin knew. . . . It was only the round of Nature. The worms eat a noxious something in the ground. The birds eat the worms. Calvin eats the birds. We eat — no, we do not eat Calvin. There the chain stops. When you ascend the scale

---

[23] The bird-lovers occasionally give themselves away. In an article in "Bird-Lore," May 1918, William Brewster tells how he frightened chipmunks away from his tulips and starlings from his cherries with a stuffed maltese and white pussy with glaring yellow eyes. The starlings, however, soon were privy to the deception and continued their depredations.

Ailurophobes and Other Cat-Haters

of being, and come to an animal that is, like ourselves, inedible, you have arrived at a result where you can rest. Let us respect the cat. He completes an edible chain." [24] It is pleasant to recall that most literary chapters on the cat are in a similar vein; even that great bird-lover, Olive Thorne Miller, inserted a highly laudatory chapter on the cat, the common, out-door cat at that, in one of her bird books.[25] The malignant cat-haters, in print, are usually commissioners or superintendents. They very frequently become feverish and sometimes even foam at the mouth. One, for instance, speaks of a blood-thirsty house-bred kitten who had never seen a bird, crouching and preparing to spring at a phonograph which was negotiating a nightingale's song.[26] I can duplicate this story. Aeroplanes frequently fly past my garret window and when they do Feathers invariably manifests the liveliest emotion, rushes to the window, gives her hunting cry; her hair bristles and she prepares to spring.

Nature, as Joseph Conrad, Thomas Hardy, Anatole France, James Branch Cabell, and some others have discovered, seldom rejects an opportunity to be ironic. It should therefore surprise no one to learn that a bird is one of the most dangerous enemies of the cat. The eagle swoops from the skies, seizes the cat along his spine with its terrible claws, mangles his head with its beak the while it flaps its gaunt and terrifying wings and bears the little beast aloft. A keeper in the eagle house at a London zoological garden informed Dr. Louis Robinson [27] that when the eagles were off their food he offered them cats. " If they won't eat cats they are about to die," he said.

Another of the most inveterate and selfish enemies of the

[24] " My Summer in a Garden."
[25] " Upon the Tree-Tops."
[26] T. G. Pearson: " Cats and Birds" in " The Art World," May 1917. I wonder if Mr. Pearson knows that game-keepers in England sometimes kill nightingales because their singing keeps the pheasants awake?
[27] " Wild Traits in Tame Animals."

77

cat is the supposed friend who goes to Palm Beach in the winter or Lake Placid in the summer and leaves puss alone in the city to shift for himself, or the tender-hearted lady who says, " I just can't bear to drown those sweet kittens." So she takes the unweaned babies away from their mother and leaves them in some public garden where they will meet a cruel death at the hands of boys or the jaws of dogs, and the mother cat suffers not only from the loss of her offspring but from a milk disease as well.[28]

It is quite a cheering thought to realize that cats sometimes hate as keenly as people, that they too contrive their little revenges and Sicilian vendettas whereby they may in some small degree compensate for the insults doled out to their race. A familiar Irish story has it that a man once severely chastised a cat for some misdemeanour, after which the feline disappeared. A few days láter the man met the cat in a narrow path. The animal glared at him with a wicked aspect and when he endeavoured to frighten her away, she sprang at him, fastening herself to his hand with so ferocious a grip that it was impossible to make her open her jaws and the creature's head actually had to be severed from her body before the hand could be extricated. The man afterwards died from his injuries. Variations of this theme have appeared in fiction. In Frederick Stuart Greene's story, " The Cat of the Cane-brake," [29] the feline revenges himself upon a woman who had mistreated him by dragging a rattle-snake to her bed and placing it on her chest. Nor must we forget the eccentric Mr. Wilde's cat in Robert W. Chambers's story, " The Repairer of Reputations." [30] In her first appearance in the tale she attacks the ugly dwarf : " Before I could move she flattened her belly to the ground, crouched, trembled, and

---

[28] I know of a case of this kind in which a friendly older cat suckled the mother until her milk disappeared.
[29] " The Metropolitan Magazine "; August 1916.
[30] " The King in Yellow."

sprang into his face. Howling and foaming they rolled over and over on the floor, scratching and clawing, until the cat screamed and fled under the cabinet, and Mr. Wilde turned over on his back, his limbs contracting and curling up like the legs of a dying spider." On a later occasion Mr. Wilde is discovered " groaning on the floor, his face covered with blood, his clothes torn to shreds. Drops of blood were scattered over the carpet, which had also been ripped and frayed in the evidently recent struggle. ' It's that cursed cat.' he said, ceasing his groans, and turning his colourless eyes to me, ' she attacked me while I was asleep. I believe she will kill me yet.' " [31] Mr. Wilde was perfectly right; the cat did kill him.

In Poe's tale, " The Black Cat " it will be recalled that the protagonist has persistently maltreated a black cat named Pluto, who in the end is responsible for handing his master over to the police as the murderer of his wife. Two old stories offer interesting corroboration of this fable. One relates how a murder had been committed in the city of Lyons and a physician requested to inquire into the particulars concerning it. Accordingly he went to the home of the murdered woman where he found her dead on the floor, lying in a pool of blood. An enormous white cat surmounted the cupboard, his eyes fixed on the corpse, his whole bearing indicative of the greatest terror. All night he kept watch over his dead mistress. The following morning, when the room was filled with soldiers, he still maintained his position, disregarding the clanking of the arms and the noisy conversation. As soon, however, as the persons under suspicion were brought in, he glared at them with particular malignancy, and then retreated under the bed. From this moment the prisoners began to lose their audacity and subsequently they confessed to the

[31] In " The Street of the Four Winds " (also in " The King in Yellow ") Mr. Chambers introduces us to a charming white cat as an antidote to his previous monster.

murder and were convicted.[32]   A similar story is to be found
in the autobiography of Miss Cornelia Wright: [33]   " An old
woman died a few years ago.   She had a nephew, to whom she
left all she possessed.   She had a favourite cat, which never
left her, and even remained by the corpse after death.   The
nephew was a lawyer, and while he was reading the will after
the funeral the cat remained restlessly outside the door of the
room, apparently adjoining that in which the old lady died.
When the door was opened the cat sprang at the lawyer, seized
him by the throat, and was with difficulty prevented from
strangling him.   The man died about eighteen months later
and on his deathbed confessed that he had murdered his aunt
to obtain possession of her money."   Edward Jesse [34] relates
a tale he had from a man who was sentenced to transporta-
tion for robbery.   He and two other thieves had broken into
the home of a gentleman who lived near Hampton Court.
While they were gathering their plunder in sacks a large black
cat flew at one of the robbers and fixed her claws in his face.

We must not forget the old nursery rhyme:

> *I love little pussy,*
> *Her coat is so warm;*
> *And if I don't hurt her*
> *She'll do me no harm.*

The cat, unlike the dog, refuses to return good for evil, or to
turn the right cheek when struck upon the left.   These revenges, however, are extreme.   A cat usually flees a persecutor
or ignores him.   But it is important to remember that this is
the animal the dog-lover sometimes calls ungrateful!

[32] " Dictionnaire d'anecdotes "; 1820; Vol. 2, p. 274.

[33] " Autobiography of Miss Cornelia Wright, lady companion to the Princess
Charlotte of Wales," two volumes, 1861; W. H. Allen and Co.; London.

[34] " Gleanings in Natural History "; London; 1838.

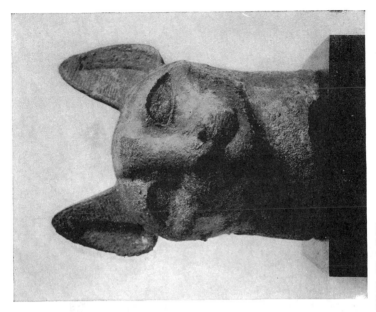

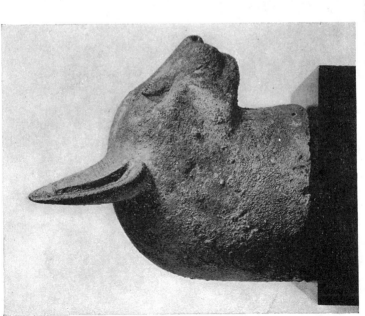

AN EGYPTIAN BRONZE HEAD OF A CAT

Courtesy of the Metropolitan Museum of Art

JAPANESE PILLAR-PRINTS BY KORIUSAI

From the collection of Arthur Davison Ficke

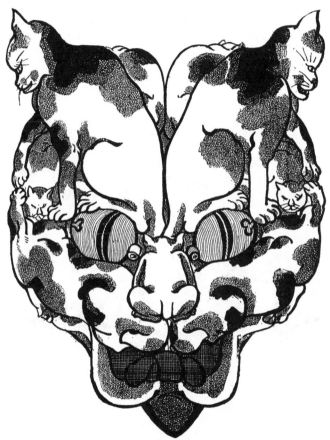

A JAPANESE FANTASY

From Champfleury's Les Chats

MINETTE WASHES

From a drawing by Gottfried Mind

"A LIFE OF LUXURY"

From a drawing by Grandville in Vie privée et publique des animaux

THE CAT IS AN ORIENTAL

From a photograph by Harriet V. Furness

"IL NE FAUT PAS FAIRE PASSER TOUS LES CHATS POUR SORCIERS"

From a drawing by Grandville in Vie *privée et publique des animaux*

PRINCE DORUS AND THE ENCHANTED CAT

From Prince Dorus by Charles Lamb; London; 1811

Chapter Four: The Cat and the Occult

Notre dame la Lune blonde
Est la patronne des bons chats.
Elle préside a leurs ébats
Avec sa grosse face ronde.

Quand le vent siffle un air de ronde,
Elle rit à leurs entrechats.
Notre dame la Lune blonde
Est la patronne des bons chats.

Mais quand, après de long pourchas,
Folle d'amour, la bande gronde,
Elle se voile et cache au monde
Le mystère impur des Sabbats
Notre dame la Lune blonde.
                              RAOUL GINESTE.

The mystical character of the cat has challenged attention, delighting her admirers and terrifying her detractors, since she strolled rather suddenly and magnificently into history about 1600 B. C. Her origin itself is veiled in the deepest mystery, for those who believe her to be a gentle descendant of some tamed wild cat must overlook the fact that of all terrestrial beasts the wild cat of today most persistently and ferociously resists all attempts at domestication. " *Peut-être est-il fée, est-il dieu,*" writes Baudelaire of puss, and again the French poet speaks of the " *chat mystérieux, chat séraphique, chat étrange.*" A writer in the " Occult Review " informs us that cats have green auras and assures us that they are the most magnetic of quadrupeds. Sir Walter Scott once observed to Washington Irving, " Ah! cats are a mysterious kind of folk. There is more passing in their minds than we are aware of. It comes no doubt from their being so familiar with warlocks and witches." Sir Walter, however, reversed cause and effect. Warlocks and witches are familiar with cats because cats are occult. Their tread is soft and noiseless. They leap lightly, and apparently blindly to the top of a high-boy littered with glass and china without disturbing an element in this brittle composition. The pupils of their eyes, wide open, vary with the light; in China it has sometimes been the fashion to tell the time of day by them; in Suffolk cats' eyes are popularly supposed to dilate with the ebb and flow of the tide. Madame Michelet asserts that it is their very transparence, their clearness, which gives these eyes their mystery, these wide open eyes which see on and beyond, which stare in an ecstatic gnostic gaze which has nothing in common with the begging or reproachful eyes of a dog. At night these eyes glisten and shine in the dark. Maister Salmon, who writes of puss in his " Compleat English Physician," published in 1693, seems to be sufficiently bewildered: " As to its Eyes, Authors say that they shine in the Night; and see better at the full, and more dimly at the change of the Moon. Also that the Cat doth vary his Eyes with the Sun; the Pupil being round at Sunrise, and long towards the Noon, and not to be seen at all at Night, but the whole Eye shining in the darkness. These appearances of the Cat's Eyes, I am sure are true; but whether they answer to the times of Day, I have never observed." The half-shut lids are even more suggestive and significant of strange thaumaturgic powers. They can be feral, too, these eyes, a fact that Prosper Mérimée has recorded in " Carmen ": " Eye of a gipsy, eye of a wolf is a Spanish proverb which signifies acute observation. If you have not the time to go to the zoological gardens to study the stare of a wolf, look at your cat when he lies in wait for a sparrow." The fur harbours electricity and sends swift currents of this lightning up

The Cat and the Occult

the arm of him who strokes the animal. Sometimes, alone with a cat in the dead silences of the night, I have watched the creature's eyes suddenly dilate, her ears point back; with arched spine a startling, unexpected, unexplained prance across the floor follows; then puss settles back again to laundry and repose as if nothing had happened. What *has* happened? What has awakened this fit of wildness? Is it some noise unheard by humans, an unwelcome smell, or some reminiscence of the terrible mediaeval nights when the cat joined the witch in her broom-stick trails across the face of the moon?

The cat walks by herself, retains her pride, her dignity, her reserve, keeps the secret of the ciborium, and gives no sign of the cupellations she has witnessed in alchemystical garrets. She is perverse, refuses to be " put " anywhere, often takes delight in manifesting her affection for some one who has an inherent dislike for her, while she frequently ignores an admirer. " You never get to the bottom of cats," says a writer in " All the Year Round." " You will never find two, well known to you, that do not offer marked diversities in ways and dispositions, and, in general, the combination they exhibit of activity and repose, and the rapidity with which they pass from one to the other, their gentle aspects and fragile forms, united with strength and pliancy, their sudden appearances and disappearances, their tenacity of life and many escapes from dangers, their silent and rapid movements, their sometimes unaccountable gatherings, and strange noises at night — all contribute to invest them with a mysterious fascination, which reaches its culminating point in the (not very frequent) case of a completely black cat."

Is it wonderful that these qualities have served to cause her to be worshipped as a god, or reviled as a demon? Animals not infrequently play important rôles in mythology and enter into the elements of religion, but no other animal, it would seem, is so intimately bound with the arcane rites of several ages as the cat, waited upon by the priests of Egypt, the

The Tiger in the House

" familiar " of witches in the middle ages, the companion of Saint Ives and Saint Gertrude, " gentlest of mystics," in Sicily sacred to St. Martha, the friend of Mohammed, the time-piece of China, and the weather-vane of Scotland and England; puss saunters with noiseless pads, through the folklore and legends of Europe, Asia, and Africa, now petted, now hated or feared, now regarded with awe or horror, now with tenderness and veneration.

The cat is not mentioned in the Bible,[1] a fact which offers consolation to many dog-lovers, and her name appears only once in the Apocrypha.[2] The allusion is significant. We learn that a cat may not only look at a king, she is also permitted to sit on a god's head. Painters of Biblical scenes have evidently regarded puss's omission as an oversight or an impertinent perversion and they have put her into their pictures while an old Arabian legend connects her creation with the story of the ark. According to this charming folk-tale the pair of mice originally installed on board this boat increased and multiplied to such an extent that life was rendered unbearable for the other occupants, whereupon Noah passed his hand three times over the head of the lioness and she obligingly sneezed forth the cat. Another oriental story which obtained wide credence has it that the first day the animals entered the ark they rested quietly in their state-rooms. The first to venture forth was the monkey who persuaded the lioness to forget her vows of fidelity. The result of this initial transgression of natural laws was not only the birth of the cat but also, the old author assures us, " the spreading of

---

[1] " In the illuminated manuscript known as Queen Mary's Psalter (1553) there is a picture of the Fall of Man, in which there is a modification of the idea which gained wide currency during the middle ages that it was the serpent-woman, Lilith, who had tempted Adam to eat the forbidden fruit. In this picture, while the beautiful grace and ample hair of Lilith are shown, instead of the usual female breast she has the body of a cat." Moncure Daniel Conway: " Demonology and Devil-lore," Vol. II, p. 301.

[2] Baruch, VI, 22.

The Cat and the Occult

a spirit of coquetry which endured during the whole of the sojourn the animals made there." Still another story is related by Pierre Palliot in " La vraye et parfaicte science des armoires " (Paris; 1664) : " The cat is more harmful than useful, its caresses are more to be dreaded than desired, and its bite is fatal. The cause of the pleasure it gives us is strange and entertaining. At the moment of the creation of the world, says the fable, the Sun and the Moon emulated each other in peopling the earth with animals. The Sun, great, fiery, and luminous, formed the lion, beautiful, sanguinary, and generous. The Moon, seeing the other gods in admiration before this noble work, caused a cat to come forth from the earth, but one as disproportionate to the lion in beauty and courage as she (the Moon) is to her brother (the Sun). This contention gave rise to derision, and also indignation on the part of the Sun, who, being angry that the Moon should have attempted to match herself with him,

> *Créa par forme de mépris*
> *En même temps une souris.*

As, however, ' the sex ' never surrenders, the Moon made herself still more ridiculous by producing the most absurd of all animals, the monkey. This creature was received by the company of stars with a burst of immoderate laughter. A flame spread itself over the face of the Moon, even as when she threatens us with a tempest of great winds, and by a last effort, in order to be eternally revenged upon the Sun, she set undying enmity between the monkey and the cat, and between the cat and the mouse. Hence comes the sole advantage which we derive from the cat."

The cat was known in Egypt at least 1600 years before the birth of Christ, as certain tablets prove. Bast or Pasht was the cat goddess, worshipped at Bubastes, and it is from this name that certain wise philologists wish to derive the word, puss; still others like to think it comes from the Latin, *pusus,*

85

The Tiger in the House

little boy, or *pusa*, little girl. Herodotus informs us that Pasht occupied a similar position among the Egyptians to that of Artemis among the Greeks; this was the Diana of the Romans. Diana, indeed, assumed the form of a cat, when Typhon forced the gods and goddesses to hide themselves in animal shapes. There is also a connection with the Norse goddesses, Freyja, the Teutonic Venus, whose chariot was drawn by cats, and Helda, who was accompanied by maidens on cats or themselves distinguished in feline form. Pasht was the goddess of light, but more than Diana, of both moon and sun. The Egyptian word *mau* signified both light and cat. Moreover the sun-god Rä was frequently referred to as The Great Cat. Puss prefers the moon; the Hindu poet says, " The cat laps the moonbeams in the bowl of water, thinking them to be milk." Diana was also the goddess of wisdom, hunting, and chastity. Wise and a huntress the cat certainly is, but chaste, never![3]

Vulson de la Colombiere, whose science was heraldry, in the " Livre de la science héroïque," speaks quaintly of the cat's relation to the moon : " *Comme le lion est un animal solitaire, aussi le chat est une bête lunatique, dont les yeux, clairvoyants et étincelants durant les plus obscures nuits, croissent et décroissent à l'imitation de la lune; car, comme la lune, selon qu'elle participe à la lumière du soleil, change tous les jours de face, ainsi le chat est touché de pareille affection envers la lune, sa prunelle croissant et diminuant au même temps que cet astre est en son croissant ou en son décours. Plusieurs naturalistes assurent que, lorsque la lune est en son plein, les chats ont plus de force et d'adresse pour faire la guerre aux souris que lorsqu'elle est faible!* "

The Egyptians shaved their eyebrows and went into mourn-

---

[3] Professor W. M. Conway says in "The Cats of Ancient Egypt" ("English Illustrated Magazine"; Vol. 7, p. 251): "Pasht for her part was lady of love and corresponded in a crude sort of way to that much nobler conception, the Aphrodite of the Greeks." Freyja, of course, was an amorous goddess.

ing when a cat died and the penalty for killing a cat was very severe. As any one who witnessed a feline death scene was often suspected of murder, Egyptian citizens took care to be as far away as possible on such occasions, not a very difficult precautionary measure, one would believe, because pussy's instinct is to conceal herself when she is sick, as she is unable to confront her enemies in that condition. G. A. Henty has chosen as the central episode for his story, "The Cat of Bubastes," the dilemma of an Egyptian who was inadvertently responsible for a cat's death. Cats were painted in fresco, sculptured in stone, and even mummified after death. The countless examples of these mummies in contemporary museums bear silent witness to the veneration in which the animal was held. There were several methods of embalming in use among the Egyptians. Of these only the most elaborate has left its record. The working classes might have their bodies soaked in an antiseptic mixture and so preserved for a time, but it was the privilege of kings and rulers alone to have their bodies imbued with costly drugs and sweet spices and to lie unchanged in their tombs for thousands of years until their mummied remains were removed from their long repose. . . . The privilege which was denied the workingman was granted to the cat.[4]

[4] "But the ghost or double of a body (in ancient Egypt) had to have a material something to be the double of. The actual body was of course best; second best was an image of it made in some lasting substance. Hence arose mummification to preserve the body, and portrait sculpture to replace it if destroyed. In later times a wealthy Egyptian was often buried with no less than some hundreds of little images in the shape of a mummy, ticketed with his name, besides one or more really fine portrait statues of him. Such statues were called *Ka* statues. If the mummy were destroyed the *Ka* could still be kept in existence by means of them. . . . As with men, so with cats; they too had their *Ka* and all the rest of it, and their *Ka* had likewise to be kept from annihilation against the great day of resurrection of cats, crocodiles and men. A rich man's cat was elaborately mummied, wound round and round with stuff and cunningly plaited with linen ribbons dyed two different colours. His head was encased in a rough kind of *papier maché,* and that was covered with linen and painted, even gilt sometimes, the ears always carefully pricked up. The mummy might be enclosed

The Tiger in the House

The fact that mummied mice have been discovered in the cat tombs has puzzled some scientists. But in the royal tombs food was always provided for the mummied ruler; what more natural than to provide food for the mummied cat! . . . We may better understand this worship of the cat if we know something of animal symbolism and credit the priests of Egypt with having known more than we do. It is well also to bring forward the testimony of Professor Maspero who is of the opinion that the worship of cats among the lower middle classes of Egypt was largely adoration of the cat herself, not of the official god incarcerated in the animal. In support of this belief he describes certain stelae in the museum of Turin. On one, belonging to the age of the eighteenth dynasty, huge figures of a cat and a swallow are painted with a table of offerings before them, as well as two kneeling scribes. Accompanying phylacteries state that these offerings are to the " good cat " and " good swallow," not to any of the state gods hidden under these forms. Further it must be taken for granted that following each inundation of the Nile every farm became an island on which mice, serpents, and insects flourished, from whose depredations the farmer depended upon the cat and the ibis to free him.

I remember a night in a villa on the Florentine hills, a

in a bronze box with a bronze *Ka* statue of the cat seated on the top. Even finer burial might await a particularly grand cat. . . . A poor man's cat was rolled up in a simple lump, but the rolling was carefully and respectfully done." W. M. Conway: " The Cats of Ancient Egypt ": " English Illustrated Magazine "; Vol. 7, p. 251.

" The cases in which the cats were placed after embalming were capital representations of the cat in life. Many of them were of carven wood, remarkably lifelike affairs, the form and even the individuality and expression being remarkably preserved. . . . Some of the cat cases are curiously decorated and some of the faces are fitted with queerly made eyes, inlaid with obsidian, or rock crystal; others are done in coloured paste." W. S. Harwood: " The Mummification of Cats in Ancient Egypt "; " Scientific American "; Vol. 82, p. 361.

There are several excellent examples of cat mummies, wound in linen of two colours, *Ka* statues in bronze and faience, and bronze enclosing boxes in the Metropolitan Museum in New York.

green Florentine night . . . a dumb curiosity seized two of us and caused us to leave our chairs on the *loggia* where the faint breeze flickered the flames of the Roman lamps and the tall bottles of golden *strega* stood half-filled, to mount the stairs, led on by a nameless questioning, and to seek the chamber directly above the spot where we had been sitting, the temporary abode of two white Persian cats. . . . The room was empty when we entered; the bright moonlight streaming in from the doorway which led to a terrace which formed the roof of the *loggia* told us that. Noiselessly, and apparently unreasonably, we crept carefully across the broad chamber and looked out. . . . I can still see the expression of horror on my companion's face, perhaps reflected on my own, as we stood just hidden by the hangings at the doorway and saw the two cats softly lift their paws from two white doves who rose unsteadily, dizzily, and lazily into the green atmosphere, while the cats rolled on their backs, stretching their claws to the air and making faint mews. . . . Did we learn why the hawk and the cat sit together in the temples of the Nile?

We lose sight of the cat in the early history of Greece [5] but that does not prove that she did not exist during this civilization. Emily James Putnam, in her ironic book, points out that the lady suffered a similar eclipse. In Rome dogs were not permitted in the Temple of Hercules but pussies were admitted. Sacerdotal cats were welcomed even in the adytum. The priests were wise to make a virtue of necessity; it is impossible to exclude cats from any place which they desire to enter. To this day they attend Christian churches of any denomination whenever they have the inclination. In Hone's " Every-day Book " there is a reference to a curious mediaeval custom, for which credit is given to Mills's " History of the Crusades:" " At Aix in Provence on the festival of Corpus

[5] Sir George Lewis thought he had proved that there were no cats in Athens, but a vase of the best period represents a cat chasing mice.

The Tiger in the House

Christi, the finest Tom cat of the country, wrapped like a child in swaddling clothes, was publicly exhibited in a magnificent shrine. Every knee was bent, every hand either strewed flowers or poured incense, and, in short, the cat on this occasion was treated in all respects as the god of the day." This curious anecdote has found wide credence and has been repeated in most of the cat books. A writer in the Catholic periodical, " The Month," however, finds little to believe in it.[6] According to this savant, King René of Anjou in 1472, although they had been in existence long before that, formulated a definite plan for the games of this day, theatrical interludes between the serious religious business. Unfortunately King René's manuscript has been lost, but a full account of the games, with curious illustrations, made just prior to the French Revolution when the Aix procession was still unshorn of its splendour, still exists and it is from that that the writer in " The Month " derives his information. There were, it seems, twelve *jeux* and the cat appeared in the first one, which was called, indeed, *The play of the cat*: One of the performers carried a tall staff with a gilt image of a calf on top of it, round it were grouped some of the Israelites, while Moses, easily recognized by his horns, and Aaron, distinguished by his breastplate, stood aloof and rebuked them. However, the chief subject of popular interest was the cat. How he came to be introduced into the picture we can only conjecture, but at any rate there he was. One of the performers carried poor Tom in his arms, muffled up in some sort of covering, probably to keep him from scratching. As the scene proceeded he tossed him up as high as he could in the air, catching him again, amid the plaudits of the crowd, with more or less dexterity. Grégoire's engraving represents the cat in

[6] " Cats in Catholic Ritual " (signed H. T.) : " The Month," Vol. 87, p. 487; London, 1896. This writer asserts that the story is not to be found in " The History of the Crusades." As I have not read this book I cannot offer corroboration of his statement.

The Cat and the Occult

the act of being tossed, and depicts the agonized expression of the victim. "We can readily understand that this bit of cruel buffoonery will have been the most popular feature of the procession," adds the Catholic author, "but we can only explain the presence of poor pussy by supposing that besides the golden calf, King René wished to suggest that the Israelites had also remembered something of the animal worship of the Egyptians. At any rate it is in this sense and this sense only that the inhabitants and priests of Aix can be described as paying divine honours to the cat."

The cat seems to have been at home in China from the fifth century, A. D., and she was introduced into Japan from China as late as the tenth century. In both these countries she generally plays a demoniac and reprehensible part in legend and folklore, although there are stories about cats who befriended mortals. Usually, however, she steals precious objects; she has the pernicious habit of producing dancing balls of fire; she wraps a towel around her head and walks the rooftop on her hind legs; sometimes she grows a forked tail and thereby becomes a nekomata. When she is ten years old she begins to talk. In China she is employed by old women to negotiate obliquities; in Japan she destroys these beldams. Her spiritual strength increases with age and she is able, if she attains the proper number of years, to effect certain transformations. This belief finds confirmation in European folklore in which it is held that a cat twenty years old turns into a witch, and a witch a hundred years old turns back into a cat. Neverthless, in spite of the animal's turpitudes, the killing of a cat was a sin for which a heavy spiritual penalty existed in Japan. The curse of the beast was said to fall not only on the man himself but on his family to the seventh generation. Sometimes the cat killed the culprit; sometimes she was satisfied to haunt him. The Persians also hesitate before slaying a cat as Djinns or Afreets often assume feline forms and the angry evicted demons are frequently willing to spend the rest of eternity haunting the person responsible for destroying their dwellings. In Egypt the Arabs believe that a Djinn takes the form of a cat when he wishes to haunt a house and the last born of twins is capable, in order to satisfy her desires, of turning herself into a cat. A traveller who had killed a cat for making ravages in his storehouse at Luxor was visited next day by a neighbouring apothecary who begged him to kill no more cats. " My daughter," he explained, " often visits you in the form of a cat to eat your dessert."

There is further the doctrine of metempsychosis to consider. There was a belief held in China that one became a cat after death. This belief caused the mighty Empress Wu to forbid cats entrance to her palace because a court lady, whom she had cruelly caused to be put to death, threatened to turn Her Royal Highness into a rat and tease her as a spectre-cat. There is a story in the " Konjaku Monogatari " of a man who was terribly afraid of cats, probably because he had been a rat in his previous existence. This belief prevailed in India, too, of course. General Sir Thomas Edward Gordon in " A Varied Life " (1906) tells the following remarkable story: " For twenty-five years an oral addition to the written standing orders of the native guard at Government House near Poona had been communicated regularly from one guard to another on relief, to the effect that any cat passing out of the front door after dark was to be regarded as His Excellency, the Governor, and to be saluted accordingly. The meaning of this was that Sir Robert Grant, Governor of Bombay, had died there in 1838 and on the evening of the day of his death a cat was seen to leave the house by the front door and walk up and down a particular path, as it had been the Governor's habit to do after sunset. A Hindu sentry had observed this, and he mentioned it to the others of his faith, who made it a subject of superstitious conjecture, the result being that one of the priestly class explained the mystery of the dogma of the transmigration of the soul from one body to another, and

The Cat and the Occult

interpreted the circumstance to mean that the spirit of the deceased Governor had entered into one of the house pets.

" It was difficult to fix on a particular one, and it was therefore decided that every cat passing out of the main entrance after dark was to be treated with due respect and the proper honours. The decision was accepted without question by all the native attendants and others belonging to Government House. The whole guard from sepoy to sibadar, fully acquiesced in it, and an oral addition was made to the standing orders that the sentry at the front door ' present arms to any cat passing out there after dark.' "

The orientals are more astute about cats than we are. They ascribe to them a language, a knowledge of the future, an extreme sensitiveness which allows them to perceive objects and beings invisible to man. They are aware that this animal wavers on the borderland between the natural and the supernatural, the conscious and the subconscious. They even allow them to have ghosts. It may be said here that an occidental clergyman has written a book [7] to prove that animals have souls and will share our future existence. A heaven without cats would, of course, be deserted for a hell with them.

In Professor de Groot's " Religious System of China " we find an early story of cat sorcery. The incident occurred in 598 A. D., under the Sui Dynasty. In that year the Emperor was about to order his brother-in-law, named Tuh-hu T'o, and his wife to commit suicide for having employed cat-spectres against the Empress and another lady, who had fallen ill simultaneously. By the personal intervention of the Empress herself and that of her younger brother they were granted their lives, but the man was divested of all his dignities and his wife was made a Buddhist nun. During the trial a female slave told the judges that T'o's mother used to sacrifice to the cat-spectres at night, on every day of the rat. Whenever

[7] Rev. J. G. Wood: "Man and Beast: Here and Hereafter."

93

a cat-spectre murdered a victim the possessions of the dead man transferred themselves automatically to the house where the beast was kept. T'o had commanded her, so the slave testified, to make the cat-spectre enter the palace in order to secure valuable presents from the Empress. When the judges had heard this confession they ordered the woman to call the spectre back, whereupon setting out a bowl of fragrant rice-gruel, and drumming against it with a spoon, she exclaimed, ' Come, pussy, remain no longer in the palace.' After a time her face turned blue and moving as if driven by some unseen force, she muttered, ' Here is the cat-spectre.' In the same year the Emperor ordered all families keeping cat-spectres to be banished to the farthest frontier regions. This act seems entirely consistent with modern governmental procedure. De Groot also tells of a hag who tormented a child and made it cry incessantly at night. She did this riding on her cat, that is on its soul as a spectral horse, but was discovered and routed by an exorcist. The cat was beaten to death and the hag starved, whereupon the child became appeased and stopped crying. The result seems worthy of almost any means.

The domestic cat was imported from China into Japan in the reign of the Emperor Ichigo (986–1011). The animal was at first a rare and high-priced luxury and consequently only the noble families could afford to keep it. How much the Emperor himself liked cats we may learn from the " O-u-ki " and the " Makura no sōshi." The former book states that " on the nineteenth day of the ninth month of the year 999 a cat brought forth young in the palace. The left and right ministers had the task of bringing up the kittens, and prepared boxes (with delicacies) and rice and clothes for them (as for newborn babes). Uma no myōbu, a court lady, was appointed wet-nurse for the kittens. The people laughed at the matter and were rather astonished." The attitude of the people does not seem to be unusual or surprising. The Emperor further bestowed the fifth rank (that of the court ladies) on a cat in the palace and gave her the name, Myōbu no Omoto (Omoto, the lady-in-waiting).

But poor puss, who began her life in Japan as a pampered pet, the favourite of the court, in less than three centuries began to be associated with demons in the popular mind. In the " Kokonchomonshu " (1254) there is a tale of a Buddhist Archbishop who received a visit from a beautiful Chinese cat, who came, like Mélisande and Mr. Warner's Calvin, apparently from nowhere. The Archbishop was vastly diverted by the antics of the graceful animal, who liked to play with a ball and was very skilful at the game. One day, by way of jest, the priest substituted a precious mamori-sword (a sacred sword with protective magical powers) for the ball. The cat seized it in her mouth, ran away, and was never seen again. " She was," remarks the author solemnly, " probably a transformed demon, who by taking the protective sword could more easily attack people."

In the " Yamato Kwai-i ki " (1708) there is an account of the strange happenings in the house of a samurai. At night, luminous balls, which no one could catch, bounded about the rooms, about three inches from the floor. Once a group of these mysterious balls illuminated a tree. The maid-servants were attacked by spirits in their sleep; one of them especially was troubled by demons. Her spinning-wheel turned of its own volition and her pillow circled as if on a pivot while she slept. In vain she sought relief from sorceresses, Shintō priests, yamabushi, and Buddhist priests; neither their charms nor their prayers assisted her. At last the master of the house saw a very old cat walking on his hind legs on the roof, with a towel belonging to the maid-servant bound round his head.[8] A slave brought down the cat with an arrow and the

[8] Pierre Loti found the following in a rare old Japanese book: " *Une certaine nuit de chaque hiver, les chats tiennent, dans quelque jardin isolé, une grande assemblée qui se termine par une ronde générale au clair de lune.*" *Vient*

house was no longer haunted. The animal was five shaku long and its tail was split (nekomata).

The " Mimi-bukuro " (1815) introduces us to talking cats, which occur in other oriental and mediaeval tales. In 1795, it seems, a cat observed, " What a pity! " when his master, the abbot of a monastery, frightened away some doves for which he had been lying in wait. The abbot seized the cat and threatened him in this manner: " It is very strange that you, an animal, can speak. You can certainly transform yourself and haunt mankind. As you have spoken once you must speak again; otherwise I shall break the commandment to spare all living beings and kill you." Whereupon puss replied in stately periods: " We cats are not the only creatures who can speak; all creatures are able to do so when they are more than ten years old. When they reach the age of twenty-four or five they can also change themselves in a miraculous way but no cat ever reaches that age. A cat who is a cross between a fox and a cat can speak before the age of ten." At the conclusion of this lesson in unnatural history the good abbot reported himself satisfied and gave the cat leave to remain in the monastery, but grimalkin took his departure with three ceremonious bows and was never seen again.

So late as 1875 a man of Toulon informed Bérenger-Féraud that one of his friends had owned a wizard cat who was accustomed to take an active part in the evening conversation, at least when it was sufficiently interesting to keep him awake. His mistress consulted him before making plans, giving her reasons for taking one course or another, and she invariably followed the cat's advice. The animal stated his preferences for meat or fish and was very indignant when his wishes were

ensuite, continues Loti, *cette clause adorable, que je recommande à l'attention de Jules Lemaitre et de tous ceux qui sont assez affinés pour comprendre le charme des chats: " Pour être admis à cette réunion, tout chat est tenu de se procurer un fichu ou un mouchoir de soie dont il se coiffe pour danser."* " Japoneries d'Automne," p. 150.

The Cat and the Occult

not respected. From time to time he disappeared for several days and the members of the household believed that he took human form during these absences. When he lay at the point of death he prayed that his body might be decently buried. His mistress not daring to inter him in a grave prepared for a human being, laid the coffin behind the cemetery wall adjacent to a Christian tomb and at the funeral the cat's soul was recommended to the care of his Creator. The fabulists all ask the cat to speak and the Cheshire Cat in " Alice in Wonderland " is as epigrammatic as an Oscar Wilde duchess. " If we had not in our intercourse with human beings acquired a certain contempt for speech we could all speak," says Hinze the Tom Cat in Ludwig Tieck's delightful play, *Der gestiefelte Kater.*

In the middle ages cats attended witches' revels, went to the Sabbath, and frequently shared the fate of the witch, which was to be drowned or toasted alive. Many witches about to be burned confessed that they had often taken the shapes of cats,

Chatte dans le jour, la nuit elle est femme,

and these confessions stimulated the persecution of the feline race. It must also be remembered that in the middle ages cats, like other animals were moral agents and could be sued or criminally tried. Trials of this sort were not rare. Again the Roman Church claimed full power to anathematize all animate and inanimate things. Doubtless these facts, added to the gleaming eyes and generally mysterious nature of the cat, her inexplicable disappearances and appearances, made it very easy for the judges to believe the witches' confessions. " What explanation can be given of the evil repute of our household friend the cat? " asks Moncure Daniel Conway.[9] " Is it derived by inheritance from its fierce ancestors of the

[9] " Demonology and Devil-Lore."

97

jungle? Was it first suggested by its horrible human-like, sleep-murdering caterwaulings at night? Or has it simply suffered from a theological curse on the cats said to draw the chariot of the goddess of beauty?" The sceptic Fontenelle told Moncrif that he had been brought up to believe that all the cats in town went to the Sabbath on the eve of Saint John's day. Therefore the peasants, in order to rid the country of sorcerers, threw all the cats they could catch into the fire on this day. Cats play a part in the horrid masonic rites described by Dr. Bataille in his " Le Diable au XIX Siècle." The she-cat is one of a dozen animals to which Dante compares his demons. Mgr. Léon Maurin, once Archbishop at Port Luis in Mauritius, writes about the sacrifices of cats by devil-worshippers at midnight on the altars of rifled churches. The devil, himself, indeed, frequently borrowed the black robe of a cat, for bad cats are usually black, as good cats are usually white. The worthy Père Bougeant writes: " *Les bêtes ne sont que des diables et à la tête de ces diables marche le chat.*" Saint Dominique, when he preached of the devil, described him as a cat. The large green or topaze fixed eyes of the inky felines contributed to the stability of the legend. There were spectre-cats, " familiars," but most often the cat was the pythoness herself in animal form. We still celebrate the union of cats and witches on Hallowe'en. How were these cat demons raised? Cornelius Agrippa in his " Occult Philosophy " (1651) says that if " Coriander, smallage, henbane and hemlock be made a fume, spirits will presently come together, hence they are called the spirit herbs. Also it is said that a fume made of the root of herb sagapen with the juice of hemlock and henbane, and the herb tapsus barbatus, red sanders and black poppy make spirits and strange shapes appear. Moreover it is said that by certain fumes certain animals are gathered together. . . ." In the " Conjurers' Magazine " (1791) there is to be found a recipe " to draw cats together and fascinate them ": " In the new moon, gather the herb Nepe, and dry it in the heat of the sun, when it is temperately hot. Gather vervain in the hour ♀ and only expose it to the air while ☉ is under the earth. Hang these together in a net, in a convenient place, and when one of them has scented it, her cry will soon call those about her that are within hearing; and they will rant and run about, leaping and capering to get at the net, which must be placed so that they cannot easily accomplish it, for they will certainly tear it to pieces." There must be other recipes in the " Grimorium Verum," the " Grimoire of Pope Honorius " and the " Grand Grimoire." But when a witch wanted to transform herself into a cat she rubbed herself with a certain ointment. This art, along with that of polishing intaglios, seems to be lost.

The Taigheirm was an infernal magical sacrifice of cats, the origin of which lies in remote pagan times, in rites dedicated to the subterranean gods, from whom particular gifts and benefits were solicited by nocturnal offerings. The word itself, in Gaelic, signifies the invocation of the house. Through Christianity these sacrifices were modified and were offered now to the infernal powers, or as they were called in the Highlands and the Western Isles of Scotland, the Black-Cat Spirits.

According to Horst's " Deuteroscopy " black cats were indispensable to the incantation ceremony of the Taigheirm, and as will presently appear, plenty of black cats. These were dedicated to the gods of the lower world or later to the foul demons of Christianity. The midnight hour between Friday and Saturday was the authentic time for these horrible practices and invocations to begin; the ceremony was protracted for four days and nights, during which period the operator was forbidden to sleep or to take nourishment.

" After the cats were dedicated to all the devils, and put into a magico-sympathetic condition by the shameful things done to them, and the agony occasioned them, one of them was at once put on the spit, and amid terrific howlings, roasted before a slow fire. The moment that the howls of one tortured cat ceased in death, another was put upon the spit, for a minute of interval must not continue if an agent would control hell; and this must continue for four entire days and nights, if the exorcist could hold out, still longer, and even if till his physical powers were absolutely exhausted, he must do so. After a time infernal spirits appeared in the shape of black cats. There came continually more and more of these cats and their howling mingled with that of those roasting on the spit was terrific. Finally a cat of monstrous size appeared with dreadful threats. The gift of second sight was usually the recompense of the Taigheirm."

One of the last Taigheirm,[10] according to Horst, was held in the middle of the seventeenth century in the Island of Mull. The spot is still marked where Allan Maclean, at that time the sacrificial priest, stood with his assistant, Lachlain Maclean. He continued his sacrifices to the fourth day when he was exhausted in mind and body and sank into a swoon.

The infernal spirits appeared, some in the early progress of the sacrifices, in the shape of black cats. The first glared at the sacrificers and cried, " Lachlain Oer " (Injurer of Cats). Allan, the chief operator, warned Lachlain that he must not waver but must keep the spit turning incessantly whatever he might see or hear. At the end of the second day a monster cat arrived with a horrid howl and assured Lachlain Oer that if he did not cease putting pussies on the spit before their largest brother arrived he would never see the face of God.

[10] John Gregorson Campbell in "Superstitions of the Highlands and Islands of Scotland " describes the Taigheirm as a " devil's supper " and he says that tradition in the West Highlands makes mention of three instances of this performance, all of which are similar: Allan the cattle-lifter (Ailein nan creach) at Dail-a-chat (subsequently called The Cats' Field) in Lochaber; Dun Lachlain in the big barn at Pennygoun in Mull; and the Children of Quithen, a small sept at Skye in a cave. The night of the day I first learned of the Taigheirm I dined with some friends who were also entertaining Seumas, Chief of Clann Fhearghuis of Stra-chur, who informed me that to the best of his knowledge the Taigheirm is still celebrated in the Highlands of Scotland.

The Cat and the Occult

" Bring on all the devils of hell and I will not stop until I have completed my work," cried Lachlain. At the end of the fourth day a black cat with fire flaming from his eyes perched on the end of a beam in the roof of the barn and his howl could be heard quite across the straits of Mull into Morven. One is not surprised to learn that on the last day Allan was wholly exhausted by the apparitions and could only utter the word " Prosperity " before he became unconscious. But Lachlain was still self-possessed and able to continue. He demanded prosperity and wealth. Both got what they asked for. It might be added that men of such nerve should be able to get anything they wanted on earth.

On his death bed Allan informed his friends that if he and Lachlain (who had died before him) had lived a little longer they would have driven Satan from his throne. When Allan's funeral cortège reached the churchyard those persons endowed with second sight saw at some distance Lachlain Oer, standing fully armed at the head of a band of black cats, from which streamed the odour of brimstone.

In some old French records an account is given of how a man buried a black cat at a spot where four cross-roads met. In the box with the c t he placed bread soaked in holy water and holy oil, sufficient to keep the animal alive for three days. His intention was to dig up his innocent victim, slay him, and make a girdle of his skin, by which means he expected to be able to transform himself into an animal and gain the gift of clairvoyance. Unfortunately for his projects, however, the buried puss was exhumed by hounds. The affair thus came to public knowledge and ended in the courts where the guilty man was condemmed for sorcery and probably subsequently burned at the stake.

One of the mediaeval grimoires gives a curious recipe by means of which a sorcerer might make himself invisible, in which a black cat again is the central figure: " Steal a black cat, buy a new pot, a mirror, a piece of flint, an agate, charcoal, and a tinder; draw water from a fountain at the exact hour of midnight; after that light your fire, put the cat in the pot, and hold the cover with the left hand without moving or looking behind you, whatever noise you may hear, and after it has boiled for twenty-four hours, always without moving or looking behind you, put the mess into a new dish, taking the meat and throwing it over the left shoulder, repeating these words: *Accipe quod tibi do et nihil amplius.* Then crunch the bones one after the other, under the teeth, from the left side, looking at yourself in the mirror, and walk backwards."

When Sir Walter Scott was a young man he went to see that curious being, the Black Dwarf, " bowed David Ritchie," in his den, a gloomy bit of hut. After they had sat together for a while the dwarf, glancing at Scott, asked, " Man, ha' ye ony poo'r? " meaning of course, supernatural power. Scott disclaimed any gift of the sort. The dwarf then stretched his finger out to a corner, where for the first time Scott became aware that a green-eyed black cat was sitting, staring at him. As the dwarf extended his finger towards the cat he cried, " He has poo'r," and Scott admitted that a strange feeling of awe and terror crept over him. A century or two earlier bowed David and his cat would have broken on the wheel. In 1607 a witch bearing the name of Isobel Grierson was burned at the stake after having been accused and convicted of entering the house of one Adam Clark in Prestonpans in the likeness of the man's own pet cat and in the company of a mighty rabble of other cats, who by their noise frightened Adam, his wife, and their servant, the last-named being dragged up and down the stairs by the hair of her head, presumably by the devil in the shape of a black man. Isobel also visited the house of a certain Mr. Brown in the shape of a cat, but being called by name she vanished, not, however, before she had caused him to fall ill of a disease of which he afterwards died. And Alice Duke, *alias* Manning, of Wincanton in Somerset, who was tried in 1664 for witchcraft, confessed that her familiar visited her " in the shape of a little cat of dunnish colour, which is as smooth as a want " and that " her familiar doth commonly suck her right breast about seven at night " after which she fell into a kind of trance. Any book on witches will furnish a score of such examples and almost all of them give a long account of the famous Rutterkin case, which has likewise been retold so frequently in books about cats that I will not repeat it here. In a story called " Ancient Sorceries " Algernon Blackwood has utilized the theme in fiction.[11] Arthur Vezin, an Englishman travelling in France, descended with his bag at some way station intending to pass the night. As the train moved slowly away one of his companions in the compartment, a stranger, leaned out of the window and whispered into his ear a long sentence of which he was only able to catch the last few words, *" à cause de sommeil et à cause de chats."* Vezin at once began to notice " the extraordinary silence of the whole place. Positively the town was muffled. Although the streets were paved with cobbles the people moved about silently, softly, with padded feet, like cats. Nothing made noise. All was hushed, subdued, muted. The very voices were quiet, low-pitched like purring. Nothing clamorous, vehement, or emphatic seemed able to live in the drowsy atmosphere of soft dreaming that soothed this little hill-town into its sleep. It was like the woman at the inn — an outward repose screening intense inner activity and purpose. Yet there was no sign of lethargy or sluggishness anywhere about it. The people were active and alert. Only a magical and uncanny softness lay over them like a spell."

Presently Vezin had the feeling that he was being spied upon and " he began to see how it was that he was so cleverly watched yet without the appearance of it. The people did nothing *directly*. They behaved *obliquely*. . . . They looked at him from angles which naturally should have led their

[11] " John Silence."

sight in another direction altogether. Their movements were oblique, too, so far as these concerned himself. The straight, direct thing was not their way evidently. They did nothing obviously. If he entered a shop to buy, the woman walked instantly away and busied herself with something at the farther end of the counter, though answering at once when he spoke, showing that she knew he was there and that this was only her way of attending to him. It was the fashion of the cat she followed. Even in the dining-room of the inn, the be-whiskered and courteous waiter, lithe and silent in all his movements, never seemed able to come straight to his table for an order or a dish. He came by zigzags, indirectly, vaguely, so that he appeared to be going to another table altogether, and only turned suddenly at the last moment, and was there beside him." At length, the daughter of the keeper of the inn returned, a beautiful, panther-like creature; she brushed past Vezin in a dark hallway, with the touch of kitten's fur, and awakened in him a most intense passion. And it was from her that he learned the secret of the town, the consecration of its folk to the ancient sorceries. He joined her and her mother in a wild but stealthily noiseless dance on the flagstones of the courtyard of the inn, and then in terror fled to his room, from whence he saw the inhabitants of the town in the guise of cats climbing from the windows, over the roofs, and leaping to the streets below. Rushing into the open he met the girl who cried: " 'Transform, Transform! . . . Rub well your skin before you fly. Come! Come with me to the Sabbath, to the madness of its furious delight, to the sweet abandonment of its evil worship! See! the Great Ones are there, and the terrible Sacraments prepared. The throne is occupied. Anoint and come! Anoint and come!' She grew to the height of a tree beside him, leaping upon the wall with flaming eyes and hair strewn upon the night. He too began to change swiftly. Her hands touched the skin of his face and neck, streaking him with the burning salve that sent

The Cat and the Occult

the old magic into his blood with the power before which fades all that is good. A wild roar came up to his ears from the heart of the wood, and the girl, when she heard it, leaped upon the wall in the frenzy of her wicked joy. ' Satan is there! ' she screamed, rushing upon him and striving to draw him with her to the edge of the wall. ' Satan has come! The Sacraments call us! Come, with your dear apostate soul, and we will worship and dance till the moon dies and the world is forgotten.' "

In the old tales human beings frequently assumed the form of cats in order the better to carry on their turpitudes. The transformation was usually accomplished, as in Blackwood's story, by the application of a magic salve. In these stories the phenomenon of repercussion is the most interesting feature. It was the belief that if you injured an animal inhabited by a witch spirit when she regained human form she still bore the marks of the injury. Variations of the belief in repercussion occur in the folk-tales of every language and evidence of repercussion was frequently introduced at witches' trials. A woodman whose dinner was stolen from him daily by a cat made many attempts to put an end to these depredations. At last, catching pussy in the act, he chopped off one of her paws, and when he returned home he observed, to his horror, that his wife had lost one of her hands. There is the similar tale of the Swabian soldier who used to visit the young woman to whom he was betrothed every evening when he was off duty. But on one occasion the girl warned him that he must never come to her on Friday because it was not convenient for her to see him then. His suspicions were accordingly aroused and the very next Friday night he set out for his sweetheart's house. On the way a white cat dogged his steps and as the animal become importunate he drew his sword and slashed off one of her hind paws, whereupon she ran away. Arriving at the girl's house he found her in bed and when he asked her what was the matter she gave a very confused reply. Noting stains of blood on the white coverlet he drew it back and saw that his betrothed was bathed in blood for one of her feet had been chopped off. " Witch! " he cried and left her. In three days she was dead.[12] There is further the history of the woman of Ceyreste whose children were always ailing, a state of affairs for which there was no natural way of accounting. A neighbour told her that she thought her mother-in-law might be responsible. " She may be a witch." The woman spoke to her husband and they determined to watch the cradles of their offspring. That very night observing a black cat crawling over the side of the baby's crib, the man struck the animal a violent blow with a club. With a howl the beast sprang through the open window and vanished. The mother-in-law had been in the habit of paying daily visits to her son's family but the next day she did not appear, nor yet the next. After a few days her son went to see her and found her in a bad temper with her hand bandaged. In response to his query as to why she had not come to his house as usual she replied in a rage: " Look at the state of my fingers. Whatever should I come to your house for? If I had been struck by a hatchet instead of a stick my hand would have been cut off and I would have had nothing but a stump." One more: the witches of Vernon in the shape of cats inhabited an ancient castle. Three or four men determined to pass the night in this castle; they were attacked by the cats and many wounds were exchanged. Afterwards the women returned to their human forms and were found to be suffering from corresponding gashes.

It seems rather surprising that Arthur Machen has not touched upon the repercussion phenomenon in any of his mystic masterpieces. Again we must turn to Algernon Blackwood, this time to his story, " The Empty Sleeve." [13] The

---

[12] Ernst Meier: "Deutsche Sagen, Sitten und Gebräuche aus Schwaben "; Stuttgart, 1852.

[13] " The London Magazine "; January 1911.

violinist Hyman " believed that there was some fluid portion of a man's personality which could be projected to a distance, and even semimaterialized there. The ' astral body,' he called it, or some such foolishness, claiming that it could appear in various forms, according to its owner's desire, even in animal forms." John Gilmer was awakened one night by a noise in the flat; seizing a Turkish sword from the wall he entered the sitting room where he saw a moving figure. The encounter and terror of both beings in the dark is described, and as the creature, which John finally recognized as an enormous cat, fled, John struck it with his weapon, almost severing one of the front legs from the body. Months afterwards the Gilmers met Hyman wearing spectacles and a beard. William pointed out to his brother the difference.

" ' But didn't you notice—'

' What? '

' He had an empty sleeve.'

' Yes,' said William. ' He's lost an arm! ' "

The supernatural plays a part in many other stories. On the twenty-sixth of March, 1782 (it is remarkable how many such miracles are carefully dated) a gentleman of wealth consulted Count Cagliostro, in an attempt to discover if his wife, who was young and beautiful, had been unfaithful to him. Cagliostro assured the anxious husband that the proof was a simple one and gave him a phial of liquid which he instructed him to drink before going to bed. " If your wife has broken her vows," he added, " you will be transformed into a cat." The husband returned home and told his wife the whole story; she laughed at his credulity but he swallowed the draught and went to bed. Rising early, the lady left him sleeping, but later as he did not appear, went to seek him, when to her astonishment she found in his place a huge black cat. She screamed, called out her husband's name, and finally knelt at the foot of the bed and begged for pardon, confessing that she had committed a sin with a handsome young soldier who had cajoled her by means of tears and tales of heroic deeds to forget her marriage vows. A story known as " The Devil's Cat " is current in North Germany: A peasant owned three beautiful cats. A neighbour begged one of these from him and obtained her. To accustom her to her new home he shut her up in the loft. At night, puss, popping her head out of the window, asked, " What shall I bring tonight? " " Thou shalt bring mice," answered the man. The cat set to work, casting all she caught on the floor till the loft was so full of dead mice that it was almost impossible to open the door and the man was employed the entire day in throwing them away by bushels. That night again the cat put her head through the window and asked, " What shall I bring tonight? " " Thou shalt bring rye," answered the farmer. In the morning the loft was stacked with rye. The man now saw the true nature of the cat and carried her back to his neighbour, " for had he given her work the third time he could never have gotten rid of her." His mistake, of course, was in not asking for gold on the second night.

It is her unusually fine nervous system, her electricity, which made the cat useful to the sorcerer, and this same nervous system, her extreme sensitiveness and susceptibility, often enable her to perform seeming miracles. In the year 1783 two cats belonging to a merchant of Messina warned him of the approach of an earthquake. Before the first shock they tried to scratch their way through the floor of a room in which they were confined. Their master, observing their fruitless efforts, opened the door for them. At two other closed doors they continued to exhibit symptoms of frantic terror and when finally set at liberty they ran swiftly through the town and made for the open fields where they began to dig. The earthquake destroyed the house they had left and several surrounding it but the merchant who, filled with curiosity over the strange behaviour of the cats, had followed them, was saved. This story has a perfectly natural explanation: the extremely

The Cat and the Occult

sensitive nervous organization of the cats was affected by the seismic disturbances long before they registered on the infinitely coarser nervous system of man, who if he ever possessed these finer perceptions has almost completely lost them, except in isolated cases. Earthquakes do not occur with sufficient frequency to obtain much evidence in this direction, but cases in which cats have warned householders of fires, sometimes saving many lives thereby, are numberless.[14]

Cats have some uncanny fashion of reckoning time. A London barrister, one of the staff of a well-known provincial newspaper, told Lindsay that his cat was accustomed to meet him regularly on a certain road on his way home from his office. There is an infallible method by which you can test your own cat in this respect. Feed him regularly at a certain hour each day for a few weeks and thereafter, if you have no clock in the house, he will inform you himself when the hour arrives. Alexandre Dumas relates a story of a clairvoyant cat which goes even further.[15] His Mysouff used to accompany him from his home in the Rue de l'Ouest every morning as far as the Rue de Vaugirard and wait for him every evening at the same point. "The curious thing was that, on such days as some chance circumstance or casual invitation tempted me to break my dutiful habits as a son and I was not going back to dine at home, Mysouff, though the door was opened for his exit as usual, positively refused to go out, and lay motionless on his cushion, in the posture of a serpent biting his own tail. It was quite different on days when I meant to return punctually. Then, if they forgot to open the door for him, Mysouff would scratch at it persistently with his claws till he got what he wanted." When Avery Hopwood visits his country-house he is accustomed to take his cat with him in his automobile. Abélard sleeps peace-

---

[14] For a particularly good example see "Lady Jule" by Francis Wilson; "Ladies' Home Journal"; November 1902.

[15] "Mes Bêtes."

fully during most of the journey, but invariably as the motor ascends a certain hill, a quarter of a mile from the house, he gets up and begins to stretch himself.

Cats in many quarters of the globe are held responsible for the weather; they are actually said to make it good or bad. In other localities they are regarded as competent barometers. This is not strange when it is remembered that cats are extraordinarily sensitive to the changes of temperature, while by storms they are sometimes affected almost to the point of madness. Colette Willy, who has more delicately expressed the psychology of cats than almost any one else, in one of her dialogues called, " l'Orage," [16] gives us what may very well be an accurate vision of a cat's mind during a hot summer tempest. Kiki-la-Doucette is speaking to Toby-Chien: " I have a headache. Do you not perceive under the nearly bare skin of my temples, under my bluish and transparent skin of an animal of fine breeding, the beating of my arteries? It is terrible! Around my forehead my veins are like vipers in convulsions and I do not know what gnome is forging in my brain. O, be silent, or at least speak so softly that the coursing of my agitated blood will cover your words." Again, " The storm is here. Gods! how I suffer! If I could only quit this skin and this fur which smother me, if I could only turn myself inside out, naked as a skinned mouse, towards the freshness! O dog, you cannot see but I feel the sparks which crackle at the tip of each of my hairs. Do not come near me: I am about to send forth a bolt of blue flame. . . ." Presently the dog describes her: " You are changed, Cat! Your drawn figure is that of a starved creature, and your hair, like burnished metal here, ruffled there, gives you the pitiful appearance of a weasel which has fallen into oil." And when the Lady approaches, Kiki mutters, " If she touches me I will devour her." Pierquin de Gemblcux [17] describes a different

[16] " Sept Dialogues de Bêtes."
[17] " Traité de la Folie des Animaux."

The Cat and the Occult

reaction to the effect of a storm in which a surplus of electricity in the air, a state of high electrical tension, sometimes produces hilarity, gaiety, noisiness, amounting occasionally to a kind of joyous mania, a morbid exuberance of animal spirits, especially in young cats.

This strange behaviour of cats during atmospheric changes has disturbed the imaginations of many peoples at many times. If a cat tears at cushions or carpets or is generally uneasy she is said to be raising a wind. This superstition is still widely prevalent in seacoast towns, on Cape Cod and elsewhere. Idle terrors of this character all have for a basis the science of divination, which neglects no token, but from effects overlooked by the ignorant ascends through a sequence of interlinked causes. This science knows, for example, that atmospheric conditions which cause a dog to howl are fatal to certain sufferers, that the monotonous wheeling of ravens, who frequent localities of murder and execution, in the air means the presence of unburied bodies. The flight of other birds prognosticates a hard winter, while others are haruspices of coming storms. It may even be stated categorically that the superstition that it is unlucky to walk under a ladder is based on an accident that has befallen some one who has done so. Perhaps the hod-carrier on the ladder has dropped a brick on his head. On that which the mystic discerns ignorance remarks and generalizes. The first sees useful warnings everywhere, the second is terrified by everything. As a matter of fact the cat with her superior nervous organism is conscious of the approach of the wind before man is and the condition of her fur alone will indicate weather changes to the careful observer.

It is a common notion that the weather will change if a cat sneezes, scratches the leg of a table, or sits with her tail to the fire. Erasmus Darwin, the grandfather of the author of " The Origin of Species," in a poem, " Signs of Foul Weather," notes the behaviour of the cat at the approach of a storm,

III

The Tiger in the House

Puss on the hearth, with velvet paws,
Sits wiping o'er his whiskered jaws.

"She useth," writes John Swan, in his "Speculum Mundi" (Cambridge, 1634), "therefore to wash her face with her feet, which she licketh and moiseneth with her tongue; and it is observed by some that if she put her feet beyond the crown of her head in this kind of washing, it is a sign of rain." In his "Hesperides" Herrick refers to this belief:

True calendars as pusses eare,
Wash't o'er to tell what change is neare.

But there is another old English saying which has it that when the cat wipes her face over her ears it is a sign of fine weather and when a cat sits with her back towards the fire it is a sign of frost. Willsford remarks quaintly enough: "Cats coveting the fire more than ordinary or licking their feet or trimming the hair of their heads and mustachios presages a storm." There is something in the superstition assuredly. Moncrif noticed that cats opened or closed their fur according to the weather and I have observed that cats lick their fur more than ordinarily in an atmosphere surcharged with moisture, just as they dry themselves with their tongues when they get wet. But cats always wash their faces after dinner, following the custom of the Romans rather than that of the Americans in this respect. A folk-tale has it that a cat caught a sparrow who observed, "No gentleman eats before washing his face." The cat relinquished his hold on the bird to prove himself a gentleman and the sparrow flew away. Since that date cats have found it wiser to wash after dinner. They also wash themselves to sleep. "Oh! that all females made as good use of their tongues," apostrophizes one Isobel Hill. If a cat's washing indicates bad weather, failure to do so indicates a sick cat. "The cat cleans her face with a look

The Cat and the Occult

of delight " is the phrase of John Clare. My Feathers puts her paw over her crown rain or shine. Who has described the operation more delightfully than Leigh Hunt? " Pussy . . . symbolically gives a twist of a yawn, and a lick to her whiskers. Now she proceeds to clean herself all over, having a just sense of the demands of her elegant person,— beginning judiciously with her paws, and fetching amazing tongues at her hind-hips. Anon, she scratches her neck with a foot of rapid delight; leaning her head towards it, and shutting her eyes, half to accommodate the action of the skin, and half to enjoy the luxury. She then rewards her paws with a few more touches; look at the action of her head and neck, how pleasing it is, the ears pointed forward, and the neck gently arching to and fro! Finally she gives a sneeze, and another twist of mouth and whiskers, and then, curling her tail towards her front claws, settles herself on her hind quarters, in an attitude of bland meditation."

The cat's relation to the weather is recognized in these United States, although different districts are not in agreement as to the meaning of the signs. In Eastern Kansas a cat washing her face before breakfast foretells rain; in New England a cat washes her face in the parlor before a shower; in Western Maine rain is assured if the cat scratches a fence. It is held also in Western Maine that when a cat is sharpening her claws the way her tail points shows the direction in which the wind will blow the next day. In Eastern Massachusetts the face of the washing cat points toward the direction from which the wind will blow. In New York and Pennsylvania the mere washing of the face signifies clear weather. If you see a cat looking out of the window you may be certain that it will storm soon, according to the inhabitants of Central Maine, where there must be continual storms because a cat in the house will spend half the day gazing out of the window. The belief in Cambridge, Massachussetts, that if the fur shines and looks glossy it is a sign that it will be pleasant the follow-ing day is credible.[18]

The belief held in Scilly Cove, Newfoundland, that a cat drowning in salt-water will bring on rain is directly in line with certain precepts of ceremonial magic. According to W. W. Skeat [19] if a Malay woman puts an inverted earthen-ware pan upon her head and then, setting it on the ground, fills it with water and washes a cat in it till the animal is nearly drowned, heavy rain will certainly follow. In this per-formance the inverted bowl is intended to symbolize the vault of heaven. A similar custom prevails in Java where usually two cats are bathed, a male and a female. Sometimes the animals are carried in procession with music. In Batavia also children carry cats around for this purpose. After duck-ing them in pools they release them. In Southern Celebes the inhabitants attempt to create a shower by carrying a cat tied in a sedan chair thrice around the parched fields, while they drench him with bamboo squirts. When the cat mews they cry, " O Lord, let rain fall upon us! " In a village of Su-matra to procure rain the women wade into the river, and splash one another. A black cat is thrown in and made to swim, and then is allowed to escape pursued by splashing women.

Other superstitions surround the cat. " In the eyes of the superstitious," writes Mr. T. F. Thiselton Dyer, " there is scarcely a movement of the cat which is not supposed to have some significance." If a cat jumps over a coffin she must be killed or great misfortune is sure to follow. The Chinese be-lieve that a cat can cause the dead to rise in this manner. As this would frequently prove awkward to the heirs and assigns cats are kept as far as possible from dead people in China. In case, however, the accident occurs it becomes nec-

---

[18] These examples are from Fanny D. Bergen's "Animal and Plant Lore, collected from the oral tradition of English speaking people."
[19] " Malay Magic."

essary to swat the resurrected dead man with a broom whereupon he will become recumbent again. "My name," declares the sorrowful vampire in James Branch Cabell's incomparable "Jurgen," "is Florimel, because my nature no less than my person was as beautiful as the flowers of the field and as sweet as the honey which the bees (who furnish us with such admirable examples of industry) get out of these flowers. But a sad misfortune changed all this. For I chanced one day to fall ill and die (which, of course, might happen to any one), and as my funeral was leaving the house the cat jumped over my coffin. That was a terrible misfortune to befall a poor girl so generally respected, and in wide demand as a seamstress; though, even then, the worst might have been averted had not my sister-in-law been of what they call a humane disposition and foolishly attached to the cat. So they did not kill it, and I, of course, became a vampire." Another superstition has it that if a cat jumps over a corpse the soul of the deceased enters its body. There is a reference to this superstition of the cat and the dead in "Bleak House." When Lady Dedlock's miserable lover dies the doctor drives Krook's cat out of the room. "Don't leave the cat there!" he says. "That won't do!" Lady Jane goes furtively downstairs, winding her lithe tail and licking her lips. In one of Ambrose Bierce's horror stories [20] a cat conceals herself in a coffin and mangles the features of the corpse. But a superstition prevails in Devonshire that a cat will not remain in a house with an unburied corpse and stories are often told of cats, who, on the death of one of the inmates of a house, have disappeared and not returned until after the funeral. According to one authority in spiritualism (Elliott O'Donnell: "Animal Ghosts") cats *scent* death, that is they smell the presence of the guiding spirit who has come to take the new soul away. "Before a death in a house I have watched a cat gradually showing signs of uneasiness. It has moved

[20] "John Mortonson's Funeral" in "Can Such Things Be?"

The Tiger in the House

from place to place, unable to settle in any one spot for any
length of time, had frequent fits of shivering, gone to the door,
sniffed the atmosphere, thrown back its head and mewed in a
low, plaintive key, and shown the greatest reluctance to being
alone in the dark." In Germany the presence of a cat on
the bed of a sick person means that death is approaching and
to this day black cats are kept away from children's cradles.
There is a legend, indeed, to the effect that cats suck children's
breaths in their sleep, a silly legend as Harrison Weir has
pointed out, for the jaw formation of the cat is not adapted
for sucking purposes. The factual foundation for this belief
is that cats, liking warm and luxurious places to lie, frequently
creep into cradles and if the cat is big enough it may happen
occasionally that a baby may be accidentally smothered.

If a kitten comes to the house in the morning it is lucky;
if in the evening it portends evil unless it stays to prevent it.
In Scotland if a white cat enters the house it is regarded as a
forerunner of sickness or trouble; if, however, a black cat
enters it is regarded as a harbinger of good luck, and he who
presumes to kill or drown the animal may expect ill luck for
nine years. The sneezing of a cat on a wedding day is said
to be a fortunate omen for the bride. In Lancashire it is regarded as unlucky to allow a cat to die in the house; hence
when they are ill they are usually drowned, which is certainly
unlucky for the cats. It is likewise a Lancashire superstition
that those who play with cats never enjoy good health. But
the magnetism of the cat and her repose should have the
most beneficial influence on human health. Louis Wain,
whose word may be said to have some weight on this subject,
offers the following evidence: "I have found as a result of
many years of inquiry and study, that people who keep cats
and are in the habit of petting them, do not suffer from those
petty ailments which all flesh is heir to. Rheumatism and
nervous complaints are uncommon with them, and pussy's lovers are of the sweetest temperament. I have often felt the

The Cat and the Occult

benefit, after a long spell of mental effort, of having my cats sitting across my shoulders, or of half an hour's chat with Peter."

Another English country superstition is that black cats will bring lovers to a girl. The rhyme goes as follows:

> *Whenever the cat o' the house is black,*
> *The lasses o' lovers will have no lack,*

and another amusing folk-rhyme has it:

> *Kiss the black cat,*
> *An' 'twill make ye fat;*
> *Kiss the white one,*
> *'Twill make ye lean.*

But what will happen if you kiss a tortoise-shell, a tabby, or a blue cat does not appear to be certain. These rhymes are to be found in Hone's " Every-Day Book " which gives us further particulars about the strange customs of cats: In Devonshire and Wiltshire it is believed that a May cat or, in other words, a cat born in the month of May, will never catch any rats or mice, but contrary to the wont of cats, will bring into the house snakes, and slow-worms, and other disagreeable reptiles. In Hungary there is a superstition that before a cat can become a good mouser he must be stolen. If a man with a cat's hair on his clothing rides, his horse will perspire violently and will soon become exhausted. If the wind blows over a cat riding in a vehicle that too will weary the horse. There is a further superstition that on the death of a tom cat the life will depart from all his unborn progeny. The Japanese have a superstition that if you rub a bamboo brush on the back of a female she can conceive of herself. In Cumberland, England, it is believed that the hair of a cat if swallowed by a human being will turn into a kitten inside him.

Cats in the Isle of Man have no tails; neither have those of the Bismarck Archipelago off the North Coast of New Guinea.

The Tiger in the House

Natives sometimes eat cats and unscrupulous neighbours might steal a cat for a meal. Accordingly in the interest of the higher morality people remove this stumbling block from the path of their weaker brothers by docking their cats and keeping the severed portion in a secret place. If now a cat is stolen and eaten the lawful owner of the animal has it in his power to avenge the crime. He need only bury the piece of tail with certain spells in the ground and the thief will fall ill. If a South Slavonian has a mind to pilfer or steal at market, he has nothing to do but to burn a blind cat, and then throw a pinch of the ashes over the person with whom he is higgling; after that he can take what he likes from the booth, and the owner will be none the wiser, having become as blind as the dead cat with whose ashes he has been sprinkled.[21]

In the United States Fanny Bergen has collected numberless examples of these curious superstitions concerning cats. In New England it is bad luck to kill a cat. In Pennsylvania it is believed that if a farmer kills a cat some of his stock will die. Cats of three colours bring luck in Canada, Washington, and Eastern Kansas. Japanese sailors share this superstition. In Eastern Kansas the possession of a tortoise-shell is a surety against fire. In New England a " smutty-nosed " cat brings prosperity to its owner and in Maine a white cat brings poverty. In Massachussetts a double-pawed cat is a lucky omen but in New York a black and white cat is sure to bring sickness to the family. The belief that it is bad luck to allow a black cat[22] to cross your

[21] From Frazer's " The Golden Bough."

[22] " I slink away, being superstitious regarding cherry-coloured cats, stepladders, and cross-eyed theatre managers," writes James Huneker in " Bedouins," p. 142.

In a poem by Susan K. Phillips, the following lines occur:

I'm no way superstitious as the person called our Mat,
When he'd none sail with the herring fleet, 'cause he met old Susie's cat.

path is pretty general in the United States and elsewhere as well. But to be followed by a black cat signifies good luck in New England and Eastern Kansas. In Eastern New England you are sure to quarrel with any one to whom you have presented a cat. In Alabama if a cat washes her face in front of several persons the first she looks at will be the first to get married. In Eastern Kansas it is unlucky to move into a house where cats have been left by former occupants. Their owners should have killed the animals. In some parts of the United States it is considered bad luck to move a cat when the family moves; in other parts it is considered bad luck *not* to move the cat. In Ohio (Hamilton County) it is believed that a child who plays with a cat will become stupid. Cats go mad if allowed to eat too much meat or if they lie much before a fire, according to authorities who live in Brookline, Massachussetts. And in Maryland there is a superstition that if you shave off a cat's whiskers you deprive him of his sense of smell! [23]

The Negro superstitions concerning cats, connected as they are with ancient African voodoo worship and noxious paludal ceremonies, are extremely curious. One has it that in the tip of every cat's tail are three hairs of the devil, which give the cat a tendency to prowl. Sandy Jenkins, the hero of James David Corrothers's " The Black Cat Club," " was dressed to kill; his linen was spotless; his clothing faultless; his cane, chrysanthemum, and patent leathers matchless," and under one arm he carried his black cat, Mesmerizer, to hoodoo his enemies. In some verses, called " De Black Cat Crossed his Luck " in this same book [24] Mr. Corrothers epitomizes the Negro feeling about the animal. An old Negro named Sambo Lee was " cotched " by a Black Cat, and cursed. Sam lost his job, was bit by a policeman's dog, beaten by the policeman, put in jail, quarreled with his wife's mother, lost his " lady-

---

[23] " Animal and Plant Lore, collected from the oral tradition of English speaking people." [24] Page 37.

lub," was worsted at fisticuffs, was robbed, and spent three
weeks in a hospital as a direct result of this curse.

> *Den to de cunjah-man Sam sped,*
> *An' dis am whut de cunjah-man said:*
> *"Black Cat am a pow'ful man;*
> *Ruinin' mo'tals am his plan.*
> *Ole Satan an' de 'Riginal Sin*
> *Am de daddy an' mammy o' him.*
> *He's got nine hunderd an' ninety-nine libes —*
> *Nineteen thousan' an' ninety-nine wibes —*
> *He's kin to cholera an' allied*
> *To smallpox on de mammy's side.*
> *An' all de ebils on de earf*
> *Stahted at de Black Cat's birf! —*
> *Jes' stop an' die right whah you's at,*
> *Ef yo' luck bin crossed by de ole Black Cat!"*
>
> *An' den Sam read in history*
> *Dat a cat crossed Pharaoh by de see,*
> *An' burried him, as sho's you bo'n,*
> *Too deep to heah ole Gabriel's ho'n!*
> *An' dat de cat crossed Jonah once,*
> *An' made him ack a regular dunce.*
> *Crossed Bonaparte at Waterloo,*
> *An' got Jeems Blaine defeated too.*
> *"Oh, Laud a-mussy now on me!"*
> *Cried Sam, " an' on dis history!"*
> *An' den Sam went an' killed de cat —*
> *Swo'e he'd make an end o' dat; —*
> *Burried him in de light o' de moon,*
> *Wid a rabbit's foot an' a silver spoon.*
> *But de Black Cat riz, an' swallered him whole —*
> *Bu'nt his house an' took his soul!*

The terrifying consequences of killing a cat are referred to
again in a poem by Virginia Frazer Boyle: [25]

[25] "I Kilt er Cat": These verses may be found on page 89 of Graham R.
Tomson's anthology, " Concerning Cats."

The Cat and the Occult

Dar's er shakin' an' er achin' ermongst dese ole bones,
And I cries in de night wid de 'miseration moans,
An' I hears sumpin 'mawkin' wid er solemn sorter groans —
    I kilt er cat!

I feels an' I knows dat dar's sumpin' ain right,
'Ca'se er black streek's er 'pearing in de broad daylight,
An' de debbil he rid my chist all night —
    I kilt er cat!

*   *   *   *   *

I wan'ers res'less laek, all erbout frough de wood,
Wid de rabbit fut fur comp'ny, but hit cain't do any good,
An' dese ole feets cain't be quiet, an' dey wouldn' ef dey could —
    I kilt er cat!

*   *   *   *   *

I drowns 'im in de water, but he sneakted out ergin,
Den I feels dat I 'mittin er mos awful kind er sin,
Fur I hangs 'im 'dout er chance an' I cain't furgit 'is grin —
    I kilt er cat!

Hab mercy on dis darky, oh! I cain't git shet er dat,
Fur I sees de porten's pintin' des es shore's I sees dis hat,
I's hoodooed wid de sperrit uv ole Jonas's black cat —
    Fur I kilt dat cat!

" Wizard cats," writes Frank Hamel, " have been known to do serious harm to those against whom they have a grudge, and it is well to be sure, if you value your life, whether you are dealing with a real animal or a ' familiar ' when you feel angry." There is, for example, the very moral story of the young man of Radnorshire who threw a stone at a cat on his wedding day. His health began to fail at once and he frequently disappeared for weeks at a time. During these periods the legend has it that he took feline form. After his death his soul entered a cat's body and the animal prowled the district at night and struck terror into the hearts of naughty children.

121

The Tiger in the House

Sailors are almost as superstitious as Negroes about cats, but the superstition assumes a more favourable form. Evidence that the sailor loves puss may be gathered from the number of words used on board ship derived from the word cat. In certain sea-coast towns in England sailors' wives keep black cats to protect their husbands at sea. The liveliness of a ship cat portends a wind and the drowning of a ship cat seems to be fatal for all on board as well as for the cat himself. Japanese sailors regard three-coloured cats (black, white, and brown), as an excellent charm against spirits and are said to be unwilling to put to sea without one. A well known superstition has it that a cat will desert a ship about to start on its last voyage and there is evidence to show that sailors have refused to undertake voyages following the desertion of the ship's cat.[26]

Charles Henry Ross in "The Book of Cats" quotes an anonymous author on the meaning of cat dreams. It is possible that Dr. Freud might not agree with these conclusions at all points: "If any one dreams that he hath encountered a cat or killed one, he will commit a thief to prison and prosecute him to the death, as the cat signifies a common thief. If he dreams that he eats the cat's flesh he will have the goods of the thief who robbed him. If he dreams that he hath the skin then he will have all the thief's goods. If any one dreams that he fought with a cat who scratched him sorely, that denotes some sickness or affliction."

[26] On page 276 of "Rabbits, Cats and Cavies," C. H. Lane quotes the following story: "The morning before the recent accident to H. M. Destroyer Salmon, that vessel was lying alongside of H. M. S. Sturgeon. Upon the former vessel dwelt two cats, the special pets of the crew, and who had never been known to show the slightest inclination to leave the ship. But on this particular morning in spite of being chased by the crew and worried by the dogs, the cats never faltered in their determination to get off the Salmon and on to the Sturgeon. And when the first-named destroyer had weighed anchor for what was to prove the disastrous voyage, the cats made one last spring as the vessels separated, and landed on the deck of H. M. S. Sturgeon."

The Cat and the Occult

There are cat remedies: a cure for erysipelas was to cut off a cat's ear (or to take three drops of blood drawn from a vein under the cat's tail) and allow the blood to drop slowly on the affected part. The brain of a cat, taken in small doses, has been used as a love potion. Ben Jonson in his *Masque of Queens,* makes a witch sing thus:

> *I, from the jawes of a gardener's bitch,*
> *Did snatch these bones and then leapt the ditch;*
> *Yet went I back to the house againe,*
> *Killed the black cat and here is the brain.*

A nostrum for preserving the eyesight was to burn the head of a black cat to ashes and have a little dust blown into the eyes three times a day. A whitlow could be cured by placing the affected finger a quarter of an hour each day in a cat's ear, and the foot of the wild cat was considered an excellent remedy for erysipelas and lameness. Cat's grease was a useful commodity but of no avail for magical or medicinal purposes unless the cat made a voluntary offering of it. T. F. Thiselton Dyer, in " English Folk-Lore," quotes Hunt as follows: " In Cornwall those little gatherings which come on children's eyelids, locally called ' whilks ' and also ' warts ' are cured by passing the tail of a black cat nine times over the place." [27]

[27] Of course Topsell in his quaint " History of Four-footed Beasts " (1658) has a good deal to say on this subject: " Alsius prescribeth a fat Cat sod for the Gowt, first taking the fat, and anointing therewith the sick part, and then wetting wool or tow in the same, and binding it to the offending place. The liver of a Cat dryed and beat to powder is good against the stone: the dung of a female Cat with the claw of an Oul hanged about the neck of a man that hath had seven fits of a Quartain Ague, cureth the same: a powder made of the gall of a black Cat and the weight of a groat thereof taken and mingled with four crowns weight of Zambach, helpeth the convulsion and wryness of the mouth: and if the gall of a Cat with the black dung of the same Cat, be burned in perfume under a woman travelling with a dead childe, it will cause it presently to come forthe: and Pliny saith that if a pin, or thorn, or fish bone, stick in one's mouth, let him rub the inside of it with a little cat's dung, and it will easily come forth. Given to a woman suffering from the flux with a little Rozen

123

The Tiger in the House

Possibly just here you may grin a little, sink comfortably into your chair, and reflect that the people of the United States are at least superior to such silly superstitions. No assumption could be more incorrect.[28] Probably every one of these beliefs has been current in some part of America at one time or another. In certain parts of England there is credence put in the statement that a cat's hair is indigestible and if one is swallowed death will ensue. It is possible that Americans do not entertain this legend but I can personally vouch for the fact that every boy I knew as a child in Cedar Rapids, Iowa, believed that a horse hair immersed in a tumbler of water would eventually turn into a snake. As for the wart cure, we learn through no less an authority than Mark Twain that such a belief existed along the banks of the Mississippi. When Huckleberry Finn enters the pages of " Tom Sawyer " [29] he carries a dead cat with him, and when Tom asks him " what dead cats is good for " Huck answers, " cure warts with." " But say,"queries Tom, " how do you cure 'em with dead cats? "

" Why, you take your cat and go and get in the graveyard 'long about midnight when somebody that was wicked has been buried; and when it's midnight a devil will come, or maybe

and oil of Roses and it stayeth the humour; and for a Web in the eye of a horse, evening and morning blow in the powder of Cat's dung and it shall be cured."

[28] There is really no panacea, mystical, moral, political, or physical, that Americans will not believe in. Moncure Daniel Conway gives the following examples in " Demonology and Devil-Lore ": " Dr. Dyer, an eminent physician of Chicago, Illinois, told me (1875) that a case occurred in that city within his personal knowledge, where the body of a woman who had died of consumption was taken out of the grave and the lungs burned, under the belief that she was drawing after her in the grave some of her surviving relatives. In 1874, according to the 'Providence Journal,' in the village of Peacedale, Rhode Island, Mr. William Rose dug up the body of his own daughter and burned her heart, under the belief that she was wasting away the lives of other members of his family." A recent criminal trial in one of the Middle Western States brought out the fact that many an American pocket, even today, carries a silver bullet as a talisman against the witch-cat.

[29] " Tom Sawyer," Chapter VI.

The Cat and the Occult

two or three, but you can't see 'em, you can only hear something like the wind, or maybe hear 'em talk; and when they're taking that feller away, you heave your cat after 'em and say, ' Devil follow corpse, cat follow devil, warts follow cat, I'm done with ye! ' That'll fetch *any* wart." [30]

We no longer burn witches and we no longer, in groups, persecute cats. Indeed puss has settled down to a life of luxury and appreciation which she has not hitherto enjoyed since the days when she watched the temple altars of the Nile, near the catadupe, or strolled among the guests at the Sultan's banquet. If she is no longer a god, at least she is still worshipped. But do not be mislead by these signs. We have forgotten the dark days but the cat remembers; the racial consciousness, the hereditary traits in cats are strong. And she will never forget her wild rides with witches, her appearances at the Sabbath, frequently attached to the belt of the pythoness, the use of her body as a casket for the soul of the sorceress, her persecution. And today, for that reason, she is more in touch with what we call the supernatural than any other animal, including man. Wood [31] gives a case of a lady and her cat simultaneously seeing and being variously affected mentally and physically by a vision of an old wrinkled hag. The lady became the victim of a helpless fascination, of paralysis of mobility and

[30] In her book, already alluded to, Fanny Bergen gives a long list of examples of cat remedy superstitions which are credited in various parts of the United States. In Eastern Kansas the skin of a black cat worn in one's clothing will cure rheumatism. In Somerset County, Maine, the blood of a black cat is used to cure shingles. In other parts of the United States it is believed that shingles may be cured by applying the freshly removed skin of a cat to the affected surface. A correspondent from Western New York wrote Mrs. Bergen in regard to this: "This is no hearsay matter with the writer, for in his boyhood he was afflicted with this disease and passed a night with the bloody skin of his favourite pussy covering his left side and the pit of his stomach." In Eastern Massachusetts this same cure is prescribed for hives, and in Salem, an old Negro was cured of consumption by this method. In Southern Illinois three hairs from the tip of a black cat's tail are sufficient to cure a felon and in the South a sty may be cured by brushing it nine times with a black cat's tail.

[31] "Man and Beast: Here and Hereafter," p. 320.

speech, while the cat, on the contrary, made frantic efforts to escape.[32] Perhaps this cat had had an unfortunate experience in some past life with the old hag; at any rate other cats have been known to entertain a vast liking for spiritualistic seances. Algernon Blackwood has written an astoundingly astute story [33] on this theme, " A Psychical Invasion," in which he contrasts the effects of the presence of spirits on a cat and a dog. In an attempt to discover the causes of certain phenomena John Silence visits a house at midnight, accompanied by a dog and a cat. " Cats in particular, he believed, were almost continuously conscious of a larger field of vision, too detailed even for a photographic camera, and quite beyond the range of normal human organs. He had, further, observed that while dogs were usually terrified in the presence of such phenomena, cats on the other hand were soothed and satisfied. They welcomed manifestations as something be-

[32] Elliott O'Donnell, in "Animal Ghosts"; William Rider and Son; London; 1913, speaks of similar experiences: " From endless experiments made in haunted houses, I have proved to my own satisfaction, at least, that the cat acts as a thoroughly reliable psychic barometer. The dog is sometimes unaware of the proximity of the Unknown. When the ghost materializes or in some other way demonstrates its advent, the dog, occasionally, is wholly undisturbed — the cat never. I have never yet had a cat with me that has not shown the most obvious signs of terror and uneasiness both before and during a superphysical manifestation." Mr. O'Donnell not only believes that cats *see* ghosts; he also believes that they *have* them. If the curious reader will turn to his book, he may find therein descriptions of the cat-spectres who have returned to haunt the scenes where they have been tortured. Mr. O'Donnell even goes so far as to assert that there may be something in the superstition that occasionally a black tom cat is the devil in animal form. " It would be idle, of course, to expect people in these unmeditative times to believe that there was ever the remotest truth underlying these so-called fantastic suppositions of the past; yet, according to reliable testimony, there are, at the present moment, many houses in England haunted by phantasms in the form of black cats, of so sinister and hostile an appearance, that one can only assume that unless they are the actual spirits of cats, earthbound through cruel and vicious propensities, they must be vice-elementals, i. e. spirits that have never inhabited any material body, and which have either been generated by vicious thoughts, or else have been attracted to a spot by some crime or vicious act once perpetrated there."

[33] " John Silence."

longing to their own region." The result of his experiment justified his faith. The dog, an unusually courageous collie, was terrified beyond belief by the presence of the spirits and lay whimpering in a corner, finally, indeed, losing his sight. But the cat! The doctor alone in the darkened room, with a low fire, waited he knew not what. " Smoke . . . began to wash. But the washing, the doctor noted, was by no means its real purpose; it only used it to mask something else; it stopped at the most busy and furious moments and began to stare about the room. Its thoughts wandered absurdly. It peered intently at the curtains; at the shadowy corners; at empty space above; leaving its body in curiously awkward positions for whole minutes together." The doctor at length fell asleep. Sometime later " a soft touch on the cheek awoke him. Something was patting him. He sat up with a jerk, and found himself staring into a pair of brilliant eyes, half green, half black. Smoke's face lay level with his own; and the cat had climbed up with his front paws upon his chest. The lamp had burned low and the fire was nearly out, yet Dr. Silence saw in a moment that the cat was in an excited state. It kneaded with its front paws into his chest, shifting from one to the other. He felt them prodding against him. It lifted a leg very carefully and patted his cheek gingerly. Its fur, he saw, was standing ridgewise upon its back; the ears were flattened back somewhat; the tail was switching sharply. The cat, of course, had awakened him with a purpose. . . . Two things he became aware of at once : one that Smoke, while excited, was *pleasurably* excited; the other, that the collie was no longer visible upon the mat at his feet. He had crept away to the corner of the wall farthest from the window, and lay watching the room with wide-open eyes, in which lurked plainly something of alarm. . . . Smoke had jumped down from the back of the arm-chair and now occupied the middle of the carpet, where, with tail erect and legs stiff as ramrods, it was steadily pacing backwards and forwards in a narrow space, uttering, as it did so, those curious little guttural sounds of pleasure that only an animal of the feline species knows how to make expressive of supreme happiness. Its stiffened legs and arched back made it appear larger than usual, and the black visage wore a smile of beatific joy. Its eyes blazed magnificently; it was in an ecstasy. At the end of every few paces it turned sharply and stalked back again along the same line, padding softly, and purring like a roll of little muffled drums. It behaved precisely as though it were rubbing against the ankles of some one who remained invisible. A thrill ran down the doctor's spine as he stood and stared. . . . For an instant, as he watched it, the doctor was aware that a faint uneasiness stirred in the depths of his own being, focussing itself for the moment upon this curious behaviour of the uncanny creature before him. There rose in him quite a new realization of the mystery connected with the whole feline tribe, but especially with that common member of it, the domestic cat — their hidden lives, their strange aloofness, their incalculable subtlety. How utterly remote from anything that human beings understood lay the sources of their elusive activities. As he watched the indescribable bearing of the little creature mincing along the strip of carpet under his eyes, coquetting with the powers of darkness, welcoming, maybe, some fearsome visitor, there stirred in his heart, a feeling strangely akin to awe. Its indifference to human kind, its serene superiority to the obvious, struck him forcibly with fresh meaning; so remote, so inaccessible seemed the secret purposes of its real life, so alien to the blundering honesty of other animals. Its absolute poise of bearing brought into his mind the opium-eater's words that ' no dignity is perfect which does not at some point ally itself with the mysterious.' " [34]

I do not remember that Hermes Trismegistus or Paracel-

---

[34] Mr. Blackwood has treated this motive again in a more sentimental vein in his story, " The Attic," in the volume entitled " Pan's Garden."

sus mentions the cat in his alchemystical formulae, but both of these philosophers sat at the feet of this animal, just as certainly as later alchemists often found the presence of grimalkin convenient or his body necessary in preparing some mixture for the arcane cauldron. Probably the sylphs, gnomes, undines, and salamanders of the Comte de Gabalis were really white, black, silver, and orange pussies. But I do not think a magic system of divination by cats, ailuromancy it would be called, has yet been evolved. He keeps his secrets too closely to afford much aid to the hierophant. He retains those instincts of transcendental sensualism, those strange currents from the past, which man and even most of the other animals, especially the domestic animals, have exchanged for the inferior benefits of " civilization." He is in touch with the infinite and unknown; he remembers the cult of the Egyptians and the strange secrets of Babylon, the apozemical soups of the sorceress. He recognizes Wotan in the storm and Katschei in the dark of the night. In the flames he sees Loge, and Aphrodite rises for him on the waves of every sea. Eros haunts his rooftops and Diana directs his hunting expeditions. Sekhet and Pasht sit in the temples of his imagination. All the gods, all the devils are his friends; he knows the fairies, the elves, and the kobolds, and stryge and vampires come when he calls. The rustling of the leaves tells him a story, warns him of a danger, and a flight of birds prophesies a fair day. The touch of a wall against his whisker presses a signal into his brain and the crackle of a dried fern under his padded paw is to him the threat of a black-handed camorra. He is Swedenborgian and Pagan, Palladian and Kabbalist, Mohammedan and Jew. He walks on the sea with Christ and on the clouds with Buddha. He promenades in the poet's brain. He understands and salutes the pale petunia; the esoteric begonia is his brother. The ithyphallic rites of Heliogabalus are as familiar to him as the cruel diversions of Gille de Retz. He

The Tiger in the House

learns the meaning of the Signs of the Zodiac, Solomon's Sigil, the Tarot, the Ibimorphic and Serapian Triads, the Pantacles of the Planets, the Ten Commandments, and Science and Health while he is yet a kitten. Far from being the apprentice of the Wizard, he is more often the Master.

Chapter Five: The Cat in Folklore

Where the cat came from is a mystery; you may believe the Noah story if you like. Wood says that the Egyptian *Felis maniculata* is the grandfather of our household pet, while Lydekker [1] summons modern authorities to prove that this progenitor was the Kaffir Cat, a yellowish cat with tiger stripes, *Felis lybica,* which still roams about northeastern Africa, hunting at night and living in holes dug by other animals. Again, *probably,* for all of this is quite as uncertain as the Noah story, the Romans brought the Egyptian cat to England some time before the fifth century and there is a theory to the effect that our modern tabby is a cross between this ancient animal and the British wild cat. This theory does not account for Persian and Angora cats at all as Egyptian cats were short-haired. A cat of Central Asia, popularly known as Pallas's cat, is suspected of the ancestry of these more aristocratic beasts. As to the *ailuros* of the Greeks, I have already intimated that current scholarly opinion, which, of course, is worth very little, has come to the conclusion that this was not a cat at all, but the snowy-breasted marten.

Where the cat is going is equally a mystery. " Every one is aware," writes Mr. Andrew Lang, " that a perfectly comfortable, well-fed cat will occasionally come to his house and settle there, deserting a family by whom it is lamented, and to whom it could, if it chose, find its way back with ease. This conduct is a mystery which may lead us to infer that cats form a great secret society, and that they come and go in pursuance of some policy connected with education, or perhaps with

[1] R. Lydekker: " The Pedigree of the Cat "; " Knowledge "; Vol. 20, p. 181; August 2, 1897.

witchcraft. We have known a cat to abandon his home for years. Once in six months he would return, and look about him with an air of some contempt. ' Such,' he seemed to say, ' were my humble beginnings.' " It must be remembered that the cat is an oriental and all orientals are mysterious. There seems to be even a canon of feline etiquette which forbids two cats to meet and pass without some display of solemn formalities, reminiscent of greetings in the Orient where time is of no particular value.

Even the derivation of the name of the cat is shrouded in darkness. From the Latin word *felis* we have extracted feline but the word *cattus* or *catus* came into use as late as the fourth century A. D. and is to be found first in the writings of an agricultural author, Palladius, who recommends that puss be kept in artichoke gardens as a protection against rodents and moles. Evagrius Scholasticus, a later Greek church historian, uses the word *catta*. Isidorus derives *cattus* from *cattare*, meaning to see, in reference doubtless to the animal's vigilance and watchfulness. On the other hand a writer in " Notes and Queries " declares that the only language, so far as he can ascertain, in which the word cat is significant is the Zend, in which the word *gatu* means a place, a particularly expressive word in this connection. His inference is that Persia is the original home of the cat and he goes on to say that the cat was probably introduced from Persia, through Spain, into Europe because the Spanish word *gato* is almost identical with the Zend. The only flaws in this brilliant philological reasoning are that the Spanish word is also almost identical with the late Latin and that Persian cats and European cats are two distinct breeds. Adolphe Pictet [2] derives *catus* from an African root: Arab, *kitt,* plural *kitât;* Syrian, *katô;* Nubian, *kadiska,* and in still other African tongues, *kaddiska* and *gada.* This ingenious etymologist further thinks that puss comes from an old Sanskrit word, *puccha,*

2 " Les Origines Indo-Européenes ou les Aryas Primitifs," Paris, 1859.

The Cat in Folklore

piccha, meaning tail. There is a suggestion of this root in the Persian *pushak;* Afghan, *pishik;* Kurd, *psig;* Lithuanian, *puize;* Irish *pus, feisag, fiseog,* and *feisain.* A still more ingenious pundit thinks that the French *chat* is an onomatope for the cat's spitting.

To come to more familiar tongues, in Dutch the word is *kat;* in Swedish, *katt;* Italian, *gatto;* Portuguese and Spanish *gato;* Polish, *kot;* Russian, *kots;* Turkish, *keti;* Welsh, *cath;* Cornish, *kath;* German, *die Katze* (a Frenchman deploring that *chat* is masculine in French, admires this choice of gender) ; Basque, *catua;* Armenian, *kitta;* Picardian, *ca, co;* Burgundian, *chai;* Catalonian, *gat.* The antique rituals in the Louvre give the Egyptian name as *mau, maï, maau.*[3] These and the Chinese word, *mao,* seem the most natural of all.

In every language allusions to the cat are sprinkled as thickly as currants in a good fruit-cake. Many of these take the form of derivative words, the formation of a good half of which is as mysterious as puss herself. Others are metaphorical or proverbial, and have a bearing on the popular ideas, prejudices, and superstitions concerning the cat. Murray's Oxford Dictionary devotes two full pages to cat and its derivative words; nor is the list in Murray by any means exhaustive. Many of the following examples are from other sources.

There are, to begin with, the sea-terms, which seem to offer cumulative evidence that the cat is a favourite marine animal. There is the cat-boat, which formerly was called merely the cat, and some students of folklore have tried to prove that this was the kind of cat Dick Whittington owned. The significance of catamaran, another variety of boat, which rights itself in a surf, is quite clear. The word is derived from the Italian, *gatta marina,* and is an allusion to the faculty the cat possesses of falling on his feet. Cat is also the name for a tackle or combination of pulleys used to suspend the anchor

[3] Some Egyptologists have read *chaou* on certain monuments.

at the cat's-head of a ship. Cat-harping is the name for a purchase of ropes employed to brace the shrouds in the lower masts behind their yards. The cat-fall is the rope employed upon the cat's-head and the cat-hook is a large hook fitted to a cat-block, by which the anchor is raised to the cat's-head. Two little holes astern, above the gun-room ports, are called cat-holes. A cat's-paw is a particular turn in the bight of a rope made to work a tackle in and it is also the rippling on the water made by light air during a calm, which resembles the slight disturbance made in a pool when a cat delicately troubles the surface with his paw. Lastly there is the terrible cat-o-nine-tails. Folklorists have discovered cross references. "How is it?" asks David Fitzgerald, "that we find the nine-tailed cat (a magical cat with no allusion to the scourge) in the legends of the Gobān Saor? And a cat with *ten* tails in Scottish counting-out rhymes, and the phrase to 'whip the cat' for to work against, among the tailors of Crieff?" [4]

Many plants are named after cats: cat-briar, an Americanism for smilax, which I offer to H. L. Mencken; cat-chop, which I have not identified; cat-haw, the fruit of the haw-

[4] "The Cat in Legend and Myth": "Belgravia"; London; November 1885. "The Norwegian *gorging* cat (whose history we once heard well related by Mr. Ralston) swallows the man and wife ('goodman' and 'goody' in the translator's dialect), a number of animals, a wedding party, and a funeral train, and the sun and moon — all of which he disgorges as wonderfully as they are swallowed down . . ." continues Mr. Fitzgerald. "In Ireland this same ancient monster appeared in at least six forms. He is Kate Kearney's cat, oldest of things (*As old as Kate Kearney's cat* is an Irish proverb). He is the proverbial *cat that ate the year.* He is the dreadful *cat a' leasa.* He is the piping cat, sculptured on ancient crosses, and figuring on tavern signs. He is the cat with two tails, cat with ten tails, cat with nine tails, of the Gobān Saor. And he is the cat in (seven-leagued) boots.— The myth further appears among the Iroquois Indians in the shape of a two-headed serpent which devours the nation, all but one man and woman; slain, however, it rolls into a lake and disgorges them all. This two-headed dragon appears in Ireland as a bi-tailed cat, as the Cat of the Fort, *cat a' leasa,* a colossal monster, circling the hill in a coil miles long. . . . The twy-tailed cat (Day and Night?) was sculptured at Holycross Abbey, Tipperary, and in the French chapel at Canterbury." Angelo de Guber-

thorne; cat-in-clover, bird's-foot trefoil; cat-keys, the fruit of the ash-tree; cat-sloe, the wild sloe; cat-succory, wild succory; cat's-head, a variety of apple and also a fossil; cat-trail, the beloved valerian; cat-thyme, a species of teucrium which causes sneezing; cat-tree, spindle tree; the familiar cat-tails and catnip; catkins, imperfect flowers hanging from trees in the manner of a cat's tail; cat's-foot, an herb; and curiously enough, cat-whin or dog-rose!

In American slang one old cat is a kind of primitive baseball game. Letting the old cat die is to allow a swing to prove that there is no such phenomenon as perpetual motion. As the swing sags back and forth eight or nine times after you have stopped pushing it this phrase possibly has reference to the nine lives of the cat. Cattycornered, meaning diagonally opposite or across, has reference to the oblique movements of the cat. Scat is an interjection used to tell puss to make a speedy departure. Pussyfoot is a term derived from the cat's padded paws and stealthy approach but no cat in the world would be in favour of prohibition of any variety. In English thieves' slang cat signifies a lady's muff. A kind of double tripod with six feet, intended to hold a plate before the fire and so constructed that in whatever position it is placed three of the legs rest on the ground is called a cat from the belief that however a cat may be thrown she always lands on her feet. The enemies of the feline race say " as false as a cat " and it is from this phrase that the terms cat's gold and cat's silver, the common names for mica, on ac-

natis, too, is infected with this familiar and somewhat silly method of trying to explain all folk-stories symbolically. In "Zoological Mythology, or the Legends of Animals," he gives it as his belief that the celebrated fable of the Kilkenny Cats may mean the mythological contest between night and twilight. God pity these men!

Moncure Daniel Conway ("Demonology and Devil-Lore") refers to a similar legend: Thor, the Norse Hercules, once tried to lift a cat, as it seemed to him, off the ground, but it was the great mid-earth serpent which encircles the whole world. Thor succeeded in lifting one paw of the supposed cat.

count of its deceptive appearance, are derived. There are sea-cats, cat-fish, cat-birds, cat-squirrels, and cat-owls, or flying cats. A French word for owl is *chat-huant*. Cat's-eye is a well-known semi-precious stone. Cat's purr is a thrill felt over the region of the heart in certain diseases. Cat's tooth is white-lead ore from Ireland; cat-brain, a soil consisting of rough clay mixed with stones; cat-dirt a kind of clay. Cat-collops is cat-meat and the cat's meat man, a familiar London figure, is frequently referred to as the pussy butcher. Cat-face is a mark in lumber wood; cat-ice, thin ice of a milky appearance from under which the water has receded. Cat-nap is a short nap taken while sitting; cat-ladder a kind of ladder used on sloping roofs of houses; cat-steps, the projections of the stones in the slanting part of the gable; cat-pipe, an artificial cat-call. Puss gentleman is eighteenth century for catamite. Kitty is a common poker term. Copy cat is a misnomer because cats never copy anybody. A common phrase for an unusual event is " enough to make a cat laugh," but the Cheshire Cat in " Alice in Wonderland " is not the only recorded example of a laughing cat. " Enough to make a cat speak " is a similar expression, but as I have pointed out in the preceding chapter, speaking cats are almost a commonplace. Cat's paw is a reference to a monkey's idle jest. Salt-cat is a mess of coarse meal placed in a dove-cote to allure strangers. A cat's walk is a little way and back. To jerk, shoot, or whip the cat means to vomit. Cat-harrow, Cat and Dog, Cat or Kit-Cat [5] are games. It was once a trick of farmers to bring a cat to market in a bag and sell it for a suckling pig to the unwary. If the purchaser discovered the deception he let the cat out of the bag; if he did not he was said to have bought a pig in a poke. Both expressions have become proverbial. An island in the Bahama group is named Cat Island and Moncrif writes of the Cape of Cats. You

[5] Kit-Cat and Cat and Dog are described in William Carew Hazlitt's " Faiths and Folklore."

may have heard of the Catskills. An ancestor of mine, Derrick Teunis Van Vechten,[6] was the founder of the extremely unimportant town in New York bearing that name. Cat was a movable pent-house used in the middle ages by besiegers to protect themselves when approaching fortifications. It was also called a cat-house;[7] something else is called a cat-house in modern times, just as certain pretty ladies in London and Geisha girls in Japan are called cats.

All languages are rich in cat proverbs, many of which appear to have been the inventions of those who believed what Buffon and Noah Webster had to say about the animal. Many others have reference to the cat's prowess and special instincts, a few to her grace and beauty. Plutarch, when in Egypt, heard the proverb, An overdressed lady is like a cat dressed in saffron. An old Chinese saying is, A lame cat is better than a swift horse when rats infest the palace. It is not the fleas of dogs that will make cats mew, is also Chinese. A Japanese proverb has it that A dog will remember a three days' kindness three years while a cat will forget a three years' kindness in three days. This may be regarded as a compliment to the intelligence of the cat. A Hindu saying is, If you want to know what a tiger is like, look at a cat; if you want to know what a thug is like, look at a butcher. I am inclined to agree with Lockwood Kipling that only the first half of this proverb is true. As cats are sometimes slung in a net in India, a proverb descriptive of sudden success is The cat is in luck; the net is torn. I was not so angry at the cat for stealing the butter as at her wagging her tail shows

[6] "Catskill was settled about 1680 by Derrick Teunis Van Vechten": Encyclopedia Americana; 1918; Vol. 6, p. 108.

[7] Morley Adams in his book, "In the Footsteps of Borrow and Fitzgerald" (p. 113), speaks of the Cat-House on the River Orwell: "This little lodge played an important part in the smuggling which took place hereabouts a century ago, the occupants, if report be true, being in league with the contraband men. When the 'coast was clear' a large stuffed cat was displayed in the window, and when the preventative men were on the look-out the cat was taken away."

that Hindu humanity is not so very different in some respects from European or American. Of a hypocrite the Hindu remarks: The cat, with mouse tails still hanging out of her mouth, says —'Now I feel good, I will go on a pilgrimage to Mecca!' The Indian cat *miyaus;* so one says to a child or a servant, What! my own cat, and *miyau* at me! The cat does not catch mice for God is a priceless bit of wisdom. Even a cat is a lion in her own lair is said of mild-tempered people who fly into sudden rages. A cat's moon is a Kashmiri expression for a sleepless night. It is also in Kashmir that they say, If cats had wings there would be no ducks in the lake. An Indian mother will say to an idle girl, Did the cat sneeze or what? A sneering proverb has it, In a learned house even the cat is learned. A sly man is said to look like a drowned cat; a live cat is said to be better than a dead tiger. It is easy to understand the meaning of The cowed cat allows even a mouse to bite its ears, but did the thing ever happen?[8]

John Hay[9] gives, A miawling cat takes no mice as a Spanish proverb but, of course, this occurs in every language. Other Spanish proverbs are They whip the cat if our mistress does not spin; The mouse does not go away with a bellyful from the cat's house; When the cats go away the mice grow saucy; Don't turn the cat out of the house for being a thief (spoken of those who expect what is contrary to nature from servants) ; Let us see who will carry the cat to water; and The meat is on the hook because there is no cat. The Portuguese say: The cat is certainly friendly but it scratches. A charming Russian proverb says: The day is young, said the cat, remembering that he could wait. Plays of cat, tears of mice is also Russian. The cat will catch fish but he does not soil his paws is German. A delightful Italian saying is: Four things are necessary for a home: grain, a cock, a cat, and a wife.

[8] These examples are from John Lockwood Kipling's "Beast and Man in India." [9] "Castilian Days."

The Cat in Folklore

The available examples of cat proverbs in English are so very numerous that I must content myself with giving only a few of them. Some of these are true folk-sayings; others have become popular through their appearance in plays and novels. Care will kill a cat. A muffled cat is no good mouser. The cat is out of kind that sweet milk will not lap. You can have no more of a cat than her skin, a proverb which does not take into account the French custom of using puss for rabbit stew.[10] When the cat winketh little wots the mouse

[10] As one of Raoul Gineste's poems has it:

> . . . sur un feu doux, dans une casserole,
> Tes morceaux chanteront l'ultime barcarolle,
> Car l'homme est sans scrupule et le lapin est cher.

" A cat," writes Browne, in his " Natural History of Jamaica," " is a very dainty dish among the Negroes." The Portuguese eat the cat, according to Darwin. The Abbé Lenoir informs us that the Chinese consider the cat excellent food and that in their provision shops enormous felines are hung up with their heads and tails on. They are bred on farms, secured by light chains, and fattened with the remains of the rice cooked for the family. Edward Topsell, who is as quotable as Bernard Shaw, and much more amusing, in his " History of Four-Footed Beasts " (1658) writes: " It is reported that the flesh of Cats salted and sweetened hath power in it to draw wens from the body, and being warmed to cure the Hemmorhoids and pains in the reins and back, according to the Verse of Ursinus. In Spain and Gallia Norbon, they eat Cats, but first of all take away their head and tail, and hang the prepared flesh a night or two in the open cold air, to exhale the savour and poison of it, finding the flesh thereof almost as sweet as a cony." Topsell, however, does not approve of this practice: " The flesh of Cats can seldom be free from poison, by reason of their daily food, eating Rats and Mice, Wrens and other birds which feed on poison, and above all the brain of the Cat is most venomous, for it being above all measure dry, stoppeth the animal spirits, that they cannot pass into the venticle, by reason thereof memory faileth, and the infected person falleth into a Phrenzie. The cure whereof may be this, take the water of sweet majoram with *terra lemnia* the weight of a groat mingled together, and drink it twice a month, putting good store of spirits into all your meat to recreate the spirits withall, let him drink pure wine, wherein put the seed of Diamoschu. But a Cat doth as much harm with her venomous teeth, therefore to cure her biting, they prescribe a good diet, sometimes taking Honey, turpentine, and Oil of Roses melt together and laid to the wound with Centory; sometimes they wash the wound with the urine of a man, and lay to it the brains of some other beast and pure wine mingled both together. The hair also of a Cat being eaten unawares, stoppeth the artery and causeth suffocation: and I have heard that when a childe hath gotten the hair

what the cat thinketh. Fain would the cat eat fish but she is
loth to wet her feet. The cat sees not the mouse ever.
Though the cat winks awhile, yet sure she is not blind. The
more you rub a cat on her back the higher she sets up her tail.
Well might the cat wink when both her eyes were out. How
can the cat help it if the maid be a fool? That that comes of
a cat will catch mice. A cat may look at a king. An old cat
laps as much as a young kitten. When the cat is away the
mice will play. The cat knows whose lips she licks. Cry
you mercy killed my cat (this was spoken of those who
played tricks and then tried to escape punishment by begging pardon). When candles are out all cats are grey. By
biting and scratching cats and dogs come together. I'll keep
no more cats than will catch mice. A cat has nine lives and
a woman has nine cats' lives. Cats eat what hussies spare.
In October not even a cat is to be found in London. A good
wife and a good cat are best at home. A cat will never drown
if she sees the shore. An ugly cat will have pretty kittens.
The cat with the straw tail sitteth not before the fire. Cats
hide their claws. The wandering cat gets many a rap. The
cat is hungry when a crust contents her. He lives under the
sign of the cat's foot (his wife scratches him). A blate cat
makes a proud mouse is a Scotch form of saying that a stupid
or timid foe is not to be feared. A dead cat feels no cold.
A piece of kid is worth two of cat. A scaulded cat fears cold
water is a translation of the French *Chat échaudé craint l'eau
froide*. As melancholy as a cat, or as melancholy as a gib-
cat is a common phrase in England. " I am melancholy as
a gib-cat or lugged bear," says a Shakespearean character.

of a Cat in his mouth, it hath so cloven and stuck to the place that it could not
be gotten off again, and hath in that place bred either the wens or the King's
evill. To conclude this point it appeareth that this is a dangerous beast, and
that therefore as for necessity we are constrained to nourish them for the sup-
pressing of small vermin: so with a wary and discreet eye we must avoid their
harms, making more account of their use than of their persons."

The Cat in Folklore

It should be explained that toms are called gib or ram-cats [11] in Northern England. In Pepys's Diary for November 29, 1667, for instance, you may read: " Our young gib-cat did leap down our stairs . . . at two leaps." To turn the cat in the pan is to reverse the order of things. Before the cat can lick her ear, of course, means never. Cats and carlins sit in the sun. Denham's " Popular Sayings " (1846) gives Every day's no yule; cast the cat a castock, which is to say spare no expense, bring another bottle of beer. In reference to the cat's elusiveness an old saying has it: He bydes as fast as a cat bound with a sacer. He can hold the cat to the sun is said of a man of extreme daring.

The French are quite as prolific as the English in proverbs referring to the cat. Note, for example, this charming aphorism, which is entirely Parisian: The three animals that spend the most time over their toilet are cats, flies, and women. To run very swiftly without tiring oneself is *courir comme un chat maigre*. Discordant music is *une musique de chats*. The sudden embarrassment which results in the loss of voice is caused by *un chat dans la gorge*. The equivalent English saying employs the humbler frog. A person who likes delicate things is *friande comme chatte*. He who writes illegibly *écrit comme un chat*. Trying to inspire pity is *faire la chatte mouillée*. To pass rapidly over a delicate situation, to skate on thin ice, to use the English parallel expression, is *passer par-dessus comme chat sur braise*. To look clean and yet not be clean is to be *propre comme une écuelle de chat*. *Vivre comme chien et chat* has its exact equivalent in English.

[11] Gib or Gyb is an abbreviation of Gilbert; in Europe this frequently became Tybalt or Tybert, Tyb or Tib. Mercutio insults Tybalt on this score. " Gibbe is the Icelandic *gabba*, to delude, and our gibber," writes Moncure Daniel Conway (" Demonology and Devil-lore "; Vol. II, p. 313). " It is the Gib cat of ' Reinicke Fuchs,' and of the ' Romaunt of the Rose.' In *Gammer Gurton* we read ' Hath no man gelded Gyb, her cat '; and in *Henry IV*, ' I am as melancholy as a gib cat.' Another cat is called Inges, that is *ignis*, fire." Another old English name for the male cat was carl-cat, and boar-cat was not uncommon.

The Tiger in the House

Dignitaries who wear fur on their costumes of ceremony are called *chats fourrés*. To look surly is *avoir une mine de chat fâché*. *Faire la chattemite* is to effect humble, flattering manners. If there is nobody present, *il n'y a pas un chat*. If by weakness or negligence one permits oneself to be deceived, *on laisse aller le chat au fromage*. *Le chat a faim quand il mange du pain* is said of those who eat what does not altogether please them, but cats often like to eat bread, indeed sometimes prefer it to other food. To expose oneself to danger without taking precaution is *prendre le chat sans mitaines*. There are several French variations of this phrase, which also occurs in English, and probably in many other languages as well. *On ne prend pas le chat sans moufles* and *Chat emmouflé ne prend pas souris* are the most common. *Gourmand comme un chat* is said of gluttons. To torment an adversary is *jouer comme le chat avec la souris*. Of a dangerous or impossible situation one says *C'est le nid d'une souris dans l'oreille d'un chat*. To watch everybody is *avoir un oeil à la poêle et l'autre au chat*. Those who are always conciliating never *jettent le chat aux jambes de personne*. *Jeter sa langue au chat* is to refuse to respond to an embarrassing question. *Acheter chat en poche* is, of course, as English as it is French. One also says in French *acheter le chat pour le lièvre,* a pretty custom which I have already touched upon. *La nuit tous les chats sont gris* I have given in its English dress; in its French form it occurs in Beaumarchais's *Le Barbier de Séville*. *A bon chat, bon rat:* for a good attack, good defence. As it is in the kitchen that the cat most frequently is scaulded one says *Chat échaudé ne revient pas en cuisine*. The meaning of the following proverbs is quite obvious: *Qui naquit chat court après les souris; On ne saurait retenir le chat quand il a goûté à la crème; Il fait le saint, il fait le chat; Qui vit avec les chats prendra goût aux souris; Les chats retombent toujours sur les pattes; Il ne faut pas faire passer tous les chats pour*

The Cat in Folklore

sorciers; Quand les chats sont absents les souris dansent,
which is our; When the cat's away the mice will play; *Faire tirer au chat les marrons du feu* is a reference to the fable of the cat and the ape. *Entendre bien chat sans qu'on dise minon* is to have the wit to comprehend things quickly. According to a thirteenth century proverb *Là où kas n'est, li souris se tient fière. Faire de la bouillie pour les chats* is to be careless. To take French leave is *emporter le chat. Avoir d'autres chats à fouetter* is to have other fish to fry. Of something insignificant one says: *Il n'y a pas de quoi fouetter un chat. Appeler un chat un chat* [12] has an English parallel. So has *Ne reveillons pas le chat qui dort. Payer en chats et en rats* is to pay in driblets. There are rhymed proverbs such as:

> *C'est chasser le chat bien tard*
> *Quand il a mangé le lard.*

> *A tard se repent le rat*
> *Quand par le col le tient le chat.*

> *Chat mioleur ne fut oncques grand chasseur,*
> *Non plus que sage homme grand cacqueteur.*

In the Temple of Liberty which Tiberius Gracchus erected in Rome, the goddess was represented holding a sceptre in one hand and a cap in the other, while at her feet reposed a cat, the symbol of freedom. " The company of soldiers, *Ordines Augustei,* who marched under the command of the Colonel of Infantry, *sub Magistro peditum,* bore on their ' white ' or ' silver ' shield, a cat of the colour of the mineral prase, which is sinople, or sea-green. The cat is ' courant ' and turns its head over its back. Another company of the

[12] Félicien Rops's motto, according to James Huneker, was " J'appelle un chat un chat." " Promenades of an Impressionist," p. 35.

143

same regiment, called ' the happy old men ' (*felices seniores*) carried a demi-cat, red, on a buckler gules; *in parma punica diluciore,* with its paws up, as if playing with some one. Under the same chief, a third cat passant, gules, with one eye and one ear, was carried by the soldiers *qui Alpini vocabantur."* [13] The Vandals and the Suevi carried a cat sable upon their armorial bearings, among the Greeks and Romans. The cat, indeed, plays no inconsiderable part in heraldry. The Burgundians used the device with the same significance of liberty and fearlessness and Clotilde, wife of Clovis the Burgundian, chose for her sigil a cat sable springing at a mouse. Other noble houses were enamoured of the emblem. We need exhibit no surprise upon learning that the Katzen family's azure shield flaunted a cat argent holding a rat or that the crest of the Della Gatta family of Naples bore a magnificent cat couchant. Two cats argent on an azure shield signified the Chetaldie family of Limoges and the motto of the Scotch Clann Chatain is " Touch not the cat but (without) a glove." [14] The Chaffardon family bore on azure three cats, or two, full face in chief. The cognizance of Richard III was a boar, passant argent, whence the rhyme which cost William Collingborne his life:

[13] Palliot: "Le Vraye et Parfaicte Science des Armoires" (Paris, 1664).

[14] Seumas, Chief of Clann Fhearghuis of Stra-chur, informs me that the Clann a Chatain (Children of the Cats) is a great clann with six tribes. The Mackintosh of Mackintosh is Chief of this Clann. I am also indebted to Fhearghuis for a translation of a song about this Clann:

> *The cats have come upon us,*
> *The cats have come upon us,*
> *The cats have come upon us,*
> *They have come upon us!*
>
> *To break in upon us,*
> *To lift the spoil,*
> *To steal the kine,*
> *To strike the steeds,*
> *To strip the meads,*
> *They have come!*

The Cat in Folklore

The Cat, the Rat, and Lovel our Dogge,
Rulen all England under an Hogge.[15]

Cervantes, it will be recalled, speaks of the " ever victorious and never vanquished " Timonel of Carcajona, Prince of New Biscay, whose shield bore a golden cat and the single word, " Miau " in honour of his lady, the lovely Miaulina, daughter of the Alfeniquen of the Algarve. More recently the tank corps of the American army carried on its machines huge black cats with snarling fangs and flashing electric green eyes and with the motto, " Treat 'em rough! " and the insignia of the Eighty-first division of the American Expeditionary Forces were wild cats. The men of this division, conscripts from North and South Carolina, Florida and Porto Rico, were the pioneers who introduced the custom of divisional emblems into the American army. According to Col. Robert E. Wyllie of the General Staff, when the Eighty-first division arrived at Hoboken, the port of embarkation, every man was wearing the wild cat on his left shoulder. General Shanks, commander of the port, immediately informed Washington army headquarters of the novel distinguishing mark of the Carolina wild cats and asked if the insignia were authorized. Before a negative reply reached General Shanks the division had sailed. When the Eighty-first landed in France the eyes of every doughboy in other divisions were focussed on the vicious feline and within the week the other divisions had invented similar insignia. So general, indeed, had the custom become that General Pershing realized that an order authorizing the decorations must follow. This authorization, so far as I know, was not issued, but the insignia were never prohibited and, as all who have seen the returning soldiers must know, they were eventually used by all divisions.

It is no longer the general custom to name shops or to label

---

[15] A. R. Frey: " Sobriquets and Nicknames "; Ticknor and Co.; Boston; 1888. The cat was William Catesby, the dog, Lord Lovel.

145

them with fantastic signboards but in the old days when such fashions were in vogue cat signs were as frequent as any others. A bookseller in London in 1612 called his shop The Cat and Parrot. Other shops, or inns, bore such quaint titles as Cat and Cage, Cat and Lion, Cat and Bagpipes, and Cat and Fiddle. The Catherine Wheel sign put up in honour of Catherine of Aragon, Queen of Henry VIII, was changed by the Puritans into Cat and Wheel! An old English tavern was called the Salutation and Cat. This is as good as the Hotel of the Virgin Mary and the Prince of Wales, which I once visited on the Italian Riviera. The name was calculated to capture both the Catholic and the English trade.

Of the French signs, *La Maison du Chat qui Pelote* (used by Balzac), *Le Chat qui Pêche,* and above all, *Le Chat Noir* are the most common. The latter once served for restaurants or bakeries but latterly it has been identified with one of the most celebrated of the Paris cabarets. The cabaret itself has passed but the name still persists. Even in New York a restaurant carries it and so does a well-known magazine. Parisian shoe-makers frequently affected *Le Chat Botté.* *Le Chat qui Fume* is a charming name. One of Anatole France's stories bears as its title the name of a little Parisian Café, *Le Chat Maigre.* An American dry-cleaning establishment uses a cat washing clothes for its trademark.

The cat leaps through so many nursery rhymes in all tongues, native and exotic, that every child must know at least half a dozen of them. The following lines seem to have been prophetic:

> *Jack Spratt*
> *Had a cat;*
> *It had but one ear;*
> *It went to buy butter,*
> *When butter was dear.*

This one is charmingly suggestive:

The Cat in Folklore

Poor Dog Bright,
Ran off with all his might,
Because the cat was after him,
Poor Dog Bright.

Poor Cat Fright,
Ran off with all her might,
Because the dog was after her,
Poor Cat Fright.

Alphabetical nursery rhymes are always popular with mothers because they are considered semi-instructive. Variations of the following lines are numberless:

A, B, C, tumble down D,
The cat's in the cupboard and can't see me.

A French version is:

A, B, C,
Le chat est allé
Dans le neige; en retournant
Il avait les souliers tous blancs.

Something like this occurs also in German, Yiddish, Russian, Patagonian, and early Australian.

The rhyme beginning

Hey, diddle, diddle,
The cat and the fiddle,

is as well known as anything in Shakespeare. Nor can there be many who have neglected to learn

Ding, dong, bell, Pussy's in the well,

or

Pussy cat, Pussy cat, where have you been?

or

The three little kittens, they lost their mittens.

147

The Tiger in the House

This is a very pleasant ditty:

> *Hey, my kitten, my kitten,*
> *Hey, my kitten, my deary;*
> *Such a sweet pet as this*
> *Was neither far nor neary.*

And this is philosophical and fatalistic:

> *Pussy-cat ate the dumplings, the dumplings;*
> *Pussy-cat ate the dumplings.*
> *Mamma stood by, and cried, " Oh, fie!*
> *Why did you eat the dumplings? "*

In many other rhymes the cat is an important figure. For instance in the epic poem about the woman who wanted to get her pig over the stile it was the cat that killed the rat, and in " A frog he would a-wooing go,"

> *A cat and her kittens came tumbling in,*
> *With a rowley powley, gammon and spinach.*

There is also the cat that killed the rat that ate the malt that lay in the house that Jack built.

The French rhymes, while often not so fantastic, are naturally lovelier. What could be more irresistible than

> *Le chat sauta sur les souris,*
> *Il les croqua toute la nuit.*
> *Gentil coquiqui,*
> *Coco des moustaches, mirlo joli,*
> *Gentil coquiqui.*

Here is another:

> *Sur ma gouttière un jour je vis*
> *Un chat de bonne mine*
> *Qui, sans s'occuper des souris,*
> *Miaulait en sourdine.*
> *Ah! il m'en souviendra,*

The Cat in Folklore

Du chat de ma voisine.
Larira,

An old Mother Goose rhyme has it that

> *Puss-cat Mew jumped over a coal;*
> *In her best petticoat burnt a great hole;*
> *Puss-cat Mew shan't have any milk*
> *Till her best petticoat's mended with silk.*

With this verse for his inspiration E. H. Knatchbull-Hugessen composed a fairy story, " Puss-Cat Mew," which is a mixture of familiar folklore elements: the ogres are the giants of Jack and the Beanstalk and Joe Brown, the miller's son who is befriended in the magic forest by a tortoise-shell cat, who, of course, at the proper moment becomes a beautiful and marriageable young lady and the daughter of no less a personage than the Queen of the Fairies, is easily recognizable. Still when I recently reread the story I again felt its charm and its thrill and the horrible man-eating ogres still inspired terror.

There are so many folk-tales about cats that some enterprising young man of the future may fill a large book with these alone. Very often the cat plays a cruel or reprehensible part in these stories but he never plays a stupid or foolish rôle. In one of La Fontaine's fables, indeed, the cat outwits even the fox. He is seldom lacking in wit; indeed he may be regarded as the Till Eulenspiegel of the animal world. It is well to remember Andrew Lang's casual remark that " Animals are always most intelligent when most depraved." Of the stories " Puss in Boots " [16] is the most familiar; some form of this fable occurs in almost every language. Mr. Lang points out that it is a " moral " story in Russia, Sicily, among the Arabs, and at Zanzibar. In these countries the cat assists the man from motives of gratitude. In France,

[16] Jules-Séverin Caillot has written a pretty sequel to this tale: "La Chatte Blanche," in " Contes après les contes "; Plon-Nourrit; Paris; 1919.

Italy, India, and elsewhere it is an immoral story; the cat is a swindler and the Marquis de Carabas is his accomplice. Gaston de Paris is convinced that the Zanzibar version is the original. In this version the man is ungrateful to the kind beast and awakes to find his prosperity a dream. "The White Cat," which the Comtesse D'Aulnoy gave to France in 1682 is a wholly pretty story in which the graceful feline with her *pattes de velours* is transformed into a princess. Gelett Burgess has symbolized this theme in a novel bearing the name of the original fable.

The tale of Dick Whittington and his cat has afforded scope for research work among the English folklorists and historians which still continues. W. R. S. Ralston writes in "The Nineteenth Century": "There used to exist in the Mercers' Hall a portrait of Whittington, dated 1536, in which a black-and-white cat figured at his left hand. A still existing portrait by Reginald Elstrack, who flourished about 1590, represents him with his hand resting on a cat. The story is told that the hand originally rested on a skull, but that in deference to public opinion a cat was substituted, which proves that the legend or the history had by that time completely spread. That is also proved by a reference to the cat legend in Heywood's *If You Know Not Me,* and by another in Beaumont and Fletcher's *The Knight of the Burning Pestle.* Newgate gaol was rebuilt by Whittington's executors, and a statue, with a cat at his feet, is said to have been set up on the gate, and to have remained there until the fire of 1666. Moreover a piece of plate on which figured 'heraldic cats' was presented to the Mercers' company in 1572; and in the house at Gloucester, which the Whittingtons occupied till 1460, there was dug up a stone, when repairs were made in 1862, on which in *basso relievo,* is represented the figure of a boy carrying in his arms a cat. The workmanship appears to be of the fifteenth century. This is all that can be said in favour of the legend. Against it, besides its inherent improbability, may be called as witnesses many folk-tales,[17] which at least suggest that the story is one of the commonplaces of fiction, capable of being associated with any historical or fictitious personage." So some destroyers of our belief in Santa Claus assure us that Whittington's cat was a boat, while others affirm that trading or buying and selling at a profit was called *achat* and probably pronounced " acat " in the fifteenth century.

Moncrif relates an enchanting Hindu story, which, it would seem to me, has not been retold sufficiently often: At the court of Salamgam, King of the Indies, a Brahmin and a Penitent each boasted that he was the most virtuous. A trial was proposed and the Brahmin offered to ascend to the Heaven of Devendiren and return therefrom with the flower of the tree called Parisadam, only indigenous to that particular celestial realm. He made good his promise, returning with the blossom to the great astonishment of all the court with the exception of the Penitent, who refused to be impressed. " My virtue is so great," he asserted, " that I can send my cat for the flower of Parisadam." He was requested to do so and immediately the adorable Patripatan ascended to the skies in full view of the King and his nobles. Now, however, Fate interfered with the Penitent's plans. The Heaven of Devendiren was inhabited by forty-eight million goddesses who had for husbands one hundred and twenty-four gods of which Devendiren was the sovereign. Now the instant the favourite goddess of the King of the Gods set her eyes on Patripatan she made up her mind to keep him for her very own. Devendiren, after he had listened to the cat, explained to the goddess that Patripatan was awaited with impatience by the court of Salamgam, that the reputation of the Penitent was

---

[17] Among the analogues of the Whittington story may be mentioned the Brittany black cat who made silver; the Danish dog who barked money; and the gold-producing horse or, as in the Midas story, a ram or swine with fleece or bristles of gold. On page 43 of W. R. S. Ralston's " Russian Folk-Tales " (Smith, Elder and Co., London, 1873) you may find a Russian story which is very similar.

at stake, and that the greatest affront one could offer to a mortal was to steal his cat. The goddess listened inattentively to this argument and finally promised, as a special favour to his godship, that she would return the beloved puss in three centuries. The court waited through this period without any other inconvenience than impatience because the Penitent by the power of his virtue was able to preserve everybody's youth. When the time had elapsed the sky reddened, and the cat appeared on a throne in a cloud of a thousand hues, bearing in his paws an entire branch of the tree of Parisadam. I believe the King awarded the *croix de vertu* to Patripatan. The only incredible part of the story is that the goddess should ever have permitted herself to be separated from a cat she had known and loved for three centuries.

One of the Japanese fairy stories translated by Lafcadio Hearn is called " The Boy Who Drew Cats." This boy, the son of a poor farmer, had been sent to a priest, so that he might be trained as an acolyte. The child, however, refused to take an interest in his new studies and spent all his time drawing cats. The old priest, realizing that the boy's talent was for art rather than for religion, sent him out into the world. In his wanderings the lad passed the night in a deserted temple but before he went to sleep he could not resist painting cats on the naked white screens. In his dreams he heard shrieks and in the morning he awakened to find an enormous goblin-rat lying dead on the floor, while the whiskers and jaws of his painted cats were red with blood.

An amusing Persian story tells of a long-sighted cat with fascinating eyes, long whiskers, and sharp teeth, who hunted like a lion in the city of Kerman. One day, perceiving the wine cellar of his house open, the cat walked in and caught a mouse. Thereafter he repented, went to the mosque, passed his paws over his face, poured water on his paws, and anointed himself as he had seen the faithful do at the hours of prayer. He swore he would never kill another mouse, praised Allah, and began to weep. The mice heard of this oath and held a celebration; a few days later the king of the mice suggested that gifts be carried to this temperate cat. So the mice brought wine, mussels stuffed with rice, raisins, and pignolia nuts; melon seeds and lumps of cheese; little cakes iced with sugar; Indian shawls and cloaks. Upon the receipt of these presents the cat reasoned thus: " I am rewarded for becoming a pious Mussulman. It is clear that Allah is appeased." Then he sprang among the mice and killed a great number of them. The others went their way in sorrow. The king of the mice, when he heard of this unwarranted assault, declared war on the cats and three hundred and thirty thousand mice went forth, armed with swords, guns, and spears. The cats on horseback came out to meet them and the armies fell upon each other. So many cats and mice were killed that finally there was no ground for the horses to stand on. At length the king of the cats was captured and condemned to execution. He was carried to the block, bound paw to paw, but he burst his fetters, darted here and there, seizing and slaying till the whole army of mice was routed and there was none left to oppose him.

Gottfried Keller's story of " Spiegel, das Kätzchen " [18] has a folk air and was probably not entirely the invention of the author. A certain wizard in a Swiss village, taking a walk one day, met a ram-cat looking very thin and miserable. He had been the favourite feline of a rich old gentlewoman, whose sudden death had left him without means of support. Now cat's grease was an invaluable ingredient in certain magical preparations, but the thaumaturgical condition prescribed that the cat must make a willing donation of it. The wizard saw his opportunity in the present situation. Spiegel was hungry and he offered him a month's luxurious living in return for his grease. The bargain was struck and the wizard

---

[18] In " Die Leute von Seldwyla," 1856.

fitted up an apartment as an artificial landscape with a little wood on a mountain and a little lake. Tiny roasted birds perched on the trees. Baked mice, seasoned with stuffing and larded with bacon, peered out of the mountain caves. Fish swam in the milk lake. Spiegel enjoyed himself but as he found himself getting very fat a ruse occurred to him. Towards the end of the month he stopped eating and grew very thin again. He continued this procedure every time his waist line increased in size until the wizard accused him of trying to escape from his bargain. It was on this day, and no other, that forcible feeding was invented! But Spiegel was again inspired; he told the wizard that he knew where 10,000 florins were buried at the bottom of a well, waiting as the wedding portion of a man who could find a beautiful and penniless maiden. The story was false. The money existed but a curse lay upon it. The wizard, however, took Spiegel on a chain to the well, saw the gold bricks and believed in them, and released his prisoner. Now the cat was the friend of an owl-companion to an old hag; with the aid of a magic net these two contrived to seize the beldam and transform her into a personable young lady. In this form she married the wizard at high noon as is the respectable custom, but at nightfall she regained her rightful shape, so that he found himself possessed of a hag for a wife and a pot of cursed gold for a dowry. Spiegel, of course, lived happily ever after.

Thomas A. Janvier found the following story among some old Mexican papers and printed it in " Stories of Old New Spain ": " It was about the year 1540 that the Reverend Father Friar Francisco de Tembleque felt stirring in his heart a good desire (that, assuredly, God put there) to build an aqueduct by which the towns of Otumba and Zempoala should be supplied abundantly with water wholesome to drink — which at that time the people of these towns were compelled to bring from springs seven leagues away. And his plan was to make an aqueduct over all that distance, carrying it across three wide valleys on no less than one hundred and thirty-six arches, and making over the deepest of the valleys one arch so great that beneath it might pass (had there been any such thereabouts) a ship under full sail. And to this work the servant of God — for so Father Tembleque was called — set himself with a stout heart; and the Indians worked for him joyfully. And at the spot where the great arch was to be, in what then was a tangle of wooded wild land, he built a little chapel to the Glory of Our Lady of Belen, and close beside the chapel he made for himself a cell so narrow that scarcely was there room within it for him to lie down to sleep.

"And God showed his love to his servant by giving to dwell with him a grey cat, which every day from the wild woodland round about brought quails for his master's sustenance; and in the season of rabbits, a rabbit. And between the servant of God and this cat there was much love.

"To Father Tembleque there came òne day a stranger, who courteously, yet with a curious particularity, questioned him about the progress of the great work that he had in hand. For certain persons of the baser sort had said in the ears of the Viceroy that Father Tembleque was wasting his time and the substance of the church in striving to do an impossible thing; and this stranger really was an alcalde of the court, whom, that he might know the truth, the Viceroy had sent thus secretly to ask searching questions and to see for himself how the work went on. And as the two communed together, behold the cat came out of the wood to where they stood in talk and laid a rabbit at his master's feet!

"When said the servant of God: 'Brother Cat, a guest hath come to us, and therefore it is necessary that thou shalt bring me this day not one rabbit, but two.'

"Hearing these words, the cat in due obedience, betook himself once more to the thicket. But the alcalde, thinking that this might be a trick that was put upon him, sent after

The Tiger in the House

the cat to spy upon him one of his own servants. And the servant presently beheld a greater wonder. For in a moment the cat met with another rabbit,[19] which he caught without any resistance at all on the creature's part, and with it returned to his master again: thus plainly showing that all had been disposed thus by God.

" And the Señor Alcalde, being so substantially assured of the miracle, returned to the Viceroy and said, ' Though it seems to be impossible to bring the water by the way that Father Tembleque hath chosen, and though the work that he hath set himself to do seems to be beyond the power of man to accomplish, yet assuredly will he succeed; for I have seen that which proves beyond a peradventure that God hath vouchsafed to him his all-powerful aid '; and he told to the Viceroy the whole of the miracle which through the cat had been wrought. Therefore did the Viceroy encourage Father Tembleque in his great work; and God's blessing continuing upon it, in seventeen years' time the aqueduct was finished — the very aqueduct through which the water comes to the towns of Otumba and Zempoala at the present day." [20]

Doubtless many miraculous cat stories are to be found in

[19] Stories of cats who have fed families are not uncommon. There is, for instance, that of the ploughman who lived at the foot of the Orchils and his cat, Mysie. The ploughman had long been ill — his home was in poverty — when the doctor said the poor man would die if his strength was not kept up by stimulants and animal food. "I put awa' my marriage gown and ring to get him wine," related the ploughman's wife, "but we had naething in the house but milk and meal. Surely, sir, it was the Lord himself that put it into that cat's head; for that same night she brought in a fine young rabbit, and laid it on the verra bed; and the next night the same, and every night the same, for a month, whiles a rabbit and whiles a bird, till George was up, and going to his work as usual. But she never brought anything after that." Agnes Repplier found a similar story in Watson's Annals, which she quotes on page 237 of "The Fireside Sphinx."

[20] Found by Mr. Janvier in MS. of Fray Agustin de Vetancourt in the Menologio Franciscano, October 1, of his Teatro Mexicano (City of Mexico; 1698; folio).

156

the archives of Negro folklore. I remember one which I have heard both Kitty Cheatham and Bert Williams tell. An itinerant Negro preacher, finding himself a long distance from the next farmhouse at an inconveniently late hour, decided to accommodate himself for the night in a deserted hut. He lighted a fire in the fireplace and settled down before it to read his Bible when suddenly a black kitten appeared. He caressed the animal and was indeed glad to have company for he began to recall a legend that the house was haunted. Presently a larger cat joined the kitten and the preacher was astonished to hear him remark, "We cain't do nothin' till Martin gits here." The old man, however, decided that his ears must have deceived him and continued to read his Bible aloud fervidly. Pretty soon along came a cat the size of a collie dog, who settled down on his haunches alongside the others. "We cain't do nothin' till Martin gits here," he remarked plaintively. The preacher's knees shook and his kinky hair began to grow straighter, but he bent over the Holy Word and began to intone the lines. But the next arrival was a cat as big as a lion. He sat down with the others and his tone was an angry deep growl as he said, "We cain't do nothin' till Martin gits here." This was too much for the preacher who dropped his Bible and fled, shouting over his shoulder, "You tell Martin when he gits here dat I cain't wait for him!"

In Russia, according to Thiselton Dyer, the cat enjoys a better reputation among the people than she does in some other countries. There is a curious legend current about Moscow that when Lucifer once tried to creep back into Paradise, he assumed the form of a mouse. The dog and the cat were on guard at the gates, and the dog allowed the evil one to pass, but the cat pounced upon him and so defeated another treacherous attempt against human felicity.

At any rate the Russian folk-tales in which puss plays a

prominent part are usually based on accurate observation of the animal's traits. The following fable of Ivan Krilof certainly epitomizes the spirit of the cat:

A certain cook, rather more educated than his fellows, went from his kitchen one day to a neighbouring tavern, leaving his cat at home to protect his store of food from the mice. But on his return he found the floor strewn with the fragments of a pie and Vaska the cat crouching in a corner behind a vinegar barrel, purring with satisfaction, and busily engaged in disposing of a chicken.

"Ah, glutton, ah, evil-doer!" exclaimed the reproachful cook. "Are you not ashamed to be seen by these walls, let alone living witnesses? You, an honourable cat up to this time, one who might be pointed out as a model of discretion! And now, think of the disgrace! Now, all the neighbours will say, 'Vaska is a rogue; Vaska is a thief. Vaska must be kept out of the kitchen, even out of the courtyard, like a ravenous wolf from the sheepfold. He is corrupt; he is a pest, the plague of the neighbourhood.'"

While the cook was delivering this discourse Vaska the cat ate the whole of the chicken.

Chapter Six: The Cat and the Law

From the epoch of the cat's godhood down to the modern moment laws have been passed to protect the cat, laws which have demanded that man treat the cat in such and such a fashion. Egyptians cat-killers were punished by death. Diodorus writes of a brave Roman soldier who was the victim of this law. It is interesting to compare this extreme measure with the old English common law which held both cats and dogs as " no property, being base by nature," but it is also well to remember that at one time in England larceny was punished by the death penalty. If a cat had been considered property the theft of a puss would have led the thief to the block or the scaffold. The English " Rule of Nuns " issued in the early thirteenth century, forbade the holy women to keep any beast but a cat. A canon of a date nearly a hundred years earlier forbade nuns, even abbesses, from wearing costlier skins than those of lambs and cats. The Welsh laws concerning domestic lions were formulated in the tenth century. In 1818 a decree was issued at Ypres in Flanders forbidding the throwing of pussies from high towers in commemoration of a Christmas Spectacle. And today the Society for the Prevention of Cruelty to Animals endeavours to make the punishment fit the crime for anyone who maliciously mistreats a cat.

But through the ages law-makers have wisely, it would seem, allowed puss to go more or less her own way, while restricting her master's actions in regard to her. I say wisely, for it cannot be considered the part of wisdom to create laws which will not be obeyed, and I think I have made it fairly clear that the cat will not obey laws. A cat makes no attempt to govern other cats and he will not tolerate such an attempt on the part of man. While other animals are leashed and muzzled, barned and fenced in, puss wanders free. The unclean dog is expelled from the mosque but grimalkin is welcomed there. She rubs her legs against the sultan's guests at dinner and attends state banquets at the White House.[1] So she sits at the prelate's table or by the humble farmer's hearth, but by night she wanders the heath or the rooftop, to view, as one poet has ingeniously explained, the surrounding country!

Even in the middle ages when it was quaintly held that animals were responsible for crimes [2] (I say quaintly because it is perfectly obvious that both the word and the idea are human inventions) and they were tried and condemned to death and to other punishments, including torture, the cat escaped.[3] In the list of these trials given by E. P. Evans [4] there is not one single case in which a cat was the defendant. The cat appears, indeed, only in the testimony of these trials. Once, for instance, a sixteenth century French jurist, Bartholomew Chassenée, complained that his clients, some rats, were prevented from appearing in court at Autun, because of a stretch of cat country that they would be forced to cross on their journey. Modern lawyers will be glad to know that Chassenée successfully defended his rats. By virtue of the old Germanic law cats often appeared as witnesses at the trials of thieves and murderers.[5]

[1] See "Slippers, the White House Cat," by Jacob A. Riis: "Saint Nicholas"; January 1908. Theodore Roosevelt was not the first of our presidents to be a cat-lover. There was at least one other, Abraham Lincoln.

[2] The middle ages cannot be held entirely responsible for these laws. It was incorporated into the Mosaic Law that an ox who killed a man was subject to death, just as if it had been a man who had murdered one of his fellows. See Exodus, XXI, 28: "If an ox gore a man or a woman, that they die; then the ox shall be surely stoned, and his flesh shall not be eaten; but the owner of the ox shall be quit."

[3] As a witch's companion she did not escape, but I have fully covered that point in a preceding chapter.

[4] "The Criminal Prosecution and Capital Punishment of Animals."

[5] Same work, p. 11.

160

The Cat and the Law

In passing it is interesting to observe that St. Ives, the patron saint of lawyers, is represented as accompanied by a cat. And here again, if it were necessary, we might invoke symbolism to explain the simple truth that holy men as well as devils found the cat the most attractive of animals. The profound wisdom, the concealed claws, the stealthy approach, and the final spring, all seem to typify the superior attorney. We should not be astonished, therefore, that Cardinal Wolsey placed his cat by his side while acting in his judicial capacity as Lord Chancellor.

The most interesting laws concerning cats were formulated during the tenth century by Howel Dda, a King of South Wales, who, perceiving that the customs of his country were being violated, called the archbishops, the bishops, the nobles, and other chosen men to meet at Y ty Gwyn ar Dav with him. The whole of Lent was spent by this body in the presence of the King in fasting and prayer; then Howel selected from the assembly twelve of the wisest men and adding to their number a doctor of laws, Blegywryd by name, committed them to the task of examining, retaining, expounding, and abrogating the laws. When the work was completed Howel sanctioned it. Wales, however, was of considerable size and it was not long before local distinctions arose which resulted in the eventual formulation of three separate Codes, Venedotian, Dimetian, and Gwentian. It is from these Codes that the following curious passages relating to cats have been extracted.

According to the Venedotian Code: The worth of a kitten from the night it is kittened until it shall open its eyes is a legal penny; and from that time until it shall kill mice, two legal pence; and after it shall kill mice, four legal pence; and so it shall always remain. The penny, at this period, was equal to the value of a lamb, a kid, a goose, or a hen; a cock or a gander was worth twopence, a sheep or a goat fourpence. The qualities of a cat, continues the Code, are to see, to hear, to kill mice, to have her claws entire, to rear and not to devour her kittens, and if she be bought and be deficient in any of these qualities, let one third of her worth be returned.

In the Dimetian and Gwentian Codes distinctions are drawn between cats and cats. The Dimetian Code says: The worth of a cat that is killed or stolen: its head is to be put downwards upon a clean, even floor, with its tail lifted upwards, and thus suspended, whilst wheat is poured about it, until the tip of its tail be covered and that is to be its worth; if the corn cannot be had, a milch sheep with her lamb and its wool is its value, if it be a cat which guards the King's barn. The worth of a common cat is four legal pence.

The Gwentian Code says: Whoever shall kill a cat that guards a house or a barn of the King or shall take it stealthily; it is to be held with its head to the ground and its tail up, the ground being swept and then clean wheat is to be poured about it until the tip of its tail be hidden: and that is its worth. Another cat is four legal pence in value.

There seem to be obvious difficulties involved in the carrying out of this law. In the first place it would appear to be necessary to capture both the thief and the stolen cat. In the second place no self-respecting cat would permit herself to be suspended by the tail. She would scratch and bite and turn and twist and curl until it would be impossible to go through with the experiment unless she were dead and certainly the Welsh judges would not kill the King's cat merely in order to punish her thief. Thirdly it would seem to be manifestly impossible to enforce this law if the King's cat happened to be a tailless Manx cat.

There are further laws: The Dimetian Code says: Whoever shall sell a cat is to answer for her not going a caterwauling every moon; and that she devour not her kittens; and that she have ears, eyes, teeth, and nails, and is a good mouser. The Gwentian Code provides that there shall be no Manx cats: The qualities of a cat are that it be perfect of

The Cat and the Law

ear, perfect of eye, perfect of teeth, perfect of tail, perfect of claw, and without marks of fire; and that it kill mice well and that it shall not devour its kittens and that it be not caterwauling on every new moon.

The importance of the cat to the community was recognized by these Welsh laws which provided that one cat was necessary to make a lawful hamlet together with nine buildings, one plough, one kiln, one churn, one bull, one cock, and one herdsman. The dog and the horse are not mentioned.

Another interesting detail of the Dimetian Code relates to the separation of man and wife: the goods and chattels were to be divided but *the husband took the cat if there was but one;* if there were others they went to the wife. The stress laid on puss at this period, her comparatively high value, leads Pennant [6] to the very credible conclusion that her importation must have been recent, as the animal breeds so rapidly that in a few years a dozen felines could populate a country.

Notwithstanding the laws of Howel the question as to whether or not the cat is a property continues to be discussed in its legal aspects down to the present day. There seems to be difference of opinion in the matter and the judgments in law suits of this character seem to depend on whether or no the judge is a cat-lover. Fortunately most judges *are* cat-lovers.

In 1865, Monsieur Richard, the *juge de paix* of Fontainebleau rendered a memorable decision. An inhabitant of the town, annoyed by cats who molested his garden, set traps and caught fifteen. The owners of the cats [7] brought the man to trial.

" Considering," said the learned judge in his opinion, " that

[6] " British Zoology."

[7] This phrase and such words as "master," "mistress," etc., which occur in this book are used purely for convenience. Of course no one ever owned a cat.

the law does not permit the individual to do justice to himself in his own person;

" That article 479 of the Penal Code, and Article 1385 of the Code Napoleon, recognize several kinds of cats, notably the wild cat, as a noxious animal for the destruction of which a reward is granted, but that the domestic cat is not affected by these articles in the eyes of the legislator;

" That the domestic cat, not being a thing of nought (*res nullius*), but the property of a master, ought to be protected by the law;

" That the utility of the cat as a destroyer of mischievous animals of the rodent kind being indisputable, equity demands the extension of indulgence to an animal which is tolerated by the law;

" That even the domestic cat is in some degree of a mixed nature, that is to say, an animal always partly wild, and which must remain so by reason of its destiny and purpose, if it is to render those services which are expected from it;

" That although the law of 1790, art. 12 *in fine,* permits the killing of poultry, the assimilation of cats with these birds is by no means correct, since the fowl species are destined to be killed sooner or later, and that they can be kept in a manner under the hand of their owners, *sub custodia,* in a completely enclosed and secure place, while this cannot be said of the cat, for it is impossible to put that animal under lock and key, if it is to obey the law of its nature;

" That the asserted right in certain cases of killing the dog, which is a dangerous animal and prompt to attack without being rabid, cannot be held to imply as a consequence the right to kill a cat, which is an animal not calculated to inspire fear, and always ready to run away;

" That nothing in the law authorizes citizens to set traps, in order, by an appetizing bait, to entice the innocent cats of an entire quarter as well as the guilty ones;

The Cat and the Law

" That no one ought to do to the property (*chose*) of another that which he would not wish to have done to his own property;

" That all goods being either movables (*meubles*) or immovables (*immeubles*) according to article 516 of the Code Napoleon, it results therefrom that the cat, contrary to article 128 of the same Code, is incontestably a movable (*meuble*) protected by the law, and therefore that the owners of animals which are destroyed are entitled to claim the application of article 479, clause 1, of the Penal Code, which punishes those who have voluntarily caused damage to the movable property of others." [8]

A similar decision was rendered in the sheriff's court at Perth, Scotland, in the late seventies. The cat had killed the plaintiff's pigeon on a neighbour's premises. The learned sheriff in his decision said:

" It was quite legitimate for the plaintiff to keep a pigeon, but just as much so for the defendant to keep a cat. The latter is more a domestic animal than a pigeon. But there are no obligations on the owner of a cat to restrain it to the house. The plaintiff's plea is that the natural instinct of the feline race is to prey on birds as well as mice. So it was argued that the owner of the cat should prevent the possibility of its coming into contact with its favourite sport. But it is equally true that the owner of a bird should exercise similar precaution to prevent its coming within the range of a hostile race. If the defendant's cat had trespassed into the plaintiff's house or aviary where the bird was secured, there might be ground for finding the owner of the cat liable for the consequences of its being at large. With parity of reason had the bird intruded itself upon the territory of the cat and there had been slain, there could have been no recourse because the owner of the bird should have prevented its escape. In the present case it appears that both

[8] This decision was afterwards disputed before the Correctional Tribunal.

the quadruped and the winged animal were in trespass on neutral territory. It was the duty of the plaintiff to take the guardianship of the bird said to be so valuable and therefore both owners are equally to blame and the case must be viewed as arising from natural law, for which neither owner without *culpa* can be answerable. The defendant being at first not sympathetic with the loss of the plaintiff, but rather put him at defiance, and forced him to prove it was the defendant's cat who slew his bird, the defendant will be acquitted but without costs." [9]

In Maine it has been decided that the cat is a domestic animal within the jurisdiction of the statute which provides that " any person may lawfully kill a dog which . . . is found worrying, wounding, or killing any domestic animal, when said dog is outside of the inclosure or immediate care of its owner and keeper." The plaintiff sued the defendant, alleging that he had killed a valuable foxhound belonging to him, and the defendant replied that he had killed it because the dog was chasing and worrying his cat. The court held that this was sufficient justification and gave an exhaustive view of the law as to felines. [10] Ingham cites a Canadian case in which the judge decided: " A person may have property in a cat and therefore an action will lie to recover damages for killing it. There may be circumstances under which it would be justifiable to kill a cat; but it is not justifiable to do

[9] Harrison Weir (" Our Cats and All About Them," p. 207) quotes an " Articled Clerk " writing in " The Standard " with regard to the illegality of killing cats: " It is clearly laid down in ' Addison on Torts,' that a person is not justified in killing his neighbour's cat, which he finds on his land, unless the animal is in the act of doing some injurious act which can only be prevented by its slaughter. And it has been decided by the case of ' Townsend v. Watken,' 9 last 277, that if a person sets on his lands a trap for foxes, and baits it with such strong-smelling meat as to attract his neighbour's cat on to his land, to the trap, and such animal is thereby killed or injured, he is liable for the act, though he had no intention of doing it, and though the animal ought not to have been on his land."

[10] " The cat a ' domestic animal' and ' property' ": " The American Law Review "; Vol. 49, p. 917.

The Cat and the Law

so merely because it is a trespasser, even though after game."

In another case the owner of a cat was not held liable to the owner of a canary bird killed by it, the court considering that cats to some extent " may be regarded as still undomesticated and their predatory habits are but a remnant of their wild nature." [11]

But an Attorney-General of the State of Maryland, evidently no felinophile, handed down a decision which was a cruel blow to the owners of cats. A certain citizen of Baltimore (I hope this was not Mencken) stole a fine maltese cat from a neighbour, who had him arrested for theft. When the case came up for trial the prisoner's counsel entered the plea that it was impossible for any one to steal a cat, as that animal is not property, and that to take forcible possession of a feline, even though it be a pet and wear a ribbon. and answer to its name, is not a legal offense.[12] The astonishing judge held the argument to be good and the more astonishing Attorney-General, to whom the case was appealed, agreed with him. The latter in his formal opinion, declared that the cat is really nothing but a wild animal, that it is of no use to man, and that the taking of a cat without the owner's consent is not an indictable offence. Since this extraordinary decision was rendered cat-owners with pussy-baskets have been seen leaving Baltimore on every train. Cats themselves, however, have as yet entered no objection to the decree, arguing doubtless that it stands to reason if a man steals you he wants you pretty badly and is therefore likely to give you more liver, fish, and other delectables than the man with whom you were living before.

In Georgia it is held to be libellous to say that a young lady said that her mama acted like a cat. Edgar Saltus has

[11] John H. Ingham: " The Law of Animals."
[12] Gertrude B. Rolfe: " The Cat in Law "; " North American Review "; Vol. 160, p. 251.

written variations on a similar theme in his story, " The Top of the Heap." [13]

It is not an uncommon occurrence for cats to be left property by will. I shall presently discuss the case of Mademoiselle Dupuy. Lord Chesterfield left life pensions to his cats and their offspring. This sounds eternal. Others have done this. In fact every few months you may read of such a will in the public prints. It is the custom of relatives in such cases to attempt to break the wills, and in most instances they have been successful. But there is at least one case in which a notable cat charity has been preserved through several centuries. About 658 of the Hegira (A.D. 1280) the Sultan, El-Daher-Beybars, having a particular affection for cats, at his death bequeathed a garden known as Gheyt-el-Qouttah (the cat's orchard), situated near his mosque outside Cairo, for the support of needy cats. This garden has been sold and resold, but until at least a comparatively recent date and probably up to the present moment, the owner still continues to carry out the terms of the will. At the hour of afternoon prayer a daily distribution of refuse from the butchers' stalls is made to the cats of the neighbourhood. " At the usual hour, all the terraces in the vicinity of the Mehkémeh (outer court) are crowded with cats; they come jumping from house to house across the narrow streets of Cairo, in haste to secure their share; they slide down the walls, and glide into the court, where, with astonishing tenacity and much growling, they dispute the scanty morsels of a meal sadly out of proportion to the number of guests. The old hands clear the food off in a moment; the youngsters and the new-comers, too timid to fight for their chance, are reduced to the humble expedient of licking the ground." [14]

There are other ways in which cats figure in the law. Marine insurance does not cover damage done to cargo by the depredations of rats, but if the owner of the damaged

[13] " Purple and Fine Women."   [14] M. Prisse d'Avennes.

The Cat and the Law

goods can prove that the ship was sent to sea without a cat he can recover damages from the shipmaster. Again, according to English law, a ship found at sea with no living creature on board is considered a derelict and is forfeited to the Admiralty, the finders, or the King, but it has often happened that, from its hatred of facing the waves, a cat remaining on board has saved the vessel from being condemned.

Periodically letters and editorials appear in the American newspapers concerning the advisability of licensing cats or in some way depriving them of their power of increasing, or restraining their actions. In the bird journals hysterical gentlemen moan loudly over the destruction of feathered songsters and demand that strong measures be taken as preventatives. I am not at all sure that laws have not been passed in certain states limiting the freedom of puss.

Nevertheless the cat preserves his liberty. As the learned judge of Fontainebleau remarked, you cannot restrain a cat without changing his nature; he might have added that you cannot change his nature. A cat will preserve his independence at any cost, even that of his life. Recently an adventurous tom climbed the switchboard of the lighting works of Cardiff, became entangled in the wires, and plunged the city in darkness. The effort cost him his life but he accomplished his purpose. Therefore senators and representatives, who find no difficulty in fettering human-kind in a hundred ways, go very slowly in formulating laws regarding the cat. They know perfectly well that the cat will refuse to obey these laws. It is amusing and delightful to observe this little animal escaping the onerous obligations of these United States, where a dog can only walk abroad on a chain with his jaw bandaged and a man is not permitted to raise a cup to his lips unless it contain lemonade or water, or to set pen to paper unless he scratches hieroglyphics that can be read without a blush by nasty-minded old gentlemen on the lookout for obscenity.

Chapter Seven: The Cat in the Theatre

Actors, playwrights, singers in opera, managers of theatres, and stage-hands have as many superstitions as Italian peasants. I have known of a tenor who, because of the presence of a rival tenor in a stage box, would not go before the footlights in his great rôle of Tannhäuser until he had performed a ludicrous and scatologic rite. An admirer once sent a handsome and expensive peacock-feather fan to Madame Modjeska. Now birds in general and peacock-feathers in particular are considered more portentous omens in the theatre than the simultaneous breaking of a mirror, sitting at table with thirteen, and facing the evil eye in any other plane of worldly existence. The gift arrived just prior to a performance of *Macbeth* and the Polish actress refused to allow the curtain to ascend until the noble count, her husband, had with his own hands consigned the offending object to the flames of the theatre furnace. These are bad luck signs. Curiously, and perversely enough, the cat, who elsewhere often signifies the most dread disaster, is a harbinger of prosperity in the theatre. A black cat is preferred; indeed, the mere presence of a black cat is sufficient to insure the success of any playhouse or any play. However a cat of another colour will do. This superstition is so wide-spread that every theatre from the Comédie Française to the People's Theatre on the New York Bowery entertains a cat, feeding her lavishly, and treating her with a respect and consideration which she seldom receives elsewhere save in the homes of cat-lovers. I myself have known a stage carpenter in the Apollo Theatre at Atlantic City to go to the butcher and spend his own money for fresh

The Cat in the Theatre

liver with which he returned to feed the cat before he went off to his own dinner. The Cécile Sorels, the Maggie Clines, the Kay Laurels, who pass the portals of the stage-door, regard themselves as fortunate if the cat so much as looks at them when they come in. If the pampered feline goes so far as to condescend a caress, rubbing herself against an actor's leg, that actor may be practically certain that David Belasco will send for him in the morning to sign a life-contract. Thus a kitten which playfully attached itself to the trailing skirt of Florence Reed's dress during a rehearsal of *Seven Days* is said to have been responsible for the subsequent success of that happy farce and the call-boy himself could have told you that Florence Reed would later become a star. After J. H. Mapleson had secured the lease of Her Majesty's Theatre in London, he passed through the door of the Opera with but £2 in his pocket, his sole balance, but, he tells us in his " Memoirs," he was assured that there was no occasion for despair when the " celebrated black cat of the theatre " rubbed herself in the most friendly way against his knees. It was the custom of Augustin Daly, after his work was done, to wait near the gallery entrance of his theatre on Thirtieth Street for a Broadway car. One night in a snow-storm a poor kitten begged his attention with a wavering mew. He picked her up and carried her back to the theatre, where she grew into cathood. At the first New York performance of Henry Irving in *Faust* the theatre cat wandered out on the open stage during the first scene; undisturbed by the thunder and lightning, from the vantage point of a canvas rock, she regarded the action with dignity and decorum. Irving afterwards remarked that he had regarded the incident as a lucky omen.

Naturally the presence of cats in theatres is frequently responsible for accidents. Puss, who is at home where she is at home, has a habit of strolling abstractedly across the stage at embarrassing moments. Sometimes she will sit through a scene, staring critically at the actors, to the vast diversion of the customers, for the presence of a cat on the stage, despite the contradictory evidence of the Irving episode, will usually excite mirth in an audience, no matter what may be the predominant mood of the play. It has therefore become a general custom to appoint a deputy whose duty it is to lock puss up before the play begins. But this is not always practicable; sometimes, too, the squire may forget to carry out his instructions. There are certain theatre cats who make it a matter of honour never to cross the stage in front of the back drop when the curtain is up and who even teach their kittens, with sundry cuffs and explanatory mews, to observe this rule. Nevertheless unexpected and unwelcome appearances of cats on the scene are not infrequent. Charles Santley, in " Student and Singer," tells how a cat almost caused the failure of *The Flying Dutchman* at its first performance in London. Santley, as Vanderdecken, had just finished his opening scene and had leaned back against a rock while he waited for Daland to make his entrance, when he heard some one behind him hiss, " Ts! Ts! " Looking out of the corner of his eye he made out that a cat was stealthily crossing the stage. Instead of letting her go on one of the men in the boat was foolishly attempting to send her back, not a very easy thing to get a cat to do under any circumstances. Being very tame and knowing all the people in the theatre she stopped to see who was calling her. " I was in dread," writes Santley, " for I knew that if the public saw her she would attract all their attention and the rest of the act would go for nothing. To my great joy the cat did not recognize the boatman, so went quietly off." Rossini told Madame Marchesi that the climax of the terrible fiasco of *The Barber of Seville* at the initial performance was the unexpected appearance of a cat on the stage which turned the already booing and hissing audience into a howling mob of mirth and necessitated the ringing down of the curtain. This incident reminds me that rude spectators sometimes express their displeasure by means of cat-calls. In the eighteenth century the cat-call was a small circular whistle, composed of two plates of tin with a hole in the centre, but more lately the small boy has learned to produce the hideous screech by placing two fingers in his mouth and whistling. The boy who has lost two front teeth is said to be better prepared by nature for making this noise. There have been occasions on which dead cats have been hurled at actors. Huckleberry Finn informs us that sixty-four dead cats were carried to the third performance of *The Royal Nonesuch* which, it will be remembered, was never given.

But now and again puss has unexpectedly been a factor in the success of a play. Just before the curtain fell on the first act of a comedy at Wallack's Theatre in New York the theatre cat walked slowly across the stage, set as a drawing-room, seated himself before the fireplace, and proceeded to wash himself. This realistic touch was very delightful and if David Belasco was in front he doubtless writhed in agonized envy that he had not introduced it into some play of his own. When the leading man and the leading woman appeared before the curtain there were calls for the cat, and the biggest round of applause greeted Tom when he came out in the actress's arms. The producer decided on the spot that the cat should become a permanent actor, but when he was called to rehearsal the next morning the results were not very satisfactory. He refused, indeed, to be made a party to any such nonsense. It was the property-boy who hit on the solution: " No cat ain't damn fool enough to let itself be trained to do extra work. Lookin' after rats and mice is Peter's job and we got to make him do the stunt along that line." Accordingly the boy held a live mouse by a cord tantalizingly near a hole in the fireplace and puss waited breathlessly each night until the end of the act when the mouse was released. On one occasion the mouse made an earlier escape and the

curtain came down with the leading woman screaming from
a chair. The account of a similar incident I owe to Channing Pollock: " On the first night of *The Little Gray Lady* in
New York I sat in the gallery and watched my play slowly fail.
Not a single laugh during the whole first act! I have never
seen a piece go so badly; it was flat, dead, and I prepared for
the funeral. The scene of the second act was a backyard,
with a fence, an alley, and an ashcan. At a certain point in
the action, chosen it would seem with meticulous precision,
the theatre cat bounded over the top of the fence, jumped
down into the ashcan and, finding it empty, jumped out again
and walked down the alley off the stage. The house howled
and roared with laughter and broke into applause; the audience, indeed, had now been warmed into an appreciative mood
and thereafter followed the progress of the play with enthusiasm. In the following performances, by the clever ruse
of laying a trail of chopped meat along the proper route and
releasing the cat at the proper moment, we were enabled to
repeat this happy accident."

This kind of acting a cat is not unwilling to perform, but
he has been called upon to do much more on the stage. Now
at home he is a natural actor. The play of the kitten, the
diversions of the grownup puss are invariably partly directed
to a human audience. Indeed a feline who lives on amicable
terms with men and women sleeps most of the time his friends
are away. Canon Liddon's famous cat loved to distract his
distinguished prelate friend. He would jump upon a bust of
Dr. Busby which stood on a bracket near the door, and
balancing himself " for one instant upon that severe and rev-
erent brow, would take a flying leap to the mantelpiece and
returning, would land with exquisite and unvarying accuracy
on the bust, repeating this performance as often as his master
desired. Liddon's great amusement was to stand with his
back to the bracket, and fling a biscuit at Dr. Busby's head,
the cat catching it dexterously, and without losing his pre-

carious foothold."[1] Wordsworth, in his description of a kitten at play, quite mistakes the nature of the artful little ball of fur when he asks:

> *What would little Tabby care*
> *For the plaudits of the crowd?*

For what else would she care, indeed? But, away from home, or constrained, the cat has a natural timidity, a natural dignity, and a feeling which amounts to an absolute aversion for the performance of silly antics which other animals, such as seals and dogs, seem to enjoy, and which elephants can be taught to execute with facility if not with desire. The showman's task becomes a heavier one because of the feline character. Animals who appear in the theatre or the circus are usually trained by being beaten or threatened with red-hot irons. In other words it is through their sense of fear that their co-operation is gained. But such tactics will be of no assistance to any one who wishes to train cats. A terrified cat will shrink and tremble but he will not jump through hoops. A cat who has been beaten will not creep up to lick the mountebank's hand.

Nevertheless a man who has won a cat's confidence can, with patience and interminable perseverance, accomplish a good deal in this direction. The easiest method is to prolong or exaggerate natural characteristics. If a cat has a natural habit of sitting on his haunches and waving his paws in the air, it is a comparatively easy matter to teach him to do this upon demand. Feathers will lie for whole minutes perfectly still on her back in the palms of my hands with one paw, perhaps, pasted to my nose, but she will often refuse to be held in any ordinary way. It is very simple, of course, to teach a cat to live at peace with animals which usually form his prey and a collection of this kind in a cage impresses a simple public. Harrison Weir describes one such family which a showman

[1] Agnes Repplier: "The Fireside Sphinx."

175

exhibited in which starlings sat on puss's head and blackbirds on his back while rabbits, white mice, rats and other such beasties thrived in the cage. The animals seemed contented and happy. At another London street corner Mr. Weir met a man who had trained cats and birds: " The man takes a canary, opens the cat's mouth, puts it in, takes it out, *makes* the cat, or cats, go up a short ladder and down another; then they are *told* to fight, and placed in front of each other; but fight they will not with their forepaws, so the *master* moves their paws for them, *each looking away* from the other." Mr. Weir witnessed other performances at the Royal Aquarium, Westminster: " On each side of the stage there were cat kennels, from which the cats made their appearance on a given signal, ran across, on or over whatever was placed between, and disappeared quickly into the opposite kennels. But about it all there was a decided air of *timidity,* and an eagerness to *get the performance over.* When the cats came out they were caressed and encouraged, which seemed to have a soothing effect, and I have a strong apprehension that they received some dainty morsel when they reached their destination." Other feats followed and the entertainment closed with an exhibition of tightrope walking in which the cats walked a rope on which white rats had been placed at intervals, without injuring the rodents. " A repetition of this feat was rendered a little more difficult by substituting for rats, which sat pretty quietly in one place, several white mice and small birds, which were more restless, and kept changing their positions. The cats re-crossed the rope, and passed over all these obstacles without even noticing the impediments in their way, with one or two exceptions, when they stopped, and cossetted one or more of the white rats, two of which rode triumphantly on the back of a large black cat." Miss Winslow [2] gives some account of Herr Techow's performing felines, who walk on their front feet, jump through hoops of fire,

[2] " Concerning Cats," p. 232.

JAPANESE WOMEN AND CAT

From a Japanese print by Utamaro in the collection of Arthur Davison Ficke

THE CAT AND THE BALL OF THREAD

From a drawing by Steinlen in Des Chats

LA MORT DE COCHON, TRAGEDIE

From an engraving in Moncrif's Les Chats

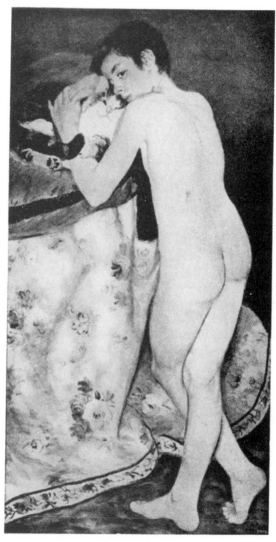

LE GARÇON AU CHAT

From the painting by Pierre Auguste Renoir

BORIS ANISFELD'S PORTRAIT OF HIS DAUGHTER, MORELLA BORISOVNA,
AND HER CAT

BANJO

From the painting by Henriette Ronner

THE ENTRANCE OF THE RESPECTABLE PUFF

From a drawing by Grandville in Vie privée et publique des animaux

COVER DESIGN FOR STEINLEN'S DES CHATS

The Cat in the Theatre

and perform other unnatural acts to the great edification of vaudeville audiences. Herr Techow told Miss Winslow that high-strung, nervous cats have the best minds but that it is difficult to keep them interested in their work. " A vagrant cat," he continued, " is the easiest to teach, the quickest to learn. Just as a street gamin gets his wits sharpened by his vagrant life, the stray, half-starved cat, forced to defend himself from foes and to snatch his living where he can, has his perceptive faculties quickened and his brain-cells enlarged. I cannot teach a kitten. I take them from a year to two or three years old, and train them three years longer before it is safe to put them on the stage with confidence in their performing the tricks they may have mastered."

Performing cats, however, are seldom to be seen in circuses or vaudeville. They are most difficult to train, not because they are stupid but because they are too intelligent to be interested in such nonsense. A cat is never vulgar and this sort of thing undoubtedly strikes a cat as vulgar. As the cat will willingly die to preserve his independence he cannot, even when he has seemingly made the compromise with the showman, be depended upon to carry out instructions. Bearing on this point Miss Repplier [3] tells a particularly significant story of a cat she saw with a troupe of performing animals at the Folies-Bergère in Paris:

" Her fellow actors, poodles, and monkeys, played their parts with relish and a sense of fun. The cat, a thing apart, condescended to leap twice through a hoop, and to balance herself very prettily on a large rubber ball. She then retired to the top of a ladder, made a deft and modest toilet, and composed herself for slumber. Twice the trainer spoke to her persuasively, but she paid no heed, and evinced no further interest in him, nor in his entertainment. Her time for condescension was past.

" The next day I commented on the cat's behaviour to

[3] " The Grocer's Cat " in " Americans and Others."

some friends who had also been to the Folies-Bergère on different nights. ' But,' said the first friend, ' the evening I went, that cat did wonderful things; came down the ladder on her ball, played the fiddle, and stood on her head.' " ' Really,' said the second friend. ' Well the night *I* went she did nothing at all except cuff one of the monkeys that annoyed her. She just sat on the ladder and watched the performance. I presumed she was there by way of decoration.' " [4]

Cats have repeatedly been drawn into cinematograph representations with success, however. I remember an elaborate film which began with a cat killing a bird, not a very difficult thing to get a cat to do, and I have seen lovely white Persians, and delightfully amusing alley cats, frisk on and off the screen in this picture and that. Adolf Bolm has told me of an electrical drama entirely performed by a cat, a bear, and a fish.

Occasionally a playwright has asked an actress to carry a cat, as dogs are often carried, on the stage. Avery Hopwood wanted his Countess with a cat to meet his Sadie Love with a dog. But an attempt or two at rehearsals decided him that the project had best be abandoned. The theme of Eugene Walter's play, *The Assassin,* was inherited blood-lust, and the audience learned that the girl-heroine was affected with the taint when she killed her pet kitten at the end of the second act. The murder was accomplished off stage and was indicated by the screams of the girl, like the crucifixion in *Aphrodite,* but in order to establish the idea of the kitten in the minds of the audience it was considered necessary to keep her on the stage during the whole act. The very youngest of kittens was secured for the purpose but even so it was no easy matter to hold her and Fania Marinoff, to

[4] It is perhaps easier for a cat to train a man than for a man to train a cat. A cat who desires to live with human beings makes it his business to see that the so-called superior race behaves in the proper manner towards him.

The Cat in the Theatre

whom the task fell, found it expedient to cut puss's claws before many rehearsals had taken place. The kitten was thoroughly jolly, good-natured, and happy on trains and in hotels, even in the dressing-room, but once the curtain had risen she was transformed into an animated fiend, whose one idea was escape. She struggled and often yowled and holding the kitten became as firmly fixed in Miss Marinoff's mind as any of her lines. At the end of Lady Gregory's play, *The Deliverer*,[5] the King's Nurseling is thrown to the King's cats:

A loud mewing and screaming is heard.
Dan's wife: What is that screeching?
Malachi's wife: It is the King's cats calling for their food.
Ard: Shove him over the steps to them.
Malachi: Will you throw him to the King's cats?
Dan's wife: A good thought. No one will recognize him. They'll have the face ate off him ere morning.
Ard's wife: Throw him to the King's cats!
They screech again. Their shadow is seen on the steps. The King's Nurseling is dragged into darkness. A louder screech is heard.[6]

Another stage cat is that in Chester Bailey Fernald's one-act play, *The Cat and the Cherub*, which is not to be confused with the story with the same title. One-Two is a delightful character in the story, but in the play the cat becomes scarcely more than a name.

There are occasions on which playwrights call upon actors to impersonate cats; the most notable example of this sort of drama is probably *The Blue Bird*. Maeterlinck, of course, is exclusively a dog-lover and the Cat does not come off very

[5] "Irish Folk-History Plays," Second Series.
[6] There is an historical precedent for this scene. A certain King of Persia, having devastated Egypt and profaned the temples, committed the final outrage in killing the sacred bull, Apis. The Egyptians were revenged; they hacked his body to pieces, and fed the morsels to the sacred cats!

well; nor is his portrait cleverly drawn. The Cat is represented as fawning on his human friends to gain his own ends, but do cats ever fawn? None that I have known do. On the other hand Hinze the Tom Cat in Ludwig Tieck's *Der gestiefelte Kater* is one of the most delightful and sympathetic cats to be found in all literature. This cat, almost white with a few black spots, is the wisest and wittiest personage in the comedy, which purports to be a dramatic version of Puss in Boots. The piece is a mad fantastic satire on the German people, the German government, and even the play form itself. In Thomas Middleton's *The Witch,* Hecate's cat plays a considerable part in the incantation scenes. In his ballet, *The Sleeping Beauty,* Tschaikovsky introduces a short dance between two cats in a scenic episode in which other heroes and heroines of the Perrault tales appear. Here, to the accompaniment of spits and meows in the orchestra, Puss in Boots has an entirely apocryphal encounter with the White Cat. The mood of this *divertissement* is humorous and Adolf Bolm has told me that it is one of the most delightful scenes in the ballet when danced at Petrograd. When Anna Pavlowa presented a version of this work at the New York Hippodrome several seasons ago I think this *pas de deux* was omitted. How many pantomimes have been constructed on the subject of cats I cannot even begin to conjecture. J. R. Planché wrote one, I know, on the theme of the White Cat, and Dick Whittington and Puss in Boots must have been figured as frequently in the London Christmas lists as any other folk or fairy story heroes.[7]

At the height of her rivalry with Taglioni, Fanny Elssler danced in a ballet called *La Chatte Métamorphosée en Femme,*

---

[7] It is interesting to know that Bernard Shaw's extravagant farce, *Passion, Poison, and Petrifaction,* was suggested by a story told by the author to the children of William Archer about a cat who by mistake lapped up a saucer of plaster of Paris instead of milk, and thereupon became petrified and was used to prop up a door!

The Cat in the Theatre

drawn by Coralli and Duveyrier from a *vaudeville* of the same title by Scribe and Melesville; the music was composed by a young winner of the *prix de Rome,* a forgotten Apollo named Montfort. There was much preliminary booming of this ballet; it was announced that, as the action passed in China, the costumes would be copied from authentic Canton models and the following paragraph went the round of the Paris journals: "Until recently, it is said, Mlle. Fanny Elssler had an unconquerable aversion for cats. Each of us has his *bête noire;* well, the *bête noire* of Fanny Elssler was a cat, even a white cat. The sight of a cat made her tremble, the mewing of a cat made her dash away on the points of her toes. But the love of art is like all love : it knows the way to triumph over fear; it knows how to vanquish the most sincere repugnances; and through devotion to her art, to give truth to her impersonation, Mlle. Elssler has had the courage to buy a little white cat, which is always with her. The perfidious animal is always by her side; and her beautiful enemy, forgetting her hate, asks inspiration of the feline, studies her graceful poses,[8] her light movements, her undulating walk, and even her defiant glare and immobile stare; sometimes she still trembles, if by chance her hand encounters the white ermine-like fur; the woman remembers her infantile terrors, and her vanquished repugnance reawakens for a moment; but the artist recalls herself to her rôle, rids herself of her weakness, draws the pretty cat towards her and bravely caresses it. The repellent animal disappears from her eyes; she sees only

[8] Rouvière, the actor, writes Champfleury, was truly feline by nature, and was haunted by a desire to represent his sensations by the brush. He fell in with Carlin, the harlequin of the Italian stage, who lived surrounded by cats, whose "pupil" he declared himself to be. A picture by Rouvière explains certain movements of that actor, who was remarkable for his quick, strange, and caressing gestures in *Hamlet.* . . . Thus might be explained certain exceptional faculties of Rouvière's, which, even after his death, might serve an instructive purpose. Those faculties were drawn from the living sources of nature, for it may be said that the contemplation of a cat is as valuable to an actor as a course at the Conservatoire.

her model; she dreams of the success she will owe to it; she hears the public applaud her and she realizes that her effort will be rewarded." [9]

The ballet was not a great success. The *vaudeville* of Scribe had been stupidly adapted and the music was uninteresting. But Fanny's performance was considered extraordinary. She played the rôle of a young Chinese Princess, in love with a student, who in turn adored his cat,

> *L'éclat d'une langue vermeille*
> *Sur deux lèvres en velours noir.*

The young man was made to believe that by means of a magic cap he could change his beloved puss into a woman. He consented to the metamorphosis and the Princess took the place of the animal. She adopted the habits of cats,[10] exaggerated their faults in order to make the young man an ailurophobe. She lapped milk from a bowl, made war on birds, played him a thousand tricks until the student was ready to take the Princess and let the cat go. All this, we learn, was carried through with astonishing effect by Fanny Elssler, who had really studied the manner of cats, captured their subtle walk, copied their gestures, their soft paw-blows, their fashion of

[9] This priceless example of 1837 puffery, so like the efforts of many present day press agents, I take from Auguste Ehrhard's charming book, "Fanny Elssler."

[10] In the "Century Magazine" for April 1891, Allan McLane Hamilton published a story called "Herr von Striempfell's Experiment," in which a scientist transplanted the brain of a cat into that of a beautiful, sensible, and dignified woman who, after her convalescence, underwent a remarkable change, acquiring feline characteristics of a familiar kind. At a formal dinner one evening she dived from her chair into the corner and caught a mouse between her teeth! Finally she died slowly and with the greatest difficulty, bearing out the nine lives superstition. In his "Recollections of an Alienist" (1916), Dr. Hamilton remarks (p. 232): "Many years ago I wrote . . . a short tale . . . which by some people was taken in dead earnest. . . . Strange to say this led to serious experimentation and I have heard of occasions when the brain grafting was actually tried with apparent success, but let us hope with no transfer of objectionable peculiarities."

stretching themselves. " The suppleness," said a writer in the " Courrier des Théâtres," " the elegant softness, the velvet agility, the spiritual vivacity, the comic expression, full of taste and charm, employed by Mlle. Fanny captivated the spectators until they believed that they had witnessed a play, whereas they had only seen a ravishing actress." [11]

I have already spoken of Mademoiselle Deshoulières's tragedy to be enacted by her mother's cat and her lovers. Moncrif has inserted in his book a quaint engraving of a fantastic performance of this piece. Mimy, Grisette, Marmuse, and Cafar in costumes of the Louis XIV epoch stalk the rooftops on their hind legs, while common cats, clothed only in fur, sedately watch the performance from various points of vantage. Cupid with his bow presides over this charming scene.

This perhaps was the last play written entirely for cats until Colette Willy's *Sept Dialogues de Bêtes* appeared in the early twentieth century, over two hundred years later.[12] And, of course, Madame Willy's work is not devoted entirely to cats! No one has written about animals with more sympathetic understanding than Colette. Pierre Loti is a careful and sensitive observer but he writes about cats objectively. Colette treats them subjectively, tries to put herself under their skins, makes them, indeed, speak for themselves. This method, of course, has obvious difficulties, the main one

[11] In Ward McAllister's " Society As I Have Found It," in the description of the ball given in honour of Lady Mandeville's visit to New York, the author writes (p. 354) : " The most remarkable costume, and one spoken of to this day, was that of a cat; the dress being of cats' tails, and white cats' heads and a bell with ' Puss ' on it in large letters."

[12] H. C. Bunner wrote a child's operetta called " Three Little Kittens of the Land of Pie," but although it is founded on the familiar nursery rhyme of the " three little kittens who lost their mittens," and although all the characters are cats, King Thomas the First, Head of the House of Grimalkin, Ringtail, Kitcat, Prince Tortoiseshell of Caterwaulia, Prince Spot of Bacquephensia, Prince Velvet of Miaouwa, Princesses Kitty, Malta, and Angora, there is not a line of the dialogue or the lyrics which suggests cat psychology or is even intended to.

being the avoidance of sentimentality, but any one who reads this book, and both lovers of cats and dogs will enjoy it, will see how well she has succeeded. These dialogues, in the form of a series of short one-act plays, between a cat, Kiki-la-Doucette, and a dog, Toby-Chien, although dated 1905, in psychological content are similar to certain phases of the modern Russian drama. Often, instead of conversing, each animal proceeds to relate his own thoughts, to think aloud. These thoughts are natural, but significant, and, of course, amusing. The book was written, indeed, "*pour amuser Willy.*" Occasionally He and She, the human companions of the animals, appear, but as subordinate figures and they are always seen from the point of view of the cat and the dog. The result is something very fine, something very near finished art.

In the opening dialogue Kiki explains her position quite neatly: "Neither the Two-footed Ones, nor you, comprehend the egoism of cats. . . . They christen thus, higglety-pigglety, the instinct of self-preservation, the chaste reserve, the dignity, the fatiguing self-denial, which comes to us from the impossibility of being understood by them. Dog of little distinction, but devoid of favouritism, do you understand me better? The cat is a guest and not a plaything. Truly I do not know in what times we live! The Two-footed Ones, He and She, have they alone the right to be sad, to be gay, to lick the plates, to complain, to be capricious? I too have *my* caprices, *my* griefs, *my* irregular appetites, *my* hours of dreamy retreat in which I withdraw from the world. . . ." There, indeed, is the whole psychology of the cat in a single speech. A little later, when the dog asks her if she has not a secret understanding with Him, she reveals a little more of her soul: "An understanding . . . yes. Secret and chaste and profound. He rarely speaks, and scratches the paper with a sound like the scratching of mice. It is to Him that I have given my avaricious heart, my precious Cat heart. And He, without words, has given me His. The exchange has made

184

me happy and reserved, and sometimes with that capricious and dominating instinct which makes us the rivals of women, I try my power on Him. For Him, when we are alone, the diabolical pointed ears which presage a bound on the paper which he scratches! For Him the tap-tap-tap of the tambourining paws through the pens and scattered letters. For Him, also, the persistent mewing which demands liberty, ' The Hymn to the Doorknob,' he smilingly observes, or ' The Plaint of the Sequestered.' But for Him also the tender contemplation of my inspiring eyes, which weigh on his bent head until he looks at me and there results a shock of souls so foreseen and so soft that I close my lids in exquisite shame. . . . She . . . moves too much, often bullies me, fans me in the air, holding my paws two by two, insists on caressing me, laughs at me, imitates my voice too well. . . ."

Toby-Chien complains that sometimes when they are playing together the cat treats him like a stranger. " Could not this be called a bad disposition? " he asks. " No," answers the cat, " a disposition only. A Cat's disposition. It is in such irritating moments that I feel, beyond doubt, the humiliating situation in which I and the rest of my race live. I can recall the time when hierophants in long tunics of linen spoke to us on bended knees, and listened timidly to our sung speech. Remember, Dog, that we have not changed. Perhaps there are days when my racial consciousness is more dominant, when everything justly offends me, a brusque gesture, a gross laugh, the sound of a door closing, your odour, your inconceivable audacity in touching me, in surrounding me with your circular bounds. . . ." There is much more of this delicately felt psychology; the effect of heat, cold, hunger, movement, a storm . . . even death, on the cat is discussed, all of this wrapped in a rather subtle French which does not lend itself very gracefully to translation.

In the last dialogue of all, there is an amusing and sudden descent to bedroom farce, a veritable Georges Feydeau comedy of ithyphallic manners, in which a visiting toy-dog is the protagonist. This little lady proves very attractive to Toby who is about to complete an easy seduction when the miniature one catching sight of the outraged Kiki sitting atop the piano and regarding the scene with a very natural horror, yelps, " A tiger, a tiger, help! " and rushes shrieking from the room. It may be remarked just here that the cat, although a passionate lover, is both modest and subtle. Dogs conduct their *amours* with little regard for public decency but a cat makes love at night in shady groves, sanctified by the natural odours of the warm earth, or in the hidden recesses of gabled roofs.

There is no dialogue in the book more characteristic, more delicious than the scene on the train. He and She are on their way to the country. Toby is loose in the compartment; Kiki, of course, has been carried in a basket. She is released at the dinner hour so that she may enjoy her chicken bone. But soon there is to be a change of cars; how is Kiki to be got back into the basket? He and She discuss this question until the cat, having completed an elaborate Roman after-dinner toilet, arches her back, spreads her claws in front of her, descends into the basket and sinks into mysterious slumber! This incident is a perfect example of the charming perversity of the cat.

Chapter Eight: The Cat in Music

Vous qui ne sauez pas ce vaut la musique,
Venez-vous en ouïr le concert manifique
Et les airs rauissants que iaprens aux Matous.
Puisque ma belle voix ren ces bestes docilles,
Je ne scaurois manquer de vous instruire tous
Ni de vous esclairsir les nottes difficiles.

In " The Question of our Speech," Mr. Henry James, who is usually precise and careful in his statements of fact, has permitted himself to say, " It is easier to overlook any question of speech than to trouble about it, but then it is also easier to snort or to neigh, to growl or to ' meow,' than to articulate and intonate." I do not know how difficult it may be to neigh or to growl or even to snort. I have never tried to make any of these sounds, but I have no confidence in my power to do so. About " meowing," however, I am not at all unenlightened and I could assure Mr. James, were he yet alive, that the vocalization of a cat is not so simple a matter as apparently he takes it to be. Felic, indeed, may be regarded as a language. Why should felines have voices and ears if they cannot speak? *"L'existence des organes,"* writes Voltaire *" entraine tout naturellement celle de leurs fonctions.*
. . . L'idée que les animaux ont tous les organes du sentiment pour ne point sentir est une contradiction ridicule." Pierquin de Gembloux expresses the theory that originally men and animals spoke a similar language. Men have expanded their mode of speech, while the animals retain their original tongues. " Between some sounds peculiar to certain animals and other sounds peculiar to the idioms of certain nations — dead or

The Tiger in the House

alive — there is very often evident a greater analogy, a more profound resemblance, a more indisputable affinity, than one really finds, three quarters of the time, between certain French words, for example, and their Latin progenitors." [1] Dupont de Nemours, a student of animals and their peculiarities, declared that while the dog used only vowel sounds, the cat in her language made use of at least six consonants, M, N, G, H, V, and F. It seems obvious to me that P, R, S, and T may be added as necessary purring and spitting consonants; the H is produced, of course, by the rapid expulsion of the breath following this very Magyar explosion of expletives, the cat's method of cursing.[2] I have never heard a cat use a V and I would like more information on this point. " Animals," writes the ingenious de Nemours, " have very few needs and desires. These needs are imperious and these desires strong. Their expression is therefore marked, but the ideas are not numerous and the dictionary short; the grammar more than simple, very few nouns, nearly twice as many adjectives, the verb nearly always taken for granted; some interjections which, as M. de Tracy has very well proved, are entire phrases in a single word: no other parts of discourse." Cats do not abuse the use of words as men do. They only use them for great moments, to express love, hunger, pain, pleasure, danger, etc. Naturally then their language is extremely poignant.

Whatever else it may be, and whether you like it or not, the cat language is musical; in her conversation, casual or passionate, pussy produces tone. As Firestone has it in Middleton's play, *The Witch,*

The cat sings a brave treble in her own language.

[1] " Idiomologie des Animaux, ou recherches historiques, anatomiques, physiologiques, philologiques, et glossologiques sur le langage des bêtes; " Paris; 1844.

[2] If anything else were needed to prove the superiority of cats, this would be the final touch. The cat is the only animal, save man, that knows how to swear, and in this department only a lumber-jack or a successful opera-singer can equal him.

188

The Cat in Music

Moncrif found her voice "*belle et grande*," but the ailuro-phobic Ronsard wrote,

Le chat cria d'un miauleux effroy.

Whatever else may be said of the cat's voice, no one can accuse this musician of plagiarism; her music is her own. Champfleury counted sixty-three notes in the mewing of cats, although he admitted that it took an accurate ear and a great deal of practice to distinguish them. On the other hand we have the testimony of the Abbé Galiani who could only discern twenty notes in the most elaborate mewing, but he found that these constituted a complete vocabulary, as no cat ever uses the same phrase except to express the same sentiment. Any one who has lived on friendly terms with a cat must be aware of the justness of this opinion; as Pierquin de Gembloux puts it, "*Chaque passion a sa note spéciale.*" Recall the trill-like purr ending in its chromatic upward run which accompanies amatory emotion in the female, the shrill cry of fright or anger, the wail of hunger, the polite but peremptory request to be let in or out, Willy's "Hymn to the Doorknob," the demand for water, which no adequate auditor will confuse with the demand for food, and the quiet purr of contentment, which, of course, is quite different from the kettle-drum purr of violent pleasure.[3] Any one who has lived on amicable terms with a cat will have no difficulty in understanding so much of her language; an interested observer may pick up much more.

[3] Charles Darwin in his "Expression of Emotions" writes: "Cats use their voices much as a means of expression, and they utter under various emotions and desires, at least six or seven different sounds. The purr of satisfaction which is made during both inspiration and expiration, is one of the most curious. The puma, cheetah, and ocelot likewise purr; but the tiger, when pleased, 'emits a peculiar short snuffle, accompanied by the closure of the eyelids.' It is said that the lion, jaguar, and leopard do not purr." Madame Michelet invented several words for different kinds of purring, in French called "*ronron*": *mourrons, monrons, mou-ous, mrrr:* "Les Chats," P. 25. She also invented a verb to express spitting (op. cit., P. XXVII).

Moncrif ("Les Chats," P. 55) quotes an extraordinary dialogue by M.

The Tiger in the House

For instance, my Feathers gives vent to what I call her " hunting cry " just before a leap at the window pane after a fly. This sound is sib to the faint creaking of a rusty hinge. The Abbé Galiani distinguished between the male and female voices, the tenor and soprano cats, and he also discovered that two sequestered pussies attended to their love-making in silence, which naturally led to the deduction that the long notes and growls of the alley fences and rooftops were calls to the foe, jealousies, bickerings, alarums and excursions, rather than amorous cries. What Pennant calls " a piteous, squalling, jarring lover " then is the jealous male about to dispose of a rival.

Others say that the gelded cat has a special cry of his own which gives him a place alongside the male sopranos of the eighteenth century. A cat, of course, cannot afford to make many concessions to man, but she finds it possible and convenient to understand the meaning of a few human words

Hauterot, which should be read aloud to make its complete effect. The scene is near the fireplace in the kitchen.

La Chatte, *voyant tourner la broche, et se débarbouillant:*
    Ç'a est bon.
Le Matou, *appercevant la Chatte, et s'approchant avec un air timide:*
    Ne fait-on rien céans?
La Chatte, *ne lui jettant qu'un demi regard:*
    Ohn.
Le Matou, *d'un ton passionné:*
    Ne fait-on rien céans?
La Chatte, *d'un ton de pudeur:*
    Oh que nenni.
Le Matou, *piqué:*
    Je m'en revas donc.
La Chatte, *se radoucissant:*
    Nenni.
Le Matou, *affectant de s'éloigner:*
    Je m'en revas donc.
La Chatte, *d'un air honteux:*
    Montez là-haut, *plus haut,* Montez là-haut.
Ensemble, *courant sur l'escalier:*
    Montons là-haut, Montons là-haut!

The Cat in Music

like " dinner and " meat." I can throw these words into the
middle of a sentence in conversation in any tone of voice and
Feathers will come bounding to the ice-chest where she knows
her meat is kept. " If you say ' Hallelujah ' to a cat, it will
excite no fixed set of fibres in connection with any other set and
the cat will exhibit none of the phenomena of consciousness,"
writes Samuel Butler. " But if you say ' M-e-e-at,' the cat
will be there in a moment, for the due connection between the
sets of fibres has been established."

The cat seldom suffers from aphonia but well-bred cats
make but few sounds. Occasionally to signify their intentions they open their mouths but do not speak. *Faute de*
mew, they resort to gestures, a matter which I have discussed
in a previous chapter.

A thousand years or so before Christ the Egyptians associated the cat with music, utilizing the graceful head and figure
of the beloved animal in the decoration of the sistra. The
sistrum consisted of a frame of bronze or brass, into which
three or four metal bars were loosely inserted, so as to produce a jingling noise when the instrument was shaken. Occasionally a few metal rings were strung on the bars to increase the sound and very often the top of the frame was
ornamented with the figure of a cat. The instrument was
used by women in performances of religious ceremonies and
its Egyptian name, Carl Engel [4] tells us, was *seshesh*. Moncrif offers readers of " Les Chats " several curious engravings of these sistra on which cats are carved in various charming attitudes. There is another engraving in this book of
a statue of the cat god holding the sistrum in such a manner
that he indicates that he knows how to use it. " Why does
this not prove a connection between instruments of music
and cats? " asks Moncrif. " The organization of cats is
musical; they are capable of giving many modulations to their

[4] " The Music of the Most Ancient Nations ": William Reeves; London.
The instrument is used by the ballet in the first act of *Aida*.

191

voices and in the different passions which occupy them they use diverse tones."

> *They no instrument use ever,*
>   *Each is his own flute and viol;*
> *All their noses trumpets are*
>   *Bellies, drums, and no denial.*
>
> *They in chorus raise their voices,*
>   *In one general intermezzo,*
> *Playing fugues, as if by Bach,*
>   *Or by Guido of Arezzo.*
>
> *Wild the symphonies they're singing,*
>   *Like capriccios of Beethoven*
> *Or by Berlioz, who's excelled*
>   *By their strains so interwoven.*[5]

The discovery of a fresco depicting a cat sitting calmly before a sistrum and a goblet led Moncrif into further dissertation which is worthy of reproduction if for nothing else than the stupendously enlightened theory of musical criticism which it introduces. This theory, exploited as it was in a "*gravement frivole*" book on cats, published in 1727, was probably not taken very seriously by Moncrif's contemporaries; there is no reason to believe, indeed, that it was taken very seriously by Moncrif himself, but it was to pop up again two hundred years later as one of the principal tenets of a certain school. The combination of cat, sistrum, and goblet, Moncrif takes as proof that cats were admitted to Egyptian banquets and that they frequently sang there.

> *Her purrs and mews so evenly kept time,*
> *She purred in metre and she mewed in rhyme.*[6]

[5] Heinrich Heine: "Mimi"; translated by Edgar Alfred Bowring.
[6] Joseph Green: "A Poet's Lamentation for the Loss of his Cat."

The Cat in Music

" Doubtless," writes the French savant, " the enemies of cats will insist that cats cannot sing, they can only caterwaul. We will content ourselves by retorting that what seems to be mewing in the cats of today proves nothing regarding the cats of antiquity, arts being subject to great revolutions; we add, with all possible discretion, that the dissonances of which these enemies complain, only indicate a lack of knowledge and taste on their part. . . . Modern music is limited to a certain division of sounds which we call tones and semitones and we ourselves are limited enough to believe that this same division is all that can be called music; therefore we have the injustice to exclude bellowing, mewing, whinneying sounds of which the intervals and relations, perhaps admirable of their kind, are beyond our understanding, because they go beyond the limits in which we are restrained. The Egyptians, no doubt, were more enlightened; they had really studied the music of animals; they knew that a sound could neither be true nor false, and that nearly always it appears to be either one or the other only because we have the habit of judging an assemblage of sounds immediately as harmony or dissonance; [7] they knew, for example, whether the cat used our scale or whether she availed herself of the tones between the half tones, which would make a prodigious difference between their music and ours; they appreciated in a chorus of toms or in a recitative, the simple or more perverted modulations, the lightness of the passages, the softness of the sounds or their piercing quality, from which, perhaps, they derived their pleasure. That this music seems to us a confused sound, a charivari, is only the effect of our ignorance, a lack of delicacy in our organs, of justice and discernment. The music of the peoples of Asia appears to us at least ridiculous. On their side they find no common sense in ours. We believe reciprocally to

[7] This phrase occurs almost word for word in Busoni's " A New Esthetic of Music "!

The Tiger in the House

hear only mewing; thus each nation, so to speak, is the cat
to the other!" [8]

Nearly a hundred years ago William Gardiner published a
curious book entitled "The Music of Nature" in which evidently it was his intention to prove that the sounds of art are
derived from the sounds of nature. The work is provided
with many tables of examples which Mr. Gardiner has taken
down in barnyard and forest, and two examples of cat cries
are given. These, however, are not very convincing as they
are necessarily expressed in the tempered scale. Any one
who has listened to a cat practising *vocalises* will have no

[8] Hiddigeigei, the Tom Cat, speaks similar words in Scheffel's "Der Trompeter von Säkkingen" (translation of Jessie Beck and Louise Lorimer); William
Blackwood and Sons; Edinburgh; 1893; P. 99):

None the less, 'tis ours to suffer
That when cat love finds expression
In the night, in sweetest numbers,
Men accord to us but scorning,
And they brand as ' caterwauling'
All our choicest compositions.
Yet, alas! 'tis ours to suffer
That these same contemptuous mortals
Call such sounds into existence
As I have been forced to hear.
Sounds like these are, surely garlands
Bound of briars, straw, and thistles,
Where the stinging nettle flaunteth.
And in view of yonder damsel,
Grasping yon abhorrent trumpet,
Can a man, with front unblushing,
Jeer when cats are making music?
Suffer, gallant heart within me,
Suffer! Times are surely coming
When the sapient human being
Will from us acquire the method
Of high feeling's right expression.
When the rude world, struggling upward
Toward the climax of all culture,
Will appreciate ' caterwauling.'
History, in the main, is righteous,
All injustice is atoned for.

194

doubt that Moncrif is quite correct in assuming that the animal makes use of smaller divisions than semitones.

So early as the sixteenth century we have a record of the cat appearing in a musical capacity in Europe, strangely enough, however, as part of an instrument and not as a voluntary vocal performer. When the King of Spain, Philip II, visited the Emperor, his father, at Brussels in 1549, among other festivities a singular procession was arranged in his honour. At its head marched an enormous bull, balancing a tiny devil between his horns, from which shot fireworks. Other quaint conceits were a youth sewed in a bear's skin seated on a prancing horse, the ears and tail of which had been cut, and the Archangel Saint Michael in gold and purple robes, holding the scales in his hands. But the most curious detail of this mad procession, and the one which awakened laughter in the usually melancholy prince, was a chariot on which a bear played the organ. In place of pipes twenty small boxes each held a cat; the protruding tails were bound to the keys of the clavier by cords so that it was only necessary to press one of these keys to produce an " infernal gallemaufry o' din." The naïve chronicler of this affair, Juan Christoval Calvete, adds that the felines were arranged in such a manner as to produce the succession of the notes of the scale, but this would have been impossible as no cat was ever limited to a monotone or by a semitone. The cat organ seems to have been comparatively common in the sixteenth and seventeenth centuries, and even as late as the eighteenth, for Weckerlin says that records have been found indicating the existence of the instrument at Saint-Germain in 1753 and at Prague in 1773. In " Musiciana " Weckerlin reproduces an old engraving of a cat organ. A gay rogue with one leg plays the instrument of torture while dogs, monkeys, asses, and cows form a choir. Champfleury found an old picture of the cat organ in Gaspard Schott's " Magia universalis " (1657) which he has reproduced in " Les Chats." And he describes Father Kircher's still more barbarous variation in which the touch of the keys drove pointed barbs into the cats at the bases of their tails. This almost reads like the experiments Professor Mantegazza describes so merrily in his " Fisiologia del Dolore."

In Champfleury's book you will also find a copy of a quaint eighteenth century woodcut of an animal tamer, carrying cats on his head and shoulders while on the table before him five cats play the viol, the bass, and the mandoline and still others appear to be singing " miaou," written on the sheets of music before them. At the top of this poster in large letters is written:

La Musique des Chats

and underneath, on a phylactery, " *Ceans lon prend pensionaires et le maistre va monstrer en ville.*" Other seventeenth century posters remain to prove that mountebanks gave concerts of cats at fairs. Valmont de Bomare [9] describes a booth at the Fair of Saint-Germain over which had been inscribed the single word, " *Miaulique.*" In the interior some cats sat on a table before a piece of music and at a signal given by a monkey they negotiated feline melodies and harmonies. The whole proceeding seems a perfect symbol for the *chef d'orchestre* and the *prime donne* at the opera. In 1758 an animal trainer named Bisset gave what he actually called a " Cats' Opera " in a hall near the Haymarket in London.

Other early engravings are more fantastic and less significant of cruelty. A common one shows us a dozen cats, Angoras, toms, blacks and whites, seated before a music desk on which the *Solfege* of Italy in oblong form lies open. The notes, however, are replaced by mice, their tails indicating the crotchets and quavers. Teniers drew a similar scene but added an owl as director and a monkey flute player. In An-

9 " Dictionnaire raisonné d'histoire naturelle "; Fourth Edition: 1800.

drew Lang's version of " The White Cat " [10] the Prince visits a luxurious apartment " upon the walls of which were painted the histories of Puss in Boots and a number of other famous cats. The table was laid for supper . . . when suddenly in came about a dozen cats, carrying guitars and rolls of music, who took their places at one end of the room, and under the direction of a cat who beat time with a roll of paper, began to mew in every imaginable key, and to draw their claws against the strings of the guitars, making the strangest kind of music that could be heard. The Prince hastily stopped up his ears; but even then the sight of these comical musicians sent him into fits of laughter." Even in nursery rhymes the cat has standing as a virtuoso. One of the most familiar speaks of " the cat and the fiddle." J. O. Halliwell [11] gives:

A cat came fiddling out of a barn,
With a pair of bagpipes under her arm.

This musical feat would have been beyond the powers of Mischa Elman or Efrem Zimbalist, but puss's vocal achievements seem to have been meagre:

She could sing nothing but " Fiddle cum fee,
The mouse has married the humble-bee."

With so many examples before them it does not seem unnatural that composers should have begun to imitate the sounds made by cats. Both in Germany and Italy, in the seventeenth century, there was produced a monstrous lot of burlesque imitative music: the cackling of hens all on one note, ending on a fifth above, the mewing of rival toms in nice chromatic order with a staccato, of course, by way of a spit were favourite pastimes of the severest German contrapuntists. Even the solemn Marcello has left two elaborate choruses, one for sopranos, the other for contraltos, who are

---

10 " The Blue Fairy Book."
11 " The Nursery Rhymes of England ": 1844.

asked to baa like sheep and mou like oxen. Frederick Niecks [12] gives us several examples in which the cat appeared. Adriano Banchieri, in his carnival farce in madrigal form (1608), has written a *" contrapunto bestiale alla mente "* (an improvised bestial counterpoint), where above the fundamental bass melody, a dog, a cuckoo, a cat, and an owl, barks (" babbau "), calls (" cuccu "), mews (" gnao "), and cries (" chiu "). . . . . Adam Krieger (1667) composed a four-part vocal fugue in which a characteristic chromatic subject is sung to " miau, miau." An instrumental example also dates from this period, the *Capriccio stravagante* (1627) by the Italian, Carlo Farina, court violinist at Dresden, with its imitations of the cackling of hens, barking of dogs, mewing of cats, etc. Examples of this kind of thing are to be found in folk-music too. Francesc Pujol's arrangement of a Catalan folk-song, *La Gata i en Belitre,* in which the male chorus imitates the mewing of cats, was recently (1920) performed by the Schola Cantorum in New York.

W. F. Apthorp says that when he was looking over the score of a new symphony (name not given) at rehearsal with Otto Dresel, the latter remarked, " Miaou! Miaou! we shall have to get another *mise en scène* for the concert; we ought to have a roof, with a ridgepole and some chimneys." So is poor pussy's voice held in disrepute. However there are examples of cat program music even in the nineteenth and twentieth centuries. There is, for instance, the spirited dialogue between Puss in Boots and the White Cat in the last act of Tschaikovsky's ballet, *The Sleeping Beauty,* in which the dancers simulate a lively scene between two cats and the orchestra imitates the sounds made by the animals including, of course, a realistic spit. G. Berthold's *Duet for Two Cats* seems to have enjoyed considerable popularity although I have never heard it sung. The single word, " miau " is vocalized by two singers to runs and scales which are sufficiently catlike

[12] Programme music.

to be amusing.   In 1917 Igor Stravinsky's *Berceuses du Chat* for a woman's voice and three clarinets were published. These are four short songs, on popular Russian texts, which have been translated into French by C. F. Ramuz.   The titles are *Sur le poêle, Intérieur, Dodo,* and *Ce qu'il a, le chat.*[13] They were evidently written by a lover of cats and they undoubtedly give one the *feeling* of cats but imitation in music is no specialty of Stravinsky and, except in the first song, in which one of the clarinets purrs, there is very little attempt made to transfer what Agnes Repplier describes as " the curious and complicated vocalism of the cat " into the range of art music.   They are strange, exotic, curious little sketches and on hearing Eva Gauthier sing them I was reminded of a passage in Algernon Blackwood's " Ancient Sorceries," [14] the passage in which Vezin listens to the invisible out-door orchestra in the enchanted town which he visits unwittingly: " He recognized nothing that they played, and it sounded as though they were simply improvising without a conductor. No definitely marked time ran through the pieces, which ended and began oddly after the fashion of wind through an Aeolian harp. . . . There was a certain queer sense of bewitchment in it all.   The music seemed to him oddly unartificial.   It made him think of trees swept by the wind, of night breezes singing among wires and chimney-stacks, or in the rigging of invisible ships; or — and the simile leaped up in his thoughts with a sudden sharpness of suggestion — a chorus of animals, of wild creatures, somewhere in desolate places of the world, crying and singing as animals will, to the moon.   He could fancy he heard the wailing, half-human cries of cats upon the tiles at night, rising and falling with weird intervals of sound, and this music, muffled by distance and the trees, made him think of a queer company of these creatures on some roof far

[13] Sung by Eva Gauthier at a concert at the Greenwich Village Theatre in New York, December 15, 1919.
[14] " John Silence."

away in the sky, uttering their solemn music to one another and the moon in chorus.

" It was, he felt at the time, a singular image to occur to him, yet it expressed his sensation pictorially better than anything else. The instruments played such impossibly odd intervals, and the crescendos and diminuendos were so very suggestive of cat-land on the tiles at night, rising swiftly, dropping without warning to deep notes again, and all in such strange confusion of discords and accords. But, at the same time a plaintive sweetness resulted on the whole, and the discords of these half-broken instruments were so singular that they did not distress his musical soul like fiddles out of tune."

One must not forget Mortimer Wilson's *Funeral of the Calico Cat*,[15] which, James Huneker avowed, " was quite tiny at the beginning of the music, but grew to monstrous proportions before its interment." There is also Edgar Stillman Kelley's *Cheshire Cat* from his *Alice in Wonderland* suite. Among Moussorgsky's *Children's Songs* you will find *The Brigand Cat*. Tom Dobson wrote a song called *The Cat* and one of the popular airs of *The Tenderfoot* concerned a tom. Another popular song of a couple of decades ago was *The Cat Came Back*. The *Me-ow* one-step, with its superb matou on the cover and its indications to the orchestra to sing the cat cries at appropriate intervals also comes to mind. It will be remembered that a rain of cats saved the day in *Hans, the Flute Player* and that a cat-o'-nine-tails plays a considerable part in " that infernal nonsense, *Pinafore*."

There have been musical cats. According to Louis Wain, the black cat of Saint Clement Danes Church in London was accustomed to climb up to the top of the organ pipes and enjoy an occasional concert alone. Perhaps a similar love for music caused the death of another puss who was found desiccated and recumbent in one of the long organ pipes of Westminster Abbey which had been out of tune for some time. John F.

---

[15] Played by the Philharmonic Society in New York; November 1918.

The Cat in Music

Runciman [16] writes: "Perhaps one reason musicians are fond of cats is that cats are extremely fond of music. But their taste generally requires a great deal of educating. I have known them even to like such songs as Mr. Galloway mentioned in the House recently — *The horse what missus dries the clothes on* and *The Boers got my daddy*. It is best to commence with a course of Bach's ' Forty-eight '— but it is necessary to close the top of the piano or you may find the instrument clogged with bits of meat, dead mice, corks, etc. The violin troubles them enormously — I believe they lose their sleep on its account, for they are always firmly convinced that it is the bow that sounds. The piano they can play by walking over the notes; but though they can knock a bow on the floor and shove it about nothing in the way of music comes of it. Mr. Balling once played the viola-alta at my house and the eyes of Felix Mendelssohn glistened with hope. The performance over the bow was duly experimented with. Alas! — no result; and Felix retired to a corner and sat there half an hour wrapt in melancholy thought." Heinrich Heine describes a similar performance on the part of his uncle's Angora, who dragged an old flute over the garret floor. An inhabitant of one of the western United States was a believer in the cat's love of music. He left all his property for the establishment of a feline infirmary. And in his will he provided that an accordion "be played in the auditorium by one of the regular nurses, to be selected for that purpose exclusively, the playing to be kept up for ever and ever, without cessation day and night, in order that the cats may have the privilege of always hearing and enjoying that instrument which is the nearest approach to the human voice." [17] Carmen Sylva desired to make her kitten, Püffchen, musical and held him, therefore, in a little fur bag in her lap whenever

[16] " My French Cats "; " Saturday Review "; London; April 2, 1904.

[17] Joseph Winthrop Moses: " Something about Cats "; " New Eclectic "; Baltimore; November 1870.

she played the piano, but Püffchen was intransigent and struggled to get away.[18] Gautier's silver-grey Angora, Zizi, was a melomaniac. Gautier describes her as listening to music with sleepy satisfaction and she would often go so far as to pick her way up and down the keys of the open pianoforte. Now my cat, Feathers, has a talent for piano playing. Sometimes she walks sedately from one end of the keyboard to the other, producing an exotic succession of tones; at other times she pounces on a group of keys, making sounds not unallied to those which Leo Ornstein evokes in *The Wild Men's Dance.* On these occasions she will leap wildly from treble to bass, tearing tone and melody to tatters, trying to paw the secret of the hidden pussy screams from the rosewood box. She has a particular penchant, after the manner of her race, for music at night and it is no rarety to awaken at 2 A. M. to hear Feathers attempting prodigious scales. There is at least one legend of a cat who furnished a composer with a theme in this fashion. One of Scarlatti's compositions bears the title, *The Cat's Fugue* (at least in modern editions) and the story goes that a stroll on the keyboard by Scarlatti's cat gave the master the subject to the fugue which is as follows:

The composition has always been popular with pianists and both Liszt, who often played it, and von Bülow have arranged editions of it. Bülow in his edition suggests that the droll suggestion of the title shall not be lost sight of during performance: " The first three measures present the mechanical promenade of the cat across the keyboard (the theme proper); the following ones exhibit the justificatory touch of the master-hand, thoughtfully arranging

[18] Carmen Sylva: " My Kittens "; " Century Magazine "; August 1908.

The Cat in Music

the first chaotic 'product of Nature.' The marks which I have added for the shading — an almost rough *forte* for the fore-phrase, and a sudden, tranquillizing *piano* for the after-phrase — will provide, I think, the simplest means for displaying this humorous contrast, a fairly consistent observance of which is to be recommended throughout." At the climax of the piece Bülow gives the following advice: "In the succeeding twenty-two measures, up to the *ff* (D minor) the cat must, so to speak, swell to a tiger — something like the poodle in Faust's study; i. e., in plain prose, there should be a continuous dramatic intensification in the effect." [19]

Sacchini, too, was beholden to cats. He could only compose, he assured his friends, when he was surrounded by them. Their presence inspired his gracious and seductive music. Weckerlin quotes the terms of the strange will of Mademoiselle Dupuy, a celebrated harpist who lived and died during the seventeenth century. She stipulated that no hunchbacks, cripples, or blind persons should be permitted to attend her funeral and she left her fortune to her cat. In Moncrif's "Les Chats" there is a delightful engraving showing the cat on the deathbed of his mistress while two attorneys are making out her testament. Mademoiselle Dupuy believed that she owed her skill as a musician to this cat, who sat beside her while she performed, manifesting pleasure or annoyance, accordingly as she played well or ill. Consequently she left him both a town and a country house with sufficient income to keep them up properly. Her relatives, however, succeeded in wresting this bequest away from the unfortunate feline, who probably was not even allowed to be present in court.

Some of the most amusing passages of Rimsky-Korsakoff's autobiography are devoted to Borodin and his ménage. The following paragraphs are descriptive of Borodin's cats: "Many cats, that the Borodins lodged, marched back and

---

[19] *The Cat's Fugue:* edited and fingered by Hans von Bülow; G. Schirmer; New York.

The Tiger in the House

forth on the table, thrusting their noses into the plates or leaping on the backs of the guests. These felines enjoyed the protection of Catherine Sergueïevna. They all had biographies. One was called Fisher because he was successful in catching fish through the holes in the frozen river. Another, known as Lelong, had the habit of bringing home kittens in his teeth which were added to the household. More than once, dining there, I have observed a cat walking along the table. When he reached my plate I drove him away; then Catherine Sergueïevna would defend him and recount his biography. Another installed himself on Borodin's shoulders and heated him mercilessly.

" ' Look here, sir, this is too much! ' cried Borodin, but the cat never moved." [20]

We learn from Heine that Meyerbeer hated cats and Old Fogy tells an apocryphal story of Brahms which is amusing enough to repeat here: " Brahms, so it is said, was an avowed enemy of the feline tribe. Unlike Scarlatti, who was passionately fond of chords of the diminished cats, the phlegmatic Johannes spent much time at the window, particularly of moonlit nights, practising counterpoint on the race of cats, the kind that infest backyards of dear old Vienna. Dr. Antonin Dvořák had made his beloved friend and master a present of a peculiar bow and arrow, which is used in Bohemia to slay sparrows. In and about Bohemia it is named in the native tongue, ' Slugj hym inye nech.' With this formidable weapon did the composer of orchestral cathedrals spend his leisure moments. Little wonder that Wagner became an anti-vivisectionist, for he, too, had been up in Brahms's backyard, but being near-sighted, usually missed his cat. Because of arduous practice Brahms always contrived to bring down his prey, and then — O diabolical device! — after spearing the poor brutes, he reeled them into his room after the manner of a trout

[20] N. A. Rimsky-Korsakoff: "Ma Vie Musicale"; Introduction et Adaptation par E. Halperine-Kaminsky; Pierre Lafitte; Paris; 1914; P. 73.

The Cat in Music

fisher. Then — so Wagner averred — he eagerly listened to the expiring groans of his victims and carefully jotted down in his note-book their antemortem remarks. Wagner declared that he worked up these piteous utterances into chamber music, but then Wagner had never liked Brahms. . . . " Baudelaire once said, " I love Wagner, but the music I prefer is that of a cat hung by its tail outside of a window, trying to stick to the panes of glass with its claws. There is an odd grating on the glass which I find at the same time strange, irritating, and singularly harmonious." Of course this was pure imaginative fiction on Baudelaire's part, who was too much attached to pussies to torture them.

Singers have usually been a little sensitive on the subject of cats, for the resemblances between a certain kind of singing and caterwauling are more than casual and in parody, burlesque, and even in criticism the soprano often finds herself side by side with the tom cat.

> *And loudest of all was heard a voice*
> *Which sounded languid and shrieking*
> *As Sontag's voice became at last,*
> *When utterly broken and squeaking.*[21]

A hundred years or so ago in London there lived a celebrated music hall performer who was called " Cat Harris " because he burlesqued the singers of the Italian Opera, imitating them in tones of the feline race. In Cassell's " Old and New London " I found the following : " When Foote first opened the Haymarket Theatre, amongst other projects he proposed to entertain the public with imitation of cat-music. For this purpose he engaged a man famous for his skill in mimicking the mewing of the cat. This person was called ' Cat Harris.' As he did not attend the rehearsal of this odd concert, Foote desired Shuter would endeavour to find him out and bring

[21] Heinrich Heine: "The Young Cats' Club for Poetry-Music"; translation by Edgar Alfred Bowring.

him with him. Shuter was directed to some court in the Minories, where this extraordinary musician lived; but, not being able to find the house, Shuter began a cat solo; upon this the other looked out of the window, and answered him with a cantata of the same sort. ' Come along,' said Shuter, ' I want no better information that you are the man. Foote stays for us; we cannot begin the cat-opera without you.' " W. T. Parke, forty years principal oboe player at Covent Garden Theatre, in his " Memoirs " tells us why Madame Catalani was almost the only great singer of the period with whom he was not acquainted. He had written a song for Miss Feron, which she sang at Vauxhall Gardens, called *The Romp, or the Great Catalani*. The song contained an imitation of Catalani in one of her airs and was intended as a compliment to the singer. However, in the recitative which introduced the air, ending with the words, " Great Catalani," it became necessary, in order to make the music accord with the poetry, to repeat a part of the name so that it read thus, " Great Cat, Great Catalani! " The result, we learn, roused Madame Catalani's ire.[22] But Jenny Lind as a child always sang to her cat, of whom she was inordinately fond. " Her favourite seat," her son is quoted as writing in Canon Scott Holland's book, " was in the window of the steward's room, which looked out on the lively street leading up to the church of St. Jacob. Here she sat and sang to the cat; and the people passing in the street used to hear and wonder." Whether Sophie Arnould cared for cats or not I do not know, but in a letter to Bélanger, dated August 2, 1801, she complains that she has not money left to keep one. We learn from J. H. Mapleson's " Memoirs " that Ilma de Murska travelled with a small menagerie, including an Angora cat which her monkey tried to kill on one occasion. Marie-Anne de Camargo kept white Angora cats with her dogs in her old age.

[22] Southey named a cat Madame Catalani; others must have done so as naturally as perfumers of today christen sweet odours after Mary Garden.

The Cat in Music

Marie Engle was fond of cats; so is Emmy Destinnova. Most singers, however, seem to prefer dogs, whose voices offer no basis for invidious comparison, and who do not object to a life of travel. There are, on the other hand, many instances recorded of cats who nursed an antipathy towards music and musicians. Pierquin de Gembloux, in his curious " Traité de la Folie des Animaux," asserts that he has known of cases in which a cat has been thrown into convulsions by the sound of singing. Some cats seem to have a sound taste in such matters, the aforementioned Mademoiselle Dupuy's cat, for example; Jenny Lind's cat, too, probably gave his mistress signs of his interest in proper tone production. Gautier's Madame Théophile, the same delightful puss who had the horrible experience with a talking parrot, was a musical amateur of taste and discretion. " Sitting on a pile of scores she listened attentively and with visible signs of pleasure to singers. But piercing notes made her nervous and at the high A she never failed to close the mouth of the singer with her soft paw. This was an experiment which it amused many to make and which never failed. It was impossible to deceive this cat dilettante on the note in question. . . ." In a letter to Samuel Butler, dated May 8, 1883, Miss Savage writes, " A lady at the Gallery was telling me about her cat; he is a most intelligent creature, and she recounted various instances of his sagacity, winding up with, ' and when I begin to play the piano, he always goes out of the room.' " . . . Eva Gauthier has told me of an experience she once had in Paris when she was singing *Der Erlkönig* in a friend's drawing-room. As she was singing the cries of the child, suddenly and entirely without warning, for she was unaware of the presence of any animal, a tiny Siamese kitten, a tawny taut ball, bounded from the next room and sprang at her throat into which he dug his claws. . . . In her charmingly personal book " Les Chats," to which I have referred so many times already, Madame

The Tiger in the House

Jules Michelet gives several examples of cats who were musical amateurs. The most interesting of these, perhaps, was Minette, who listened to her mistress singing old folk-songs of the province where she had lived as a child. "If I sang a simple air, spun out in a low voice, like a nurse's humming, she kept her place, raising her eyes dreamily to mine. But if the air was melancholy, if there were tears in my voice, she began to be agitated. Her obvious uneasiness, however, indicated a certain kind of pleasure. If the tone raised and mounted to that accent of acute grief which is precisely the tone of a violin, Minette gave signs of sickly excitement. The *Serenade* of Schubert, for example, imploring in its restrained passion, slow at first, sombre as a song of night; this prayer which, from the profound depths, rises to ardent supplication, and takes as witness the bird, its sighs, the emotional silence of Nature,— this supreme cry of a wounded heart succeeded in creating the greatest excitement in Minette. Never, I believe, did a woman's soul exhibit greater grief. She sat on my knees, her eyes fastened only to my lips. If I continued, she placed her two paws on my breast, relaxing herself in a nervous swoon. Her voice recalled that shivering mew which in the cat says so many things. Her eyes, in spite of the bright light, were dilated, as they are in a state of apprehension or suffering. If I still continued to mount higher, with a firm gesture, entirely human, she applied her two rigid paws to my mouth and sealed my lips." This little scene of Minette's may have been excusable. Madame Michelet herself admits that she was no musician; her singing of Schubert *lieder* may have been unendurably trying to a feline melomaniac.

Elsewhere in her book,[23] Madame Michelet educes the interesting theory that while cats are often painfully affected by sounds of nearby musical instruments, the faint tinkle of music in the distance often gives them a pleasurable sensation,

[23] "Les Chats," P. 30.

The Cat in Music

" inspires them with an amiable madness." Dining with some friends one night opposite the Café Turc, in which a ball was being given, she was astonished to see nine cats on the roof, directly over the dance hall, nine cats, grey, brown, and black in the soft light of the evening. These cats silently and gravely moved across the sky in some esoteric relation to the music. With arched backs, tails held high or lopped off, stiff legs, stretched, steel ham-strings refalling to each measure, they manifested a marvellous precision. Occasionally when the band played a fast quadrille they leaped about quite insanely.

Another and fearsome link binds the cat to music, the terrible catgut. Swift gives this example of weak wit in his " Art of Punning": " Why are rats and mice so much afraid of bass-viols and fiddles? Because they are strung with catgut." And in his verse with the gruesome title, " The Music of the Future," [24] Oliver Herford comments on the matter as follows:

The politest musician that ever was seen
Was Montague Meyerbeer Mendelssohn Green.
So extremely polite he would take off his hat
Whenever he happened to meet with a cat.

" It's not that I'm partial to cats," he'd explain;
" Their music to me is unspeakable pain.
There's nothing that causes my flesh so to crawl
As when they perform a G-flat caterwaul.

Yet I cannot help feeling — in spite of their din —
When I hear at a concert the first violin
Interpret some exquisite thing of my own
If it were not for catgut I'd never be known.

And so, when I bow as you see to a cat,
It isn't to her that I take off my hat;
But to fugues and sonatas that possibly hide
Uncomposed in her — well — in her tuneful inside!"

[24] "The Bashful Earthquake"; Charles Scribner's Sons; New York; 1900.

The Tiger in the House

" No sounds are so captivating as those made by the men of sin who rub the hair of the horse to the bowels of the cat," writes Artemus Ward, and Addison in one of his Spectator essays remarks that the cat has contributed more to harmony than any other animal, " as we are not only beholden to her for her wind music but for our string music in general." The truth is, however, that violin strings are not and never have been, so far as is known, fashioned of catgut; they are really made of lambs' intestines. Why they are called catgut is another etymological mystery.

Chapter Nine: The Cat in Art

" It is odd that, notwithstanding the extreme beauty of cats, their elegance of motion, the variety and intensity of their colour, they should be so little painted by considerable artists," writes Philip Gilbert Hamerton.[1]   " Almost all the pictures of cats which I remember were done by inferior men, often by artists of a very low grade indeed.   The reason for this is probably that although the cat is a refined and very voluptuous animal, it is so wanting in the nobler [2] qualities as to fail in winning the serious sympathies of noble and generous-hearted men."   The reason for this is probably nothing of the sort. To begin with it may be stated categorically that artists as a class, and painters in particular, are seldom " noble and generous-hearted men."   Then, although so well-known an animal painter as Rosa Bonheur seldom painted the cat, preferring to dally with his less subtle brother, the lion, and Sir Edwin Landseer, after two youthful attempts,[3] sought easier subjects, nevertheless I can scarcely recall the name of a single artist of note who has not at one time or other made an effort

[1] " Chapters on Animals," P. 52.

[2] " To bestow such epithets as 'generous' and 'noble' on a dog for pulling a drowning man out of the water, or scratching him out of a snow-drift, is fully as irrational as it would be to call the swallow and cuckoo intrepid explorers of the dark continent, or to praise the hive-bees of the working caste for their chastity, loyalty, and patriotism, and for their profound knowledge of mathematics as shown in their works." W. H. Hudson: " The Great Dog-Superstition": " The Book of a Naturalist"; George H. Doran Co.; New York; 1919.

[3] Landseer painted *The Cat Disturbed* in 1819 and *The Cat's Paw* in 1824. In the former picture puss is persecuted and her nerves are upset by the intrusion at meal-time of a pair of ill-bred terriers.

to draw a cat, and almost all of them have failed. The simple fact of the matter is that under any ordinary circumstances the animal is too difficult to paint. The artist, indeed, who would succeed at feline portraiture, must first of all have a certain understanding and sympathy for cats, and then he must devote his lifetime to their study. Landseer decided he could not give so much time to one form and so he set himself more facile tasks.

The beauty of the cat is very deceptive, for under the grace of the furry exterior lie concealed steel-like muscles. Now the artist who indicates the grace and softness usually misses the strength and the artist who seizes the strength usually does so at the expense of other qualities. The cat's eye alone, an eye skilfully blending innocence and mystery, an eye which changes with the hours of the day, offers insuperable difficulties. "Nothing is so difficult," observes Champfleury, "as to paint the cat's face, which as Moncrif justly observes, bears a character of 'finesse and hilarity.' The lines are so delicate, the eyes so strange, the movements subject to such sudden impulses, that one should be feline oneself to attempt to portray such a subject." With every movement, with every thought, the cat varies in expression, contour, and markings. The cat's character, too, must be taken into consideration. No self-respecting cat has any leanings towards a career as an artist's model.

"She is willing," writes Arthur Tomson, from some experience, "to be observed at times when the performance under scrutiny is entirely of her own direction. But let a cat imagine for one moment that she is under some sort of compulsion, and very speedily she will let you know who is master. If one wishes her to lap milk, and provides her with the means of doing so, she will sit up and wash herself; if one wishes her to wash herself she will chase her tail; if it is a sleeping attitude that one is studying she will scamper off. No sort of training, or affection, or love of good food will turn the cat

The Cat in Art

into a perfect assistant to any artist. Neither will any sort of compulsion." [4]

But the greatest obstacle to painting the cat is the obstacle that any portrait painter must be prepared to meet. The technique of painting may be acquired; one may learn how to paint bodies and faces, arms, legs, hands and ears, characteristics, in short, but how few portrait painters can paint character; how few can go beyond externals. It is exactly this final touch that felinophiles miss in pussy pictures. The painter has painted a cat, perhaps, satisfactorily enough, but *whose* cat? One of the most celebrated painters of cats, Henriette Ronner, is a great offender in this respect. All of Madame Ronner's cats and kittens have a tendency to look precisely alike; they have little or no character.

Contemporary artists were often inclined, naturally enough, to paint Théophile Gautier surrounded by his feline harem. He sometimes posed in Turkish costume, squatting on cushions and overrun with cats. He admitted that there was little exaggeration in these pictures and that the portraits of himself were admirable, but it was hard to induce him to praise the cat portraits. He missed the peculiar and characteristic features: where was the curve of Zuleika's snow-white breast, the deep repose of Zulema's folded paws, or the eloquent elevation of Zobeide's jet-black tail? " Painting cats," he used to say, " is a question of genius, my dear boys."

Nevertheless one meets with the cat in nearly all forms of art from the time of the early Egyptians down to the present day. Curiously enough she is not a conspicuous figure in Roman or Greek art but perhaps her absence may be accounted for on the same ground as that on which Mrs. Emily James Putnam accounts for the disappearance of the Athenian lady.[5]

[4] For these and other reasons the cat is also very hard to photograph. The best photographs are instantaneous, as the mere breathing of a cat will blur the fur in a time exposure.

[5] " Anything that is necessary tends to become an evil, and the wife's dynas-

The Tiger in the House

At any rate there are comparatively few examples of art dealing with cats in the Greek and Roman collections. The two notable exceptions are a Grecian urn of the best period and a bas-relief in the Capitoline Museum on which a young woman is represented who tries to teach her cat to dance while she plays the lyre, the cat naturally preferring to snap at a duck.[6] Even more curious is the neglect of the cat in ecclesiastical architecture. The demons sculptured in the mediaeval cathedrals were often put there to plant terror in such matters in the hearts of the people, but although cats and witches were ever so chummy, demon cats do not raise their hideous fangs in these churches. What few cats do appear in these carvings seem pleasant enough in intention.

In Tarragona Cathedral, Havelock Ellis notes the broadly humorous sculptured scene in the cloisters " where we see a solemn procession of rats joyfully bearing on a bier a demurely supine cat, who, a little farther on, is again seen vigorously alive and seizing one of her unfortunate bearers while the rest are put to flight — the most insignificant sculpture in the cathedral, but perhaps the most interesting, the sacristan observes smilingly." [7] In the first scene tabby lies on a litter borne by rats and mice and preceded by a train of rodents bearing banners, vessels of holy water, aspergills, crosiers, and censers. The executioner, a rat bearing an ax, marches under the litter. This stately pageant is followed by the more lively scene in which the cat springs up and catches a rat while the rest disperse in all directions.[8]

tic importance, which was her very *raison d'être,* operated to her disadvantage as a source of romantic interest." Emily James Putnam: " The Lady "; Sturgis and Walton Co.; New York; 1910; P. 13.

[6] But there is proof enough that classical antiquity loved the cat. Among the objects unearthed at Pompeii was the skeleton of a woman bearing in her arms the skeleton of a cat, whom perhaps she gave her life to save.

[7] " The Soul of Spain," P. 290.

[8] A reproduction of this bas-relief may be found in G. E. Street's " Gothic Architecture in Spain "; Vol. II, P. 34.

The Cat in Art

In Great Malvern Abbey rats may be seen hanging a cat in the presence of owls who are looking on with an air of legal wisdom and judicial gravity. In the Cathedral of Rouen a cat chases a mouse round a pillar in the nave. In Albert de Brule's choir-stalls in San Giorgio Maggiore in Venice, representing scenes from the life of St. Benedict, several cats are introduced. On one stall puss is quarrelling with Benedict's raven; on another she is eating a mouse under the couch of a sleepy brother, whom the saint is endeavouring to waken. There are two droll cats in the choir of the old Minster in the Isle of Thanet.

Champfleury found a fifteenth century capital of a " hideous animal " in the Museum of Troyes and a door-lintel at Ricey-Haute-Rive with a bas-relief of a cat in company with hens, a fox, and a rat. Viollet-le-Duc, the restorer of the Château of Pierrefonds, ornamented the dormer windows of the inner court with cats in different postures. Champfleury has chosen a mother with a kitten between her teeth for reproduction.

In the pictures of the early Italian, Flemish, and Spanish masters the cat frequently appears, seldom, if ever, I must admit, very well painted. Nevertheless she is to be found in *Annunciations, Holy Families, Last Suppers,* and *Marriage Feasts at Cana* indiscriminately. I have no doubt that some painter has included her with the elders among the furtive observers of Susanna's plight. Bassano painted and repainted the departure from the Ark and invariably in these pictures a big, brindled, self-satisfied cat leads the procession, for it has pleased the artist to follow the Arabian rather than the Biblical legend. Occasionally, indeed, puss is already frightening a rabbit or pouncing on a dove. In Tintoretto's *Leda* a tabby snaps at a duck.

In the Vatican Gallery hangs an *Annunciation* by Baroccio in which a great silver cat sleeps on the Virgin's work and in another painting by the same artist to be seen at Budapest a tranquil cat on a cushion regards the visiting angel through

half-opened sleepy eyelids.   What are angels to her, indeed?
Another cat characteristically indifferent to angelic visitations
may be observed in the *Annunciation* of Federigo Zucchero on
the portico of the hospital of Santa Maria Nuova at
Florence and the cat also appears in two frescos by Puccio in
the choir of the cathedral at Orvieto.   In the one Saint Ann's
great white cat arches her back, lifts her tail, and drives a
dog from the room; in the second, while others are occupied
looking at the newly born Virgin she stands on her hind legs
and helps herself to some food on a little table.   In Baroccio's
famous altar-piece, *La Madonna del Gatto* in the National
Gallery in London, the cat, of course, is the centre of interest.
The infant St. John holds a struggling bird high over his head
and the cat rises towards it.   In Ghirlandajo's celebrated
fresco of *The Last Supper* in the refectory of the Monastery
of San Marco in Florence a most intelligent cat scowls dis-
approvingly at Judas.   Benvenuto Cellini, too, places a cat
at the feet of Judas in one of his bas-reliefs.   Is it possible
that this juxtaposition may be regarded as uncomplimentary
to the animal?   The cat in Veronese's *The Marriage at Cana*
is not the most easily remembered detail of this large canvas.
Many of Veronese's pictures contain cats but so carelessly
painted that they might be taken for weasels or lap-dogs.
Benozzo Gozzoli painted the cat in the scene of the Ark on
the walls of the Campo Santo at Pisa and a black cat with
amber eyes occupies herself watching the maids washing the
new-born Virgin in the Oratorio of San Bernardino at Siena.

" The picture which of all others, however, best illustrates
the temper of the cat as the Italians knew her two hundred
years ago, and as we know her today, was painted by Luca
Giordano, and hangs in the Imperial Gallery of Vienna,"
Agnes Repplier observes with some humour.   " It is another
presentation of that ever familiar theme, the birth of the
Blessed Virgin.   Saint Ann sits upright on her bed.   Saint
Joachim enters the door.   The spacious room is full of attend-

ants, engaged in waiting on their mistress, in airing the baby linen, in washing and admiring the infant. Everybody is busy and excited. Everybody save Saint Ann is standing, or kneeling on the floor. There is, in fact, but one chair in the room. On that chair is a cushion, and on that cushion sleeps, serene and undisturbed, a cat."

Many Flemish artists painted cats. In Hieronymus Bosch's *The Birth of Eve* a fierce puss is devouring an innocent tadpole and in van Tulden's *Orpheus Taming the Beasts,* while the other animals seem to be lulled pleasantly by the music, the cat is on the point of attacking a lion. These pictures are in the Prado Museum at Madrid. In the genre pictures of the Dutch school cats naturally play their decorative part, basking by the great stoves, or frisking with kittens, or stealing meat. Jan Steen, Jordaens, Jan Fyt, Willem van Mieris and Rembrandt all occasionally included cats in their designs. In Munich there is an *Annunciation* by Hendrick met de Bles in which the Blessed Virgin's cat, a handsome white beast, sleeps by her mistress's side.

Fragonard painted a cat or two. In Jan Breughel's *Paradise Lost* in the Louvre the cat sleeps contentedly while our parents are being driven forth. This is perfectly catlike; it also serves to remind us that God did not drive cats out of the Garden. In Franz Floris's *Garden of Eden* puss lies stretched between the feet of Adam and Eve. The cat sleeps again beneath the elevated stove in Lebrun's unsophisticated *Sleep of the Infant Jesus in the Louvre.* Watteau painted a delicious *Chat malade,* rolled up like a baby in the arms of his little mistress, who is weeping. An Italian comedy doctor, with skull-cap and eye-glasses, attends the invalid with a majestic air, while the cat himself makes a face like a spoiled child at the smell of the medicine. There is a puss in Velázquez's *Las Hilanderas.* Gainsborough's *Child with a Cat* in the Metropolitan Museum in New York is a familiar picture but the child is painted with more care than the cat.

The Tiger in the House

One could go on and on listlessly with this dull catalogue. These cats have no great interest but they serve to indicate that puss roamed home and studio with as much freedom three centuries ago as she does today. The old Italian and Dutch artists introduced grimalkins into their pictures because they saw them about the place, but they only introduced them as decoration or ornament, like vine-leaf or vase, chair or table, although Hamel [9] suggests that occasionally they may have wished to indicate the animal spirit that dwells in human beings: " Sir Joshua Reynolds painted two portraits of young girls, one holding a cage with a mouse in it, the other a kitten. The former is called *Muscupula* and the latter *Felina,* and it may be surmised that he intended to show in their features the imitative sympathy young children have with young animals." This tendency may be studied in more modern painting. Boris Anisfeld has painted his daughter, Morella Borisovna, with her hand on the head of a black and white puss. Both girl and cat have a band of black hair over their eyes and as the expression in each case is nearly identical the artistic intention of the painter is obvious. A red-haired lady in a picture which hangs in a corridor of the Hotel Astor carries her counterpart, a red and white pussy, sound asleep in her lap. Renoir, too, was conscious of the relationship between animals and people. In *Le garçon au chat,* (1868) a superb example of languid grace, beauty, and indolence, a boy stands in a luxurious attitude with his arm drawn round a luxurious cat. The faces are brought close together and there is a decided resemblance between the two. In *La femme au chat* (1878–9) a country girl sleeps with a cat asleep in her lap. These cats, it may be added, are extremely well painted. It was not Renoir's custom to approach any subject in a half-hearted way.

There have been, however, painters who devoted themselves to the cat, who painted cats with accessories, instead of cats as

[9] " Human Animals," P. 42.

accessories. There was, for example, Gottfried Mind, to whom Madame Lebrun once gave the sobriquet of the " Raphael of Cats," a name by which he continues to be known to this day, although his work bears as little relation to Raphael's as the Belgian Shakespeare's bears to that of the author of *Timon of Athens*. Of Hungarian origin Mind was born at Berne in 1768; he died in 1814. He consecrated his life to painting bears and cats, mostly cats, animals to which he was devoted. When in 1809 an epidemic of madness broke out among the cats of Berne and a general massacre followed Mind was inconsolable [10] although he saved his own Minette. The painter and his cats were inseparable and his Minette was always by his side. Sometimes she would sit upon his knees while kittens perched on his shoulders and rather than disturb his friends he would remain in one attitude for hours. To his cats he was unfailingly polite and affable but he treated men with the same scant courtesy that Jeremy Bentham allotted to humans.

I have not seen any of Mind's original drawings; indeed I have seen but few reproductions of his work. These are interesting and indicate a deep talent for cat painting. Depping writes of him (" Biographie Universelle ") : " His pictures were, one might almost say, cat-portraits; he gave every shade of expression to their soft and cunning faces; he lent infinite variety to the graceful attitude of kittens playing with their mother; he depicted the silky coat of the cat perfectly; in short the cats painted by Mind seemed to be alive." This praise of Mind's work may be a little excessive, but his fame as one of the earliest of the cat painters is still considerable.

Delacroix painted cats which resembled tigers more than

[10] Once when a similar epidemic broke out among her cats and Mabel Dodge found it necessary to put several of them out of their misery, especially to protect the few who had not succumbed to the contagion, a guest walked the streets of Florence saying to whomever would listen, "Murder has been committed at the Villa Curonia!"

household pets and his pupil, Louis Eugène Lambert, [11] was a celebrated cat painter. His *Family of Cats* did hang in the Luxembourg Gallery in Paris; perhaps it does still. On this rather conventional canvas the mother sits on the table and superintends the antics of her mischievous kittens.

Of Henriette Ronner, whom writers on two continents and an island or two united to honour on her seventieth birthday, I cannot speak with any enthusiasm. She painted cats all her life and several albums devoted to her pictures of pussies have been published. I have one or two of these myself. These pictures are sentimental; they are " story pictures," but that is not their worst fault. They are carelessly observed, superficial. In such a canvas as her *Banjo* Madame Ronner can be very ingratiating, but in such a picture she has said all that she ever says. It is apparent at once that this lady, who painted cats for several decades, never learned more about them than the most casual observer would know at first glance. She makes no attempt at differentiation; one of her cats looks much like any other. They are usually represented in families, a fond mother looking on while the babies play in and out of work-baskets, on chess-boards, in empty bird-cages or clocks. The sort of thing for which, no doubt, you could depend upon an immediate purchaser, who would sign a cheque with an added encomium, " My, aren't they sweet! " Well, of course, they are. Madame Ronner caught a certain playful streak in kittens although some of her kittens are almost as wooden as Henry IV doors; she caught texture in fur; her arrangements are sometimes happy; but she never, it seems to me, captured the soul of the cat, because *au fond*, Madame Ronner was a Belgian *bourgeoise* and it takes an aristocrat with a Persian soul to understand the soul of a cat.

[11] His work may be studied in " Les Chiens et les Chats d'Eugène Lambert," by G. de Cherville; Paris; 1888. This book is illustrated with six etchings (all of cats) and one hundred and forty-five drawings of cats and dogs.

The Cat in Art

Champfleury shoots most of his enthusiastic sky-rockets to celebrate an obscure English painter named Burbank and claims to have discovered him, but Mrs. Hoey in her translation of " Les Chats " exposes the French writer in the following footnote: " M. Champfleury has drawn upon his imagination for these facts. In Graves' Dictionary of Artists, Burbank is described as an animal painter who exhibited twenty-seven pictures in London between the years 1825–1872, twelve of them in the Royal Academy." Champfleury says, " A few years ago I saw a wonderful water-colour drawing, representing a cat's head, life-size, in the studio of Dantan, the sculptor. In this picture there were melted and mingled certain qualities which make a Holbein, or a plodding clockmaker, a Denner, or a forger of bank notes. It would be useless to attempt to describe the eyes of the animal as they looked into the face of the spectator. The pen becomes useless before the marvellous tints of those eyes. And yet here was a painter whose brush was capable of rendering strange looks. . . . This painting is the result of the prolonged attention of an observer whose fault is that of coldness. Excessive application and exactness have the counter quality of lessening the enthusiasm of the artist. Cold and correct, passionate and incorrect; so few men are quite perfect! . . . So great is the importance that I attribute to Burbank that I venture to assert, if the cat painted by this artist were placed among the ancient drawings in the Louvre, not only would it hold an honourable place there, but it would attract the attention of all who are capable of appreciating the interpretation of truth." To some, who have seen only such reproductions of Burbank's work as Champfleury offers, this description may seem a trifle exaggerated; to others, I dare say, it will not.

Edouard Manet painted cats several times. There is, for instance, the etching of the cat among flowers, which he made for the edition de luxe of Champfleury's volume which is not, to be sure, very convincing evidence of his skill in this direction.

But the poster he painted for this book, the celebrated *Rendez-vous des Chats,* in which a superb black carl-cat is paying attention to a white queen among the chimney tops, while their tails are flaunted in the face of the rising moon, is amazing. On the bed of the nude *Olympia* a black cat arches his back. It was probably the artist's somewhat ribald intention to suggest the familiar of a modern sorceress. This cat, soon known as "the cat of Monsieur Manet," for a time enjoyed a *succès de scandale.* Now that the picture has reached the Louvre it has become old hat and neither the lady nor her pussy are much talked about any more.

Aubrey Beardsley occasionally painted cats, and as well may be imagined he painted them black. Wicked demon cats are the cats of Aubrey Beardsley. In Aymer Vallance's iconography of Beardsley's work he notes a design for Meinhold's Romance, " Sidonia the Sorceress " with the demon-cat, Chim. William Morris criticized this drawing unfavourably and it is almost certain that Beardsley destroyed it. Among his grotesques for " Bon Mots " is one of a woman with a cat, an eldritch beast with spread claws and a horrid face. Vallance mentions a Pierrot with a black cat which I have not seen. For the large paper edition of Poe's " Tales of Mystery and Wonder " (Stone and Kimball; Chicago; 1895) Beardsley made four drawings, of which the one for The Black Cat is perhaps the most striking.

I do not believe I have ever found cats in art which so completely satisfied me as the cats of Grandville. Jean-Ignace-Isadore Gérard, who called himself Grandville, was born at Nancy, September 15, 1803, and he died March 17, 1847. He was an illustrator and he designed lovely and amusing pictures for the works of Béranger, the Fables of Florian, Lavalette, and La Fontaine, " Gulliver's Travels " and " Robinson Crusoe." Even in these cats may be found but for the finest examples of his drawings of felines you must turn to " Les Métamorphoses du Jour," " Les Animaux Peints

Par Euxmêmes," "Album des Bêtes," "Cents Proverbes," and especially, "La Vie Privée et Publique des Animaux." When I first opened this latter book, indeed, I simply chortled for joy as I experienced an enthusiasm which I had never before felt for the cats of any artist. The sickly sentiment of Madame Ronner, the commonplaces of Burbank, even the drawings of Mind had left me more or less as they found me, but the drawings of Grandville gave me the requisite thrill.

When I stumbled upon Grandville's drawings, almost by accident, for they are not reproduced in any of the cat books I have seen and the volumes in which they originally appeared are now very rare, I almost shrieked for joy. Here are cats! I shouted: Here, indeed, are cats! For Grandville not only solved the conflicting problems of grace and strength, he also solved the far more difficult problems of individuality and expression.[12] You, who have a favourite grimalkin or matou or tabby queen, you know that your cat *looks* different from the cat in the next block. His gestures are different; his eyes are different. But cat painters, as a whole, have not felt this difference. That is why, although they have painted many cats, few cat pictures remain in the memory. You remember the details of a set of Goya prints because, while each is infused with the strong personality of the artist, each suggests something new, just as you forget a set of Charles Dana Gibson prints because every one suggests the same thing as its neighbour, which is nothing at all. In the latter nineties a popular song proclaimed that *All coons look alike to me.* A paraphrase of this idea seems to have been the principal inspiration of cat painters, who apparently have said to themselves: "We must learn how to paint fur, how to paint strength, how to paint grace, how to paint eyes, etc.," but they have seldom perceived that they must also learn how to paint character. Indeed it may never have occurred to

[12] Grandville asserted that he had observed seventy-five different expressions in cats.

The Tiger in the House

Madame Ronner to consider whether or not cats have character. If it did occur to her she never made the slightest attempt to put this idea into her pictures.

Now Grandville never, or hardly ever, except in the homely illustrations for " Robinson Crusoe," or for Béranger's poems, draws a cat in an ordinary situation. He surrounds his cats with fantastic touches, dresses them in clothes, asks them to use furniture, but so sure is his touch, so correct his feeling, that for days after I had seen his cats it did not seem right to me that Feathers should not march on her hind paws and wear gowns. These gowns, these attitudes, these gestures, seemingly human and uncatlike, all fall into place and become indispensable attributes of cat character. Recall the little minx in an ermine robe reclining on a couch. No one ever saw a real cat in a gown from the Rue de la Paix; no one ever saw a real cat lying in the attitude affected by this little lady, very nearly the same as that in which Caro-Delvaille painted Madame Simone, and yet any one would recognize this puss should she walk through the doorway to confront the picture, so strongly does the drawing suggest character. So, too, you would know the Chinese cat, or the demure and frightened female on the roof, vacillating between the white agathodemon and the black kakodemon cats while the chimney pots grin disapproval. In " Cent Proverbes " to illustrate *A bon chat, bon rat,* Grandville has drawn an adorable matou in a top coat with a portmonaie projecting from his pocket, high hat held behind his back, and bouquet, bowing to a rat dressed as a lady of the ballet. The scene is the stage of the Opéra. The picture of the kittens playing with a mouse-doll while mama knits under a stuffed rat in a glass case is also very amusing. So is the scene from Balzac's story [13] in which Beauty meets her Bohemian lover on the rooftop and almost yields to his impetuous importunities. Indeed, the saucy ex-

[13] Peines de Cœur d'une Chatte Anglaise " in " Vie Privée et Publique des Animaux."

pression of the *costaud*, Brisquet, is fascinatingly caught. But my eternal favourite is the engraving illustrating the entrance of the respectable Puff in the same story, Puff whose manners were those of a cat who had seen the court and the world; he had two valets in his service; he ate from Chinese porcelain; he only drank black tea; he went to drive in Hyde Park; he was about to enter parliament; Puff, "*milord matou!*" This resplendent orange and black Angora is introduced to little white Beauty as a possible mate. He comes into the hall, walking, of course, on his hind paws; he wears a gorgeous overcoat and he holds a silk hat, while two monkey flunkeys carry his tail. His eyes bulge with naïve vanity and poor Beauty, overcome by this splendour, curtseys before him. This to me is the acme, the alpha and omega, the A and Z, the Carpaccio and Shakespeare, the Gluck and Stravinsky, the Napoleon and Mohammed of all cat pictures. Grandville has not only created one cat character herein, he has created two. If you have ever seen a superb Persian matou enter a room in which he was expected to perform the ceremony described in Chapter XXII of James Branch Cabell's "Jurgen" you will be in a better position to understand and appreciate this very extraordinary drawing.

Louis Wain's [14] rakish London cats are amusing; he is not so keen an observer as Grandville; nor yet so good a draughtsman, and yet there is much to admire in these ribald pussies who smoke cigars and ride motorcycles. There is really a good deal of character in these drawings. Wain is especially successful at depicting ram-cats. In most of his pictures the eyes are emphasized to such an extent that they seem almost to epitomize the cat, but I think his feeling in this matter has been correct; the eyes are undoubtedly the most important single feature of the cat. Wain once remarked that drawing felines was as difficult as drawing circles freehand.

[14] "Wain's Annual" and elsewhere; Wain has illustrated a number of books and made innumerable postcards and calendars.

The Tiger in the House

There should be a word for Lady Chance's [15] exceedingly delightful wash drawings of cats. Lady Chance has stepped in upon puss in many of the interesting moments of her life, but perhaps her supreme achievement is her drawing of the cat with the closed eyes. These little sketches are full of mystery and charm. Arthur Tomson's [16] drawings are more conventional and certainly not as interesting. There is a fascinating verisimilitude about Harrison Weir's [17] drawings. His cats, mostly in commonplace attitudes, have *body*. They are honest and they are not sentimental. On the other hand they are entirely bereft of mystery. Mrs. Janvier's [18] pictures are entertaining. Like Grandville and Louis Wain she has half humanized her cats, dressed them up and asked them to walk upright. The two knights who struggle for the Princess Catina's love in the picture called *Taunting Mews* are most aggressive, splendid beasties, and in *Crawley Mews* she has drawn some curious and strange animals.

Elisabeth F. Bonsall has illustrated several American cat books. In " The Book of the Cat " [19] she has an opportunity in full-page coloured illustrations to exhibit the range of her talent. Her cats are more often thoughtful and dignified than playful. They gaze into the fire or at the observer with half-shut eyes, they sleep sprawled across open books. But in pieces of rapid action such as the kitten playing with the leaves or the toms on the roof she is less successful.

Of the moderns Steinlen is probably the greatest of the cat artists. His book " Des Chats " (*" dessins sans paroles "*) is a joy. Steinlen made many posters of cats (they serve decorative purposes as well or better than Chéret's dashing

[15] Mrs. W. Chance: "A Book of Cats."
[16] Graham R. Tomson: " Concerning Cats."
[17] Harrison Weir: "Our Cats, and All About Them."
[18] Catherine A. Janvier: "London Mews."
[19] " The Book of the Cat," with facsimiles of drawing in colour by Elisabeth F. Bonsall and with stories and verses by Mabel Humphreys; F. A. Stokes Co.; 1903.

barmaids) and the cover for this book is a revision in colour of a celebrated poster, *Lait pur stérilisé* . . . . A grey tabby claws the skirts of a child bearing a bowl of milk; a black cat rubs calinely against her leg, while a tortoise-shell, a black Persian, and a brown tabby yowl pleasantly and expectantly. An orange tabby, a little aloof, arches his back and says, " Please! " Other cats are seen rapidly approaching.

Steinlen is the only painter, past or present, who has been successful in drawing cats in action [20] and this volume bears testimony to his ability in this direction. The sheets of this large folio are filled with drawings in black and white. They are like the films of a cinema reel; each picture gives us a little more knowledge of movement. Observe, for instance, the page entitled, *Poor Little Mouse!* on which three Siamese cats shake a rodent out of a trap and capture it. Every detail of this incident is set down with rare fidelity to both movement and the nature of the animal. The horrible end of a goldfish teaches us that all cats who attempt indoor fishing do not meet the tragic death of Gray's celebrated Selima. The cat with the ball of yarn is a masterpiece of carefully observed action and the kitten with the burning cigar is equally diverting. The page described as *Miaulements* is a delightful miscellany of mothers carrying their babies, or suckling them, and toms fighting. There are eleven heads on this page, careful cat portraits, each differentiated as to character and temperament. On the page called *Paresse,* Steinlen has permitted himself to draw cats in repose, yawning, stretching cats, cats arching their backs, cats sleeping in a dozen or more attitudes. All these are done very surely in a few convincing strokes. The character of the cats is well differentiated in all of these vibrant pages. The dignified black Persian who is the victim

[20] Renouard comes near to doing so. There are several pages devoted to cats in his volume entitled " Croquis d'Animaux." I feel sure that both Benjamin Rabier and Caran d'Ache must have drawn cats, but I do not seem to be able to find any among such drawings of theirs as I have at hand.

of a baby with a wooden horse is a very different animal from the black cat who steals the butter from the baby's bread.

Oliver Herford's specialty is kittens for whom, undoubtedly, he has a peculiar feeling. These kittens are suffused with more life than any Henriette Ronner ever painted. They are roguish, innocent, rakish, wistful, but always adorable balls of fur, for it is ever his fancy to paint babies of the Persian tribe. Mr. Herford's [21] kittens are scattered through most of his volumes of poetry and through many magazines as well, but the perusal of two books, " The Rubáiyát of a Persian Kitten " and " A Kitten's Garden of Verses " will give you an excellent idea of his work. Observe, for instance, the smug, short-legged, snub-nosed kitten who sits opposite the lines called " Happy Thought ":

> *The world is so full of a number of mice*
> *I'm sure that we all should be happy and nice.*

This surely is Vachel Lindsay's good kitten who wore his ribbon prettily and washed behind his ears. The picture called *Foreign Kittens,* too, is very attractive to me. A Persian kitten in characteristic attitude watches through a window some common cats on the back fence. This puss is observed from the back and she has been well observed. *The Whole Duty of Kittens* is quite as pleasing. More celebrated, more amusing, and perhaps better drawn are the illustrations for " The Rubáiyát." How perfect is the branch of pussy-willows, for example. How much at times kittens resemble pussy-willows and caterpillars!

It was with Oliver Herford that Fania Marinoff and I met a particularly kitten-like caterpillar. One fine day in summer we all stopped together to look at some fuzzy red caterpillars that promenaded on the branches of the shrubs inside the railing of Gramercy Park. One lusty little fellow, deter-

---

[21] Oliver Herford's monogram is in the form of a cat. He calls it his " Cat-of-Arms."

mined no doubt to see the world, tumbled out on the sidewalk, and with the most terrific speed made for the kerb. Fania, determining to save his life, picked him up and put him gently back on the earth inside the fence. He immediately started out again and in a short time was back at the kerb. Now I picked him up and tossed him a yard or so on the grass back of the grating. He returned with an air of abandoned persistence which gave one the idea that he knew what he wanted to do. Mr. Herford next assumed the rôle of the god in the car and tossed him still farther back. Will you believe it that this obstinate kitten-like, fuzzy, red, baby caterpillar came back a third time and before our astonished gaze walked across the street to the Players' Club, where for all I know he may have spun his cocoon and turned into a butterfly or a fairy!

But the early Egyptians, the Chinese, and other orientals have probably made better art out of the cat than any one else, for the simple reason that they have seldom attempted to draw or model the animal realistically. Their sculpture, their frescos, their woodblocks are generally fantastic or conventionalized. Thus they have expressed the essential mystery of the most mysterious of living beings. The old bronze cats of the Egyptians are still full of the breath of life. You may study several examples in the Metropolitan Museum in New York. There you may see two bronze cases for cat mummies, each of which supports a cat figure in bronze, one crouching, the other seated upright. Both of these objects are endowed with a soft green patina. There also you may find several exquisite blue faience figures of cats, and an entire case is filled with bronzes. The figures are mostly in the same position, seated, but they are all beautiful. One head, especially, was formed by the artist in honest love. It is perhaps the finest cat-head in the history of art, transcendent in its dignity, nobility, and mystery.

The Japanese and the Chinese too are almost invariably

successful in depicting the domestic tiger, no matter in what medium they work. They begin by forgetting the fur and it is on the technique of painting fur that most occidental painters waste their time, I think. Arthur Davison Ficke once told me that the secret of Japanese painting was that the artist never worked from a model; he worked from memory. The result is that when he drew a cat on his block he was drawing his *feeling* for the cat. Hokusai made innumerable coloured prints of cats, some of which are reproduced in Champfleury's book, and all of which have charm and grace. There is an adorable cat in the first Kiyonobu's print of *The Princess and the Kitten*,[22] a prancing, frantically exhilarating creature. And cats wander in and out of the work of Harunobu, Kiyomitsu, Koriusai, Kitao Masanobu, and Buncho. The Mongolians, too, love to represent the cat in porcelain. I have a Chinese cat, Chuang Tzŭ, ivory porcelain spotted with black, who sits recumbent on his four paws, gazing with his eternal eyes into the mystic maze of the centuries. He has already visited four continents and he has forgotten that time exists. Other Japanese and Chinese artists have represented the cat asleep or just about to awaken, or playing, but always with the grace of love, the understanding of sympathy, and the unescapable oriental touch of mystery. These artists because they never say too much, have expressed without apparent difficulty what European artists almost always fail to express. A row of these exotic images from China would recreate the wonder of the animal, if she should suddenly become extinct. The art of feeling the hidden recesses of feline reserve is now, it would seem, exclusively Asiatic.

[22] There is a story to this picture. Josan No Miya, The Princess, was an aristocratic young person much sought after by the youths of the region, but she remained in seclusion until one day when her cat, startled by the noise of the young men come into the courtyard to woo, escaped from her, she impulsively ran after it.

Chapter Ten: The Cat in Fiction

In the second of his imaginary dialogues with Edmund Gosse, George Moore complains of the absence of animals in "Tom Jones" and "Vanity Fair." "Both books lack intimacy of thought and feeling. No one sits by the fire and thinks what his or her past has been and welcomes the approach of a familiar bird or animal. I do not remember any dog, cat, or parrot in ' Vanity Fair,' and I am almost certain that ' Tom Jones ' is without one. . . . I have forgotten their names but I am conscious of the presence of dogs and cats in Dickens's pages." It is true that animals play an important rôle in prose fiction, more important than is often realized, for a book without animals is seldom a living book. Cats sleep by the fire or frisk across the leaves of many a romance. In "Bleak House" alone there are three cats: Krook's snarling Lady Jane, who follows her master, as Charmian followed Cleopatra, or perches hissing on his shoulder: she is the symbol of his mystery; the Jellybys' cat, who, more often than not, disposes of poor Mr. Jellyby's morning milk; and the nameless cat of Mr. Vohles, the lawyer. Then there is Mrs. Pipchin's old cat, little Paul Dombey's friend, who coiling himself in the fender purrs egotistically, "while the contracting pupils of his eyes looked like two notes of admiration." In "Père Goriot," Madame the Keeper of the Pension is accompanied on her introduction by her cat, Mistigris. In the end, all her boarders having deserted her, it is announced as a final blow that Mistigris has disappeared. "Cats are very graceful and very clean," proclaims Mrs. Penniman to her brother in "Washington Square," when the good doctor suggests the drowning of the kittens. And in "A Small Boy

231

and Others," Henry James remarks that he rubbed himself against the Seine-front in Paris, " for endearment and consecration, as a cat invokes the friction of a protective piece of furniture." Somewhere George Eliot has written: " Who can tell what just criticisms the cat may be passing on us beings of wider speculation? " Chattie, a very impersonal puss, plays a small part in the opening scenes of " Robert Elsmere." Jean Jacques Rousseau in " Emile " comments upon the analogy between the curiosity of the child and that of the cat: " Observe a cat entering a room for the first time: it searches and smells about, it is not quiet for a moment, it trusts nothing until it has examined and made acquaintance with everything. Just in the same way would a child who was beginning to walk, and, so to speak, entering upon the unknown space of the world, demean itself." Nor must we forget Don Quixote's adventures in the castle of the Duke of Villahermosa. Chanting a love-song in his chamber at midnight, the knight is suddenly disturbed by a prodigious caterwauling and ringing of bells. " Such was the din of the bells and the squalling of the cats, that though the duke and the duchess were the contrivers of the joke, they were startled by it, while Don Quixote stood paralysed with fear: and as luck would have it, two or three of the cats made their way in through the grating of his chamber, and flying from one side to the other, made it seem as if there was a legion of devils at large in it. . . . Don Quixote sprang to his feet, and drawing his sword, began making passes at the grating, shouting out, ' Avaunt, malignant enchanters! Avaunt ye witchcraft working rabble! I am Don Quixote of La Mancha, against whom your evil machinations avail not nor have any power.' " When the duke ran in and laid hold of a cat attached to the knight's nose, the knight called out, " Let no one take him from me; leave me hand to hand with this demon, this wizard, this enchanter; I will teach him, I myself, who Don Quixote of La Mancha is." The cat, however, snarled and held on. In Thomas Love Peacock's " Gryll Grange," we get a less goetic view of the cat. The fragment may be regarded as autobiographical: " In all its arrangements his house was a model of order and comfort; and the whole establishment partook of the genial physiognomy of the master. From the master and mistress to the cook, and from the cook to the tom cat, there was about the inhabitants a sleek and purring rotundity of face and figure that denoted community of feelings, habits, and diet; each in its kind, of course, for the master had his port, the cook her ale, and the cat his milk, in sufficiently liberal allowance." In " The Hill of Dreams," " Lucian leant back and roared with indecent laughter till the tabby tom-cat who had succeeded to the poor dead beasts looked up reproachfully from his sunny corner, with a face like the reviewer's, innocent and round and whiskered." Again Lucian meets a cat: " In the back street by which he passed out of the town he saw a large ' healthy ' boy kicking a sick cat; the poor creature had just strength enough to crawl under an outhouse door; probably to die in torments. He did not find much satisfaction in thrashing the boy, but he did it with hearty good will." In Henry Handel Richardson's " Maurice Guest," " Peter, the Fursts' lean cat, had sneaked stealthily in upon this, to him, enchanted ground and, according to the fancier, had caused the death from fright, of a delicate canary, although the culprit had done nothing more than sit before the cage, licking his lips." Wotan, the one-eyed cat in this book is a memorable figure. Catulle Mendès, too, had a fancy for naming cats after Wagnerian heroes. Naming cats is beyond the powers of the ordinary brain. Samuel Butler asserts that it is the test of literary power: " They say the test of this is whether a man can write an inscription. I say, ' Can he name a kitten?' And by this test I am condemned, for I cannot." [1] Peter Whiffle

---

[1] Samuel Butler was inspired when he wrote these lines in his note-book. Out of every ten names sent in for registry with the Cat Fanciers' Federation

once named two cats, George Moore and George Sand. Eventually they had children. The King turns to Perion, " fierce, tense, and fragile, like an angered cat," in Mr. James Branch Cabell's " The Soul of Melicent " and " He who hunts with cats will catch mice " is another figure from this book. The incorrigible Jurgen tells of a ghost who once haunted him who " towards morning took the form of a monstrous cat, and climbed upon the foot of my bed: and there he squatted yowling until daybreak." [2] And Jurgen, speaking of the glory of the number nine, mentions the Muses, the lives of a cat, and how many tailors make a man. Kipling compares an engine leaping across a bridge to a cat streaking along a fence. " You closed your eyes while he was kissing you like a cat being stroked," is a figure from Octave Mirbeau's " Chez l'illustre écrivain." Achmed Abdullah, in " The Honorable Gentleman," says that love is like " wings upon a cat, like rabbits' horns, like ropes made of tortoise hair." Charles-Henry Hirsch, in " ' Petit ' Louis, Boxeur," describes a professional pugilist as " *leste comme une chatte.*" Her little head . . . " as smooth as a cat's," writes Gelett Burgess in " The White Cat." " He knows no more about the world," remarks a character in Mr. Chambers's " The King in Yellow," " than a maiden cat on its first moonlight stroll." Peter, one of Mr. Dreiser's " Twelve Men," tested his skill " by embalming a dead cat or two after the Egyptian

nine are returned because they have already been used. The lack of imagination or invention most people display in christening pussies is almost beyond credence.

[2] In nightmare an oppression and suffocation are felt and one's fancy immediately conjures up a spectre to lie on one's bosom. Scott writes of a man dying, first afflicted by the vision of a large cat which came and disappeared he could not tell exactly how, but the man liked cats and became almost indifferent to the spectre until it turned into a gentleman-usher dressed " as if to wait upon a Lord Lieutenant of Ireland, a Lord High Commissioner of the Kirk, or any other who bears on his brow the rank and stamp of delegated sovereignty." The hallucination finally took the form of a skeleton, and the patient died under the effects of this visitation. " Demonology and Witchcraft," P. 30.

manner." In this same book Culhane, the solid man, asserts, "a dog . . . eats what he needs, and then stops. So does a cat," which, as Mr. Dreiser adds, is by no means true. In Richard Middleton's "The Ghost Ship," you may read, "As a rule the cat kept me company, and I was pleased with his placid society, though he made my legs cramped. I thought that I too would like to be a cat." And again, "Like a cat I wanted to dream somewhere where I would be neglected by friends and foes alike." Yet again, "Then there was the vision of two small feet that moved a long way off, and Toby would watch them curiously as kittens do their tails, without knowing the cause of their motion." The postillion in "Lavengro" uses a wonderful cat figure in his description of a priest: "My mother had a sandy cat, which sometimes used to open its mouth wide with a mew nobody could hear, and the silent laugh of that red-haired priest used to put me wonderfully in mind of the silent mew of my mother's sandy-red cat." "Growling to herself, something after the manner of an old grimalkin when disturbed," is a figure from "The Bible in Spain."

Pierre Loti invariably writes of cats with a sympathy and a comprehension that partakes of the mystic ("stranger than strange" is Henry James's description of the performance), and his fondness for the little animal causes him to mention her frequently. Sometimes, in his books, she appears in person; sometimes her qualities are used figuratively. In "Japoneries d'Automne," he speaks of the "*mousmés aux yeux de chat.*" Rarahu, the quaint little heroine of "Le Mariage de Loti," which reminds us that the author visited the South Seas before Stevenson or Gauguin or Strickland the protagonist of "The Moon and Sixpence," loved a cat, a mournful beast named Turiri, who was sick a good deal and followed her mistress about, howling mournfully and eating blue butterflies. She arched her back at the nude Chinaman who tried to seduce Rarahu with presents, and once, after a hegira, she created a havoc at a feast by leaping on the table and disturbing the cups and plates in very uncatlike fashion. Plumket, one of the characters of the book, was called by the Tahitians, " *Oeil de Chat.*" Loti's cat figures are always descriptive: *Rarahu avait des yeux d'un noir roux, pleins d'une langueur exotique, d'une douceur caline, comme celle des jeunes chats quand on les caresse.*" Another: " *avec une prestesse de jeune chatte nerveuse et courroucée.*" Still another: " *Comme deux chattes qui vont se rouler et s'égratigner les deux petites se regardaient.*" He hears some Chinese actors, " *avec des voix de chats de gouttières.*"

His biographical pictures of his two cats, Moumoutte Blanche and Moumoutte Chinoise, are perhaps the most careful studies of cats that exist. Who that loves either Loti or pussies does not know them? In " Une bête galeuse," [3] his subject is a tom cat suffering from mange, the dread leprosy of cats, which has eaten the fur away from his head and made it impossible for him further to make his toilet. Loti rescues this poor beast from the wall where he has climbed to die and with the aid of a groom in the stables gives him chloroform. And with that unerring personal touch which is one of his passwords into the company of the immortals, he awakens our pity much more than our horror for the poor dumb brute who as he is dying fixes Loti with his eyes which seem to say, " It was to kill me you rescued me. . . . And you see, I am letting you do it. . . . It is too late. . . . I shall sleep." And the poor sick head drops in the writer's hand.

There is another harrowing study of a sick cat in the last pages of " En Rade." Huysmans, of course, spares the reader nothing. This lank, half-starved beast, belonging to Aunt Norine, came into the monotonous lives of Jacques and Louise. At first very wild, he rapidly became tame and " he rested finally sleeping with Louise, taking her throat between his paws from time to time, and through friendliness rubbing

[3] " Le Livre de la Pitié et de la Mort."

his head against her cheek." A little later Huysmans describes the animal: " The fact is that this cat, thin as a hundred nails, carried his pointed head in the form of a pike's jaw and as the climax of disgrace had black lips; his fur was ashen grey, waved with rust, a vagabond's garment, with the hair dull and dry. His hairless tail was like a cord with a little tuft at the end and the skin of his belly, torn, no doubt, in a fall, hung like a fetlock of which the dirty hair swept the ground. Were it not for his enormous caline eyes in the green fluid of which golden gravel circled incessantly, he would have been, under his poor and changeable coat, a low son of the race of the gutters, an unspeakable cat." Presently he began to die, suffering the most exquisite agony, an agony, which readers of Huysmans may well believe, is protracted for pages and discussed in detail. Indeed it may be said that this incident shares with the birth of the calf the dramatic interest of the book. It is carefully observed. When Louise tried to alleviate his suffering, " he cried at each effort and she dared not aid him because his poor body seemed to be a clavier of pain which resounded to each touch." [4] Finally Louise placed an apron over the poor beast and left him.

This cat was a composite picture of two of Huysmans's own cats. The death scene is a transcription of the final struggles of Barre-de-Rouille, a big red tabby gutter cat, who was a wonderful hunter and caught bats from Huysmans's balcony at night. He appears in his healthier days as one of the characters of " En Ménage." A later occupant of Huysmans's household, Mouche, an ugly grey cat, sat for the description of the feline in " En Rade," and appears more characteristically in " La-Bas." A true philosopher, he assists, curious but calm, at the most intimate diversions of Durtal and his mistress, while his green eyes seem to say, " How useless all

[4] This description is proof that Huysmans was well acquainted with cats, if any such proof were needed. A cat is never able to locate pain. If his foot hurts he will yowl if you touch his breast.

this is!" Mouche was an affectionate cat who waited for
Huysmans at the door and purred sympathetically when he
entered.

It is highly probable that Balzac meant his " Peines de
Cœur d'une Chatte Anglaise " [5] to be something more than a
cat story. There is every reason to believe, indeed, that it
may be regarded as an ingenious satirical comparison of the
French and British manners of making love, an ironic
commentary on Anglo-Saxon respectability. Whether J.
Thomson, the English translator of the book in which it appeared, felt that this satire was too keen for English minds
or whether he was shocked by certain rather lively passages
in the original, at any rate he saw fit to omit it from his version.
This story of the demure English puss brought up in a strict
household where she is taught to read the Bible and suppress
her desires is delicious. The cats of Albion, according to Balzac, are always respectable and never *natural*. To the simple
white Beauty comes the remarkable and splendid Puff, a
superb Angora who is so bored that he goes to sleep in front
of his prospective mistress but she, with her lack of experience, infatuated by his languor and magnificence, falls an
easy victim. She marries him but he continues to sleep every
night and she continues to suppress her desires. One night,
however, while he is asleep, her curiosity overcomes her mod-
esty and she ascends to the rooftop where she makes the
acquaintance of a rowdy French *maquereau* cat named Brisquet, who immediately finds it convenient to assail her timid
heart with such effective ammunition that I think I cannot do
better than to reproduce his impassioned appeal in full in the
original French:

*" Dear Beauty, de longtemps d'ici la nature ne pourra
former une Chatte aussi parfaite que vous. Le cachemire de
la Perse et des Indes semble être du poil de Chameau comparé*

[5] " Vie Privée et Publique des Animaux."

à vos soies fines et brillantes. Vous exhalez un parfum à faire évanouir de bonheur les anges, et je l'ai senti du salon du Prince de Talleyrand, que j'ai quitté pour accourir à ce déluge de sottises que vous appelez un meeting. Le feu de vos yeux éclaire la nuit! Vos oreilles seraient la perfection même si mes gémissements les attendrissaient. Il n'y a pas de rose dans toute l'Angleterre qui soit aussi rose que la chair rose qui borde votre petite bouche rose. Un pêcheur chercherait vainement dans les abîmes d'Ormus des perles qui puissent valoir vos dents. Votre cher museau fin, gracieux, est tout ce que l'Angleterre a produit de plus mignon. La neige des Alpes paraîtrait rousse auprès de votre robe céleste. Ah! ces sortes de poils ne se voient que dans vos brouillards! Vos pattes portent mollement et avec grâce ce corps qui est l'abrégé des miracles de la création, mais que votre queue, interprète élégant des mouvements de votre cœur, surpasse: oui! jamais courbe si élégante, rondeur plus correcte, mouvements plus délicats ne se sont vus chez aucune Chatte."

You will not be able to believe that any woman's virtue would be proof against such an attack, but Beauty fled from it . . . only to return a few nights later. She began to feel drawn towards the rooftops as Louise felt the call of Paris, and when Brisquet began to talk carelessly about his conquest and she began to murmur in her sleep, " *Cher petit homme!* " in French, Puff at last woke up, dragged his unfortunate wife to Doctors' Commons, and secured a divorce. A little later Brisquet was stabbed in the back and the disgraced Beauty was left entirely alone. The irony of the story lies in the fact that her husband has never satisfied her longings and she has throughout been afraid to yield to her lover. The little *déclassée* at the end of the tale is as pure as the virgin of the beginning.

In Balzac's " Une Fille d'Ève," the musician Schmuke has a magnificent Angora named Murr: *" Je l'ai nommé Murr "* remarks his master, " *pur clorivier nodre crant Hoffmann te Perlin, ke ché paugoube gonni.*" Hoffmann's cat Murr, indeed, was something more than a literary philosopher. The death of Murr was one of the profound events in this fantastic writer's life. To his friend Litzig he wrote on November 30, 1821 : " In the night between the twenty-ninth and thirtieth of November, my dear pupil, the cat Murr, went to sleep to relive in a better life, after short but violent suffering. He was four years old and full of hope. Those who know that I weep will understand my grief and will respect it — by their silence."

There are many felines in the novels of Émile Zola. He began by putting two, one black, the other white, in his "Nouveaux Contes à Ninon." In the foyer of the theatre of Bordenaire in " Nana " there is an enormous red cat who has an aversion for the odour of the gum which the old comedian Bosc rubs on his cheeks in order to attach his beard. In " La Faute de l'Abbé Mouret " there are three cats, country cats, like Zola's cats at Médan. The black one is called Moumou. There is also François, the cat with the hard, ironic, cruel gaze, of the diabolic stare in " Thérèse Raquin." Zola's own favourite was Minouche of " La Joie de Vivre," a little white cat with delicate airs, whose tail twitched with disgust at the sight of mud, but who nevertheless ventured four times a year into the soft mud of the brooks. Zola was an ardent ailurophile and there were always several cats at Médan.

In that inconceivably stupid, pretentious, highfalutin, and altogether reprehensible bundle of nonsense called " Eugene Aram," Bulwer-Lytton has drawn an extraordinarily life-like picture of a cat. As every human character in the book is made of wax, or wood, or sand, and as cats are infinitely more difficult to individualize and describe than men, this feat must be set down as one of some importance. Jacobina, for so is the grimalkin called, belongs to Corporal Bunting, whom

THE PRINCESS AND THE CAT

From the Japanese print by Kiyonobu I, in the collection of Arthur Davison Ficke

BEAUTY AND BRISQUET

From a drawing by Grandville in Vie privée et publique des animaux

"A LITTLE LION, SMALL AND DAINTY SWEET"
From a copyright photograph by Harriet V. Furness

"JAMAIS CHATTE NE FUT SI BELLE,
JAMAIS CHATTE NE ME PLUT TANT"

From a photograph by Harriet V. Furness

THE CAT AND THE ALCHEMYSTICAL CAULDRON

From a photograph by Harriet V. Furness

THE TOMB OF MADAME DE LESDIGUIERES'S CAT

From an engraving in Moncrif's Les Chats

RENDEZ-VOUS DE CHATS

From a poster by Edouard Manet

FEATHERS ALERT

From a photograph by Harriet V. Furness

The Cat in Fiction

she loves with a unique devotion, which, of course, is returned, for cats only display this emotion when it is richly deserved. Corporal Bunting calls her " daughter, wife, friend," and the brindled Jacobina rubs her sides against his leg and purrs.

Under the tutelage of the corporal she had become a remarkable animal, learning to fetch and carry, to turn over head and tail like a tumbler, to run up his shoulder, " to fly as if she were mad at any one upon whom the corporal saw fit to set her; and, above all, to rob larders, shelves, and tables, and bring the produce to the corporal, who never failed to consider such stray waifs lawful manorial acquisitions. These little feline cultivations of talent, however delightful to the corporal, had, nevertheless, rendered the corporal's cat a proverb and byword in the neighbourhood. Never was a cat in such bad odour; and the dislike in which it was held was wonderfully increased by terror,— for the creature was signally large and robust, and withal of so courageous a temper, that if you attempted to resist its invasion of your property it forthwith sat up its back, put down its ears, opened its mouth, and bade you fully comprehend that what it feloniously seized it could gallantly defend. . . . Various deputations had, from time to time, arrived at the corporal's cottage requesting the death, expulsion, or perpetual imprisonment of the favourite. But the stout corporal received them gruffly, and the cat went on waxing in size and wickedness, and baffling, as if inspired by the devil, the various gins and traps set for its ·destruction."

Miss Repplier relates an anecdote of a Southern gentleman who brought suit in a court of law against his next-door neighbour for alienating the affections of his cat. The testimony declared that a certain maltese puss was the plaintiff's sole companion who spent her evenings devotedly by the side of her master. This happy life was broken into by the advent of a widow who rented the adjoining house and garden. Puss visited the new neighbour and was welcomed. Soon she began to pass her days there, but the gentleman overlooked this as he was away until sundown and only began to miss his cat when dinner time arrived. A little later, however, the fickle maltese stayed away at night, and when brought back by force, sulked and glowered in corners until she could again escape. The widow declared in court that an intelligent cat had the right to choose her own friends and surroundings and, however the suit ended, one may be sure that the cat continued to exercise her own preferences.

In his very amusing "Zut," the talented Guy Wetmore Carryl has related a similar story, the story of a cat who lived in the *épicerie* of Jean-Baptiste Caille in the Avenue de la Grande Armée in Paris. Zut was "a white Angora cat of surpassing beauty and prodigious size. She had come into Alexandrine's possession as a kitten, and, what with much eating and an inherent dislike for exercise, had attained her present proportions and her superb air of unconcern. It was from the latter that she derived her name, the which, in Parisian argot, at once means everything and nothing, but is chiefly taken to signify complete and magnificent indifference to all things mundane and material: and in the matter of indifference Zut was past-mistress. Even for Madame Caille herself, who fed her with the choicest morsels from her own plate, brushed her fine fur with excessive care, and addressed caressing remarks to her at minute intervals throughout the day, Zut manifested a lack of interest that amounted to contempt. As she basked in the warm sun at the shop door, the round face of her mistress beamed upon her from the little desk, and the voice of her mistress sent fulsome flattery winging towards her on the heavy air. Was she beautiful, mon Dieu! In effect all that one could dream of the most beautiful! And her eyes, a blue like the heaven, were they not wise and calm? Mon Dieu, yes! It was a cat among thousands, a mimi almost divine." Now Madame Alexandrine Caille bore a rich

The Cat in Fiction

resentment against Espérance Sergeot and her husband, the proprietors of the very smart hair-dressing shop immediately adjoining the grocery, and this resentment was increased when one day she perceived Zut sitting in the doorway of this shop. Zut had been allured and fascinated by the sweet odours, the mirrors, the soft cushions, and when Espérance fed her cream and fish, she capitulated and purred as she had not been in the habit of purring for Alexandrine. Her mistress tore puss away from this life of shameless luxury but Zut returned and bore kittens at the hair-dresser's. Now on this point the Parisian law is explicit: kittens belong to the owner of the premises on which they are littered; the owner of the cat has no standing in the matter. Zut was delivered of one pure white kitten, while the rest were " any other colour," mottled types. Espérance concludes the situation and the story by retaining the prize and sending Zut and the rest of her brood back to the grocery.

Rudyard Kipling, dropping into an appropriate folklore style, has written a delicious story called, " The cat that walked by himself." [6] We are told how the cave man and his woman persuaded the dog and the horse and the cow to give up their freedom in return for food and protection; but the cat made a bargain with the woman whereby he is offered milk and a place under the roof by the hearth in return for doing only what he cares to do and would do naturally if he were wild, play and catch mice. " The Cat keeps his side of the bargain. He will kill mice and he will be kind to babies when he is in the house, just so long as they do not pull his tail too hard. But when he has done that, and between times, he is the Cat that walks by himself, and all places are alike to him. Then he goes out to the Wet Wild Woods or up on the Wet Wild Trees or on the Wet Wild Roofs, waving his wild tail and walking by his wild lone."

[6] " Just So Stories."

The Tiger in the House

Ambrose Bierce, too, curiously enough, approached the cat in the folklore spirit, writing about him in the fable form, and like the other fabulists somewhat paraphrased those who have gone before him. His three feline fables [7] are short enough so that I can give them complete.

" A cat was looking at a King, as permitted by the proverb.

" ' Well,' said the Monarch, observing her inspection of the royal person, ' how do you like me? '

" ' I can imagine a King,' said the Cat, ' whom I should like better.'

" ' For example? '

" ' The King of the Mice.'

" The sovereign was so pleased with the wit of the reply that he gave her permission to scratch his Prime Minister's eyes out."

" A Cat fell in love with a handsome Young Man, and entreated Venus to change her into a woman.

" ' I should think,' said Venus, ' you might make so trifling a change without bothering me. However, be a woman.'

" Afterward, wishing to see if the change were complete, Venus caused a mouse to approach, whereupon the woman shrieked and made such a show of herself that the Young Man would not marry her."

" Hearing that the Birds in an aviary were ill, a Cat went to them and said that he was a physician, and would cure them if they would let him in.

" ' To what school of medicine do you belong? ' asked the Birds.

" ' I am a Miaulopathist,' said the Cat.

" ' Did you ever practice Gohomœopathy? ' the Birds inquired, winking faintly.

" The Cat took the hint and his leave."

[7] "Fantastic Fables"; G. P. Putnam's Sons; 1899.

The Cat in Fiction

In "Blind Alley," Mr. W. L. George has written a book about the effect of the war on an upper middle class English family. Every character in the story, save alone the cat, comes to the end of a blind alley as the result of the world conflict and Mr. George seems to imply that England and the world in general have come to the end of a blind alley too. But through the general agitation, prostration, sex excitement, stupidity, folly, worry, and anxiety of the book, calmly walks Kallikrates, the orange Persian cat. Now if Mr. George intended anything at all by this cat, and he must have intended a good deal because Kallikrates opens and closes the book and, along with an otherwise unmentioned creature named Russet, receives half the dedication, he intended to convey his superiority to any of the human beings about whom he has written. There is about this feline an abstraction from things real, a separation of spirit from matter, a meditativeness, which place him on a plane considerably higher than that of the human philosophy which occasionally for brief periods sustains the people of the book. "Kallikrates," murmurs Sir Hugh, "If you were a man I don't think you would have joined up." . . . And again: "Ah! Kallikrates didn't care. He went on purring, and drinking milk, and begging for toast. And when he wanted you he put an enormous paw, lined with orange velvet, upon your knee. And when he didn't want you he just walked away, leaving behind him a trail of contempt. Oh! fortunate cat, aloof from all passions and all responsibilities, centre of his visible world, on whom no emotions are enjoined and that dwells on an Olympus below the crest of which loves and duties hang pale as clouds. Like a god, looking down without emotion or curiosity on little servant men." Later, in the midst of war, Sir Hugh apostrophizes the superb feline eunuch: "'Sultan! Debauchee! Don Juan! Casanova! Petronius! Demetrios! Marguerite of Navarre and Maria Monk! Thou dost contain all their sensuous souls, Oh, Kallikrates, lascivious and epicene!

The Tiger in the House

Is this not for thee a world of velvet and down, padded against all shocks, running with the milk of Canaan and the honey of Hymettus? When the last constellations faint and fall, as thine own Sussex poet says, thou shalt neither faint nor fall.' He poked the cat suddenly in the ribs: ' Get up! you fat yellow pig. Don't you know that there's a revolution going on in Russia? Don't sit there, and purr, and be superior to such things. I'll have no Plato in this house urging me to moderation and aloofness. What do you think I keep you for? Charity brat! Not to sit there like a sham Socrates, pleading by your inaction that life and death are the same thing.' Kallikrates very slowly rose, yawned enormously, stretched and lay down again on his side, his rosy nose hidden between his hind paws. Alone, a watchful strip of yellow eye showed that he was ready to bite and claw if the sacred fur of his belly was touched. For a moment Sir Hugh thought only of his cat's beauty. Then he came to regret that in the present times beauty should be so little cared for, so easily abandoned, when little mortals took to political agitation." And at the end of the book we leave the delightful Kallikrates on Sir Hugh's desk: " A long stare of his amber eyes assured him that nothing dangerous lay there. So slowly, cautiously, he sank down, one after the other folded the velvet gauntlets of his paws, composed his squat head into the sumptuous silk of his ruff. His eyelids began to droop, the watchful strip of gold below them grew less and less. He breathed louder; by degrees there purred forth from his throat the soft song that conceals neither joy, nor pain, nor hope, but is all content, uncritical and faith eternal in the permanence of aloof good things in an unchanging world."

In many novels the cat has appeared as a domestic accessory, a necessity of the fireside; in others he has played a part in the drama, lived his little life, or died his little death, but, for the first time, in " Blind Alley " he emerges as a critic and philosopher, and a true superior to man.

Chapter Eleven: The Cat and the Poet

In that remarkable volume in which Cesare Lombroso attempts to prove that all men of genius are tainted with insanity he makes a complete case against Charles Baudelaire. The charges are that he wrote three poems about cats. But if three poems would put the poet of the " Fleurs du Mal " in Bedlam, Madame Deshoulières, who wrote more than a dozen, Heinrich Heine, Joseph Victor von Scheffel, Raoul Gineste, and Oliver Herford would have to be strait-jacketed and given the water cure! Why, one might ask the learned professor, were he still alive, is it any more evidence of insanity to choose puss for the subject of a rhyme than a mountain or a man, not to speak of a Greek vase or a skylark? And doubtless the good doctor would lay a portentous finger on his lip and ejaculate a ponderous and all-knowing " ah! " which might settle the question so far as he was concerned, but which might leave us in some doubt as to the validity of his preposterous conclusions. But these men of science, in their valiant attempts to prove something, stop at nothing. " They show a want of knowledge that must be the result of years of study," Oscar Wilde once sapiently remarked.

Poets, I believe, are more closely in touch with the spirit of grimalkin, the soul of a pussy-cat, than either prose writers or painters. They should be, because poets are mystics, at least the great poets are mystics, speaking like the oracle or the clairvoyant, words that come, of which they themselves may not even understand the meaning. And the poet knocks at gates which sometimes open wide, disclosing gardens to which entrance is denied to those who stumble to find truth in

reason and experience. Faith is needed to comprehend the
cat, to understand that one can never completely comprehend
the cat.

Puss rambles in and out of verse from an early date.
Doubtless Babylonians, Zends, and shaggy Patagonians wrote
poems about the cat. She appears in Greek poetry and early
Persian. Lope de Vega is reported to have celebrated her
bewildering beauty and Saadi refers to her in his " Gulistan."
Tasso indited a sonnet to her. One Domenico Balestieri in
1741 published in Milan a volume entitled " Tears upon the
death of a cat," [1] in which two hundred and eighty-five pages
in several languages are consecrated to the memory of a single
tabby.

English poets have not neglected the cat; nor on the whole
have they been unkind to her, but generally they have been
quite content to describe her as a hunter of rats and mice and
birds, as a fireside companion, or as a plaything. By a curious irony the cat denotes the commonplace as often as she does
the mystic. She is the complement of the peasant's hearth
and the shop-keeper's friend, just as surely as she is the astrol-
oger's apprentice and the familiar of the pythoness.
Goldsmith strikes this common chord of C major when he
writes:

> *Around, in sympathetic mirth,*
> *Its tricks the kitten tries;*
> *The cricket chirrups on the hearth,*
> *The crackling fagot flies.*

Robert Herrick sounds the same harmony:

> *A cat I keep,*
> *That plays about my house,*
> *Grown fat with eating*
> *Many a miching mouse.*

[1] I have found frequent references to this work, but have never seen the book itself.

The Cat and the Poet

Another example from this writer is prettier:

> *Yet can thy humble roof maintaine a quire*
> *Of singing crickets by thy fire;*
> *And the brisk mouse may feast herselfe with crumbs,*
> *Till that the green-eyed kitling comes.*

Even Gautier and Heine, to whom cats were something of a religion,[2] devoted passages in their poems to the domestic possibilities of puss.

Seldom, indeed, until recently at least, has there seemed anything mysterious about the cat to the English poet; to his unobservant eyes she has appeared as matter-of-fact an animal as the cow or the dog, although differing in external appearance and character from either. It is only in the late nineteenth and the twentieth century that cat-worship has been revived in England and that the strange complexities of her occult nature have come to be admired again.

One of the earliest of the English bards, John Skelton, treats her harshly, but he is writing a poem about a sparrow. Naturally, therefore, he calls down vengeance

> *On all the whole nacyon*
> *Of cattes wylde and tame;*
> *God send them sorowe and shame!*
> *That cat especyally*
> *That slew so cruelly*
> *My lytell pretty sparowe.*[3]

[2] "*Les pachas aiment les tigres; moi j'aime les chats,*" wrote Théophile Gautier; "*les chats sont les tigres des pauvres diables. Hormis les chats, je n'aime rien. . . .*"

[3] Canning probably wrote the first bird-poem in which the sympathy lies with the cat:

> *Tell me, tell me, gentle Robin,*
> *What is it sets thy heart a-throbbing?*
> *Is it that Grimalkin fell*
> *Hath killed thy father or thy mother,*
> *Thy sister or thy brother,*
> *Or any other?*

The Tiger in the House

Chaucer writes:

> *For whoso woldè senge a cattès skyn,*
> *Thenne wolde the cat wel dwellen in hir in;*
> *And if the cattès skyn be slyk and gay,*
> *She wol nat dwelle in housè half a day.*
> *But forth she wol, er any day be dawed,*
> *To shewe hir skyn, and goon a-caterwawed.*

The characters of Shakespeare frequently allude to the cat, but none of them seems to be her friend. We can bear

> *A harmless necessary cat,*

which is not entirely a gnostic view, from Shylock, and Antonio's

> *For all the rest,*
> *They'll take suggestion as a cat laps milk,*

in *The Tempest* has become a commonplace of English speech. Lady Macbeth says,

> *Letting I dare not wait upon I would,*
> *Like the poor cat i' the adage,*

and the picture of feline caution is an accurate one, but Romeo cries,

> *Every cat and dog,*
> *And little mouse, every unworthy thing,*

which is paralleled by the remark of Cornelius in *Cymbeline,*

> *Creatures vile, as cats and dogs,*
> *Of no esteem.*

> *Tell me but that,*
> *And I'll kill the cat.*
> *But stay, little Robin, did you ever spare*
> *A grub on the ground or a fly in the air?*
> *No, that you never did, I'll swear;*
> *So I won't kill the cat;*
> *That's flat.*

Raoul Gineste also takes the part of the cat in *Le Serin.*

The Cat and the Poet

We may at least be glad to find dogs included in this diatribe. Lysander shouts at Hermia:

Hang off, thou cat, thou burr: vile thing, let loose!

And Bertram says of Parolles in *All's Well:*

I could endure anything before but a cat, and now he's a cat to me,

and later:

He is more and more a cat,

and again:

He's a cat still.

It is only in *Macbeth* that one gets a portent of the mystery of the cat; only in *Macbeth* that Shakespeare seems to realize the relation of puss to the occult.

Thrice the brinded cat hath mewed

is the line that saves Shakespeare.

Pope refers casually to the practice, prevalent then as now, of leaving money to cats, in the line,

endow a college or a cat.

George Tuberville wishes he were a cat so that he could protect his mistress from mice:

The Mouse should stand in Feare,
So should the squeaking Rat;
All this would I doe if I were
Converted to a Cat.

The fabulists, of course, regard all animals from the moral point of view. Under the circumstances the cat may be said to come off well. In Edward Moore's fable, " The Farmer, the Spaniel, and the Cat," the dog complains because the cat is given food:

The Tiger in the House

They only claim a right to eat,
Who earn by services their meat.

Whereupon, in the very best Rollo book style:

I own (with meekness Puss reply'd)
Superior merit on your side;
Nor does my breast with envy swell,
To find it recompens'd so well.
Yet I, in what my nature can,
Contribute to the good of man.
Whose claws destroy the pilf'ring mouse?
Who drives the vermin from the house?
Or, watchful for the lab'ring swain,
From lurking rats secures the grain?
From hence, if he awards bestow,
Why should your heart with gall o'erflow?
Why pine my happiness to see,
Since there's enough for you and me?

Thy words are just, the Farmer cry'd,
And spurn'd the snarler from his side.

Gay wrote three fables about the cat and in two of them, " The
Rat-catcher and the Cats " and " The Man, The Cat, the
Dog, and the Fly," he treats of puss from the same utilitarian
point of view.   But in " The Old Woman and Her Cats," in
which he touches on the subject of witchcraft, he plunges a
little deeper into his theme:

A wrinkled Hag, of wicked fame,
Beside a little smoky flame
Sat hov'ring, pinch'd with age and frost;
Her shrivell'd hands, with veins embossed,
Upon her knees her weight sustain,
While palsy shook her crazy brain:
She mumbles forth her backward pray'rs,
An untam'd scold of fourscore years.
About her swarm'd a num'rous brood
Of Cats, who lank with hunger mew'd.

The Cat and the Poet

Teas'd with their cries, her choler grew,
And thus she sputter'd: Hence, ye crew.
Fool that I was, to entertain
Such imps, such fiends, a hellish train!
Had ye been never hous'd and nurs'd,
I, for a witch, had ne'er been curs'd.
To you I owe, that crowds of boys
Worry me with eternal noise;
Straws laid across, my pace retard;
The horse-shoe's nail'd (each threshold's guard);
The stunted broom the wenches hide,
For fear that I should up and ride.

Tabby's reply is the wail of all the cats of the middle ages:

'Tis infamy to serve a hag;
Cats are thought imps, her broom a nag;
And boys against our lives combine,
Because, 'tis said, your cats have nine.

In Peter Pindar's " Ode to Eight Cats " the poet wishes he too were a cat for somewhat the same reason that Walt Whitman exalts the animals, because they do not need lawyers and preachers and furniture. While these stanzas are, like so much of English verse concerning puss, purely external, they have humour and a certain limited kind of observation and as they are not to be found in the other cat books or anthologies I will quote them here, omitting the four moralizing verses:

AN ODE TO EIGHT CATS

Belonging to Israel Mendez, a Jew

SCENE: *The street in a country town; Time: Midnight; The poet at his chamber window.*

Singers of Israel, O ye singers sweet,
Who with your gentle mouths from ear to ear,
Pour forth rich symphonies from street to street,
And to the sleepless wretch, the night endear!

253

The Tiger in the House

Lo, in my shirt, on you these eyes I fix,
Admiring much the quaintness of your tricks!
Your friskings, crawlings, squalls, I much approve;
Your spittings, pawings, high-raised rumps,
Swelled-tails and Merry-Andrews jumps,
With the wild ministrelsy of rapturous love.

How sweetly roll your gooseberry eyes,
As loud you tune your amorous cries,
And loving, scratch each other black and blue!
No boys in wantonness now bang your backs,
No curs, nor fiercer mastiffs, tear your flax,
But all the moonlight world seems made for you.

     *   *   *   *   *

Good gods! Ye sweet love-chanting rams!
How nimble are you with your hams
To mount a house, to scale a chimney top,
And peeping from that chimney hole,
Pour in a doleful cry, the impassioned soul,
Inviting Miss Grimalkin to come up:

Who, sweet obliging female, far from coy,
Answers your invitation note with joy,
And scorning 'midst the ashes more to mope;
Lo! borne on Love's all-daring wing
She mounteth with a pickle-herring spring,
Without the assistance of a rope.

Dear mousing tribe, my limbs are waxing cold —
Singers of Israel sweet, adieu, adieu!
I do suppose you need now to be told
How mnch I wish that I was one of you.

No feline poem is better known than Thomas Gray's " On the death of a favourite cat, drowned in a tub of gold-fishes," but Gray again only deals in externals. " Demurest of the tabby kind," the pensive Selima is drawn with the broadest strokes. The poem is graceful but it can be said of it that it

The Cat and the Poet

scarcely scratches the surface of the subject of cats. William Cowper's two cat poems, in one of which there occurs a catastrophe [4] much like that around which "The Bride of the Mistletoe" is built, are still external but they, too, are very pleasing. The picture of the kittens playing with the forked tongue of the viper is charming and "The Retired Cat" almost tastes of the mystic flavour. There is something intensely feline in the description of the poet's cat:

> Sometimes her ease and solace sought
> In an old empty watering-pot;
> There wanting nothing save a fan,
> To seem some nymph in her sedan,
> Apparell'd in exactest sort,
> And ready to be borne to Court.

One of Matthew Prior's poems to a cat is a version of the Aesop Fable which relates the story of the cat who was changed into a woman by Venus. His "Lines on a Reasonable Affliction," which Graham R. Tomson includes in her collection, scarce refer to the cat at all. I certainly shall not linger over the sentimental and silly verses which Rumpelstilzchen and Hurlyburlybuss are alleged to have written to Robert Southey. No cat, it would seem, could write so ill. Nor need one stop to admire Tom Hood's verses, "Puss and Her Three Kittens." But Joanna Baillie seems to have been trembling on the verge of the discovery of the psychic nature of the cat. In her poem she describes a kitten at play with exquisite felicity and she asks:

> Whence hast thou then, thou witless Puss,
> The magic power to charm us thus?
> Is it, that in thy glaring eye,
> And rapid movements we descry,
> While we at ease, secure from ill,

---

[4] François Coppée once remarked that all cats die a tragic death. "There is not," he said, "a single case on record of a cat who died in his bed!"

The Tiger in the House

The chimney corner snugly fill,
A lion darting on his prey?
A tiger at his ruthless play?

Wordsworth sings of a " kitten's busy joy." Shelley was
surely not inspired when he wrote his lines on an esurient cat
and Keats's sonnet, in the nature of a query to his cat, is very
unimaginative. The poet is content to ask how many frays
puss has fought, how many rats and mice he has captured.
A subtler artist would have sought more occult information,
asked concerning the temples of the Nile and the Witches'
Sabbath, asked of Cardinal Wolsey and the Archbishop of
Taranto, asked of Victor Hugo and Madame Deshoulières
and the doors of Isaac Newton.[5] Landor reasons with his
Chinchinillo in the matter of pigeon-slaughter, apparently with
small result:

> *I doubt his memory much, his heart a little,*
> *And in some minor matters (may I say it?)*
> *Could wish him rather sager.*

This from the man who spoiled a cook and a bed of violets
simultaneously! C. S. Calverley's " Sad Memories " are an
impertinent invasion of the sacred arcane mysteries of the cat
mind, about which the poet, of course, proves that he knows
nothing. We need not pause over Tennyson's verses, " The
Spinster's Sweet-arts " but pass on to the modern writers who,
it would seem, are more conversant with the mystic essence of
the cat than their earlier brethren.[6] Mr. A. C. Benson, to be

[5] Isaac Newton had a large hole cut in his door for his old cat and a small
one for his kittens! These cat doors, which afford easy egress or ingress to
the animal, still exist in some Andalusian towns, according to Somerset
Maugham ("The Land of the Blessed Virgin"; Heinemann; 1905). Their
disappearance in England and France is proof, according to Miss Repplier,
of the advanced esteem in which the cat is held, for now people open and
shut doors for her when she asks to get in or out.

[6] This is probably due to French influence. The modern English poets may
have studied Baudelaire.

The Cat and the Poet

sure, falls in with the dog-lovers in his apostrophe to the panther of the hearth:

> *Cold eyes, sleek skin, and velvet paws,*
> *You win my indolent applause,*
> *You do not win my heart.*

We really must go back to Matthew Arnold, for it is in his
picture of Atossa that the cat enters her great period in English poetry. Here the poet almost achieves a French understanding of the cat:

> *Cruel, but composed and bland,*
> *Dumb, inscrutable, and grand;*
> *So Tiberius might have sat,*
> *Had Tiberius been a cat.*

Mr. Swinburne's

> *Stately, kindly, lordly friend,*
> *Condescend*
> *Here to sit by me, and turn*
> *Glorious eyes that smile and burn,*
> *Golden eyes, love's lustrous meed,*
> *On the golden page I read.*

is perhaps a little sentimental, but Richard Garnett's " Marigold " is magnificent:

> *She moved through the garden in glory, because*
> *She had very long claws at the end of her paws.*
> *Her back was arched, her tail was high,*
> *A green fire glared in her vivid eye;*
> *And all the Toms, though never so bold,*
> *Quailed at the martial Marigold.*

But no other English poet, it seems to me, has so well sounded
the depths of cat nature, so well suggested the soul of the
mystic mammal, as Graham R. Tomson (Mrs. Rosamund
Ball Marriott Watson) in her three verses. The plea to the
puss in another world:

The Tiger in the House

Nor, though Persephone's own Puss you be,
Let Orcus breed oblivion — of me,

is irresistibly appealing; so is the description in " Arsinoë's Cats ":

A little lion, small and dainty sweet
(For such there be!)
With sea-grey eyes and softly stepping feet.

The sonnet to the Chat Noir is Baudelairean in its harmonies, and although like the others, it has been often quoted, I make no apology for reprinting it:

Half loving-kindliness and half disdain,
Thou comest to my call serenely suave,
With humming speech and gracious gestures grave,
In salutation courtly and urbane:

Yet must I humble me thy grace to gain —
For wiles may win thee, but no arts enslave,
And nowhere gladly thou abidest save
Where naught disturbs the concord of thy reign.

Sphinx of my quiet hearth! who deignst to dwell
Friend of my toil, companion of mine ease,
Thine is the lore of Ra and Rameses;
That men forget dost thou remember well,
Beholden still in blinking reveries,
With sombre sea-green gaze inscrutable.

William Watson's " great Angora . . . throned in monumental calm . . . immobile, imperturbable," too, sticks in the memory.

American poets do not all come off very well in their cat poems. Bret Harte's " Miss Edith's Modest Request " is not inspired; it might have been written by anybody for any newspaper. Nor can I find much to delight me in the " Two Cats " of Ella Wheeler Wilcox, although the lady herself

The Cat and the Poet

was a passionate felinophile. Her mother treated cats rudely and used to throw them out of doors at night. Little Ella protested: "Put him out a-walkin', mama, put him out a-walkin'." Somewhat later in life Mrs. Wilcox (then Miss Wheeler) wrote a song called, "Mother, Bring my Little Kitten." "It was supposed," Mrs. Wilcox explains in her priceless book, "The Worlds and I," "to be a dying child asking for her pet, which she feared she might not meet in heaven. It was mere sentimental stuff, of no value, of course. But the 'Funny Man' on the Waukesha Democrat (I think that was the paper) poked much fun at me, and said I ought to follow my song with another, 'Daddy, do not drown the puppies.'" Mrs. Wilcox took the suggestion as a cat laps milk and published the new poem in one of the Wisconsin papers. The refrain ran as follows:

> *Save, oh, save one puppy, daddy,*
> *From a fate so dark and grim —*
> *Save the very smallest puppy —*
> *Make an editor of him.*

Mrs. Wilcox adds that her brother Ed liked these lines better than any others she ever wrote. I am inclined to believe that Ed exhibited excellent literary judgment.

However I do not wish to speak unkindly of journalistic verse. I found the following stanzas by Miriam Teichner in a newspaper and, as they touch a phase of our subject not elsewhere dealt with in this volume, I should like to reproduce them. Any one who has eaten in these restaurants (and which of us has not?) will recall

THE TABLE D'HÔTE CAT

> *Now are we come on troublous times,*
> *So I will sing unruffled rhymes.*
> *This one is written, hoping that*
> *The table d'hôte-ish pussy cat,*

259

The Tiger in the House

That creature base and unrefined,
Will for the nonce, distract your mind.

Imagine lives (the cat boasts nine)
Spent in the flow of thin red wine!
See where the cocktail-sired bon mot
Inspires the luckless beast with woe.
Hedged in a brush of table legs,
See how she dodges, skulks and begs
For chicken bones, or thin and pale,
The sardine's limp anaemic tail.

It's wrong — all wrong. That cat should be
Out scouring alleys, blithe and free,
A tiny lion, jungle wise,
Or dreaming with ecstatic eyes
Before a homey hearth. But here
In this too hectic atmosphere
How must all life seem stale and flat!
Pity the table d'hôte-ish cat.

In " Feline Philosophy by Thomas Cat," Walter Léon Hess in fifty " caterwauls " has written a long epic in free verse. There is little about the cat in these pages, however; Thomas tells the sordid story of his masters. But the following lines have point:

How lucky to be a cat
Free to accept or — refuse
What is offered!

Oliver Herford's drawings are perhaps more important than his verses, but he occasionally writes some very charming lines. This paraphrase, for example, is delightful:

Kittens, you are very little,
And your kitten bones are brittle,
If you'd grow to Cats respected,
See your play be not neglected.

The Cat and the Poet

Smite the Sudden Spool, and spring
Upon the Swift Elusive String,
Thus you learn to catch the wary
Mister Mouse or Miss Canary.[7]

The ending is quite terrible:

But the Kittencats who snatch
Rudely for their food, or scratch,
Grow to Tomcats gaunt and gory,—
Theirs is quite another story.

Cats like these are put away
By the dread S.P.C.A.
Or to trusting Aunts and Sisters
Sold as sable Muffs and Wristers.

" The Whole Duty of Kittens " should be engraved in every kitten's mind:

When Human Folk at Table eat,
A Kitten must not mew for meat,
Or jump to grab it from the Dish,
(Unless it happens to be fish).

And this puts the question very neatly:

To Someone very Good and Just,
Who has proved worthy of her trust,
A Cat will sometimes condescend —
The Dog is Everybody's friend.

One of the most celebrated of the German poets devoted many of his poems to cats, a great many more than the three that Baudelaire wrote to prove to an Italian pedant that he was crazy. And the eccentric German Jew seems to have been attached to the little animal. I have found a description of

[7] This and the following two examples are from " The Kitten's Garden of Verses "; Charles Scribner's Sons; 1911.

the poet's days in the garret of his uncle :[8]   " The only creature living there being a fat Angora cat that was not especially given to cleanliness and that only rarely with her tail wiped the dirt and cobwebs away from the old rubbish that was stored there. . . . But my heart was still in the bloom of youth. . . . Everything appeared to me in a fantastic light, and the old cat herself seemed to me like a bewitched princess, who might perhaps suddenly be set free from her animal shape, and show herself in her former beauty and splendour. . . . But the good old fancy times are over; cats remain cats."

Another German poet, Joseph Victor von Scheffel, has made Hiddigeigei, the Tom Cat, one of the principal figures of his long poem, " Der Trompeter von Säkkingen." Aside from his dramatic and philosophic importance in this romance, Hiddigeigei has thirteen songs. A restaurant in Capri has been named in his honour.

But it has remained for the French poet to capture the grace, the idle charm, the magnificence, and the essential mystery of the cat; and the French poet has seldom failed to do so. The fabulists, to be sure, have not been so unerring. However, they have followed the folklore suspicion that the cat is a hypocrite and a successful rogue rather than the English fabulists' idea that puss is a Sunday School teacher. In Florian's Fable of the " Two Cats," the lazy old matou says to the lean laborious tom,

> *Va, le secret de réussir,*
> *C'est d'être adroit, non d'être utile.*

This may be true. Florian's more celebrated Fable concerns the " Cat and the Mirror." After puss has examined both sides of the glass in an effort to find the other cat he settles back, quite satisfied.

[8] T. W. Evans: " The Memoirs of Heinrich Heine "; George Bell and Sons; London; 1884.

The Cat and the Poet

Que m'importe, dit-il, de percer ce mystère?
Une chose que notre esprit,
Après un long travail, n'entend ni ne saisit,
Ne nous est jamais nécessaire.[9]

This is true feline philosophy.

La Fontaine makes the cat out a monster, a rogue, a Till Eulenspiegel, but he has been praised for doing so. " Observe," writes M. Feuillet de Conches to Champfleury, " how thorough is La Fontaine's knowledge of the cat. Rominagrobis is not Rodilardus. La Fontaine has painted the cat as he studied it, under all its aspects, and with the skill of a master. La Fontaine is the Homer of cats. And pray, what was La Fontaine himself, if not a genuine cat? That he loved the owners of the house I am glad to believe, but he loved the house itself still more. He was always curling himself up in it again. His answer to M. d'Hervart: ' I was going there! ' is a cat's answer." The Duchesse de Bouillon, a true lover of cats, asked her friend, La Fontaine, to give her a copy of every fable in which her favourite animal appeared. M. Feuillet de Conches found these precious autographs in an old garret among some ancient papers of the Bouillon estate.

The French précieuse, Madame Deshoulières, amused herself by writing a long series of poems in epistolary form between her cat, Grisette, and other cats, between her cat, Grisette, and Cochon, the dog of M. le Maréchal le Duc de Vivonne, who was the brother of Madame de Montespan. Passages from these poems are delightful.

[9] There is a well-known and oft-repeated story of a cat who, for the first time seeing his own reflection in the mirror, tried to fight it. Meeting with resistance from the glass, he next ran behind the mirror. Not finding the object of his search, he again came to the front, and while keeping his eyes deliberately fixed on the image, felt around the edge of the glass with one paw, whilst with his head twisted around to the front he assured himself of the persistence of the reflection. He never afterwards condescended to notice the mirror. . . . My cats never pay the slightest attention to mirrors.

The Tiger in the House

Tata, the cat of Madame la Marquise de Montgras writes of Grisette:

> *Jamais chatte ne fut si belle;*
> *Jamais chatte ne me plut tant,*

and Dom Gris, the cat of Madame la Duchesse de Béthune, in his love letter explains:

> *Tout matou que je suis, j'ai l'âme délicate.*

Mittin, the cat of Mademoiselle Bocquet, charmingly describes Grisette:

> *On ne vous vit jamais souiller vos pattes,*
> *Innocentes et délicates,*
> *Du sang des souris et des rats.*
> *En amour vous avez les plus belles manières;*
> *Vous n'allez point, par des cris scandeleux,*
> *Promener sur les toits la honte de vos feux,*
> *Ni vous livrer aux matous des gouttières.*

And Mittin's description of himself is irresistible:

> *J'appuie adroitement ma patte sur les bras*
> *De ceux qui sont assis à table.*
> *Si leur faim est inexorable,*
> *Ma faim ne se rebute pas;*
> *Et, d'un air toujours agréable,*
> *Je tire du moins charitable*
> *Les morceaux les plus délicats,*
> *Qu' à la fin il me tend d'une main libérale.*
> *Enfin, quoique je sois un chat des mieux nourris,*
> *Je chasse d'une ardeur qui n'eut jamais d'égale.*
> *Nul matou mieux que moi ne chasse dans Paris;*
> *Et je prétends qu'un jour mon amour vous régale*
> *D'une hécatombe de souris.*[10]

---

[10] Freely translated as "Grisette Dines" the first few lines of this excerpt from a long poem appear in Miss Repplier's anthology, "The Cat." But, it will be observed that it is *not* Grisette who dines.

The Cat and the Poet

Béranger, too, is interested in the cat in love. He writes of the amorous female:

> Tu réveilles ta maîtresse,
> Minette, par tes long cris;
> Est-ce la faim qui te presse?
> Entends-tu quelque souris?
> Tu veux fuir de ma chambrette,
> Pour courir je ne sais où;
> Mia-mia-ou: que veut Minette?
> Mia-mia-ou! c'est un matou.[11]

But of all Frenchmen, Baudelaire came the nearest to appreciating and expressing the esoteric nature of cats; he felt that they represented a phase of the occult science. His three poems to cats are mystic masterpieces and no other poet has been able to create works to rival them. Of Baudelaire's love for pussies, Gautier writes: " As I am speaking of the individual tastes and little eccentricities of the poet, let me say that he adored cats, who like him, are fond of perfumes, and easily thrown into a kind of ecstatic epilepsy by the smell of valerian. He loved these charming creatures, tranquil, mysterious, and gentle, with their electric shudderings, whose favourite attitude is the elongated pose of sphinxes, who seem to have transmitted their secrets to them. They wander about the house with velvet tread, like the genius of the place, or come and sit upon the table near the writer, keeping company with his thought, and gazing at him out the depths of their dark golden pupils with an intelligent tenderness and a magic penetration. It might almost be said that cats divine

---

[11] One might devote a volume to the study of the love-habits of the cat, which are cruel and fascinating. It is diverting to know that once mating is accomplished the male and female quarrel, thus setting an excellent example that is followed generally by the human race. In the mating process, sometimes with blooded cats a matter of days, both male and female often refuse all food! The soft purring call of the female is more amorous than the cooing of a dove.

the idea which descends from the brain to the tip of the pen, and that, stretching out their paws, they wished to seize it in its passage. They like silence, order, and quietness, and no place is so proper for them as the study of a man of letters. With admirable patience they wait until he has finished his task, emitting a guttural and rhythmic purr as a sort of accompaniment to his work. From time to time they gloss with their tongue some ruffled spot in their fur, for they are clean, fastidious, coquettish, · and permit no irregularities in their toilet, but always in a calm and discreet way, as if they were afraid to distract or annoy. Their caresses are tender, delicate, silent, and have nothing in common with the noisy and gross petulance which belongs to dogs, upon whom nevertheless, has been bestowed all the sympathy of the vulgar. All these merits were fully appreciated by Baudelaire, who has more than once addressed to cats some fine bits of verse,— the ' Fleurs du Mal ' contains three, — and often he has them flitting across his compositions as characteristic accessories. Cats abound in the verse of Baudelaire as dogs in the paintings of Paolo Veronese, and are a kind of signature. I should add that among the pretty creatures, so pleasant by day, there is a nocturnal side, mysterious and cabalistic, which is very seductive to the poet. The cat with his phosphoric eyes, which serve him as lanterns, and sparks flying from his back, fearlessly haunts the darkness, where he encounters wandering phantoms, sorcerers, alchemists, necromancers, resurrectionists, lovers, pickpockets, assassins, drunken patrols, and all those obscene larvae which sally forth and do their work only at night. He has the air of having heard last Sunday's sermon, and readily rubs himself against the lame leg of Mephistopheles. His serenades under the balcony, his *amours* on the rooftops, accompanied with cries like those of a strangled child, lend him a passably satanic aspect, which to a certain point justifies the repugnance of diurnal and practical

The Cat and the Poet

minds, for whom the mysteries of Erebus have no charm. But a Dr. Faust in his cell, encumbered with flasks and instruments of alchemy, will like always to have a cat for companion. Baudelaire himself was a voluptuous cat, indolent, with velvety ways, and full of force in his fine suppleness, fixing upon men and things a look of restless penetration, free, voluntary, hard to hold, but without perfidy withal, and faithfully attached to every one to whom he had once given his independent sympathy." [12]

Jules Lemaitre, François Coppée, Paul Verlaine, Joseph Boulmier, and Hippolyte Taine all wrote poems about cats. Verlaine's " Femme et Chatte " is nervous and electric and should have been set to music by Debussy. We must thank Lemaitre for the lines,

> *et je salue en toi, calme penseur,*
> *Deux exquises vertus: scepticisme et douceur.*

Taine's twelve sonnets to his three cats, Puss, Ebène, and Mitonne, were written in the fall of 1883 and were not intended for publication. After his death, however, they appeared in the Literary Supplement of the " Figaro " for March 11, 1893, without the authorization of the writer's heirs and executors. They have not been included in his collected works and as a result they are difficult to procure. Such specimens of them as I have been able to find may be placed with the very best cat poems. This one, for instance, dedicated to Puss, is wholly pleasing:

> *Le plaisir, comme il vient; la douleur, s'il le faut,*
> *Puss, vous acceptez tout, et le soleil là-haut,*
> *Quand il finit son tour dans l'immensité bleue,*
> *Vous voit, couchée en circle, au soir comme au matin,*
> *Heureuse sans effort, résignée au destin,*
> *Lisser nonchalamment les poils de votre queue.*

[12] From Gautier's preface to "Fleurs du Mal," P. 33. (Calmann-Lévy; Paris).

The Tiger in the House

Charles Cros's lines are likewise adorable:

> *Chatte blanche, chatte sans tache,*
> *Je te demande dans ces vers*
> *Quel secret dort dans tes yeux verts,*
> *Quel sarcasme sous ta moustache?*

But the white cat without a spot refused to reply. Cats occasionally have spoken in China, the South of France, or Alice's Wonderland, but never for the purpose of giving their secrets away. Indeed one of the oldest affinities cats have with alchemists and philosophers is their capacity for keeping secrets.[13] Imagine a frank dog present at the discovery of the *magnum opus.* "Gold! Gold!" murmurs the delighted alchemist, and the dog, barking with delight, jumps on his master, upsetting the crucible and retort and destroying the secret. But the cat would gaze through his half-closed, sleepy eyelids, "dumb, inscrutable, and grand."

Of the modern French writers Raoul Gineste and Alfred Ruffin have devoted books of poems to cats and Lucie Delarue-Mardrus has written much verse which shows that she has an affinity with the mystic beast. The following lines were first quoted (from manuscript) in "Claudine s'en va."[14] I do not know that they have appeared elsewhere.

POUR LE CHAT

> *Chat, monarque furtif, mystérieux et sage,*
> *Sont-ils dignes, nos doigts encombrés d'anneaux lourds,*
> *De votre majesté blanche et noire, au visage*
> *De pierrerie et de velours?*

---

[13] "An intending magus shall be discreet and faithful; he shall never reveal what he has been told by a spirit. Daniel was commanded to set a seal on several matters; Paul was forbidden to reveal what he beheld in his ecstasy. The importance of this ordination cannot be exaggerated." "Theosophia Pneumatica"; Frankfort; 1686.

[14] P. 47.

The Cat and the Poet

Votre grâce s'enroule ainsi qu'une chenille;
Vous êtes, au toucher, plus brûlant qu'un oiseau,
Et, seule nudité, votre petit museau
Est une fleur fraîche qui brille.

Vous avez, quoique rubanné comme un sachet,
De la férocité plein vos oreilles noires,
Quand vous daignez crisper vos pattes péremptoires
Sur quelque inattendu hochet,

En votre petitesse apaisée ou qui gronde
Râle la royauté des grands tigres sereins;
Comme un sombre trésor vous cachez dans vos reins
Toute la volupté du monde . . .

Mais, pour ce soir, nos soins vous importent si peu
Que rien en votre pose immobile n'abdique:
Dans vos larges yeux d'or cligne un regard boudhique,
Et vous vous souvenez que vous êtes un Dieu.

Madame Delarue-Mardrus has also written an apostrophe to Maut, the goddess with the head of a cat.[15]   The goddess responds with a " *surnaturel, formidable ronron:*

O vous, mes soeurs, je suis la chatte-femme.
Je possède, de par ma tête, plus qu'une âme,
Reconnaissez en moi votre animalité.

Adorez-moi!   Je suis l'instinct et son mystère.
Je suis l'amour, le charme et la fatalité,
Tant qu'il demeurera des femmes sur la terre.

Gineste meets the cat in many moods.   " Conversion " is a satire on those who like animals when they find them useful. " A cat," writes Margaret Benson, " must either have beauty and breeding, or it must have a profession."   Monsieur Prud'-homme went further than this; he insisted, apparently, that all cats should have a profession.

---

[15] " Souffles de Tempête."

269

The Tiger in the House

Monsieur Prud'homme a dit: Je n'aime pas le chat;
C'est un être cruel et traître, il égratigne;
Le chien, ami de l'homme, est, au contraire, digne
De toute mon estime; il lèche qui le bat.

Le chat, gourmand fieffé, ne lèche que le plat,
C'est un voleur subtil, un paresseux insigne,
Un animal d'humeur fantasque ou bien maligne,
Un coureur sans vergogne, un serviteur ingrat.

Or, voici que Prud'homme est près d'une tendresse
Subite pour le chat qu'il flatte, qu'il caresse,
Qu'il couche près de lui, qu'il nourrit à gogo;

Sa concierge éclaira d'un mot son égoïsme,
Affirmant que les chats prennent le rhumatisme;
Et sa personne est fort sujette au lombago.

Alfred Ruffin, too, has devoted an entire book to poems about cats. The following lines from his " Le Livre des Chats " are entitled:

LE CHAT EXILÉ

Je ne me suis jamais senti fort attristé
Des pleurs que verse un roi sur la terre étrangère:
Ces gens-là regrettant bien plus la royauté
Que la simple patrie à nous autres si chère;

Mais un honnête chat banni de son foyer,
Un chat qui n'a jamais convoité de couronne,
Sur sa juste douleur sait mieux m'apitoyer,
Car je connais le prix de ce qu'il abandonne.

L'asile où l'enchaînait depuis des jeunes ans
Le doux et fort lien des libres habitudes,
Ces murs à le frôler devenus caressants,
Ces fentes du plancher, objet de tant d'études,

The Cat and the Poet

Ce toit où s'asseyant il bâillait près du ciel,
Ces caves dont ses yeux éclairaient le mystère,
Tout cet immeuble enfin dont le maître réel
C'était lui, bien plutôt que le propriétaire,

Voilà ce qu'on lui prend! pour Québec ou Chatou
Dans la planche ou l'osier, une main assassine
Emballe miaulant l'infortuné matou:
Entendez-vous gémir l'arbre qu'on déracine?

Ah! l'amour du pays, dont l'humaine raison
Arbore en nos drapeaux la noble idolâtrie,
C'est l'instinctif amour du chat pour sa maison:
Les chats auraient sans l'homme inventé la patrie!

Et l'animal, au seuil de son logis nouveau
Vers des cieux inconnus jetant sa plainte vaine,
Fournirait pour un cadre aussi poignant tableau
Qu'Alighieri pleurant sur les bords de la Seine.

The Epilogue to this book, too, I feel that I must permit my
readers to enjoy:

Le chat est beau dans un salon,
Il est beau dans une mansarde,
Beau sur les genoux de Ninon
Comme aux pieds d'une campagnarde;

A son aise dans tout décor,
C'est un hôte aussi présentable
Sous des plafonds lambrissés d'or
Que sous les poutres d'une étable;

Et tel minet qui vit le jour
Au fond d'une arrière-boutique,
Dès qu'on le produit à la cour
Y paraît un prince authentique.

271

The Tiger in the House

Mais le chat au regard des sots
Est marqué de plus d'une tare,
Et le premier de ses défauts
C'est de n'être pas assez rare.

" Noble et beau, soit, mais si banal
Qu'on ne le vend pas, on le donne!
Souvent même on jette au canal
Ses enfants dont ne veut personne! "

Toujours d'ailleurs il s'est fait tort
Par excès de bon caractère :
Il est de trop facile abord,
Ce noble est trop égalitaire.

Accueillant pour tous les habits,
Riche ou pauvre, qui veut l'embrasse ;
Je crois même que des bandits
Il ne détourne pas sa face.

Mais il est en cela pareil,
Sur la terre où sa grâce abonde,
Au plus grand des rois, au Soleil
Qui luit gratis pour tout le monde!

It has happened, perhaps naturally enough, that some of the best poems on cats have been inspired by death. When Joachim du Bellay's cat, Bélaud, died in 1558, the poet wrote a very long epitaph in honour of his little friend. It is a lovely tribute :

C'est Bélaud, mon petit Chat gris :
Bélaud, qui fut par avanture
Le plus bel oeuvre que Nature
Fit onc en matiere de Chats :
C'étoit Bélaud, la mort aux Rats,
Bélaud, dont la beauté fut telle,
Qu'elle est digne d'être immortelle.

272

The Cat and the Poet

He describes the animal's physical appearance, his character and habits, at length. Here is a pretty passage:

Mon Dieu! quel passe-temps c'étoit
Quand ce Bélaud vire-voltoit,
Folatre au tour d'une pelotte?
Quel plaisir, quand sa tête sotte
Suivant sa queue en mille tours,
D'un roüet imitoit le cours!
Ou quand assis sur le derrière
Il s'en faisoit un jarretière,
Et montrant l'estomac velu,
De panne blanche crespelu,
Sembloit, tant sa trogne étoit bonne,
Quelque Docteur de la Sorbonne!

Domenico Balestieri's anthology of poems in several languages devoted to the memory of a single cat is not available. George Huddesford's mock-heroic " Monody on the Death of Dick, an Academical Cat," is easier to examine.

Ye Rats, in triumph elevate your ears!
Exult, ye Mice! for Fate's abhorred shears
Of Dick's nine lives have slit the catguts nine;
Henceforth he mews 'midst choirs of Cats divine!

Thus Huddesford writes and, after describing the variety of cats who mourn Dick's fall he says:

Though no funereal cypress shade thy tomb,
For thee the wreaths of Paradise shall bloom,
There, while Grimalkin's mew her Richard greets,
A thousand Cats shall purr on purple seats.
E'en now I see, descending from his throne,
Thy venerable Cat, O Whittington!
The kindred excellence of Richard hail,
And wave with joy his gratulating tail.
There shall the worthies of the whisker'd race
Elysian Mice o'er floors of sapphire chase,

273

The Tiger in the House

Midst beds of aromatic marum stray,
Or raptur'd rove beside the Milky Way.
Kittens, than eastern houris fairer seen,
Whose bright eyes glisten with immortal green,
Shall smooth for tabby swains their yielding fur,
And to their amorous mews, assenting purr; —
There, like Alcmena's, shall Grimalkin's son
In bliss repose,— his mousing labours done,
Fate, envy, curs, time, tide, and traps defy,
And caterwaul to all eternity!

There is perhaps an unwonted strain of frivolity in these lines which is not entirely lacking in the following:

Ci repose pauvre Mouton,
Que jamais ne fût glouton;
J'espère bien que le roi Pluton,
Lui donnera bon gîte et croûton.

But the epitaph for the cat of Madame Lesdiguieres, inscribed on his monument, is charming, wistful, and pathetic:

Ci-gît une Chatte jolie:
La Maîtresse qui n'aima rien,
L'aima jusques à la folie;
Pourquoi le dire? on le voit bien.

François de la Mothe le Vayer who, when he was not writing of the most abstruse matters, found it agreeable to create sonnets on cats, composed an epitaph for Marlemain, the favourite cat of Madame la Duchesse du Maine, which has been translated by Edmund Gosse.

Puss passer-by, within this simple tomb
Lies one whose life fell Atropos hath shred;
The happiest cat on earth hath heard her doom,
And sleeps for ever in a marble bed.
Alas! what long delicious days I've seen!
O cats of Egypt, my illustrious sires,

The Cat and the Poet

You who on altars, bound with garlands green,—
Have melted hearts, and kindled fond desires,—
Hymns in your praise were paid, and offerings too,
But I'm not jealous of those rights divine,
Since Ludovisa loved me, close and true,
Your ancient glory was less proud than mine.
To live a simple pussy by her side
Was nobler far than to be deified.

Ludovisa, of course, was the duchess.

These French epitaphs are filled with pity and tenderness and almost a divine sympathy with cats. All the epitaphs in English do not boast these qualities. We cannot, for example, think too highly of Whittier's effort:

Bathsheba: To whom none ever said scat,
No worthier cat
Ever sat on a mat
Or caught a rat:
Requies-cat.

Clinton Scollard's elegy on Peter, aged twelve, is an extended expression of pity for the poet himself on his loss of the " king of mousers, who no longer rubs his velvet fur against the poet's trousers." Vachel Lindsay's " Dirge for a Righteous Kitten " is better. Gray's celebrated gold-fish tub catastrophe may be taken as an epitaph in spirit and so may Sir Frederick Pollock's " Tom of Corpus," in a more robust vein. Christina Rossetti wrote verses entitled " On the Death of a Cat, a friend of mine age ten years and a half." A more subtle example is the following, which appeared in the " London Star," November 3, 1795, " imitated in English from the Latin of Dr. Jortin: "

Worn out with age and dire disease, a cat,
Friendly to all save wicked mouse and rat,
I'm sent at last to ford the Stygian lake,
And to the infernal coast a voyage make.

The Tiger in the House

Me Proserpine received and smiling said:
" Be blessed within these mansions of the dead.
Enjoy among thy velvet-footed loves,
Elysian's sunny banks, and shady groves!"
" But if I've well deserved (O gracious Queen),
If patient under sufferings I have been,
Grant me at least one night to visit home again,
Once more to see my home and mistress dear,
And purr these grateful accents in her ear:
' Thy faithful cat, thy poor departed slave
Still loves her mistress, e'en beyond the grave.'"

The cat may be said to have a mystic affinity with the perfect circle, the symbol of mystery, without beginning and without end. Through the centuries she is now worshipped or adored, now cherished as an essential of the household, a mouse-enemy. However man regards the cat does not affect the attitude that animal has towards man, which remains gently tolerant at best and aggressively feral at worst. The poet, sometimes, has seized this superiority of the cat and exalted it, perfumed it with exotic words, waved the incense of the grand phrase before it, and anointed it with the holy oil of inspiration. The poet, alone, can feel the hallucination of the circle. However it is not of *any* poet I speak. One poet alone, perhaps, has sufficiently comprehended the true significance of the cat to give his comprehension form, the poet of the " Flowers of Evil."

Dans ma cervelle se promène,
Ainsi qu'en son appartement,
Un beau chat, fort, doux, et charmant,
Quand il miaule, on l'entend à peine,

Tant son timbre est tendre et discret;
Mais que sa voix s'apaise ou gronde,
Elle est toujours riche et profonde,
C'est là son charme et son secret.

Chapter Twelve: Literary Men Who Have Loved Cats

Au lieu d'un os rongé qu'en dînant je te jette,
Si mon argent devait payer ce que tu vaux,
Oh! combien envers toi serait lourde ma dette,
Aimable inspirateur de mes plus chers travaux!
ALFRED RUFFIN.

Even in the dark ages the cat was the friend of the intelligent man, for the sorcerers and alchemists were the philosophers of the period and those who persecuted sorcerers and cats were the philistines. In our day the cat is as essential to the literary workshop as he was formerly to the alchemystical laboratory. French writers, especially, have made a fetish of the soft and independent little fellow animal. Hardly an author of distinction during the nineteenth century in Paris who did not surround himself with harems of long-haired Persian beauties. Prosper Mérimée, Théophile Gautier, Victor Hugo, Charles Baudelaire, Paul de Kock, André Theuriet, Émile Zola, Joris Karl Huysmans, Jules Lemaitre, Pierre Loti, Octave Mirbeau, and Anatole France all loved cats. Those in this list who are yet alive still do love them. Maupassant stands out as a solitary figure opposed to the cult, for I gather from his rather unsympathetic essay [1] on cats that he neither understood nor cared for them. The others revived cat-worship, for which there are sufficient reasons. Dogs are noisy, restless, clumsy, and dirty. As W. H. Hudson has remarked they are useful and therefore should be relegated with other useful animals to their proper

---

[1] " Sur les Chats " in the volume entitled, " La Petite Roque."

The Tiger in the House

place in the stables and the fields.[2] Two or three dogs about the house are sufficient to distract the attention and to claim one's time, but it is possible to endure, nay to enjoy, the companionship of seventeen or more pussies, especially if they are aristocratic pussies. They keep themselves faultlessly clean and have no odour. They walk about noiselessly. Persian cats seldom mew and when they do their voices are modulated like those of well-bred people. They offer a pleasing exterior to the eye; their velvet backs invite caresses. When a man is tired a cat does not excite his nerves; when he is rested he can turn to puss for play. It is but fair to state, however, that the cat has his own ideas about such matters. "When I play with my cat who knows whether she diverts herself with me, or I with her!" writes Montaigne

[2] The dog with all his new propensities, remains mentally a jackal, above some mammalians and below others; nor can he outlive ancient, obscene instincts which become increasingly offensive as civilization raises and refines his master man. How did our belief in the mental superiority of this animal come to exist? Doubtless it came about through our intimacy with the dog, in the fields where he helped us, and in our houses where we made a pet of him, together with our ignorance of the true character of other animals. In the Orient the dog is an unclean animal. His instincts still persist. He may be shut up in an atmosphere of opopanax and frangipani for twelve hundred years and he will love the smell of carrion still.
The moral of all this is, that while the dog has become far too useful for us to think of parting with it — useful in a thousand ways, and likely to be useful in a thousand more, as new breeds arise with modified forms and with new unimagined propensities — it would be a blessed thing, both for man and dog, to draw the line at useful animals, to put and keep them in their place, which is not in the house, and to value them at their proper worth, as we do our horses, pigs, cows, goats, sheep, and rabbits.
But there is a place in the human heart, the female heart especially, which would be vacant without an animal to love and fondle, a desire to have some furred creature for a friend . . . and this love is unsatisfied and feels itself deprived of its due unless it can be expressed in the legitimate mammalian way, which is to have contact with its object, to touch with the fingers and caress. Fortunately such a feeling or instinct can be amply gratified without the dog. W. H. Hudson in "The Great Dog-Superstition." Goethe was among those who hated dogs and Mephistopheles appeared to Faust in the form of a poodle.

278

in an essay [3] vindicating natural theology from the objections of some of his opponents. " We entertain one another with mutual follies, struggling for a garter; and if I have my time to begin or to refuse, she also has hers. It is because I cannot understand her language that we agree no better; and perhaps she laughs at my simplicity in making sport to amuse her."

It is perfectly possible (a fact which I have proved scores of times myself) to work not only with a cat in the room, but with a cat on one's shoulder or in one's lap. In a draughty room, indeed, the cat makes a superior kind of paper-weight! Cats, to be sure, love to play on tables with loose papers and pens, but a little care will keep them from doing damage, and how welcome is the soft paw tap on the pen with the look of surprise that invariably follows, to the tired writer.

As an inspiration to the author I do not think the cat can be over-estimated. He suggests so much grace, power, beauty, motion, mysticism. The perfect symmetry of his body urges one to achieve an equally perfect form. His colour and his line alone would serve to give any imaginative creator material for several pages of nervous description; on any subject, mind you, not necessarily on the cat himself. As for his intelligence, his occult power, they are so remarkable that I sometimes feel convinced that true cat-lover authors are indebted even more deeply than they believe to " cats of ebony, cats of flame " for their books. The sharp, but concealed claws, the contracting pupil of the eye, which allows only the necessary amount of light to enter, the independence, should be the best of models for any critic; the graceful movements of the animal who waves a glorious banner as he walks silently should stir the soul of any poet. The cat symbolizes, indeed, all that a good writer tries to put into his work. I do not wonder that some writers love cats; I am only surprised that all writers do not love cats.

There is another explanation for the almost general fasci-

[3] " Apologie de Raimond Sebond."

nation the cat has for the literary man. Writers as a class
are irritable, temperamental, captious, and sensitive. They
find in the soft grace, the urbanity, the reserve and the dignity
of the cat exactly the softening qualities they require to smooth
the ruggedness of life. Indeed the cat is as nearly as possible
what many a writer would like to be himself.

Some writer's cats have been celebrated so often that I see
small occasion for giving them much space in this volume.
Dr. Johnson's Hodge, for instance, who ate oysters and annoyed Boswell. If it had not been, indeed, that Boswell was
by way of being ailurophobic, we should doubtless have heard
more about Hodge who was one of the good doctor's joys.
Nor need we linger over Scott's Hinse of Hinsefield, for a
fondness for cats came late in the life of the author of
" Waverley," at heart a dog-lover. But it is worth while to
note Scott's account of his visit to the Archbishop of Taranto
at Naples, " a most interesting old man, whose foible is a
passion for cats." Sir Walter was delighted with the ecclesiastical pets. " One of them," he wrote in his journal, " is a
superb brindled Persian, a great beauty, and a particular
favourite. I remember seeing at Lord Yarmouth's house a
Persian cat,[4] but not so fine as the Bishop's." Scott was not
the only traveller who described his meeting with these cats.
Sir Henry Holland, lamenting the death of his friend, the
Archbishop, wrote, " His cat and the Archbishop sitting together as they generally did, made a picture of themselves, the
former looking the more austere theologian of the two."
And Lady Morgan's report is irresistible : " The first day we
had the honour of dining at the palace of the Archbishop of
Taranto at Naples, he said to me, ' You must pardon my passion for cats, but I never exclude them from my dining room
and you will find they make excellent company.' Between the
first and second courses, the door opened, and several enor-

[4] In the early nineteenth century Persian cats were comparatively rare in
England.

Literary Men Who Have Loved Cats

mously large and beautiful Angora cats were introduced by the names of Pantalone, Desdemona, Otello, etc. They took their places on chairs near the tables, and were as silent, as quiet, as motionless, and as well behaved as the most *bon-ton* table in London could require. On the Bishop requesting one of the chaplains to help the Signora Desdemona, the butler stepped to his lordship, and observed, ' My lord, la Signora Desdemona will prefer waiting for the roasts.' "

Steele makes delicate domestic allusions to puss in " The Tatler." His first actions on arriving home were to stir his fire and to stroke his cat. Night after night he sat between her and a little dog. " They both of them sit by my fire every Evening and wait my return with Impatience; and, at my entrance, never fail of running up to me, and bidding me Welcome, each of them in its proper Language. As they have been bred up together from Infancy, and have seen no other Company, they have acquired each other's Manners; so that the Dog gives himself the Airs of a Cat, and the Cat, in several of her Motions and Gestures, affects the Behaviour of the little Dog." Byron was lavish in his hospitality to animals. At Ravenna at one time he had five cats, eight dogs, ten horses, an eagle, a crow, a falcon, five peacocks, two guinea hens, and an Egyptian crane. Shelley was appalled by these beasts and birds but Byron found them all delightful. Miss Edgeworth and the Brontës kept cats. Carlyle had a soot-black kitten who begged tidbits from him at the table and ate them on the floor to the annoyance of Mrs. Carlyle who, during an absence, wrote to her maid, Jessie: " As long as she attends Mr. C. at meals (and she doesn't care a sheaf of tobacco for him at any other time) so long will Mr. C. continue to give her bits of meat and driblets of milk, to the ruination of the carpets and hearthrugs." There is a familiar story about Dickens and a kitten first called William, but later, for good reasons, Williamina, who to attract the author's attention, persisted in putting out a candle by which he was reading.

The Tiger in the House

And a portrait exists of Mr. Gladstone reading with a cat on his knee.

Jeremy Bentham, the apostle of utilitarianism, childless, and wifeless, lived in his house in London, surrounded by piles of books. Occasionally he was visited by admirers whom he turned away or treated with rudeness. Madame de Staël, for instance, sought an interview, and sent in her card. Charming Mr. Bentham wrote on it, " Mr. Bentham has nothing to say to Madame de Staël, and he is quite certain that Madame de Staël can have nothing to say to him," and sent it down to her! But he adored his pussy-cats. His favourite was a cat named Langbourne, who afterwards became Sir John Langbourne, and still later the Reverend Sir John Langbourne, D. D.

John Payne, the author of " The Masque of Shadows " and the translator of Villon, was possessed of an Angora cat, named Parthenopæus, who was accustomed to leap on Payne's shoulders and coil himself half way round his neck. Horace Walpole delighted in cats and Gray's letter to him on the death of a beloved beast has become a classic. In 1852 Thomas Griffiths Wainewright, the writer-poisoner, the friend of Lamb, of whom W. Carew Hazlitt and Oscar Wilde have written, died of apoplexy with his cat beside him, his sole living companion, " for whom he had evinced an extraordinary affection." Enough, it would seem, has been written concerning Southey's cats and Matthew Arnold's Atossa.

George Borrow had a deep affection for animals. One of his biographers, Herbert Jenkins, says that his horse, Sidi Habismilk, would come to a whistle and would follow him about, and his two dogs and his cat would do the same. When he went for a walk the dogs and the cat would set out with him, but the cat would turn back after accompanying him for about a quarter of a mile. When a favourite cat was so ill that he crawled away to die in solitude, Borrow went in search of him, and discovering the poor creature in the garden-hedge, carried him back into the house, laid him in a comfortable place, and watched over him until he died. But his care of the much persecuted " ecclesiastical cat " at Llangollen, referred to elsewhere in this volume, is the best evidence of his warm feeling for pussies. Walter Pater, it seems, had two long-haired Persians to grace his hearth and to sit at his table, and Andrew Lang was a passionate felinophile. His black cat, Mr. Toby, his grey Persian, Master of Gray, and the abandoned Gyp should go into any biographical dictionary of cats.

That strange intransigent genius, Samuel Butler, who, aside from his own writings and the music of Handel, found little in art to interest him, appears to have been fonder of cats than he was of men, in this respect resembling Jeremy Bentham. But he did not surround himself with exotic Persians after the fashion of many another author. The common cats of London were good enough for him, and the passages in his Note-Books and letters which refer to this passion are vibrant with interest. Early in 1873 Butler seems to have presented his equally eccentric correspondent, Miss Savage, with a cat, which she called after the name Butler first gave to the pseudonymous author of " The Fair Haven." " I have named your cat ' Purdoe,' a good name for a cat," Miss Savage writes March 10, 1873. " I baptised it with ink." Miss Savage makes reference in other letters to other pussies, Clara and Tybalt. Butler writes to her September 22, 1884, " My cat is better, and though it looks old and battered is not otherwise amiss. I am extremely sorry to hear of your bereavement. Shall you cat again? " In November of the same year he writes, " How is your cat? Mine is *so* stupid. She does not even know how to catch rats and mice. Our servant says she catches them by the tail, instead of at the back of the neck. What is to be done with her? " Butler's friend, Pauli, was in the habit of ringing the bell, if he saw a cat sitting on the doorstep, so that the owner might take the beast in. Butler was delighted with this idea and once tried it himself, but made the mistake of waiting until the servant opened the door when he explained why he had rung, only to learn that the cat did not belong to these people and that they had been trying very hard to get rid of it. In the meantime Butler seems to have lost his own cat. He writes to Miss Savage, " Don't offer me your cat. If my cat does not come back I don't mean to have a cat for some time. Jones has a real love of a cat, and when my mice get bad I will fetch it down for a day or two." In his " Note-Books " Butler records that Prince, Jones's cat, once picked up a little waif in the court and brought it home, " and the two lay together and were much lovelier than Prince was by himself." It was this same Prince that caused a child who was playing with him one day to exclaim, " Oh! it's got pins in its toes," an incident that the author used in " The Way of All Flesh." By the fall of 1885 not only Miss Savage but Butler's sister seem to have been determined that he should " cat again." He writes the latter on October 21, 1885, " No, I will not have a Persian cat; it is undertaking too much responsibility. I must have a cat whom I find homeless, wandering about the court, and to whom, therefore, I am under no obligations. There is a Clifford's Inn euphemism about cats which the laundresses use quite gravely: they say people come to this place ' to lose their cats.' They mean that, when they have a cat they don't want to kill and don't know how to get rid of, they bring it here, drop it inside the railings of our grass-plot and go away under the impression that they have been ' losing ' their cat. Well, this happens very frequently and I have already selected a dirty little drunken wretch of a kitten to be successor to my poor old cat. I don't suppose it drinks anything stronger than milk and water, but then, you know, so much milk and water must be bad for a kitten that age — at any rate it looks as if it drank; but it gives me the impression of being affectionate, intelligent, and fond of mice, and I believe, if it had a home, it would become more respectable; at any rate I will see how it works." It seems to have worked well, for six months or so later we read that the cat has become a mother. As a wet-nurse Butler was a failure. He writes to his sister in March 1886, " My kittens came and alas, went! One after another died for want of sufficient nourishment. This being their mother's first confinement, she had forgotten to make the milk necessary to feed her offsprings, and so one after another starved in spite of all I could do. I had found homes for three out of the four and was sorry to lose them. They were exceedingly pretty while they lasted, but none of them lived as long as four days. The cat frequently came and told me that things were not going right, and I soon found out what the matter was, but I could not do anything." Butler is perhaps the first and the last amateur cat-fancier to find beauty in kittens three days old. As for the lack of nourishment, probably he did not feed the mother enough; in any case it never seems to have occurred to him that kittens can be raised on a bottle as easily as human babies. In October 1886 the cat became a mother again while he was absent on a journey and he writes his sister that the kittens are " well and strong but as wild as little tigers through not having been habitually caressed." [5]

Like Butler, George Moore prefers the occidental cat. His cats, however, have not been waifs from Clifford's Inn. Cats appear now and again in his books and generally a generous-sized tom cat wanders about his home in Ebury Street. One of these is described in " Salve," [6] " a large, grey and affectionate animal upon whom Jane, without the aid of a doctor, had impressed the virtue of chastity, so successfully that he never sought the she, but remained at home, a quiet, sober animal that did not drink milk,[7] only water, and who, when

[5] These examples are from " Samuel Butler " by Henry Festing Jones; Macmillan and Co.; London; 1919, and " The Note-Books of Samuel Butler."

[6] P. 25; English edition.

[7] Many common cats are brought up on milk and they cannot be said to dislike it, but no cat breeder would think of giving milk to his cat, and a

thrown up to the ceiling, refrained from turning round, content to curl himself into a ball, convinced that my hands would receive him — an animal to whom I was so much attached that I had decided to bring him with me in a basket; but a few weeks before my departure he died of a stoppage in his entrails, brought about probably by a morsel of sponge fried in grease — a detestable and cruel way of poisoning cats often practised by porters. . . ." Moore and his Jane attempted in every conceivable way to alleviate Jim's sufferings, " but he neither ate nor drank and lay down stoically to die. Death did not come to him for a long while; it seemed as if he would never drop off, and at last, unable to bear the sight of his sufferings any longer, Jane held his head in a pail of water, and after a few gasps the trial of life was over. It may have been that he died of the fur that he licked away collecting in a ball in his entrails, and that there is no cause for me to regret the sovereign given to the porter when the great van drove up to my door to take away the bedroom and kitchen furniture." Some time later George Moore took another cat into his family, a large black tom cat with green eyes, who makes his appearance in an interview published in the " Fortnightly Review," [8] an interview which Moore later worked into a chapter for " Avowals." For this is his famous defence of censored literature, a defence which immediately preceded his decision to publish his own books privately to avoid all future arguments with the Comstocks and Sumners, and this defence was originally made before the great black tom cat of Ebury Street, who sat as judge in an arm-chair, listening gravely, but with some astonishment, to his master's plea, blinked his green eyes and finally fell asleep. Fontenelle

Persian cat, brought up on meat, will not touch it. Frequently, therefore, they die of starvation, when they are old and have lost their teeth. But a cat without a carnivorous diet is a weak cadaverous cat. It may be mentioned here that it is essential that prey be freshly killed. Cats will not eat carrion or stale food of any kind.

[8] " The Fortnightly Review "; October 1917.

tried a similar experiment once, but with less success. He rehearsed a discourse before his cat, but the animal refused to listen and left his presence. Always talking, Fontenelle followed him from room to room, upstairs and down, until at length the cat escaped to the roof! [9] But the great black tom cat of Ebury Street is dead. " I am sorry to tell you," Moore wrote me in December 1919, " that my last cat was run over, a dear cat, one of the most intelligent I have ever had, who did not mind a cuff for jumping on the table, but would not forgive you if you turned him down from your knee."

Théophile Gautier has written a book about his cats, his black and white dynasties, but delightful as these pages are they have been worn thread-bare by repetition and quotation. No felinophile, however, who has thus far passed it by should miss reading " La nature chez elle et la ménagerie intime." Pussies, exquisite or suffering, wander in and out of nearly all of Pierre Loti's books. " Vies de deux chattes " is possibly the most perfect prose yet dedicated to the charms of these gentle beasts. You may read it in French, in translation, or summarized or quoted in a dozen cat books. His studies of cats in " Reflets sur la route sombre " are less familiar. How charming, for example, is this: " A cat is watching me. . . . He is close at hand, on the table, and thrusts forward his dimly thoughtful little head, in which some unwonted flash of intelligence has just entered. Whilst servants or visitors have been on the spot, he has scornfully kept out of the way, under an armchair, for no other person than myself is allowed to stroke his invariably immaculate coat. But no sooner does he perceive that I am alone than he comes and sits in front of me, suddenly assuming one of those expressive looks that are seen from time to time in such enigmatical, contemplative animals as belong to the same genus as himself. His yellow eyes look up at me, wide open, the pupils dilated by a mental

[9] Moncrif: "Les Chats," P. 103.

The Tiger in the House

effort to interrogate and attempt to understand: 'Who are you, after all?' he asks. 'Why do I trust you? Of what importance are you in the world?' In our ignorance of things, our inability to know anything, how amazing — perhaps terrifying — if we could but see into the curious depths of these eyes and fathom the *unknowable* within the little brain hidden away there. Ah! if only for a moment we could put ourselves in its place and afterwards remember, what an instantaneous and definite solution — though no doubt terrifying enough — we might obtain of the perplexing problem of life and eternity!

"And now he is about to sleep, maybe to dream, on this table at which I am writing; he settles down as close to me as possible, after stretching out his paw towards me two or three times, looking at me as though craving permission to leap on to my knees. And there he lies, his head daintily resting on my arm, as though to say: 'Since you will not have me altogether, permit this at least, for I shall not disturb you if I remain so.'

"How mysterious is the *affection* of animals! It denotes something lofty, something superior in those natures about which we know so little. And how well I can understand Mohammed, who, in response to the chant of the *muezzin* summoning him to prayers, cut off with a pair of scissors the hem of his cloak before rising to his feet, for fear of disturbing his cat, which had settled down thereon to sleep."

Alexandre Dumas was an enormously prodigal and fecund person. He wrote a monstrous lot; he lived a lot; he ate a lot; his establishment was always crowded and among the crowds of people played crowds of pets, which he has described in "Mes Bêtes." The reader, however, will not carry away from this book the impression that Dumas was especially fond of animals, although there is a touching picture drawn of the English pointer, Pritchard. The vultures, cats, monkeys, and macaws about the place were mostly cared for by the gardener, Michel, who adored animals. Dumas was amused by them, much as was Byron.

Chateaubriand, on the other hand, was a discerning admirer of cats. Under all circumstances, he occupied himself with cats, as an ambassador, as an exile, and at the close of his life when he ruled over the literary world from the retirement of Abbaye-aux-Bois. Champfleury finds him " of all writers on this theme, the best, the most enthusiastic." " Do you not know some one, *near here,*" he asked his friend, Comte de Marcellus, " who is like a cat? I think myself, that our long familiarity has given me some of his ways." Space and Time did not permit his friend to send him Huysmans, who is described by Arthur Symons as looking like a cat,[10] or Walt Whitman, of whom Edmund Gosse [11] has said, " If it be true that all remarkable human beings resemble animals, then Walt Whitman was like a cat — a great old grey Angora Tom, alert in response, serenely blinking under his combed waves of hair, with eyes inscrutably dreaming," or La Fontaine or Baudelaire.[12] When he went on an embassy to Rome Chateaubriand received a cat as a gift from the Pope. " He was called Micetto," writes M. de Marcellus. " Pope Leo the Twelfth's cat, which came into the possession of Chateaubriand, could not fail to reappear in the description of that domestic hearth where I have so often seen him basking." Chateaubriand has immortalized his favourite: " My companion is a large grey and red cat, banded with black. He was born in the Vatican, in the loggia of Raphael. Leo the Twelfth reared him on a fold of his white robe, where I used to look at him with envy when, as ambassador, I received my

---

10 " ' He gave me the impression of a cat,' some interviewer once wrote of him; ' courteous, perfectly polite, almost amiable, but all nerves, ready to shoot out his claws at the least word.' And indeed there is something of his favourite animal about him. The face is grey, wearily alert with a look of benevolent malice." "Figures of Several Centuries," P. 270.

11 " Critical Kit-Kats," P. 103; London; 1896.

12 See Pages 263 and 267.

audiences. The successor of Saint Peter being dead, I inherited the bereaved animal. He is called Micetto, and surnamed ' the Pope's cat,' enjoying in that regard much consideration from pious souls. I endeavour to soften his exile, and help him to forget the Sistine Chapel, and the vast dome of Saint Angelo, where far from earth, he was wont to take his daily promenade." [13]

Barbey d'Aurevilly's Demonette outlived her master and was subsequently cared for by Louise Read. Her name was Desdemona, " Demonette to her intimate friends," Barbey used to explain. She was given to the writer-dandy in 1884 by Madame Constantin Paul, and he at once installed her as the favourite in his home, even allowing her to sprawl on his manuscript while he worked. She also sat by him with her paws on the table at his meals, receiving the choicest morsels from his hands. Léon Ostrowski made a sketch of this scene which appeared in the " Revue Illustrée " for January 1, 1887. " Eyes of gold on a piece of black velvet ": thus Barbey described her. When Spirito was born, Barbey cried, " My cat has made a misalliance! " But eventually he became deeply attached to Spirito, who was infinitely more tender than the Archduchess Demonette, as he sometimes called her. At Valognes he had a cat-companion whom he called Grifette but he missed the Archduchess and Spirito and he wrote, " How lovely Demonette with her black fur, this Mauritian princess, would be here in this great yellow room (the disguise of the brunettes)! Alas I have not my cats, my nocturnal companions, to caress." After the death of Barbey, Demonette could not be induced to leave his bed. An expression of terror and fright shone from her eyes. Three days later four kittens were born before their time, three of them dead; the fourth tiny little beast seemed to inherit his mother's despair.

Champfleury spent many agreeable hours discussing cats with Prosper Mérimée, who found cats excessively sensitive,

[13] " Mémoires d'Outre Tombe."

a trait which he deplored, and exceedingly polite. " In that," he said, " the animal resembles well-bred persons." In one of his letters Mérimée writes of *" un vieux chat noir, parfaitement laid, mais plein d'esprit et de discretion. Seulement il n'a eu que des gens vulgaires et manque d'usage."* Champfleury also describes Victor Hugo and his cat: " It takes an essentially feminine and poetic nature to understand the cat. In my youth I used to visit at a house in the Place Royale; the salon was hung with tapestry and decorated with Gothic ornaments; in its centre stood a large red ottoman, on which a huge cat was seated, awaiting the homage of visitors with grave dignity. This was the favourite cat of Victor Hugo, whom, in his ' Lettres sur le Rhin ' he calls Chanoine, because of his indolence and idleness." Saint-Beuve's Palémon was permitted to range undisturbed through the critic's precious manuscripts. Among the guests who came to the house he had a natural preference for Théophile Gautier. Huysmans once said, " In the matter of animals I love only cats but I love them unreasonably for their qualities and in spite of their numerous faults. I have only one but I could not live without a cat." But later he wrote, " I have been and still am a diligent friend of the feline race, but since the death of my last cat I do not own one; my affection is then for the present entirely platonic." This feeling that there will never be another, after the death of a cat, is pretty generally distributed, but in time another usually comes. Stéphane Mallarmé held that a cat was a necessary adjunct of the home. He completed it, polished the furniture, softened the angles, and gave the place mystery. He was the last bibelot, the supreme touch! Mallarmé's Lilith was sketched by Whistler.[14] François Coppée named one of his cats Bourget, who unlike his namesake, became a great fighter until finally his ears were torn to lace. His nickname was Zézé and he lived to be

[14] There is a reproduction of this sketch on P. 251 of Paul Mégnin's book, "Notre Ami le Chat."

twenty years old. Coppée owned two more celebrated cats, Loulou and Mistigris. These pussies had their own physician, M. Bourrel, who once remarked, to Coppée's delight, " These are not the first literary cats that I have had the honour of caring for. I was also the physician for the cats of M. Paul de Kock." Paul de Kock, indeed, was a true *félinophile enragé*. His property at Lilas was surrounded by a wall and within the enclosure pussies roamed at their leisure. His neighbours were familiar with his weakness and whenever they found a stray cat, they carried it to him. They did not even take the trouble to ring the bell at the gate. The cat was tossed over the wall to join the vast family already there. Frédéric Mistral loved his cat, Marcabrun. Catulle Mendès was attracted towards cats by their beauty. Aside from Mime, who committed suicide on account of certain alterations, he owned Fasolt and Fafner, who during their and his lifetime, dined at his table. Georges Courteline had a fondness for the rakish *apache* cats of the Butte Montmartre and he named them the Purotin of the Rue de Ruisseau, Charles Scherer, alias l'Infâme, alias la Terreur de Clingnancourt, la Mère Dissipée, le Petit Turbulent, and the Rouquin de Montmartre. When Ernest la Jeunesse came to Paris from Nancy he brought five cats with him, Elsa, Thaïs, Paphnuce, Bérénice, and Boudolha. From the names we would gather that these became twenty-five before the year was out. This list, you will observe, is not short. Indeed a history of the French felinophiles might serve as the literary history of France. In this connection it is interesting to remember that François Coppée, Catulle Mendès, André Theuriet, A. Sylvestre, Octave Mirbeau, Eugène Lambert, Steinlen, Pierre Mégnin, and Maurice Vaucaire served on the jury of the first cat-show [15] in Paris.

[15] Cat-shows have undoubtedly done much to raise this little animal in the estimation of unbelievers. They have also made it a great incentive to improve breeds. It is unfortunate, however, that cat-shows at present are so

Literary Men Who Have Loved Cats

"The Black Cat" is perhaps not the story of a cat-lover; nevertheless Poe loved cats, and there are those who even assert that Baudelaire inherited this passion from Poe, and took it over together with the other paraphernalia of the alchemist's retreat. At any rate a visitor to Poe in Fordham in 1846, describes this scene in his cottage: "There was no clothing on the bed, which was only straw, but a snow-white counterpane and sheets. The weather was cold and the sick lady (Mrs. Poe) had the dreadful chills that accompany the hectic fever of consumption. She lay on the straw bed, wrapped in her husband's great coat, with a large tortoise-shell cat in her bosom. The wonderful cat seemed conscious of her great usefulness. The coat and the cat were the sufferer's only means of warmth, except as her husband held her hands and her mother her feet." Mrs. Poe died in January 1847. Lafcadio Hearn, it may well be imagined, was a felinophile. "Very much do I love cats," he writes in "Kottō," "and I suppose that I could write a large book about the different cats that I have kept, in various climes and times, on both sides of the world." Alas, Hearn never wrote this book, which might have been his masterpiece, but pussies stroll through his other works.

Mark Twain completely capitulated to grimalkin; cats, indeed, it would seem were one of the necessities of life to him. In "Pudd'nhead Wilson" he says, "A home without a cat, and a well-fed, well-petted, and properly revered cat, may be a perfect home, *perhaps,* but how can it prove its title?" Cat comparisons, cat allusions, cat descriptions, cat figures, cats and kittens abound in his stories. Twain even mentions cats in his early lecture on Artemus Ward.[16] In "Following the Equator," somewhere in the Orient he remarks the ab-

largely in the hands of professional breeders, who are anxious to advance the prices of their "stock." The cat-shows in both England and France were started by artists, authors, and rich amateurs. It would be a good thing if more people in these classes would interest themselves in American cat-shows.

[16] Don C. Seitz: "Artemus Ward," P. 140.

The Tiger in the House

sence of the cat from a fauna otherwise satisfactory. " And yet," he observes plaintively, " a cat would have liked the place." In " The Stolen White Elephant " we read: " We saw upwards of a million cats in Bermuda, but the people are very abstemious in the matter of dogs. Two or three nights we prowled the country far and wide, and never once were accosted by a dog. It is a great privilege to visit such a land." [17] Mr. Clemens wrote several stories about cats and he was once photographed with a kitten. Naturally there were always cats in his home (Like George Borrow, Samuel Butler, and George Moore he specialized in the domestic variety) and I have been told that when he played billiards, his cat frequently watched him from one corner of the table. In a letter to " Saint Nicholas " [18] he speaks of Sour Mash, Apollinaris, Zoroaster, Blatherskite, " names given them, not in an unfriendly spirit, but merely to practise the children in large and difficult styles of pronunciation."

All readers of " Roughing It " will remember Tom Quartz, " who wouldn't let the Gov'ner of Californy be familiar with him," and who " never ketched a rat in his life —'peared to be above it. You couldn't tell *him* nothin' 'bout placer diggins —'n' as for pocket mining, why he was jest born for it. He would dig out after me an' Jim when we went over the hills prospect'n, and he would trot along behind us for as much as five mile; if we went so fur. An' he had the best judgment about mining ground — why you never see anything like it. When we went to work, he'd scatter a glance around, 'n' if he didn't think much of the indications, he would give a look as much as to say, ' Well, I'll have to get you to excuse *me*,' 'n' without another word he'd hyste his nose in the air and shove for home. But if the ground suited him, he would lay low 'n' take a look, an' if there was about six or seven grains of gold *he* was satisfied — he didn't want no

[17] " Some Rambling Notes of an Idle Excursion "; P. 74.
[18] This letter was republished in " Cat Stories from Saint Nicholas."

better prospect 'n that —'n' then he would lay down on our coats and snore like a steamboat till we'd struck the pocket an' then get up 'n' superintend." In due time quartz mining became fashionable. One day Tom, asleep on the coat, was forgotten when the fuse was lit, and when the explosion followed he rose in the air with the shower of rock. Thereafter Tom " shoved off " for home as soon as any one lit a fuse.

" When Tom was sot once, he was *always* sot, and you might a blowed him up as much as three million times 'n' never a broken him of his cussed prejudice agin quartz mining." Theodore Roosevelt must have enjoyed this story for he named a White House cat, Tom Quartz. This cat once playfully challenged the dignity of Joe Cannon.[19]

Henry James's love of cats is a more esoteric matter. Less is probably known about this writer's private life than about the life of any man equally prominent. He was seldom, if ever, interviewed, and anecdotes of his adventures and personal habits did not appear in the magazine sections of the Sunday newspapers, or in " The Ladies' Home Journal." Nevertheless one writer has asserted that Henry James often worked with a cat on his shoulder,[20] a statement I should not have credited uncorroborated, but in a paper by S. B. Wister [21] I found the following: " The prettiest of Princess's ways was a fashion she had of rearing on her hind legs, pressing her little pink nose against the face that bent over her, and at the same time patting the cheeks with her forepaws. She reserved this caress for her mistress almost exclusively, making a rare exception in favour of her master, but for nobody else save once, memorably for Mr. Henry James. It was very rapid, very endearing, and had a touch of condescension about

[19] This incident is related in " Theodore Roosevelt's Letters to His Children."
[20] Marvin R. Clark: " Pussy and Her Language."
[21] " Temple Bar "; January 1896.

it which was characteristic of her attitude towards man and beast."

In William Dean Howells's " My Literary Passions " that author tells us how in his youth he wrote a " mock-heroic epic of a cat fight, studied from the cat fights in our back yard, with the wonted invocation to the Muse, and the machinery of partisan gods and goddesses. It was in some hundreds of verses, which I did my best to balance as Pope did, with a cæsura falling in the middle of the line, and a neat antithesis at either end." Further pussies decorate the progress of Mr. Howells's many volumes and in " Familiar Spanish Studies " I found convincing evidence of this writer's real love for cats, for it would seem that he would turn away from Goya and El Greco to pet and talk to cats in Spain.[22] I was somewhat astonished to learn that this idiosyncrasy had not grown further, for Mr. Howells wrote me, " We are a cat family as opposed to dogs, but I have no great personal passion for cats." Perhaps not, yet in one of his books,[23] Mr. Howells has made a very personal study of a cat named Jim who lived at Kittery Point. " Unless one has lived at Kittery Point, and realized from observation and experience, what a leading part cats play in society, one cannot feel the full import of this fact. Not only has every house in Kittery its cat, but every house seems to have its half-dozen cats, large, little, old, and young; of divers colours, tending mostly to a dark tortoise-shell.[24] With a whole ocean inviting to the tragic rite, I do not believe there is ever a kitten drowned in Kittery; the illimitable sea rather employs itself in supplying the fish to which ' no cat's averse,' but which the cats of Kittery demand to have cooked. They do not like raw fish; they say it plainly,

[22] " In Gerona Cathedral there was a cat who would stroll about in front of the *capilla mayor* during the progress of mass, receiving the caresses of the passersby," writes Havelock Ellis in " The Soul of Spain," P. 14.
[23] " Literature and Life."
[24] Mr. Howells probably means tabby.

and they prefer to have the bones taken out for them, though they do not insist upon that point."

Jim scented the odour of broiled mackerel in the air about the Howells kitchen and dropped in one evening " with a fine casual effect of being merely out for a walk, and feeling it a neighbourly thing to call. He had on a silver collar, engraved with his name and surname, which offered itself for introduction like a visiting card. He was too polite to ask himself to the table at once, but after he had been welcomed to the family circle, he formed the habit of finding himself with us at breakfast and supper, when he sauntered in like one who should say, ' Did I smell *fish?* ' but would not go further in the way of hinting.

" He had no need to do so. He was made at home, and freely invited to our best not only in fish, but in chicken, for which he showed a nice taste, and in sweet-corn, for which he revealed a most surprising fondness when it was cut from the cob for him. After he had breakfasted or supped he gracefully suggested that he was thirsty by climbing to the table where the water-pitcher stood and stretching his fine feline head towards it. When he had lapped up his saucer of water, he marched into the parlour, and riveted the chains upon our fondness by taking the best chair and going to sleep in it in attitudes of Egyptian, of Assyrian majesty. His arts were few or none; he rather disdained to practise any; he completed our conquest by maintaining himself simply a fascinating presence. . . ."

Thomas A. Janvier was a great ailurophile. Tabbies and silvers insinuate themselves smilingly into the pages of many of his books. " Not that I would depreciate one single beast — no, not even the hippopotamus in order to give cats a better standing; " he writes,[25] " for all of them in their severally

[25] In his essay, " The Cats of Henriette Ronner "; " The Century Magazine "; October 1893.

appointed places, have those first good qualities wherewith
they have been endowed by their creator. . . . But to some
natures — of which, I confess, mine own is one — the super-
eminence of the cat over every other animal, save man alone,[26]
is so obtrusive a certainty that there surely is no denying it."
Edmund Clarence Stedman was an admirer of cats.   In 1895
he owned a great maltese called Babylon and Mrs. Stedman
a long-haired blue called Kelpie.   Sarah Orne Jewett is a cat-
lover and the old gentlewomen of her books usually are felinophiles too.   Mrs. Frances Hodgson Burnett exhibited her
Dick at the first New York cat-show.   Mary E. Wilkins is
devoted to puss and she has written several stories about him.
I especially remember the dreary old New England spinster
who lost her Willy, and who thereupon became very wicked,
figuratively cursed her Maker, and refused to go to meetin'.
Willy was eventually discovered in the cellar where the spinster herself had unwittingly locked him up.   I think Miss
Repplier must love cats with a fervour equal to her adoration
of the eighteenth century English essayists.   At least they
share an equal importance in her books.   Her study of a kitten, her portraits of Agrippina, Claudius Nero, and Lux
are among the treasures of felinature, and yet Miss Repplier
seems always a little afraid that she loves her cats more than
they love her.

Cats appear somewhere in nearly all the books of Edgar
Saltus, which is but fitting in the works of a son of the
French diabolists, but the only story he has written which
directly concerns puss is about a girl,

qui miaulait d'un ton fort doux.

Saltus's passion for the animal is as intense as that of
Baudelaire.   Like the author of the " Fleurs du Mal " he
stops to converse with every grimalkin he meets on the street.
Indeed wherever he goes, which to be sure is next to nowhere,

[26] To me this exception seems unduly cautious and unnecessary.

for Saltus is a recluse, the cats he meets receive more attention from him than men. In "The Anatomy of Negation," one reads, "Throughout the middle ages no sorcerer was considered well-equipped without a sleek black cat, an animal to which, like many a sensible mortal, the devil appears to have been greatly attached." In "Mr. Incoul's Misadventure" there is a Thibetan cat. In "The Paliser Case" there is a cat with "long hair, the colour of smoke, a bushy tail, the eyes of an angel, and a ferocious moustache."

But of all American cat-lovers I think perhaps Charles Dudley Warner deserves first place. . . . "I only had one cat," he once said, "and he was more of a companion than a cat. When he departed this life I did not care to do as many men do when their partners die, take a second." The wonderful Calvin appears briefly in the delightful chapters of "My Summer in a Garden," which Samuel Butler sent to Miss Savage warning her to keep silent if she did not like it, "for I cannot bear to have people disagree with me." After Calvin's death Warner wrote a special paper about him, which is included in later editions of this work. This essay is a masterpiece of sympathetic prose and one of the best cat portraits that has been given to us by a literary man. Calvin, it seems, walked one day a full-grown cat into the home of Mrs. Harriet Beecher Stowe. "It was as if he had inquired at the door if that was the residence of the author of 'Uncle Tom's Cabin,' and, upon being assured that it was, had decided to dwell there." Later when Mrs. Stowe moved to Florida, Calvin was entrusted to the Warner family of which he was a beloved member until his death eight years later.

"He was of royal mould, and had an air of high breeding. He was large, but he had nothing of the fat grossness of the celebrated Angora family; though powerful, he was exquisitely proportioned, and as graceful in every movement as a young leopard. . . . His coat was the finest and softest I have ever seen, a shade of quiet maltese; and from his throat downward underneath, to the white tips of his feet, he wore the whitest and most delicate ermine; and no person was ever more fastidiously neat. In his finely formed head you saw something of his aristocratic character; the ears were small and cleanly cut, there was a tinge of pink in the nostrils, his face was handsome, and the expression of his countenance exceedingly intelligent — I should call it even a sweet expression if the term were not inconsistent with his look of alertness and sagacity.

" Although he had fixed notions about his own rights, and extraordinary persistency in getting them, he never showed temper at a repulse; he simply and firmly persisted till he had what he wanted. His diet was one point; his idea was that of the scholars about dictionaries,—' to get the best.' He knew as well as any one what was in the house, and would refuse beef if turkey was to be had; and if there were oysters, he would wait over the turkey to see if the oysters would not be forthcoming. And yet he was not a gross gourmand; he would eat bread if he saw me eating it, and thought he was not being imposed on.

" The intelligence of Calvin was something phenomenal, in his rank of life. He established a method of communicating his wants, and even some of his sentiments; and he could help himself in many things. There was a furnace register in a retired room, where he used to go when he wished to be alone, that he always opened when he desired more heat; but never shut it, any more than he shut the door after himself. . . . I hesitate a little to speak of his capacity for friendship and the affectionateness of his nature, for I know from his own reserve that he would not care to have it much talked about. We understood each other perfectly, but we never made any fuss about it; when I spoke his name and snapped my fingers, he came to me; when I returned home at night, he was pretty sure to be waiting for me near the gate, and would rise and saunter along the walk, as if his being there was purely accidental,— so shy was he commonly of showing feeling. There was one thing he never did,— he never rushed through an open doorway. He never forgot his dignity. If he had asked to have the door opened, and was eager to go out, he always went out deliberately; I can see him now, standing on the sill, looking about at the sky as if he was thinking whether it were worth while to take an umbrella, until he was near having his tail shut in.

" His friendship was rather constant than demonstrative. When we returned from an absence of nearly two years, Calvin welcomed us with evident pleasure, but showed his satisfaction rather by tranquil happiness than by fuming about. He had the faculty of making us glad to get home. It was his constancy that was so attractive. He liked companionship, but he wouldn't be petted, or fussed over, or sit in any one's lap a moment; he always extricated himself from such familiarity with dignity and with no show of temper. If there was any petting to be done, however, he chose to do it. Often he would sit looking at me, and then, moved by a delicate affection, come and pull at my coat and sleeve until he could touch my face with his nose, and then go away contented."

Like Loti, Mr. Warner touches our hearts very deeply in the death scene, a scene which is very sincerely, very beautifully written. An animal who can inspire such prose as " Calvin " and " Vies de deux chattes " has certainly served his purpose in this world.

Chapter Thirteen: Apotheosis

Les bêtes sont au bon Dieu;
Mais la bêtise est à l'homme.
VICTOR HUGO.

I have written, how skilfully I cannot tell, on the manners and customs of the cat, his graces and calineries, the history of his subjugation of humankind. Through all the ages, even during the dark epoch of witchcraft and persecution, puss has maintained his supremacy, continued to breed and multiply, defying, when convenient, the laws of God and man, now our friend, now our enemy, now wild, now tame, the pet of the hearth or the tiger of the heath, but always free, always independent, always an anarchist who insists upon his rights, whatever the cost. The cat never forms soviets; he works alone.

We have much to learn from the cat, we men who prefer to follow the slavish habits of the dog or the ox or the horse. If men and women would become more feline, indeed, I think it would prove the salvation of the human race. Certainly it would end war, for cats will not fight for an ideal in the mass, having no faith in mass ideals, although a single cat will fight to the death for his own ideals, his freedom of speech and expression. The dog and the horse, on the other hand, perpetuate war, by group thinking, group acting, and serve further to encourage popular belief in that monstrous panacea, universal brotherhood.

For the next war man will build ships which can make sixty or seventy knots an hour; submarines will skim through five thousand leagues of the sea with the speed of sharks; and airships will fly over cities, dropping bundles of TNT.

Apotheosis

Saïgon, Berlin, Cairo, Paris, Madrid, and even Indianapolis are doomed to disappear. Man himself will become extinct; crude, silly man, always struggling against Nature, rather than with Nature behind him, helping him forward and across, beyond the abysses and torrents and landslides of existence. And presently everything we know will be over, another cycle of years will begin, and a new " civilization " will arise.

For man has persistently, and perhaps a little intentionally, misunderstood the Prometheus legend. Prometheus was the enemy, not the friend, of man. The fire which he brought to earth was a devastating flame and Zeus, the Nature God, chained him to a rock to protect humanity. This misuse of holy things, this turning of good to the account of evil, this misapplication of natural principles to unnatural practices are the commonplaces of history, the foundations of our present state, and the causes of all misery.

But the cat will survive. He is no such fool as man. He knows that he must have Nature behind him. He also knows that it is easier for one cat alone to fit into the curves of Nature than two cats. So he walks by himself. For Nature here and Nature there are two different Natures and what one cat on one side of the fence has to do is not what another cat on the other side of the fence has to do. But the great principles are obeyed by all cats to such an extent that twenty, a hundred, a thousand cats will willingly give their lives, which they might easily save, to preserve an instinct, a racial memory, which will serve to perpetuate the feline race. The result will be that, after the cataclysm, out of the mounds of heaped-up earth, the piles and wrecks of half-buried cities, the desolated fields of grain, and the tortured orchards, the cat will stalk, confident, self-reliant, capable, imperturbable, and philosophical, He will bridge the gap until man appears again and then he will sit on new hearths and again will teach his mighty lesson to ears and eyes that again are dumb and blind. Shylock's doom was foretold by Shakespeare from the moment

the poet asked the poor creature to say, " the harmless necessary cat." For it is possible, nay probable, that the cat,
unlike man who forgets his previous forms, remembers, really
remembers, many generations back; that what we call instinct
may be more profound than knowledge. And so Providence
wisely has not allowed the cat to speak any language save his
own.

We may dominate dogs, but cats can never be dominated
except by force. They can be annihilated, at least a few of
them can, but never made servile or banal. The cat is
never vulgar. He will not even permit God to interfere with
his liberty and if he suffers so much as a toothache he will refuse all food. He would rather die than endure pain. Thus,
like the Spartan, he preserves the strength of his stock. He
may at any moment change his motto from *Libertas Sine
Labore* or *Amica Non Serva* to *Quand Même*.

There is, indeed, no single quality of the cat that man could
not emulate to his advantage. He is clean, the cleanest, indeed, of all the animals, absolutely without odour or soil when
it is within his power to be so. He is silent, walking on
padded paws with claws withdrawn, making no sound unless
he wishes to say something definite and then he can express
himself freely. He believes in free-speech, and not only believes in it, but indulges in it. Nothing will make a cat stop
talking when he wants to, except the hand of death.

He is entirely self-reliant. He lives in homes because he
chooses to do so, and as long as the surroundings and the
people suit him, but he lives there on his own terms, and never
sacrifices his own comfort or his own well-being for the sake
of the stupid folk with whom he comes in contact. Thus
he is the most satisfactory of friends. Among men (or
women) it is customary to say, " We're dining with the Ogilvies tonight. We don't want to go but they'll never forgive
us if we don't." Meanwhile the Ogilvies are muttering,
" Good God! This is the night those horrible Mitchells are

coming to dinner. I wish they would telephone that they cannot come. Perhaps their motor will break down on the way!" The cat neither gives nor accepts invitations that do not come from the heart. If he tires of his friends sometimes, so do I. If he wishes to move he does so. Perhaps to another house, perhaps to the wilds. If he is suddenly thrown on his own resources in the country he can support himself on the highway; he can even support himself in town under conditions that would terrify that half-hearted, group-seeking socialist, the dog. The cat is virile, and virility is a quality which man has almost lost. St. George Mivart insisted that the cat rather than man was at the summit of the animal kingdom and that he was the best-fitted of the mammalians to make his way in the world.[1] I agree perfectly with St. George Mivart. I do not see how it is possible for any one to disagree with him. But the cat makes no boast of his pre-eminent position; he is satisfied to occupy it. He does not call man a " lower animal " although doubtless he regards him in this light. I have dwelt at some length on his occult sense. It can scarcely be overestimated. He has not lost the power of gesture language. With his tail, with his paws, his cocking ears, his eyes, his head, the turn of his body, or the waving of his fur, he expresses in symbols the most cabalistic secrets. He is beautiful and he is graceful. He makes his appearance and his life as exquisite as circumstances will permit. He is modest, he is urbane, he is dignified. Indeed, a well-bred cat never argues. He goes about doing what he likes in a wellbred superior manner. If he is interrupted he will look at you in mild surprise or silent reproach but he will return to his desire. If he is prevented, he will wait for a more favourable occasion. But like all well-bred individualists, and unlike human anarchists, the cat seldom interferes with other people's

---

[1] St. George Mivart: "The Cat," P. 492: "The organization of the cat-tribe may be deemed superior, because it is not only excellent in itself, but because it is fitted to dominate the excellences of other beasts."

rights. His intelligence keeps him from doing many of the fool things that complicate life. Cats never write operas and they never attend them. They never sign papers, or pay taxes, or vote for president. An injunction will have no power whatever over a cat. A cat, of course, would not only refuse to obey any amendment whatever to any constitution, he would refuse to obey the constitution itself.

Feathers is very tired of this book. She has told me so more than once lately. Sometimes with her eyes, gazing at me with impatience while I write. Sometimes with her paws, scratching scornfully at the sheets of paper as I toss them to the floor. Sometimes on my writing table she insinuates herself between me and my work. When I began this book she was a kitten, a chrysanthemum-like ball of tawny, orange, white, and black fuzzy fur, and now she is about to become a mother. Yes, while I have been writing a book, Feathers has experienced teething, love, and now soon will come maternity. It makes me feel very small, very unimportant. What I have done in fourteen months seems very little when it is compared with what she has done.

The mystery of life deepens for her. Her eyes are slightly drawn. She is less active and she wishes more repose. She needs the warmth of my knees, where she desires to sleep uninterrupted by the sound of clicking keys. She is pleading with me to come to an end. And I cannot resist her prayer. See, Feathers, I am nearly done. I am writing the last page. You can come to me now and spend the hours of preparation in my lap, and I offer, rather than this poor book, to test myself as a literary man, after Samuel Butler's method, by naming your yet unborn kittens. I shall call them, if Nature gives you five, and the sexes permit, Aurélie, Golden Feathers, Coq d'Or, Prince Igor, and Jurgen.

March 4, 1920.
New York.

Bibliography and Index

The obligations incurred in the preparation of this book have been many and deep. I wish to thank my wife, Fania Marinoff, for suggesting the charming title, Mrs. Harriet V. Furness for her admirable photographs of cats, of which I have used so many, and Mr. Arthur Davison Ficke, for photographs of Japanese prints in his collection. The cover design is from a medal struck in 1725, now in the French National Library. For the rest the bibliography will express my gratitude.

Bibliography

This bibliography makes no pretence to being complete. It includes very few books that I have not read myself, very few books, indeed, which are not in my own library. An exhaustive bibliography on the subject of cats would undoubtedly fill a very large volume all by itself. But this one is more nearly complete than any other which exists; as a matter of fact it is the only bibliography on the subject that I know save Mr. Babington's, which covers only a small and select private library, and which makes no mention of periodical literature. I have not in all cases listed first editions; generally I have mentioned the special edition I have consulted. As for errors and omissions I shall be only too glad to receive news of them as at some future time, in another publication, I may extend the present list. Any one who has suggestions to make may address me care of my publisher, Alfred A. Knopf, 730 Fifth Avenue, New York City.

I

BIBLIOGRAPHY

Babington, Percy L.: A Collection of Books about Cats; fifty-four copies printed by J. B. Peace, M.A. at the University Press, Cambridge, England; August 1918.

II

GENERAL

Champfleury (pseudonym of Jules Husson): Les Chats; J. Rothschild; Paris; 1870. The fifth edition is an *édition de luxe,* and includes a lithograph in colour by Marie Champfleury, after Burbank, other illustrations in colour, etchings by Edouard Manet, Eugène Lambert, Armand Gautier, Crafty, and Marie Champfleury, besides numerous illustrations in the text.

Bibliography

This book was translated by Mrs. Cashel Hoey, with supplementary notes, under the title: The Cat Past and Present; G. Bell and Sons; London; 1885. The illustrations are from the original French edition.

Chance, Mrs. W. (later Lady): A Book of Cats, being a discourse on cats with many quotations and original pencil drawings; J. M. Dent and Co.; London; 1898. E. P. Dutton and Co. published an American edition the same year.

Clark, Marvin R.: Pussy and Her Language, including a paper on the wonderful discovery of the cat language by Alphonse Leon Grimaldi, F.R.S., etc. Published by the author; New York; 1895.

Gautier, Théophile: La Nature Chez Elle et la Ménagerie Intime; Bibliothèque-Charpentier; Paris.

Landrin, Alexandre: Le Chat: zoologie, origine, historique, moeurs, habitudes, races, anatomie, maladies, jurisprudence; Georges Carré; Paris; 1894. With one illustration.

Marks, Anne: The Cat in History, Legend, and Art: Elliot Stock; London; 1909. The illustrations are by the author.

Mégnin, Paul: Notre Ami le Chat, with a preface by François Coppée; J. Rothschild; Paris; 1899. With two hundred illustrations (drawings and photographs), many of which are from Champfleury's book.

Michel, Gustav: Das Buch der Katzen; Hermann Weisbach; Weimar; 1876. With twenty-six illustrations from drawings.

Michelet, Madame Jules: Les Chats; E. Flammarion; Paris. Gabriel Monod edited this book which Madame Michelet left in manuscript at the time of her death.

Moncrif, F. A. Paradis de: Les Chats; Quillan; Paris; 1727. There are nine drawings by Charles Coypel, engraved by the Comte de Caylus, and ornamental woodcut head and tail pieces. In 1728 an edition of this book was published at Rotterdam, the engravings for which were made from Coypel's drawings by Otten. Les Chats was published anonymously.

Percheron, Gaston: Le Chat: histoire naturelle; hygiène; maladies; Firmin-Didot et Cie.; Paris; 1885. Illustrations from drawings.

Repplier, Agnes: The Fireside Sphinx; Houghton, Mifflin and Co.; Boston; 1902. The illustrations are by Elisabeth F. Bonsall.

Bibliography

Ross, Charles Henry: The Book of Cats, a chit-chat chronicle of feline facts and fancies, legendary, lyrical, medical, mirthful, and miscellaneous; Griffith and Farran; London; 1868. With twenty illustrations by the author.

Simpson, Frances: The Book of the Cat; Cassell and Co., Ltd.; London; 1903. With twelve coloured plates and nearly three hundred and fifty illustrations in the text from drawings and photographs.

Weir, Harrison: Our Cats and All About Them, their varieties, habits, and management; and for show, the standard of excellence and beauty; described and pictured; R. Clements; Tunbridge Wells; 1889. This book was published in America by Houghton, Mifflin and Co.; Boston, the same year. With numerous illustrations by the author. There is a large paper edition of the English issue.

Winslow, Helen M.: Concerning Cats, my own and some others; Lothrop Publishing Co.; Boston; 1900. Illustrated with photographs.

III

VARIETIES, BREEDING, CARE, AND DISEASES

Aspinwall, Grace: Pussies, Plebeian and Royal; Good Housekeeping; August 1909; Vol. 49, P. 178. Illustrated with photographs.

Barton, Frank Townend: The Cat: its points and management in health and disease; Everett and Co.; London; 1908. Illustrated with photographs and drawings.

Bennett, I. D.: Cat Fancy; American Homes and Gardens; November 1913; Vol. 10, P. 380. Illustrated with photographs.

Betelle, Mabel Nicholson: One-cat Cattery and how to make it pay; Country Life in America; January 15, 1912; Vol 21. Illustrated with photographs.

Bosworth, Isabella Essex: The Care and Training of the House Cat; Country Life in America; November 1907; Vol. 13, P. 72. Illustrated with photographs.

Brown, C.: Cats as Money-makers; Harper's Bazaar; August 1912; Vol. 46, P. 388. Illustrated with photographs.

Bibliography

Brown, Elizabeth Frances: The Popular Persian Cat; The Country-side Magazine; October 1915; Vol. 21, P. 218.

Cat Culture; Spratt's Patent (Am.) Ltd.; Newark, N. J. Pamphlet. Illustrated with photographs.

Champion, Dorothy Bevill: Everybody's Cat Book; New York; 1909. Illustrated with photographs. This book, one of the latest and best for the breeder of Persian cats, is easily procurable.

Clayton, G. V.,: A Treatise on the Cat; published by the author; Chicago. Pamphlet.

Cornish-Bond, Mabel: Cat Raising as a Business; Munsey's Magazine; 1901. Vol. 25, P. 841. Illustrated with photographs.

Crandall, Lee S.: Pets; their history and their care; Henry Holt and Co; New York; 1917. Illustrated with photographs.

Cust, the Honourable Lady: The Cat: its history, diseases, and management; Henry J. Drake; London.

Daniels, Dr. A. C.: The Cat Doctor: home treatment for cats and kittens; published by the author; Boston; 1911. Pamphlet.

Diehl, J. E.: The Domestic Cat: different breeds and varieties, how to keep and rear them, together with a treatise of their diseases — with symptoms and remedies for them; Associated Fanciers; Philadelphia; 1899. Pamphlet.

Ewart, J. Cossar: The principles of breeding and the origin of domesticated breeds of animals; U. S. Department of Agriculture; Bureau of Animal Industry; 1912. With especial reference to the theories of telegony [1] and saturation.

Farrington, E. I.: A Palace for Cats; Technical World; August 1914; Vol. 21, P. 900. Illustrated with photographs.

Hall, Kate A.: Cat Farming in California; Overland Monthly; April 1907; N. S. Vol. 49, P. 299. Illustrated with photographs.

Hill, J. Woodroffe: The Diseases of the Cat; William R. Jenkins; New York; 1903. Illustrated with photographs.

Huidekoper, Rush Shippen: The Cat, a guide to the classification and varieties of cats and a short treatise upon their care, diseases, and

---

[1] Telegony is the name given to the hypothesis that the offspring of a known sire sometimes inherit characteristics from a previous mate of their dam. Prof. James Cossar Ewart: The Penicuik Experiments, 1899, put telegony to the test and found it wanting. Romanes also was against it after investigation.

Bibliography

treatment; D. Appleton and Co.; New York; 1895. With over thirty illustrations from drawings and photographs.

James, Robert Kent: The Angora Cat: how to breed, train and keep it; with additional chapters on the history, peculiarities and diseases of the animal; James Brothers; Boston; 1898. Illustrated with photographs.

Jennings, John: Domestic and Fancy Cats: a practical treatise on their antiquity, domestication, varieties, breeding, management, diseases, exhibition and judging; L. Upcott Gill; London; 1893. Illustrated with drawings. The second edition, revised and considerably enlarged, illustrated with photographs, appeared in 1901. This book may be recommended to the breeder.

L. H. F.: Her Serene Highness, the Cat; Harper's Bazaar; May 26, 1900; Vol. 33, P. 222. Illustrated with photographs.

Lane, Charles Henry: Rabbits, Cats and Cavies: descriptive sketches of all recognized exhibition varieties with many original anecdotes; J. M. Dent and Co.; London; 1903. With over one hundred illustrations by Rosa Bebb.

Martling, Harriet: Cats of Leisure and Lineage; Overland Monthly; 1900; Vol. 36, P. 460. Illustrated with photographs.

Miller, Olive Thorne (Harriet Mann Miller): Our Home Pets; how to keep them well and happy; Harper and Brothers; New York; 1894. Pages 195-230 are devoted to cats. Illustrated with drawings.

Morrison, F.H.S.: The Aristocratic Persian Cat; Country Life in America; September 1908; Vol. 14, P. 446. Illustrated with photographs by A. Radclyffe Dugmore and others.

Neel, Edith K.: Cats: how to care for them in health and treat them when ill; Boericke and Tafel; Philadelphia; 1902. Illustrated with photographs and drawings. This small manual, which is easily procurable, may be recommended.

Roberts, Walter T.: Some Celebrated Cats and Their Owners; Cassell's Magazine; London; 1904; Vol. 38, P. 77. Illustrated with photographs.

Roderick, Virginia: The Aristocracy of Cats; Everybody's Magazine; 1909; Vol. 20, P. 216. Illustrated with photographs.

Rule, Philip V.: The Cat: its natural history, domestic varieties, management and treatment; with an essay on feline instinct by

Bibliography

Bernard Perez; Swan Sonnenschein, Lowery and Co.; London; 1887. The illustrations are from drawings.

Rydall, E. H.: The Care of the Cat; Country Life in America; August 1907; Vol. 12, P. 444. Illustrated with photographs.

Saint Maur, Kate V.: Caring for Home Pets; Woman's Home Companion; July 1910; Vol. 37, P. 26.

Simpson, Frances: Cats for Pleasure and Profit; Sir Isaac Pitman and Sons, Ltd.; London; 1909. This is a new and revised edition; the original title was Cats and All About Them. With twenty-five illustrations from photographs.

Stables, Gordon: Cats, their humane and rational treatment; Chambers's Journal; September 8, 1883; Vol. 60, P. 572.

Stables, William Gordon: Cats, their points and characteristics, with curiosities of cat life, and a chapter on feline ailments; Dean and Smith; London; 1874. Illustrated with a photographic frontispiece of the author sitting with a retriever, cat, and starling, and seven chromo-lithographs of prize cats, two on each plate and one of an Abyssinian cat.

Stables, William Gordon: The Domestic Cat; G. Routledge and Sons; London; 1876.

Stanwood, Harriet B.: Persian Cats for Profit; Country Life in America; April 1915; Vol. 27, P. 90. Illustrated with photographs.

Stecker, C. H.: The common-sense care of Angora cats; Suburban Life; November 1907; Vol. 5, P. 285. Illustrated with photographs by Jessie Tarbox Beals and W. F. Sleight.

The Types of Cats; Suburban Life; March 1908; Vol. 6, P. 184.

Voogt, Gos de: Our Domestic Animals, their habits, intelligence and usefulness; translated from the French by Katherine P. Wormeley; edited for America by Charles William Burkett; Ginn and Co.; Boston; 1907. The section on the cat begins on P. 73. Illustrated with photographs, some of them coloured.

Wellington, Arthur: Beautiful Pets; Bostonian (National Magazine); February 1896; Vol. 3, P. 459. Illustrated with photographs.

Bibliography

IV

NATURAL HISTORY

Aristotle: History of Animals; translated by Richard Cressell; Bohn Libraries; London; 1862.

Benton, J. R.: How a falling cat turns over; Science; New York; January 19, 1912; N. S. Vol. 35, P. 104. This is a letter in answer to W. S. Franklin.

Bingley, Reverend W.: Animal Biography or Popular Zoology; Three volumes; London; 1813.

Buffon, Georges Louis Leclerc: Histoire naturelle, générale, et particulière; Paris; 1749-67.

Cochrane, Robert: Four Hundred Animal Stories; W. and R. Chambers; Edinburgh; 1897. Cats, Chapter VI, P. 196. Illustrated.

Doncaster, L.: Sex-limited Inheritance in Cats; Science; August 2, 1912; N. S. Vol. 36, P. 144:

Dureau de la Mallu: The Cat: researches in regard to the ancient history of our domestic animals; Edinburgh New Philosophical Journal; July-October 1829; Vol. 7, P. 309.

Elliot, Daniel Giraud: A monograph of the Felidae or Family of the Cats; Published for subscribers by the author; London; 1883, large folio, with forty-three magnificent coloured plates by J. Wolf.

Fabre, Jean-Henri-Casimir: Our Humble Friends, familiar talks on the domestic animals; translated from the French by Florence Constable Bicknell; Century Co.; New York; 1918. Illustrated with drawings. Chapter XXVI, P. 239, The Cat.

Fairchild, David: Cats as Plant Investigators; Science; October 19, 1906; N. S. Vol. 24, P. 498.

Franklin, W. S. How a falling cat turns over in the air; Science; 1911; N. S. Vol. 34, P. 844. This is a letter.

Howe, Freeland, jr.: A case of abnormality in cats' paws; American Naturalist; July 1902; Vol. 36, P. 511. Illustrated with diagrams.

Hudson, W. H.: The Book of a Naturalist; George H. Doran Co.;

New Yɔrk; 1919. A friendly rat, P. 232; The great dog-superstition, P. 238.

Jesse, Edward: Gleanings in Natural History; John Murray; London; (new edition) 1838. Two volumes.

Little, C. C.: Preliminary note on occurrences of a sex-limited character in cats; Science; May 17, 1912; N. S. Vol. 35, P. 784.

Lydekker, R.: The Pedigree of the Cat; Knowledge; August 2, 1897; Vol. 20, P. 181.

Miles, Alfred H.: 1001 Animal Anecdotes; Frederick A. Stokes Co.; New York; His Grace the Cat, P. 67. With sixteen original drawings and photographs by Winifred Austen and others.

Miller, Mrs. Hugh: Cats and Dogs, or notes and anecdotes of two great families of the animal kingdom; T. Nelson and Sons; London; 1872. Illustrated. The first six chapters are concerned with the domestic cat and his wild relatives. Juvenile.

Miller, Olive Thorne (Harriet Mann Miller): Queer Pets at Marcy's; E. P. Dutton Co.; New York; 1880. Illustrated by J. C. Beard. Juvenile.

Natural History Anecdotes; Leisure Hour; January 30, 1875; Vol. 24, P. 74. All cat anecdotes.

Nicol, Dr. John: The Best Cat Story Yet; Scientific American; October 28, 1905; Vol. 93, P. 339.

Pennant, Thomas: British Zoology; printed for Benj. White; London; 1776. Four volumes. The cat is in Volume 1.

Pocock, R. I.: The question of our two types of tabby cat; Nature; September 8, 1910; Vol. 84, P. 298.

Poulton, Edward B.: Observations on heredity in cats with an abnormal number of toes; Nature; 1883; Vol. 29, P. 20; November 11, 1885; Vol. 35, P. 38; a letter from J. Herbert Wood: November 18, 1885; Vol. 35, P. 53; a letter from William White: December 9, 1885; Vol. 35, P. 125. Illustrated with drawings of paws.

Puss's Pedigree; Literary Digest; October 27, 1917; Vol. 55.

Robinson, Louis: Wild Traits in Tame Animals, being some familiar studies in evolution; William Blackwood and Sons; Edinburgh and London; 1897; The Cat, Chapter IX, P. 227. Illustrations by S. T. Dadd. This book will entertain the casual reader and stimulate the student.

Bibliography

Rope, G. T.: Cats with abnormal tastes; The Zoologist; October 1915; Series 4, Vol. 19, P. 393. Cats as vegetarians, etc.

Topsell, Edward: The History of Four-footed Beasts; E. Cotes; London; 1658. Cats on P. 81 with illustration. A quaint and amazing book.

Valmont de Bomare, Jacques-Christophe: Dictionnaire raisonné d'histoire naturelle; Lyon-Paris; (fourth edition) Year VIII (1800). Fifteen volumes.

Vickers, H. M.: Origin of the domestic " blotched " tabby cat; Nature; September 8-15, 1910; Vol. 84, Pages 298 and 331.

White, C. A.: Permanence of domestic instinct in the cat; Knowledge; April 11, 1884; Vol. 5, P. 243. C. G. D. Roberts and Mary E. Wilkins Freeman have based stories on this incident of a cat who made shift to live in the wilds for a year, when deserted, but who was friendly to humans when they appeared.

Whiting, Phineas W.: The tortoise-shell cat; American Naturalist; August 1915; Vol. 49, P. 518.

V

ANATOMY AND BIOLOGY

Anthony, R.: Considérations anatomiques sur la région sacro-caudale d'une chatte appartenant à la race dite " anoure " de l'île de Man; Bulletins de la Société d'Anthropologie de Paris; Paris; 1899; Séries IV, Vol. 10, P. 303. Illustrated.

Buchanan, Lieut. Col. A. (I. M. S. M. A. M. D.): Cats as Plague Preventers; British Medical Journal; London; October 24, 1908; Vol. 2, P. 1231.

Darwin, Charles: The Descent of Man and Selection in Relation to Sex; John Murray; London. Two volumes.

Darwin, Charles: The Origin of Species; John Murray; London.

Darwin, Charles: The Variations of Animals and Plants Under Domestication; John Murray; London.

Davison, Alvin: Mammalian Anatomy, with special reference to the cat; P. Blakiston's Sons and Co.; Philadelphia; 1903.

Fritz, W.: Über einen Sinnesapparat am Unterarm der Katze nebst Bemerkungen über den Bau des Sinusbalzes; Zeitschrift für wissen-

Bibliography

schaftliche Zoologie; Leipzig; 1909; Vol. 92, P. 291. Illustrated.

Gorham, Frederick P., and Ralph W. Tower: A Laboratory Guide for the Dissection of the Cat; Charles Scribner's Sons; New York; 1903. Illustrated with charts drawn by F. P. Gorham.

Hall, G. Stanley and C. E. Browne: The Cat and the Child; Pedagogical Seminary; Worcester, Mass.; 1904; Vol. 11, P. 3.

Huber, John B. (M. D.): The Disease Carrying Cat; Collier's; August 14, 1915; Vol. 55.

Hyde, Henrietta: Collateral circulation in the cat after ligation of the postcava; Kansas University Quarterly; July 1900; Vol. 11, P. 167.

Liadze, Wissarion: Die Backen — und Lippendrüsen des Hundes und der Kätze; E. Birkhäuser; Basel; 1910. Illustrated.

Lyon, Goffrey A.: Alimentary parasites of felis domestica; Science; September 7, 1906; N. S. Vol. 24, P. 313.

Millard, Bailey: War Declared Upon the Cat; Illustrated World; November 1915; Vol. 24, P. 339. Illustrated with photograph.

Miller, William Snow: Variations in the distribution of the bile duct of the cat; Transactions of the Wisconsin Academy of Sciences, Arts, and Letters; Madison, Wisconsin; 1904; Vol. 14, P. 621.

Mivart, St. George: The Cat: an introduction to the study of backboned animals, especially mammals; John Murray; London; 1881. Charles Scribner's Sons issued an American edition the same year. With two hundred illustrations from drawings.

Morris, Harry Waldo: The carotid arteries and their relation to the circle of willis in the cat; Proceedings of the Iowa Academy of Science for 1906; Des Moines; Vol. 13, P. 251.

Osborne, Caroline A.: The Cat: a neglected factor in sanitary science; Pedagogical Seminary; Worcester, Mass.; 1907; Vol. 14, P. 439.

Reighard, Jacob and H. S. Jennings: The Anatomy of the Cat; Henry Holt and Co.; New York; 1901. With one hundred and seventy-three drawings by Louise Burridge Jennings.

Stowell, T. B.: The Cat: the glossopharyngeal, the accessory and hypoglossal nerves in the domestic cat; Read before the American Philosophical Society; March 2, 1888. Pamphlet.

Wilder, Burt G., and S. H. Gage: Anatomical Technology as Applied to the Domestic Cat; an introduction to human, veterinary,

Bibliography

and comparative anatomy; A. S. Barnes and Co.; New York; 1882.

Wilder, Burt Green: The Anatomical Uses of the Cat; D. Appleton and Co. New York; 1879. Pamphlet.

Wilder, Burt G.: The Brain of the Cat: preliminary account of the gross anatomy; Read before the American Philosophical Society, July 15, 1881. Pamphlet with fourteen plates.

VI

PSYCHOLOGY

Burroughs, John: The Animal Mind; Atlantic Monthly; November 1910; Vol. 106, P. 622.

Burroughs, John: Animal Wit Indoors and Out; Atlantic Monthly; February 1912; Vol. 109, P. 196.

Burroughs, John: Do Animals Think?; Harper's Magazine; February 1905; Vol. 110, P. 354.

Burroughs, John: The Reasonable but Unreasoning Animals; The Outlook; December 14, 1907; Vol. 87, P. 809.

Burroughs John: Ways of Nature; Houghton, Mifflin and Co.; Boston; 1905.

Cesaresco, the Countess Evelyn Martinengo: The Place of Animals in Human Thought; Charles Scribner's Sons; New York; 1909. Illustrated.

Darwin, Charles: The Expression of the Emotions in Man and Animals; John Murray; London. Illustrated.

Dixon, Royal: The Human Side of Animals; Frederick A. Stokes Co.; New York; 1918. Illustrated with photographs.

Evans, E. P.: Evolutionary Ethics and Animal Psychology; D. Appleton and Co.; New York; 1898.

Groos, Karl: Die Spiele der Thiere; Gustav Fischer; Jena; 1896. Translated with the co-operation of the author as the Play of Animals, by E. L. Baldwin, with a preface and an appendix by J. Mark Baldwin; D. Appleton & Co.; New York; 1898.

Hachet-Souplet: L'Intelligence des Chats: Bulletin de l'Institut Géneral Psychologique; Année III; Paris; 1903; P. 128.

Bibliography

Holmes, S. J.: Studies in Animal Behaviour; Richard G. Badger; Boston; 1916.

Lindsay, W. Lauder: Mind in the Lower Animals; D. Appleton and Co.; New York; 1880. Two volumes.

Lloyd, Morgan C.: Animal Behaviour; Edward Arnold; London; 1900.

Menault, Ernest: L'Intelligence des Animaux; Paris; 1869 (second edition). Illustrated by E. Bayard, A. Mesnel, etc. Le Chat, Pages 264–70. Charles Scribner and Co., in 1869, published an illustrated translation of this book as The Intelligence of Animals.

Mills, T. Wesley: The Cat; The Dog; The Cat and the Dog Compared; McGill University; Papers from the Department of Physiology; Montreal; 1896. Pamphlet.

Mills, Wesley: The Nature and Development of Animal Intelligence; Macmillan Co.; New York; 1898.

Perrens, F. T.: Mémoires de Mes Chattes; Revue Scientifique; Paris; 1899. Séries IV, Vol. 12, Pages 417, 461, and 491, and Vol. 15 (1901), P. 398.

Pierquin de Gembloux: Traité de la Folie des Animaux; Paris, 1859.

Romanes, George John: Animal Intelligence; D. Appleton and Co.; New York; 1883; Chapter XIV, P. 411, is devoted to the cat.

Romanes, George John: Essays (edited by C. Lloyd Morgan); Longmans, Green, and Co.; London; 1897.

Romanes, George John: Mental Evolution in Animals; Kegan Paul, Trench and Co.; 1883.

Shepherd, W. T.: The discrimination of articulate sounds by cats; American Journal of Psychology; July 1912; Vol. 23, P. 461.

Shepherd, W. T.: Tests in adaptive intelligence in dogs and cats, as compared with adaptive intelligence in Rhesus monkeys; American Journal of Psychology; April 16, 1915; Vol. 26, P. 211.

Smith, E. M.: The Investigation of Mind in Animals; Cambridge University Press; 1915.

Thompson, Edward P.: The Passions of Animals; Chapman and Hall; London; 1851.

Thorndike, Edward L.: Animal Intelligence: Experimental Studies; Macmillan Co.; New York; 1911. Illustrated with diagrams.

Vevey, Artault de: Des Actes Raisonnés chez le Chat; Bulletin de l'Institut Géneral Psychologique; Paris; 1903; Année III; P. 13.

Bibliography

Washburn, Margaret Floy: The Animal Mind, a text book of comparative psychology; Macmillan Co.; New York; 1908.

Watson, Rev. John Selby: The Reasoning Power in Animals; Reeve and Co.; London; 1867. The cat, Chapter XXV, P. 247; Chapter XXX, P. 322.

VII

LANGUAGE

Bolton, H. Carrington: The Language used in talking to domestic animals; Judd and Detweiler; Washington, D. C.; 1897. Pamphlet. Cats, P. 40.

Bougeant, G. H.: Amusement philosophique sur le langage des bestes; Paris; 1739.

Pierquin de Gembloux: Idiomologie des Animaux, ou recherches historiques, anatomiques, physiologiques, philologiques, et glossologiques sur le language des bêtes; A la Tour de Babel; Paris; 1844.

VIII

HUMANITARIAN

Brewster, Edwin Tenney: The City of 4,000,000 cats; McClure's Magazine; New York; 1912; Vol. 39, P. 54. Illustrated with photographs.

Gohier, Urbain: Les Bêtes; Librairie Léon Vanier; Paris; 1911. Les chats au cirque, P. 34.

Helps, Sir Arthur: Some talk about animals and their masters; Strahan and Co.; London; 1873.

Kindness to Animals, illustrated by stories and anecdotes; W. and R. Chambers; London and Edinburgh; 1877. Anecdotes of cats, P. 85.

Salt, H. S.: Animals' Rights; with an essay on vivisection in America by Albert Leffingwell, M. D.; Macmillan and Co.; New York and London; 1894.

Bibliography

IX

CATS AND BIRDS

Barrett, E. N.: The Bird-Cat Question; The Outlook; December 27, 1916; Vol. 114, P. 965.

Brewster, William: A Blameless Cat; Bird-Lore; May 1918; Vol. 20, P. 211.

Cats and Birds; Bird-Lore; September 1915; Vol. 17, P. 408.

Chapouille, Arthur: A plea for puss and her victims; Good Housekeeping; May 1911; Vol. 52, P. 564.

Forbush, Edward Howe: The Domestic Cat: bird killer, mouser, and destroyer of wild life; means of utilizing and controlling it; Wright and Potter Printing Co; Boston; 1916. This is a pamphlet issued by the State of Massachusetts. Forbush is (or was) the State Ornithologist. Illustrated with drawings and photographs.

Forbush, Edward Howe: Facts About Cats; Bird-Lore; March 1915; Vol. 17, P. 165.

Forbush, Edward Howe: What are we going to do about the cat?; Ladies' Home Journal; March 1917.

The House-Cat Indicted; Current Opinion; April 1917; Vol. 62, P. 289.

Hunt, Emily G.: How to enjoy both birds and cats; Country Life in America; February 1915; Vol. 27, P. 52. Illustrated with photographs.

Mason, Walt: The Conservation of Cats; Collier's; November 8, 1913; Vol. 52.

Pearson, T. Gilbert: Cats and Birds; Art World; May 1917; Vol. 2, P. 202. Illustrated with photographs.

Professor R. J. H. de Loach writes about the house cat; Home Progress; March 1914; Vol. 3, P. 326.

A Question for unprejudiced consideration: the house cat; Bird-Lore; January 1915; Vol. 17, P. 54.

Raymond, William: The marauding cat; Country Life (English); June 5, 1915; Vol. 37, P. 780. With four illustrations from photographs.

Bibliography

X

LAW

Cat, a "domestic animal" and "property"; The American Law Review; December 1915; Vol. 49, P. 917.

Evans, E. P.: The Criminal Prosecution and Capital Punishment of Animals; William Heinemann; London; 1906. Illustrated with engravings.

Ingham, John H.: The Law of Animals, a treatise on property in animals, wild and domestic, and the rights and responsibilities arising therefrom; T. and J. W. Johnson; Philadelphia; 1900.

Rogers, R. Vashon: Cats; The Green Bag; Boston; August 1891; Vol. 3, P. 350.

Rolfe, Gertrude B.: The Cat in Law; North American Review; February 1895; Vol. 160, P. 251.

XI

FOLKLORE AND RELIGION

Bérenger-Féraud, Laurent-Jean-Baptiste: Réminiscences populaires de la Provence; Ernest Leroux; Paris; 1885.

Bérenger-Féraud, Laurent-Jean-Baptiste: Superstitions et Survivances, étudiées au point de vue de leur origine et de leurs transformations; Ernest Leroux; Paris; 1896. Two volumes.

Bergen, Fanny D.: Animal and Plant Lore, collected from the oral tradition of English speaking people, with an introduction by Joseph Y. Bergen; Houghton, Mifflin, and Co.; Boston; 1899.

Buckner, E. D.: The Immortality of Animals, and the relation of man as guardian from a Biblical and philosophical hypothesis; George W. Jacobs and Co.; Philadelphia; 1903.

Budge, E. A. Wallis: The Gods of the Egyptians or Studies in Egyptian Mythology; Methuen and Co.; London; 1904. With ninety-eight coloured plates and one hundred and thirty-one illustrations in the text.

Campbell, John Gregorson: Superstitions of the Highlands and Islands of Scotland; James MacLehose and Sons; Glasgow; 1900.

Bibliography

Collin de Plancy, J.: Dictionnaire Infernal; Paul Mellier; Paris; 1844 (third edition).

Conway, Moncure Daniel: Demonology and Devil-lore; Henry Holt and Co.; New York; 1879. Two volumes with numerous illustrations.

Dyer, T. F. Thiselton: The Cat and its Folk-lore; Gentleman's Magazine; May 1882; N. S. Vol. 28, P. 604.

Dyer, T. F. Thiselton: English Folk-lore; Hardwicke and Bogue; London; 1878.

Ennemoser, Joseph: The History of Magic; translated from the German by William Howitt; Bohn's Library; London; 1854; Two volumes.

Fitzgerald, David: The Cat in Legend and Myth; Belgravia; London; November 1885; Vol. 58, P. 98.

Fornaro, Carlo de: White Lotus: the legend of the cat's eye; Marcus and Co.; New York; 1901. Illustrations by the author.

Frazer, J. G.: The Golden Bough, a study in magic and religion; Macmillan and Co.; London. Third edition in twelve volumes, 1911-15.

Gubernatis, Angelo de: Zoological Mythology, or the legends of animals; Trübner and Co.; London; 1872. Two volumes. Vol. 2, Chapter VII, P. 41, for the cat.

Hamel, Frank: Human Animals; Frederick A. Stokes Co.; New York; 1915.

Hargrove, Ethel C.: The Psychic Significance of the Cat; Occult Review; London; 1917; Vol. 25, P. 337.

Harwood, W. S.: The mummification of cats in ancient Egypt; Scientific American; June 9, 1900; Vol. 82, P. 361.

Hazlitt, William Carew: Faiths and Folklore: a dictionary; a new and alphabetically arranged edition of Brand's Antiquities; Reeves and Turner; London; 1905.

Hearn, Lafcadio: Japanese Fairy Tales; The Boy Who Drew Cats, P. 29; Boni and Liveright; New York; 1918. Originally published in Japan with charming illustrations.

Hone, William: The Every-Day Book; Thomas Tegg; London; 1826-1830. Three volumes.

James, Hartwell: The Cat and the Mouse: a book of Persian fairy tales; edited with an introduction by Hartwell James; Henry

Bibliography

Altemus Co.; Philadelphia; 1906. With forty illustrations by John R. Neill.

Kipling, John Lockwood: Beast and Man in India, a popular sketch of Indian animals in their relations with the people; Macmillan and Co.; London; 1891. Cats, P. 282. Illustrated with drawings.

Lean's Collectanea: Collections by Vincent Stuckey Lean of proverbs, English and foreign, folklore, and superstitions, also compilations towards dictionaries of proverbial phrases and words, old and disused; J. W. Arrowsmith; Bristol; 1902. Five volumes.

Meller, Walter Clifford: A Brief for Animal Immortality; G. Bell and Sons; London; 1911.

O'Donnell, Elliott: Animal Ghosts; William Rider and Sons; London; 1913. Cats, P. 3–56.

Phipson, Emma: Animal Lore in Shakespeare's Time; Kegan Paul, Trench and Co.; London; 1883.

Ralston, W. R. S.: Krilof and his fables; Strahan and Co.; London; 1869. The following are cat stories: The Pike and the Cat, P. 27; The Cook and the Cat, P. 45; The Cat and the Nightingale, P. 167; and The Wolf and the Cat, P. 171. Illustrated with drawings.

The Rat's Plaint: translated from the Chinese by Archibald Little; T. Hasegawa; Tokyo; 1891. Illustrated with many drawings in colour.

Rozan, Charles: Le chat dans les proverbes; Monde Moderne; Paris; 1901; Vol. 13, P. 650. Illustrated with drawings.

Visser, Dr. M. W. de: The Dog and the Cat in Japanese Superstition; Transactions of the Asiatic Society of Japan; 1909; Vol. 37, P. 1.

Wood, Rev. J. G.: Man and Beast: Here and Hereafter; George Routledge and Sons; London; 1875 (?).

XII

FICTION

Aesop: Three Hundred Fables, translated by Rev. Geo. Fyler Townsend; George Routledge and Sons; London; 1867. The Cat and the Cock, P. 27; The Cat and the Birds, P. 46; The Cat and the

Bibliography

Mice; P. 103; and The Cat and Venus, P. 214. This edition is illustrated by Harrison Weir.

Alden, W. L.: The Cats of Piacenza; Harper's Monthly; August 1906; Vol. 113, P. 398. Illustrated by May Wilson Preston.

Alden, W. L.: Cat Tales: eleven somewhat fantastic stories about cats; Digby, Long and Co.; London; 1905. Illustrated by Louis Wain.

Aldrich, Thomas Bailey: The Story of a Cat, translated from the French of Émile de la Bédollière; Houghton, Osgood and Co.; Boston; 1878. With many designs in silhouette by Hopkins. There is a French nursery rhyme on this subject which you may find on P. 234 of Miss Repplier's The Fireside Sphinx, or translated on P. 169 of Miss Repplier's The Cat.

Allen, Willis Boyd: The Head of Pasht; E. P. Dutton and Co.; New York; 1900. There is a head of Pasht on the cover and on the title page.

Archibald the Cat, and other sea yarns, by " the old sailor "; " out of The World "; published by the New York World; New York; 1878. The title story is the only cat story. The illustrations are by F. S. Church.

Babcock, Edwina Stanton: From the Diary of a Cat; Harper's Magazine; August 1904; Vol. 109, P. 487. Illustrations by Strothmann.

Bacon, Peggy: The True Philosopher and other cat tales; The Four Seas Co.; Boston; 1919. Illustrated with etchings by the author.

Balzac, Honoré de: Peines de cœur d'une chatte anglaise; first published in Vie Privée et Publique des Animaux. In the edition of Balzac (Oeuvres Complètes) issued by Calmann Lévy, Paris, 1879, this story is to be found in Vol. 21, Oeuvres Diverses.

Bell, J. J.: Mr. Pennycook's Boy; Harper and Brothers; New York; 1905. Poor Pussy, P. 263.

Bell, J. J.: Wanted — A Pussy-Mew; The Bellman; March 3, 1917; Vol. 22, P. 236.

Bierce, Ambrose: Can Such Things Be?: Collected Works; Neale Publishing Co.; New York and Washington; 1910. John Mortonson's Funeral, P. 252, is a cat story.

Bierce, Ambrose: Fantastic Fables; G. P. Putnam's Sons; New York;

Bibliography

1899; The Cat and the King, P. 27; The Cat and the Youth, P. 159; The Cat and the Birds, P. 161.

Blackwood, Algernon: The Empty Sleeve; The London Magazine; January 1911; P. 552.

Blackwood, Algernon: John Silence: Physician Extraordinary; John W. Luce and Co.; Boston; 1909. Case I: A Psychical Invasion, and Case II: Ancient Sorceries, are cat stories.

Blackwood, Algernon: Pan's Garden; Macmillan and Co.; London; 1912. The Attic, P. 137, is a cat story. Illustrated by W. Graham Robertson.

Brouse, Marian M.: The cat that tried to be stylish; Woman's Home Companion; April 1914. Illustrated by Kerr Eby.

Bulwer-Lytton, Edward: Eugene Aram.

Burgess, Gelett: The White Cat; A. Wessels Co.; New York; 1908. This is a story of dissociated personality in which the fairy tale of The White Cat is used as a symbol.

Caillot, Jules Sevérin: Contes après les contes; Plon-Nourrit et cie.; Paris; 1919. La Chatte Blanche, P. 67.

Carroll, Lewis: Alice in Wonderland. Illustrated by John Tenniel.

Carroll, Lewis: Through the Looking Glass. Illustrated by John Tenniel.

Carruth, Hayden: The Adventures of Jones; Harper and Brothers; New York; 1895. The Cat Motor, P. 7 and The Wild-cat Frightener, P. 48.

Carryl, Guy Wetmore: Zut, and other Parisians; Houghton, Mifflin Co.; Boston; 1903. The title story is a cat story.

Chambers, Robert W.: The King in Yellow; F. Tennyson Neely; Chicago — New York; 1895. The Repairer of Reputations and The Street of the Four Winds are cat stories.

Corrothers, James David: The Black Cat Club, Negro humor and folklore; Funk and Wagnalls; New York; 1902. Illustrated by J. K. Bryans.

Davey, Robert M.: The Pinckney Street Cats; New England Magazine; September 1911; N. S. Vol. 45, P. 40.

Ensign, Hermon Lee: Lady Lee and other animal stories; A. C. McClurg; Chicago; 1902. Union Square Jim, P. 67 and Baby and the Kitten, P. 171 are cat stories. Illustrated by J. Carter Beard.

Bibliography

Felissa: or the life and opinions of a kitten of sentiment; J. Harris; London; 1811. With twelve coloured plates. Methuen and Co., London, reprinted this book in 1903.

Fernald, Chester B: The Cat and the Cherub, and other stories; The Century Co.; New York; 1896. One-Two, the white and blue Angora, appears in The Cat and the Cherub and The Cruel Thousand Years. With one illustration by Grace Wetherell. The cover design depicts the cat and the cherub.

France, Anatole: Le Crime de Sylvestre Bonnard; Calmann-Lévy; Paris.

Freeman, Mary E. Wilkins: Understudies; Harper and Brothers; New York; 1901. The Cat is the title of the story.

Freeman, Mary E. Wilkins: A Humble Romance and other stories; Harper and Brothers; New York; 1887. An Object of Love, P. 266, is a cat story.

George, W. L.: Blind Alley; T. Fisher Unwin; London; 1919.

Graham, R. B. Cunninghame: Success, and other sketches; Duckworth and Co.; London; 1902. Terror, P. 109.

Greene, Frederick Stuart: The Cat of the Cane-Brake; Metropolitan Magazine; August 1916; Vol. 44. Illustrations by Worth Brehm.

The Guardian Cat: Every Saturday; October 12, 1872. Reprinted from Chambers's Journal.

Hamilton, Allan McLane: Herr von Striempfell's Experiment; The Century; April 1891; Vol. 41, P. 89.

Hamm, Margherita Arlina: The Cat Coquette; The Century; October 1905; Vol. 70, P. 823. Illustrations by Jay Hambidge.

Hearn, Lafcadio: Fantastics and Other Fancies; Houghton, Mifflin and Co.; Boston; 1914. The Little Red Kitten, P. 33.

Henty, G. A.: The Cat of Bubastes: a tale of ancient Egypt; Blackie and Son; London; 1889.

Hubbard, Elbert: Pig-Pen Pete, or Some Chums of Mine; Roycrofters Shop; East Aurora, N. Y.; 1914. The Black Cat, P. 157; Our Emmiline, P. 169.

Huysmans, J. K.: En Rade; Plon-Nourrit et Cie; Paris.

Jackson, Gabrielle E.: Little Comrade: the story of a cat, and other animal stories; D. Appleton and Co.; New York; 1905. With a picture of Little Comrade. Juvenile.

Bibliography

Jackson, Helen (H. H.): Cat Stories: Letters from a Cat; Mammy Tittleback and her Family; The Hunter Cats of Connorloa; Little Brown and Co.; Boston; 1903. The illustrations for the first two stories are by Addie Ledyard; those for the last from photographs and drawings. Juvenile.

Janvier, Thomas A.: From the South of France; Harper and Brothers; New York; 1912. Illustrations by Frank Craig. Madame Jolicœur's Cat, P. 137.

Janvier, Thomas A.: In the Sargasso Sea; Harper and Brothers; New York; 1898. Cat in Chapter XXXII, P. 236 et seqq.

Janvier, Thomas A.: The Passing of Thomas, and other stories; Harper and Brothers; New York; 1900. The title story is a cat story. Illustrations by Charles Dana Gibson.

Janvier, Thomas A.: Stories of Old New Spain; D. Appleton and Co.; New York; 1891. San Antonio of the Gardens is a cat story.

Kari: Madame Tabby's Establishment; Macmillan and Co.; London; 1886. Illustrations by Louis Wain. Juvenile.

Keller, Gottfried: Spiegel, das Kätzchen, in Die Leute von Seldwyla; 1856.

Kendall, May: Billy; Longman's Magazine; December 1903; Vol. 43, P. 163.

Kipling, Rudyard: In Black and White: The Sending of Dana Da is a cat story.

Kipling, Rudyard: Just So Stories: The Cat that Walked by Himself. With illustrations by the author.

Knatchbull-Hugessen, E. H. (M. P.): Puss-Cat Mew, and other stories for my children; Harper and Brothers; New York; 1871. With illustrations. The first story is the only cat story. Juvenile.

Loti, Pierre: Le Livre de la Pitié et de la Mort; Calmann-Lévy; Paris. This book contains two cat stories: Une bête galeuse, P. 27, and Vies de deux chattes, P. 47. The latter, translated by M. B. Richards as Lives of Two Cats and illustrated by C. E. Allen, was published by Dana Estes and Co.; Boston, 1902.

Loti, Pierre: Le Mariage de Loti; Calmann-Lévy; Paris.

Lyman, Edward Branch: Me'ow Jones, Belgian Refugee Cat, his own true tale as written down by E. B. L.; George H. Doran; New York; 1917. Illustrated by Julia Daniels.

Bibliography

Mirbeau, Octave: La Vache Tachetée; Ernest Flammarion; Paris. Le petit gardeur de vaches, P. 40, is a cat story.

Morley, Charles: Peter: a cat o' one tail: his life and adventures; G. P. Putnam's Sons; New York-London; 1892. Illustrated by Louis Wain, Peter's proprietor.

Mulford, Prentice: The Family Cat; Hood's Comic Annual for 1874; London; P. 50.

A parable for philanthropists: Atlantic Monthly; December 1919; Vol. 124, P. 861.

Patteson, S. Louise: Pussy Meow: the autobiography of a cat, with an introduction by Sarah K. Bolton; George W. Jacobs and Co.; Philadelphia; 1901. Illustrated with drawings and photographs, Juvenile.

Peple, Edward: A Night Out; Moffat, Yard and Co.; New York; 1909. Frontispiece by R. L. Goldberg.

Picard, Gaston: La confession du chat; with a preface by J.–H. Rosny, ainé; Albin Michel; Paris; 1919. The title story is the only cat story.

Pinski, David: Temptations; Brentano's; New York; 1919. The Black Cat.

Poe, Edgar Allan: The Black Cat.

Polko, Elise: Musical Sketches; Sturgis and Walton Co.; New York; 1909. Translated from the fifteenth German edition. The Cat's Fugue, P. 82. This is the story of Scarlatti and his cat.

Porter, Eleanor H.: The Tie that Binds; Houghton, Mifflin Co.; 1919. Illustrated by Helen Mason Grose. The Cat and the Painter, P. 1.

Porter, Eleanor H.: The Cat that played Cupid; New England Magazine; June 1905; N. S. Vol. 32, P. 461.

Powell, G. H.: Animal Episodes, and studies in sensation; George Redway; London; 1896. The Blue Dryad, P. 68, is a cat story.

Puckett, G. A.: Ten Kittens; Burton Publishing Co.; Kansas City, Mo. Illustrated by Helen Walley.

Pyle, Katherine: Stories of Humble Friends; American Book Co.; 1902. Illustrated by the author. Little Brown Hen, P. 13; Flora and her cat, P. 118; Limpety, P. 138; What became of the kittens, P. 178. Juvenile.

Rameau, Jean: Le Chat Nouveau-Riche; Le Petit Journal; Paris;

Bibliography

December 9, 1919. Translated by William R. McPherson as The Nouveau Riche Cat this story appeared in the New York Tribune, February 15, 1920.

Rideout, Henry Milner: The Siamese Cat; Duffield and Co.; New York; 1919.

Robert, Charles G. D.: Neighbours Unknown; Macmillan Co.; New York; 1911. Illustrated by Paul Branscom. How a cat played Robinson Crusoe, P. 173.

Roberts, Morley: The Man Who Stroked Cats, and other stories; Eveleigh Nash; London; 1912. The title story is the only cat story.

Russell, Robert Howard: The Delft Cat, and other stories; R. H. Russell; New York; 1896. Illustrations by F. Berkeley Smith. Juvenile.

Saltus, Edgar: Purple and Fine Women; Ainslie Publishing Co.; New York; 1903. The Top of the Heap, P. 207, is a cat story.

Saunders, Marshall: Pussy Black-Face or the story of a kitten and her friends: a book for boys and girls; L. C. Page and Co.; Boston; 1913. Illustrations by Diantha Horne Marlowe. Juvenile.

Seton, Ernest Thompson: Animal Heroes: being the histories of a cat, a dog, a pigeon, a lynx, two wolves, and a reindeer and in elucidation of the same over two hundred drawings by the author; the designs for cover, title-page, and general makeup by Grace Gallatin Seton; Charles Scribner's Sons; New York; 1905. The Slum Cat is the first story.

Sologub, Feodor: The Little Demon. Translated by John Cournos and Richard Aldington; Martin Secker; London; 1916.

Southworth, May E.: The Great Small Cat and Others: seven tales; Paul Elder and Co.; San Francisco; 1914. Illustrated with photographs and decorated by Pedro J. Lemos.

Stables, Gordon: Shireen and her Friends: pages from the life of a Persian cat; Jarrold and Sons; London; 1894. Three full-page illustrations by Harrison Weir. This book is dedicated to Swinburne and his poem, To a Cat, is reprinted in it. L. C. Page and Co. in Boston printed an American edition.

Swain, Miranda Eliot: Daisy, the autobiography of a cat; Noyes Brothers; Boston; 1900. With a photograph of Daisy.

Bibliography

Tarkington, Booth: Penrod and Sam; Doubleday, Page and Co.; New York; 1916. Illustrated by Worth Brehm.

Twain, Mark: Dick Baker's Cat; Screams; 1871. Later incorporated in Roughing It; American Publishing Co.; Hartford; 1872; P. 439.

Twain, Mark: Jim Wolfe and the Cats; New York Sunday Mercury; 1867; Garrett's 100 Choice Selections, No. 17; 1879; This story was also published in Hood's Comic Annual for 1874 under the title, A Yankee Story by G. R. Wadleigh. It is included in the anthology, Werner's Readings: Cats and Kittens, P. 244.

Twain, Mark: The Man Who Fought Cats; Practical Jokes; John Camden Hotten; London; 1872.

Twain, Mark: The Stolen White Elephant, etc.; James R. Osgood and Co.; Boston; Some Rambling Notes of an Idle Excursion, P. 74, for some Bermuda cats.

Vie Privée et Publique des Animaux; études de moeurs contemporains, publiées sous la direction de M. P.-J. Stahl, avec la collaboration de Messieurs de Balzac, L. Baude, É. de la Bédollière, P. Bernard, J. Janin, Ed. Lemoine, Charles Nodier, George Sand, L'Heretier, Alfred de Musset, Paul de Musset, Madame M. Ménessier-Nodier, Louis Viardot. J. Hetzel; Paris; 1842. Two volumes. Illustrations by Grandville. The cat stories are Peines de cœur d'une chatte anglaise by Balzac; Vol. 1, P. 89, and Peines de cœur d'une chatte française by P.-J. Stahl; Vol. 2, P. 165. The edition of 1867 is in one volume. Translated by J. Thomson as Public and Private Life of Animals, this book was published in London by Sampson Low, Marston, Searle, and Rivington in 1877, but Balzac's story is omitted from this version. Most of Grandville's drawings are retained.

Weyman, Stanley J.: The Cat and the King; McClure's; October 1895; Vol. 5, P. 438.

White, Eliza Orne: Brothers in Fur; Houghton, Mifflin Co.; Boston; 1910. Illustrated with photographs. Juvenile.

Wilkinson, Elizabeth Hays: Peter and Polly; Doubleday, Page and Co.; New York; 1912. Illustrated with photographs in colour by Cornelia Clarke. Juvenile.

Willy et Colette Willy: Claudine à l'Ecole; Paul Ollendorff; Paris.

Willy et Colette Willy: Claudine à Paris; Paul Ollendorff; Paris.

Bibliography

Willy et Colette Willy: Claudine en Ménage; Mercure de France; Paris; 1902.

Willy et Colette Willy: Claudine s'en va; Paul Ollendorff; Paris.

Woodrow, Mrs. Wilson: The Cat and the Countess; American Magazine (Leslie's Monthly); August 1905; Vol. 60, P. 373. Illustrated with drawings.

Worts, George F.: The Cat and the Burglar; Everybody's Magazine; April 1920; Vol. 42, No. 4, P. 54.

Zola, Émile: Nouveaux Contes à Ninon; Bibliothèque-Charpentier; Paris. This book contains the story Le Paradis des Chats. Translated by Edward Vizetelly as Stories for Ninon this book was issued in London in 1895 by William Heinemann.

XIII

ESSAYS

About Cats; London Society; January 1872; Vol. 21, P. 69. Signed, Philo-felis.

Achard, Émile: The history of my friends or home life with animals; translated from the French; G. P. Putnam's Sons; New York; 1875. Illustrated with drawings. Matapon the First, P. 180.

Addison, Joseph: Cat-calls; The Spectator; Thursday, April 24, 1712.

Addison, Joseph: Moll White and her cat; The Spectator; Saturday, July 4, 1711.

Ailurophobia: Current Literature; August 1905; Vol. 39, P. 186. Quotations from S. Weir Mitchell and Andrew Lang.

Affable Hawk: Cats; The New Statesman: Books in General; February 28, 1920.

Anecdotes of the Cat: Chambers's Miscellany; Edinburgh; Vol. 6.

Atkins, J. B.: Side-Shows; Christophers; London; 1908. The New Cat, P. 1.

Atom: Cats; Everyman; London; November 8, 1919.

Barnicoat, C. A.: The Cat and the Human; Temple Bar; London; 1906; N. S. Vol. 2, P. 162.

Bibliography

Bates, Katherine Lee: Sigurd Our Golden Collie and other comrades of the road; E. P. Dutton and Co.; 1919. Catastrophes, P. 324.

Belloc, Hilaire: On Nothing and Kindred Subjects; Methuen and Co.; London; 1908. On Them is an essay on cats.

Benson, Margaret: The Soul of a Cat, and other stories; William Heinemann; London; 1901. Illustrations from· photographs and drawings by Henriette Ronner. G. P. Putnam Sons issued the American edition in New York the same year. The papers of interest to cat-lovers are: Preface, P. V.; The Soul of a Cat, P. 1; The Mysterious Ra, P. 85; Mentu, P. 97; Epilogue, P. 141.

Borrow, George: Wild Wales. The ecclesiastical cat appears in Chapter VII and also elsewhere in the book.

Boyle, Frederick: Taming Animals; Living Age; June 3, 1911; Vol. 269, P. 599. From the Cornhill Magazine.

Broderip, W. J.: Zoological Recreations; Henry Colburn; London; 1849 (new edition with alterations). Cats, Part II, P. 191.

Bullen, Frank T.: Cats on Board Ship; The Spectator; April 8, 1899; Vol. 82, P. 484.

C. T. L.: Some cats I have known: a reminiscence; Old and New; Boston; April 1873; Vol. 7, P. 462.

The Cat; Household Words; April 18, 1857; Vol. 15, P. 369. This is a review of Lady Cust's book with some additional matter.

The Cat — Ancient and Modern; Chambers's Journal; March 16, 1878; Vol. 55, P. 171.

Cats; Chambers's Journal; July 3, 1875; Vol. 52, P. 430.

Cats; Chambers's Journal; March 23, 1872; Vol. 49, P. 177.

Cats: with some account of the Tooten Toon; Chambers's Journal; April 11, 1868; Vol. 45, P. 225. This is a review of Ross's book with a good deal of additional matter.

Cat Stories; All the Year Round; June 7, 1862; Vol. 7, P. 308.

The Cat About Town; The Spectator; Vol. 80, P. 197.

The Cat and the Bell-Collar; Atlantic Monthly; August 1913; Vol. 112; P. 282.

Cats in Catholic Ritual; The Month; London; August 1896; Vol. 87, P. 487.

Cats and Dogs; Leisure Hour; December 6, 1862; Vol. 2, P. 788.

Bibliography

Cats as Government Servants; World Today; December 1910; Vol. 19, P. 1416. Illustrated with photographs.

The Cat in Literature; The Spectator; Vol. 80, P. 300.

The Cat as Wild Animal; The Spectator; September 12, 1896; Vol. 77, P. 333.

Catacaustic Reflections; Atlantic Monthly; February 1915; Vol. 115, P. 285.

The Cat as an Unconscious Humorist; The Spectator; August 2, 1890; Vol. 65, P. 145.

The Cat Lady; The Outlook; June 10, 1911; Vol. 98, P. 287.

The Cat Show at the Crystal Palace; Saturday Review; October 20, 1883; Vol. 56, P. 500. This was the fifteenth annual cat show in London.

A Chapter on Cats; Chambers's Journal; January 10, 1852; Vol. 17, P. 27.

A Chapter on Cats; The Knickerbocker Magazine; December 1839, P. 556.

Clark, Harriet Woodward: An unappreciated suburbanite; Suburban Life; September 1907; Vol. 5, P. 172. Illustrated with a photograph.

A Climbing Cat; The Living Age; December 21, 1912; Vol. 275, P. 759. From The Spectator.

Concerning Cats; Appleton's Journal; New York; May 27, 1871; Vol. 5, P. 613.

Concerning Cats; Leisure Hour; 1883; Vol. 32, Pages 48, 94, 161, 224. Illustrated with drawings.

Conway, W. M.: The Cats of Ancient Egypt; English Illustrated Magazine; January 1890; Vol. 7, P. 251.

Coulson, G. J. A.: Cats; New Eclectic; Baltimore; August 1869; Vol. 5, P. 172.

Curiosities of Cats; Once a Week; London; December 26, 1863; Vol. 10, P. 16.

Cursory Cogitations Concerning Cats; Blackwood's; November 1839; Vol. 46, P. 653.

Day, Clarence, jr.: The Great Cats in This Simian World; Alfred A. Knopf; New York; 1920. Illustrated by the author.

De Forest, J. W.: The Cats of Antiquity; Atlantic Monthly; May 1874; Vol. 33, P. 556.

Bibliography

De Forest, J. W.: Modern Cats: Atlantic Monthly; June 1874; Vol. 33, P. 737.

Docquois, Georges: Bêtes et Gens de Lettres; Flammarion; Paris; 1895. With a cover in colours by Steinlen.

Douglas, A. Donald: Of Cats; The Forum; March 1914; Vol. 51, P. 415.

Dumas, Alexandre: My Pets, translated by Alfred Allinson from Mes Bêtes; with sixteen illustrations by V. Lecomte; the Macmillan Co.; New York; 1909.

Durand, James: A Household Pet; Cosmopolitan; January 1887; Vol. 2, P. 312.

Employment for Cats; The Living Age; October 15, 1910; Vol. 267, P. 184. From The Spectator.

A Few Words About Cats; Temple Bar; November 1881; Vol. 63, P. 378.

Froude, James Anthony: Short Studies on Great Subjects: First Series; Longmans Green; London; 1867 (second edition). The Cat's Pilgrimage, P. 419.

Gautier, Théophile: Baudelaire and the Cat; in Gautier's preface to Fleurs du Mal, Pages 33, 34, 35; Calmann-Lévy; Paris.

Goldsmith, Gertrude: The Serpent in Eden; Suburban Life; July 1913; Vol. 17, P. 12. Illustrated with photographs.

Gosse, Edmund: Gossip in a Library. Cats is an essay on Augustin Paradis de Moncrif.

Graves, C. L.: The Diversions of a Music Lover; Macmillan and Co.; London; 1904; A Musical Celebrity, P. 219.

G. Y.: " Mole "; The Spectator; January 13, 1912; Vol. 108, P. 51.

Hamerton, Philip Gilbert: Chapters on Animals; Seeley, Jackson and Halliday; London; 1874. With twenty etchings by J. Veyrassat and Karl Bodmer. Chapter IV, P. 43, is devoted to cats.

Havet, Mireille: La maison dans l'oeil du chat; Georges Crès et cie; Paris; 1917. Avertissement de Colette Willy. Dessins de Jeanne de Lanux. Two pieces in this book concern cats, the title paper, P. 65, and Le chat, P. 151.

Hearn, Lafcadio: Kottō: being Japanese curios with sundry cobwebs; Macmillan and Co.; New York; 1902. Illustrations by Genjiro Yeto. Pathological, P. 217, is a cat paper.

Bibliography

Herendeen, Anne: The Case of Mouser vs. Bowser; Everybody's Magazine; July 1919; Vol. 41, P. 41. Illustrations by Oliver Herford.

The History of Cats; Saturday Review; May 6, 1882; Vol. 53, P. 558.

Hopkins, Tighe: Cats; Leisure Hour; 1895; Vol. 44, P. 107. Illustrations by Louis Wain and A. Seiger.

Howe, Arthur L.: Abolishing the stray cat nuisance; Suburban Life; January 1911; Vol. 12, P. 20. Illustrated with photographs.

Howells, W. D.: Literature and Life; Harper and Brothers; New York; 1902. Jim, in Staccato Notes of a Vanished Summer, P. 261.

Hunt, Leigh: The Cat by the Fire; first published in The Seer, this essay is to be found in the volume of selected papers in Walter Scott's Camelot series.

In Praise of Cats; Living Age; January 9, 1909; Vol. 260, P. 124. From The Nation.

Jerome, Jerome K.: Idle Thoughts of an Idle Fellow; Field and Tuer; London. On Cats and Dogs, P. 77.

Jerome, Jerome K.: Novel Notes; Simpkin, Marshall, Hamilton Kent, and Co.; London; 1893. Chapter VI (illustrated by Louis Wain) is devoted to cats.

Kidd, W.: Love me, love my cat; Leisure Hour; November 28, 1861; Vol. 10, P. 75.

L. J. S.: Cats and Poets; Lippincott's; February 1885; Vol. 35, P. 177.

Lang, Andrew: At the Sign of the Ship; Longman's Magazine; Vol. 2, P. 463; February 1888 (Puss in Boots); P. 571; March 1888 (Arsinoë's Cats); Vol. 25, P. 215; December 1894; P. 320; January 1895 (cats and dogs); Vol. 31, P. 92; November 1897; P. 465; March 1898; P. 558; April 1898 (ailurophobia); Vol. 34, P. 280; July 1899; P. 380; August 1899 (with Walter Pollock's poem, Le chat devant la guerre); Vol. 35, P. 93; November 1899; Vol. 44, P. 85; May 1904; Vol. 45, P. 382; February 1905. So far as I know these extremely interesting notes by Andrew Lang have not been collected in book form.

Larrabee, W. H.: Cats and their Friendships; Popular Science Monthly; New York; May 1890; Vol. 37, P. 91. Illustrated with drawings.

Bibliography

Larrabee, W. H.: The Intelligence of Cats; Popular Science Monthly; January 1891; Vol. 38, P. 368.

Lautard, Henri: Chiens et Chats: la sympathie envers les animaux; Le Correspondent; Paris; 1906; Vol. 219 (N. S. Vol. 183), P. 999.

The License of the Cat; Living Age; May 3, 1913; Vol. 277, P. 309. From The Spectator.

Lord, J. K.: Cats; Leisure Hour; July 27, 1867; Vol. 16, P. 474.

Loti, Pierre: Reflets sur la Sombre Route; Calmann-Lévy; Paris. Chiens et Chats, P. 49. Translated by Fred Rothwell as On Life's Byways, this book was issued in London in 1914 by G. Bell and Sons, Ltd. Dogs and Cats is on P. 34.

Lucas, E. V.: Landmarks; Macmillan Co.; New York; 1914. The Black Cat, Chap. X, P. 60.

Lynd, Robert: The Book of This and That; Mills and Boon, Ltd.; London; 1915. On Black Cats, P. 137.

Marquis, Don: Prefaces; D. Appleton and Co.; New York; 1919. Preface to a Cat Show Catalogue, P. 57.

Maupassant, Guy de: La Petite Roque; Paul Ollendorff; Paris. Sur les chats, P. 185.

Mayo, Isabella Fyvie: The Calumniated Cat; Humane Review; London; April 1902; P. 38.

Miller, Olive Thorne (Harriet Mann Miller): Upon the Tree Tops; Houghton, Mifflin and Co.; Boston; 1897. The Idyl of an Empty Lot, Chap. XI, P. 192, is about cats.

Mitchell, S. Weir: Cat Fear; Ladies' Home Journal; March 1906.

Moses, Joseph Winthrop: Something About Cats; New Eclectic; Baltimore; November 1870; Vol. 7, P. 604.

My Cats; Once a Week; London; August 22, 1863; Vol. 9, P. 245.

Notes on Cats; The Spectator; August 2, 1913; Vol. 3, P. 171.

On Black Cats; London Magazine; March 1822; Vol. 5, P. 285.

Our Family Cats; Leisure Hour; February 19, 1857; Vol. 6, P. 117.

Outside Pets; Blackwood; December 1903; Vol. 174, P. 766.

Owlett, F. C.: The Cat in Literature; Bibliophile; London; October 1908; Vol. 2, P. 82. Illustrated with drawings.

Panton, J. E.: Cats and Kittens, or in defence of the cat; English Illustrated Magazine; March 1890; Vol. 7, P. 450. Illustrated by Louis Wain.

Bibliography

Phoenix's Feline Attachment; The Knickerbocker Magazine; July 1857, P. 87. A meeting of cats to consult concerning John Phoenix's feline attachment; idem; September 1857.

Puss; Chambers's Journal; October 9, 1880; Vol. 57, P. 646.

Pussy's bit in the war; Literary Digest; December 6, 1919; Vol. 63.

Pussy's Notable Friends; Chambers's Journal; Edinburgh; November 14, 1891; Vol. 68, P. 734.

A Question of Animal Ethics; The Spectator; October 7, 1911; Vol. 107, P. 541.

Repplier, Agnes: Americans and Others; Houghton, Mifflin Co.; Boston; 1912. The Grocer's Cat, P. 273.

Repplier, Agnes: Essays in Idleness: Houghton, Mifflin and Co.; Boston; 1893. Agrippina, P. 1.

Repplier, Agnes: Essays in Miniature; Houghton, Mifflin Co.; 1899; Old World Pets, P. 182.

Repplier, Agnes: In the Dozy Hours; Houghton, Mifflin and Co.; Boston; 1894. A. Kitten, P. 16. This is a charming account of Agrippina's son, Claudius Nero.

Reserve and the Cat; Scribner's Magazine; March 1919.

Riis, Jacob A.: Slippers, the White House Cat; Saint Nicholas; January 1908; Vol. 35, P. 202. With an illustration.

Robinson, Phil: The Poets' Beasts; Chatto and Windus; London; 1885. Some Poets' Cats, P. 337.

Runciman, John F.: My French Cats; Saturday Review; London; April 2, 1904; Vol. 97, P. 424.

St. Clair, George: The Cat and the Moon; Gentleman's Magazine; London; 1901; Vol. 290, P. 251.

Saint-Victor, Paul de: Les Chats; L'Artiste; Paris; 1870, P. 368.

Sanborn, Kate: My Literary Zoo; D. Appleton and Co.; New York; 1896. The paper on cats begins on P. 75.

Sandy; The Spectator; March 13, 1915; Vol. 114, P. 366.

A Short Paper on Cats; Leisure Hour; February 12, 1857; Vol. 6, P. 107.

Southey, Robert: The Doctor; Longmans, Green and Co.; London; 1865 (edition in one volume). Contains Memoirs of Cats' Eden and Memoirs of the Cats of Greta Hall.

Spaulding, Thomas Marshall: The Army Cat; Overland Monthly; December 1919; Vol. 74, P. 437.

Bibliography

Spencer, Herman: Mark Twain and the Cat; Harper's Weekly; February 9, 1907; Vol. 51, P. 194.

Stables, Gordon: A Plea for Pussy; Leisure Hour; 1888; Vol. 37, P. 813.

Stories of Cats; Chambers's Journal; December 11, 1886; Vol. 63, P. 791.

Stray Thoughts on Stray Cats; Argosy; London; March 1894; Vol. 57, P. 252.

Strong, Prof. Herbert A.: The Cat; Chambers's Journal; June 1, 1916; Ser. 7, Vol. 6, P. 356.

Strong, H. A.: Some notes on the cat and the rat and the testimony of language as to their early history; Academy; London; January 28, 1893; Vol. 43, P. 81. In the Academy for February 4, 1893, P. le P. Renouf has a corrective letter.

Sylva, Carmen: My Kittens; Century; August 1908; Vol. 76, P. 538. Illustrated with photographs.

Toussenel, Alphonse: L'esprit des bêtes; zoologie passionelle; mammifères de France; E. Dentu; Paris; 1858 (third edition). Le Chat, P. 226. Translated by M. Edgeworth Lazarus as Passional Zoology, or Spirit of the Beasts of France.

Trueblood, Sarah E.: Cats by the Way; J. B. Lippincott Co.; Philadelphia; 1904. Illustrations by the author.

Uncle Sam's feline force of mail guardians; Literary Digest; April 12, 1919; P. 46.

Van Tricht, Victor: Nos Familiers; Paul Godenne; Namur; 1890 (third edition). Vol. 1: Les familiers de la maison: chiens et chats.

Vere, Schele de: Pussy; Harper's Monthly; March 1870; Vol. 40, P. 481. The illustrations are mostly from Champfleury's Les Chats.

Warner, Charles Dudley: My Summer in a Garden; Houghton, Mifflin, and Co.; Boston. Fields, Osgood, and Co. issued this book in 1870. Mr. Warner's Calvin appears in it several times. When Calvin died Mr. Warner wrote a special paper about him which first appeared, I think, in the Houghton, Mifflin edition of 1882, and has since been included in all subsequent editions.

Webb, Charles Henry: Uncared-for Cats; Lippincott's; August 1894; Vol. 54, P. 246.

Bibliography

What has become of the half-million war cats?; Literary Digest; May 10, 1919.

What the cat thinks of the dog; Unpopular Review; July 1918; Vol. 10, P. 205.

Willy, Colette: La Paix Chez les Bêtes; Georges Crès et cie.; Paris; 1916. Frontispiece by Steinlen. Contains the following cat essays: Poum, P. 1; Prrou, P. 17; La Shah, P. 35; Le Matou, P. 45; Nonoche, P. 93; La Mère Chatte, P. 105; Le Tentateur, P. 113; Automne, P. 127; Le Naturaliste et la Chatte, P. 135; Ricotte, P. 153; Conte pour les Petits Enfants des Poilus, P. 221.

Wilson, Francis: Lady Jule; Ladies' Home Journal; November 1902. Illustrated with photographs.

Wister, S. B. (the first installment is signed C. B.): Cats and Their Affections; Temple Bar; December 1895; Vol. 106, P. 557; and January 1896; Vol. 107, P. 84.

Wood, Eugene: Mah-ow!; Delineator; July 1917; Vol. 91, P. 12. Illustrations by H. L. Drucklieb. This paper was written by a canophilist who hates cats.

Wood, Rev. J. G.: Bible Animals: Longmans, Green, Reader, and Dyer; London; 1869. The Cat, P. 36.

Wood, Rev. J. G.: Glimpses into Petland; Bell and Daldy; London; 1863. Pages 1-84 about the cat, Pret. With a frontispiece by Walter Crane.

Wynter, Andrew: Fruit Between the Leaves; Chapman and Hall; London; 1875. Two volumes. Eccentric Cats, Vol. 2, P. 108.

XIV

THEATRE

Bunner, H. C.: Three Operettas; Harper and Brothers; New York; 1897. The Three Little Kittens of the Land of Pie, P. 3. Music by Oscar Weil. Illustrations by C. D. Weldon.

Deshoulières, Mademoiselle Antoinette Thérèse: La Mort de Cochon (chien de M. le Maréchal de Vivonne); tragédie. Collected Works of Madame and Mademoiselle Deshoulières, and Moncrif: Les Chats, P. 190.

Fernald, Chester B.: The Cat and the Cherub: a play in one act;

Bibliography

Samuel French; Ltd.; New York and London; 1912. Although some of the same characters appear, this is not a dramatization of the story which bears the same name. The play was produced at the Lyric Theatre, London, October 30, 1897.

Lopez, John S.: The Theatre Cat; Harper's Weekly; January 4, 1908; Vol. 52, P. 22. Illustrated by Henry Raleigh.

Maeterlinck, Maurice: L'Oiseau Bleu; féerie en six actes et douze tableaux. Performed for the first time at the Art Theatre in Moscow, September 30, 1908.

Middleton, Thomas: The Witch.

Tieck, Ludwig: Der gestiefelte Kater — ein Kindermärchen in drei Akten (1797); P. 161, Vol. 5: Collected Works; Berlin; 1828. An abbreviated translation, Puss in Boots, by Lillie Winter, is to be found in The German Classics (edited by Kuno Francke); German Publication Society; New York; Vol. 4, P. 194.

Todhunter, John: The Black Cat; Henry and Co.; London; 1895. A play in three acts, performed by the Independent Theatre (J. T. Grein, director) December 8, 1893, at the Opera Comique, London.

Walter, Eugene: The Assassin; produced at the Collingwood Opera House, Poughkeepsie, New York, on the afternoon of May 30, 1917. Not published.

Willy, Colette: Sept Dialogues de Bêtes; Mercure de France; Paris; 1905 (fifth edition). There is a preface by Francis Jammes and a portrait of the author after a painting by Jacques Blanche. Translated by Maire Kelly as Barks and Purrs, with many illustrations, the English version was published by Desmond Fitzgerald; New York; 1913.

XV

MUSIC

Berthold, G.: Duet for Two Cats, with pianoforte accompaniment; Augener and Co.; London.

Dobson, Tom: The Cat (words by James Stephens); in The Rocky Road to Dublin; Oliver Ditson Co.; Boston; 1919.

German, Edward: The First Friend (words by Rudyard Kipling);

Bibliography

in Just So Song Book; Doubleday, Page, and Co.; New York; 1919.

Kaufman, Mel B.: Me–ow: one-step; Sam Fox Publishing Co.; Cleveland; 1918.

My Musical Critic; Atlantic Monthly; January 1894; Vol. 73, P. 139.

Scarlatti, Domenico: The Cat's Fugue.

Stravinsky, Igor: Berceuses du Chat; four songs for a woman's voice and three clarinets; arranged for piano by the composer. Popular Russian songs put into French by C. F. Ramuz; Edition Ad. Henn; Geneva; 1917. I, Sur le poêle; II, Intérieur; III, Dodo; IV, " Ce qu'il a, le chat."

Tschaikovsky, P.: La Belle au Bois Dormant; ballet; Opus 66; P. Jurgenson; Moscow. No. 23 is a Pas de Caractère between Puss in Boots and the White Cat. This is on P. 168 of the piano score.

XVI

ART

Bate, Francis: Mr. Arthur Tomson's pictures and studies of cats at the Dutch Gallery; The Studio; London; November 15, 1893; Vol. 2, P. 65. Illustrated with drawings by Arthur Tomson.

Boston, Frederick J. and Elizabeth S. Tucker: Cats and Kittens; with numerous full-page colour-plates after paintings in water colours by F. J. Boston, and with decorative borders and other designs, together with new stories and verses by E. S. Tucker; Frederick A. Stokes Co.; New York; 1895. Juvenile.

The Cat Painter (Gottfried Mind); The Penny Magazine; London; March 1, 1834; Vol. 3, P. 86.

Cherville, G. de: Les Chiens et les Chats d'Eugène Lambert; Librairie de l'Art; Paris; 1888. Illustrated with six etchings of cats and one hundred and forty-five drawings of cats and dogs.

Claudy, C. H.: Cats and Cameras; Photographic Times-Bulletin; New York; 1904; Vol. 36, P. 145. Illustrated with photographs by the author.

Englemann, Richard: Die Katzen im Altertum; Jahrbuch des Kaiser-

Bibliography

lich Deutschen Archaeologischen Instituts; Berlin; 1900; Vol. 14, P. 136. With illustrations.

Evans, E. P.: Animal Symbolism in Ecclesiastical Architecture; Henry Holt and Co.; New York; 1896. With seventy-eight illustrations.

Grandville (Jean-Ignace-Isadore Gérard): Album des Bêtes, à l'usage des gens d'esprit; J. Hetzel; Paris. There are many plates of cats but they are all from Les Métamorphoses du Jour and the Vie Privée et Publique des Animaux. Louis Moens in Brussels issued an edition of this book in 1864.

Grandville: Cent Proverbes; H. Fournier; Paris; 1845.

Grandville: Les Métamorphoses du Jour; Gustav Havard; Paris; 1854. The plates are coloured and there are many of cats.

Grandville: Physionomie du Chat; Magasin Pittoresque; Paris; 1840; P. 11. With thirteen engravings from drawings by Grandville.

Grandville: Vie Privée et Publique des Animaux; J. Hetzel; Paris; 1842.

Hall, Eugene J.: Peter and Polly; Country Life in America; January 1, 1911; Vol. 19, P. 212. A series of photographs by Cornelia Clarke.

Hamerton, Philip Gilbert: Chapters on Animals; Seeley, Jackson and Halliday; London; 1874. Chapter XV, P. 221: Animals in Art.

Havard, Henry: Henriette Ronner, un peintre de chats; E. Flammarion; Paris; 1891. Illustrated with photogravures of the artist's paintings and reproductions of drawings in the text.

Howe, William Norton: Animal Life in Italian Painting; George Allen; London; 1912. Illustrated.

Humphreys, Mabel: The Book of the Cat; Frederick A. Stokes Co.; New York; 1903. With facsimiles of drawings in colour by Elisabeth F. Bonsall. Large folio with binding of grey flannel stamped with kitten heads.

Janvier, Catherine A. (Mrs. Thomas A.): London Mews; Harper and Brothers; New York; 1904. Folio. Illustrations in colour and text by Mrs. Janvier. Dedicated "'To T. A. J., lover of cats.'"

Janvier, Thomas A.: The Cats of Henriette Ronner; Century Maga-

344

Bibliography

zine; October 1893; Vol. 46, P. 852. With illustrations from paintings by Madame Ronner.

Keller, Otto: Zur Geschichte der Katze im Altertum; Mitteilungen des Kaiserlich Deutschen Archaeologischen Instituts; Rom; 1908; Vol. 23, P. 40. With twelve illustrations.

Pollock, Walter Herries: Pictures of Cats; Magazine of Art; Vol. 7, P. 89. Illustrated with drawings by Mind and others.

Ranck, Edwin Carty: A Famous Photographer of Cats (Charles E. Bullard); American Magazine; April 1915; Vol. 79, P. 56. Illustrated with photographs.

Renouard: Croquis d'Animaux; Gillot; Paris. This is a folio book of drawings; there are several pages of interesting cats.

Ronner, Henriette: Cats and Kittens; Cassell and Co.; London; 1894. Descriptive text by M. Vachon, translated by Clara Bell. The twelve plates and the sketches in the text are entirely different from those in the Spielmann volume.

Spielmann, M. H.: Henriette Ronner, the painter of cat life and cat character; Cassell and Co.; London, 1891. Illustrated with twelve Goupil photogravures from her paintings, a portrait, and reproductions of her sketches in the text. Folio. A popular edition was issued in 1892.

Sprigg, Stanhope: Louis Wain's Method of Work; Cassell's Magazine; London; November 1898; Vol. 26, P. 563. Illustrated with drawings by Wain and his photograph.

Steinlen, Théophile Alexandre: Des Chats; images sans paroles; Ernest Flammarion; Paris; 1898. Large folio. Twenty-six plates of drawings, all of cats, except one which is of white mice; the covers bear a fine lithographic version of the famous poster, Lait pur stérilisé.

Thompson, Ernest Seton: Studies in the Art Anatomy of Animals; Macmillan and Co.; London; 1896. Illustrated with many plates by the author.

Tomson, Arthur: An Artist on the Cat in Art; Century Magazine; New York; 1910; Vol. 80, P. 370. Illustrations from drawings by the author.

Wain, Louis William: Louis Wain's Annual, 1901, and several years following; George Allen and Sons; London. Illustrated by Wain

Bibliography

with many fantastic and comic pictures of cats, several full pages,
many in colour. Paper covers with lithographs of cats.

Winans, Walter: Animal Sculpture; G. P. Putnam's Sons; New
York; 1913. Illustrated with photographs.

XVII

ANTHOLOGIES

Cat Stories, retold from St. Nicholas (edited by M. H. Carter); Cen-
tury Co.; New York; 1904. On P. 4 is a letter from Mark
Twain, reprinted from St. Nicholas, where it was addressed to
Edwin Wildman. Illustrated with drawings and photographs.

Pender, Mrs. Frederick W.: Cats and Kittens, compiled and arranged, and original poems by Mrs. F. W. P.; Edgar S. Werner
and Co.; New York; 1906. This is No. 35 of Werner's Readings and Recitations. Illustrated with drawings and photographs.

Repplier, Agnes: The Cat: being a record of the endearments and
invectives lavished by many writers upon an animal much loved
and much abhorred; collected, translated, and arranged by Agnes
Repplier; Sturgis and Walton; New York; 1912. Illustrated by
Elisabeth F. Bonsall.

Tomson, Graham R. (Mrs. Rosamund Ball Marriott Watson): Concerning Cats: a book of poems by many authors; T. Fisher Unwin;
London; 1892. Illustrations by Arthur Tomson (W. Ball).
The American edition was issued by the Frederick A. Stokes Co.
the same year.

Van Vechten, Carl: Lords of the Housetops: thirteen cat tales;
Alfred A. Knopf; New York; 1921.

XVIII

POETRY

As many of the following poems are to be found in one or more of
the cat anthologies, I have given these references for convenience. Cats
and Kittens, of course, refers to Mrs. Pender's Work; The Cat, to
Miss Repplier's, and Concerning Cats, to Mrs. Tomson's.

Bibliography

Alnaharwany, Ibn Alalaf: On a cat that was killed as she was attempting to rob a dove-cote; translated from the Arabic and rendered freely by " Dr. Carlyle ": The Cat, P. 42.

Arnold, Matthew: Poor Matthias; from Later Poems. The Atossa episode from this: The Cat, P. 84; Cats and Kittens, P. 182; Concerning Cats, P. 10; The Fireside Sphinx, P. 177.

Auld Bawthren's Song: The Cat, P. 34; Concerning Cats, P. 85; The Fireside Sphinx, P. 169.

Baillie, Joanna: The Kitten: Concerning Cats, P. 55; The Cat (abbreviated), P. 16.

Bates, Katherine Lee: Hudson's Cat: in Sigurd Our Golden Collie, P. 322.

Baudelaire, Charles: Fleurs du Mal; édition définitive; Calmann-Lévy; Paris. Le Chat, P. 135; Le Chat, P. 161; Les Chats, P. 189. These are all published in French in Concerning Cats; there is an English translation of Les Chats on P. 67 of The Cat; English translations of Le Chat (2) and Les Chats, Pages 16, 17 of Mrs. W. Chance's A Book of Cats; English translation of Le Chat (1), Cats and Kittens, P. 115.

Baylor, Adelaide S.: Adventures of Miss Tabby Gray; W. A. Wilde Co.; Boston; 1913. Illustrated by Josephine Druce. Juvenile.

Benserade, Isaac de: Labyrinthe de Versailles; Amsterdam; 1682 (?). Published in four languages, French, English, German, and Dutch. The original edition in French appeared in Paris in 1677. Fables, with curious engravings of the fountains. The cat pieces are: Le chat pendu et les rats, Le conseil des rats, Le singe et le chat, La souris, le chat, et le petit coq.

Benserade, Isaac de: Sonnet (on the emasculation of a cat belonging to Madame Deshoulières): Moncrif: Les Chats, P. 74.

Benson, A. C.: The Cat. In The Cat, P. 3 and The Fireside Sphinx, P. 284.

Béranger, Pierre Jean de: La chatte. See Works of Béranger.

Boulmier, Joseph: A Ma Chatte Coquette: Concerning Cats, P. 133.

Boulmier, Joseph: A Mon Chat Gaspard: Concerning Cats, P. 134.

Boyle, Virginia Frazer: I kilt er cat; Love Songs and Bugle Calls; A. S. Barnes and Co.; New York; 1906; P. 222. Concerning Cats, P. 89.

Bibliography

Brown, C. Helton: Peter (a kitten buried at sea); The Spectator; June 21, 1913; Vol. 110, P. 1058.

Brown, Hattie: Catoninetales: a domestic epic, comprising a very true and dismal pathetic narration of the ends of a most worthy cat Kok Robyn beginning with his first death and burial and the inquest thereupon; Lawrence and Bullen; London; 1891. 330 numbered copies. Edited and illustrated by W. J. Linton. According to the editor, Hattie Brown was " a young lady of colour lately deceased at the age of fourteen."

Burgess, Gelett and Burges Johnson: The Cat's Elegy; A. C. McClurg and Co.; Chicago; 1913. Illustrated.

C. B.: The Terrific Legend of the Kilkenny Cats. In Helen M. Winslow's Concerning Cats, P. 168. An abbreviated version in Concerning Cats, P. 101.

Calverley, C. S.: Sad Memories: Concerning Cats, P. 67; The Cat, P. 127.

The Cameronian Cat: Concerning Cats, P. 99.

Carlton, Will M.: Baron Grimalkin's Death: Cats and Kittens, P. 126.

Carryl, Guy Wetmore: How a Cat was annoyed and a Poet was booted; Grimm Tales Made Gay; Houghton, Mifflin and Co.; Boston; 1902. Illustrations by Albert Levering.

A cat may look upon a king; an epistolary poem on the loss of the ears of a favourite female cat. By J. A. Belcher, esq. in his ms., " To . . .": Concerning Cats, P. 53.

A Cat's Conscience: The Cat, P. 55.

Cat Tails; D. Lothrop Co.; Boston; 1887. Illustrated with many drawings. Juvenile.

The Cattie Sits in the Kiln-Ring Spinning: Concerning Cats, P. 107; The Cat, P. 170.

Les Chats: idile; from the Arabian (?): Moncrif: Les Chats, P. 114.

Concerning a Certain Tom Cat, the companion and friend of one Widow Tomkins, but whom she left locked up in her room without either milk or mice: Ross: The Book of Cats, P. 185; Concerning Cats, P. 96 (abbreviated).

Coolidge, Susan: Hodge, the Cat: The Cat, P. 81; Cats and Kittens, P. 117.

348

Bibliography

Coppée, François: Sonnet to Henriette Ronner: Paul Mégnin's Notre Ami le Chat, P. VIII.

Corrothers, J. D.: De Black Cat Crossed His Luck: The Black Cat Club, P. 37; Cats and Kittens, P. 124.

Cowper, William: The Colubriad: Concerning Cats, P. 28; The Cat, P. 154.

Cowper, William: The Retired Cat: Concerning Cats, P. 30; The Cat, P. 144; Cats and Kittens, P. 236.

Davies, W. H.: The Cat: Living Age; August 30, 1919; Vol. 302, P. 571. From the Westminster Gazette.

Delarue-Mardrus, Lucie: Pour le Chat; Willy et Colette Willy: Claudine s'en va, P. 47.

Delarue-Mardrus, Lucie: A la Déesse Maut, à Tête de Chat: Souffles de Tempête; Bibliothèque-Charpentier; Paris; 1918; P. 74.

Deshoulières, Madame et Mademoiselle: Oeuvres; two volumes; Stéréotype d'Herman; Paris; 1803. The cat poems are all by Madame: Lettre en chansons à M. Deshoulières; 1677; P. 55. Moncrif quotes part of this, Les Chats, P. 97 and Gosse translates a stanza in his essay in Gossip in a Library; Concerning Cats (Gosse's translation), P. 45. Épître de Tata, chat de Madame la Marquise Montglas, à Grisette, chatte de Madame Deshoulières; October 1678; P. 55; Moncrif, P. 169. Réponse de Grisette à Tata, P. 56; Moncrif, P. 171. Blondin, chat des Jacobins de la rue Saint-Honoré, à sa voisine Grisette, sur les rimes de la pièce précédente, P. 58. Dom Gris, chat de Madame la Duchesse de Béthune, à Grisette, P. 59. Mittin, chat de Mademoiselle Bocquet, à Grisette, P. 61. Regnault, chat de A. . . ., à Grisette, P. 65. Réponse de Tata à Grisette, P. 65; Moncrif, P. 173. Réponse de Grisette à Tata, P. 67; Moncrif, P. 176. Grisette, à M. le Maréchal Duc de Vivonne, qui faisoit semblant de croire que Madame Deshoulières avoit fait un mauvais rondeau qui couroit le monde, P. 69. Épître de Cochon, chien de M. le Maréchal de Vivonne, à Grisette, P. 72. Résponse de Grisette Cochon, P. 73. Réponse de Cochon à Grisette, P. 75. Réponse de Grisette à Cochon, P. 77; Moncrif, P. 179. Réponse de Cochon à Grisette, P. 80. Réponse de Grisette à Cochon, P. 83; Moncrif, P. 184. Rondeau à M. le Duc de Vivonne, sur ce qu'il soutenoit, en plaisantant, qu'elle étoit auteur du mauvais

Bibliography

rondeau dont il a été parlé dans l'épître de Grisette; 1678; P. 84.

Docquois, Georges: Rondels pour les chats de François Coppée: I. Bourget; II. Petit-Loulou; III. Mistigris. In Bêtes et Gens de Lettres, P. 70.

Du Bellay, Joachim: Epitaphe d'un Chat: Moncrif: Les Chats, P. 156.

Epitaph: Ci repose pauvre Mouton: Ross: The Book of Cats, P. 55.

Epitaph: Imitated in English from the Latin of Dr. Jortin: Concerning Cats, P. 47.

Epitaph for the cat of Madame de Lesdiguieres: Moncrif, P. 104; The Fireside Sphinx, P. 74.

Feydeau, Georges: Le Petit Ménage: Mégnin's Notre Ami le Chat, P. 259; illustrated by the actor, Saint-Germain.

Florian, Jean Pierre Clarisse: Fables. The Cat fables are: Le Chat et le Miroir; Le Chien et le Chat; Le Chat et la Lunette; Les Deux Chats; l'Hibou, le Chat, l'Oison, et le Rat; Le Chat et les Rats; and Le Chat et le Moineau. There is an edition illustrated by Grandville.

Gardiner, Ruth Kimball: The Cat: The Cat, P. 11.

Garnett, Richard: Marigold: Concerning Cats, P. 78; The Cat, P. 164; The Fireside Sphinx, P. 290.

Garnett, Richard: To a cat which had killed a favourite bird (after Agathias): Concerning Cats, P. 50; The Cat, P. 41; The Fireside Sphinx, P. 15.

Gay, John: Fables. The Fables about cats are The Rat-catcher and the Cats; Concerning Cats, P. 38, and The Cat, P. 132; The Old Woman and her Cats; and The Man, The Cat, the Dog, and the Fly.

Gineste, Raoul: Chattes et Chats, avec une préface par Paul Arène; Marpon et Flammarion; Paris; 1892. All the poems in this book are about cats.

Gray, Thomas: On the death of a favourite cat drowned in a tub of gold-fishes: Concerning Cats, P. 25; The Cat, P. 158; Cats and Kittens, P. 232; The Fireside Sphinx, P. 135; Ross: The Book of Cats, P. 260.

Green, Joseph: A poet's lamentation for the loss of his cat: Cats and Kittens, P. 261.

Bibliography

Guyot-Desherbiers: a long poem on cats, parts of which are quoted in Mégnin's Notre Ami le Chat, Pages 66, 70, 73, 74, and 111, and in Landrin's Le Chat, P. 69, 89, 91, 93, 94, 101, 148, 149, 150. According to Landrin, Guyot-Desherbiers was the maternal grandfather of Alfred de Musset, who sent the poem to Jean Gay, who published it in his Les Chats.

Harte, Bret: Miss Edith's Modest Request: Cats and Kittens, P. 138.

Hay, Elijah: The King Sends Three Cats to Guenevere: Others; December 1918.

Heine, Heinrich: Poems, translated by Edgar Alfred Bowring; George Bell; London; 1884. P. 46, Sonnet No. 7, (another translation in Concerning Cats, P. 74): Hüt dich, mein Freund, vor grimmen Teufelsfratzen; P. 117, No. 6, Clarissa; P. 129, Songs of Creation; P. 162, No. 6, The Old Chimneypiece (two stanzas of this, translated by Sir Theodore Martin, P. 14, The Cat); P. 455, Romancero, Retrospect; P. 506, Red Slippers: Rote Pantoffeln: Gar böse Katze, so alt und grau; P. 529, Mimi: Bin kein sittsam Bürgerkatzchen; P. 533, The Young Cats' Club for Poetry-Music: Der philharmonische Katerverein. Mrs. Browning translated two stanzas of a poem by Heine beginning, " The neighbour's old cat often came to pay us a visit "; to be found in Vol. 6, P. 165 of Mrs. Browning's Complete Works; Thomas Y. Crowell and Co.; and in Kate Sanborn's My Literary Zoo, P. 85.

Herford, Oliver: The Bashful Earthquake; Charles Scribner's Sons; New York; 1900; contains the following poems on cats: The Music of the Future, P. 9; Song, P. 11; The Tragic Mice, P. 38; Illustrations by the author.

Herford, Oliver: The Kitten's Garden of Verses; Charles Scribner's Sons; New York; 1911. Illustrated by the author.

Herford, Oliver: The Laughing Willow; George H. Doran; New York; 1918. The Town Cat, P. 65, and The Catfish, P. 108.

Herford, Oliver: The Rubáiyát of a Persian Kitten; Charles Scribner's Sons; New York; 1904. Illustrations by the author.

Herford, Oliver: At the Photographers: Cat Stories from St. Nicholas, P. 20; An Open Letter: Cat Stories, P. 71 and Cats and Kittens (called A Mirror Cat), P. 30; The Audacious Kitten:

Bibliography

Cat Stories, P. 178 and Cats and Kittens, P. 184. Illustrations by the author.

Hess, Walter Léon: Feline Philosophy by Thomas Cat; Richard G. Badger; Boston; 1919. The illustrations are mostly from Harrison Weir's book.

Hood, Thomas: Puss and Her Three Kittens: Cats and Kittens, P. 87.

Huddesford, George: Monody on the Death of Dick, an Academical Cat; Collected Poems in two volumes; printed for J. Wright; London; 1801; Vol. 1, P. 131.

Hugues, Clovis: Les Petits Chats; in Percheron's Le Chat, P. 22.

Idem Carmen Germanice Redditum: Concerning Cats, P. 79.

Katzenleben, Baroness de (pseudonym): The Cat's Tail: being the history of Childe Merlin; William Blackwood; Edinburgh; 1831. With three etchings and copies in colour by George Cruikshank.

Keats, John: To a Cat: Concerning Cats, P. 73.

The Kilkenny Cats: Helen M. Winslow's Concerning Cats, P. 169.

King, Ben: That Cat: Cats and Kittens, P. 78.

Kipling, Rudyard: The First Friend; in Just So Stories.

La Fontaine, Jean de: Fables. The cat fables are Le Chat, la Belette, et le petit Lapin; Le Chat, le Cochet, et le Souriceau; Le Chat et les deux Moineaux; Le Chat et le vieux Rat; Le Chat et le Renard; Le Chat et le Singe; Le vieux Chat et la jeune Souris (translated in The Cat, P. 54); La querelle des Chats et des Chiens, et celle des Chats et des Souris; La Chatte métamorphosée en Femme (Concerning Cats, P. 126); and La Chatte, la Laie, et l'Aigle.

Lamb, Charles: Prince Dorus; printed for M. J. Godwin; London; 1811. Illustrated with coloured engravings. The cat Minon plays a part in this tale in rhyme and there are two pictures of him. A facsimile of this book was printed in 1890.

Lament for Tabby, or the Cat's Coronach: The Cat, P. 72; Concerning Cats, P. 48.

La Mothe le Vayer, François de: Epitaphe de Marlemain (favourite cat of Madame la Duchesse du Maine): Moncrif, P. 106; Gosse (trans.) Gossip in a Library, P. 180; Concerning Cats, P. 46 (Gosse's translation); The Cat, P. 71 (Gosse's translation); The Fireside Sphinx, P. 74 (Gosse's translation).

Bibliography

Landor, Walter Savage: Chinchillo (addressed to his child, Carlino):
Cats and Kittens, P. 134.

Lemaitre, Jules: Sonnet: Concerning Cats, P. 135; The Fireside
Sphinx, P. 283. The last six lines of this sonnet, translated, The
Cat, P. 37.

Levesque, Madame: Minet (1736): part of this poem is published on
P. 173 of Mégnin's Notre Ami le Chat.

Lindsay, Vachel: The Congo; Macmillan Co.; New York; 1914.
The cat poems are The Mysterious Cat, P. 38, and Dirge for a
Righteous Kitten, P. 40.

Locker, Frederick: Loulou and her Cat: Concerning Cats, P. 80.

Lowell, Amy: Pictures of the Floating World; Macmillan and Co.;
New York; 1919. To Winky, P. 193.

Maine, Duchesse du: Rondeau Marotique: Moncrif, P. 96. The
envoy, translated by Gosse, P. 179, Gossip in a Library; The Cat,
P. 70; and Concerning Cats, P. 44.

Menard, M.: Sonnet: Moncrif, P. 134.

Monkhouse, Cosmo: The Cat and the Canary: Concerning Cats,
P. 82.

Moore, Edward: Fables; T. Heptinstall; London; 1799. The
Farmer, the Spaniel, and the Cat.

Mother Tabbyskins: Concerning Cats, P. 110.

La Musique des Chats: Champfleury: Les Chats, P. 71; Concerning Cats, P. 123.

Pikhson, J. Rheyn: Tawny Tom and Tabby Gray: The Knickerbocker Magazine; June 1842; P. 517.

Pindar, Peter (John Wolcot): An Ode to Eight Cats: Works; edition of Jones and Co.; London; P. 246.

Pollock, Sir Frederick: Tom of Corpus: The Cat, P. 110; The
Fireside Sphinx, P. 288.

Poor Puss: Concerning Cats, P. 119.

Prior, Matthew: Lines on a reasonable affliction: Concerning Cats,
P. 43.

Prior, Matthew: To my Lord Buckhurst, very young, playing with a
cat: Concerning Cats, P. 41; The Cat, P. 36.

Rives, Amélie: My Cat: McClure's Magazine; May 1920. Decoration by Oliver Herford.

Ronsard, Pierre de: Le Chat: Concerning Cats, P. 124.

Bibliography

Rossetti, Christina: On the death of a cat, a friend of mine age ten years and a half; New Poems; Macmillan and Co.; London; 1896. P. 313.

Ruffin, Alfred: Le Livre des Chats; Alphonse Lemerre; Paris; 1908. All the poems in this book are about cats.

Saint Gilles, Chevalier de: Le Renard et le Chat: Moncrif, P. 168.

Scarron, Paul: Épître à Madame de Montatere: Moncrif, P. 99.

Scheffel, Joseph Victor von: Der Trompeter von Säkkingen: ein Sang vom Oberrhein. Hiddigeigei, the Tom Cat, appears in the poem, and there are thirteen Lieder des Katters Hiddigeigei. Translated as The Trumpeter, from the two hundredth German edition by Jessie Beck and Louise Lorimer, with an introduction by Sir Theodore Martin, K. C. B., this book was issued by William Blackwood and Sons; Edinburgh and London; 1893.

Schofield, Lily: Tom Catapus and Potiphar, a tale of ancient Egypt; Frederick Warne and Co.; London. Illustrated with many drawings in colour.

Scollard, Clinton: Peter, an elegy: The Cat, P. 119.

Shelley, Percy Bysshe: Verses on a Cat: Concerning Cats, P. 71.

Skelton, John: The Boke of Phyllyp Sparowe: Vol. 1, P. 51, The Poetical Works of John Skelton, with notes by Rev. Alexander Dyce; two volumes; Thomas Rodd; London; 1843. The cat episode from this long narrative poem may be found in The Cat, P. 47.

Sonnet sur la chatte de Madame de Lesdiguieres: Moncrif, P. 89.

Southey, Robert: Southey's Cats write their master: Cats and Kittens, P. 263.

Stephens, James: The Cat.

Stevens, D. K.: The Lyrics of Eliza; Century Co.; New York; 1911. Illustrated by Katherine Maynadier Browne. Juvenile.

Swinburne, Algernon Charles: To a Cat: The Cat, P. 68. A different version is to be found in Gordon Stables's story, Shireen and her Friends.

Taine, Hippolyte: Douze sonnets inédits de Taine; Figaro; Paris; Supplement Littéraire; March 11, 1893. I, Le Bonheur; II, La Societé; III, La Religion; IV, Les Souvenirs; V, Les Pénates; VI, La Philosophie; VII, L'Enseignement; VIII, La Pratique; IX, L'Enfance; X, La Sensibilité; XI, Le Point de Vue; XII,

Bibliography

L'Absolu. Published posthumously without the consent of the author's heirs and executors. They carry this inscription: A trois chats, Puss, Ebène et Mitonne, domiciliés à Menthon-Saint-Bernard, Haute-Savoie, ces douze sonnets sont dediés par leur ami et serviteur, H. Taine, novembre, 1883. Pratique, in French, The Fireside Sphinx, P. 194; translated, in The Cat, P. 33.

Tennyson, Alfred Lord: The Spinster's Sweet-arts; Works of Tennyson; Macmillan and Co.; London, 1893; Vol. 10, P. 70.

Tomson, Graham R.: Arsinoë's Cats (imitation in the manner of the later Greek poets, circa A. D. 500): Concerning Cats, P. 51; The Cat, P. 65; The Fireside Sphinx, P. 14.

Tomson, Graham R.: Dedication: Concerning Cats, P. 3.

Tomson, Graham R.: To my cat: le chat noir: Concerning Cats, P. 76; The Cat, P. 61; The Fireside Sphinx, P. 281.

Tregellas, John Tabois: Grammer's Cat and Ours: Concerning Cats, P. 92;

Tuberville, George (attributed to): The Lover, whose Mistresse feared a Mouse, declareth that he would become a Cat if he might have his desire: Concerning Cats, P. 36; The Cat, P. 8; The Fireside Sphinx, P. 132.

Verlaine, Paul: Femme et Chatte: Concerning Cats, P. 132.

Watson, William: A Study in Contrasts: Collected Poems; John Lane Co.; London; 1899; P. 188.

Wells, Carolyn: A Serious Question: Cat Stories from St. Nicholas, P. 166. Illustrated by Oliver Herford.

Wells, Carolyn: The Timid Kitten: Cats and Kittens, P. 58.

Wilcox, Ella Wheeler: Two Pussy-Cats: The Pet Cat; The Tramp Cat: Cats and Kittens, P. 105.

Wordsworth, William: The Kitten and the Falling Leaves: Concerning Cats, P. 61; The Cat (abbreviated), P. 29; Cats and Kittens (abbreviated), P. 122.

XIX

MISCELLANEOUS

Chapin, Howard Millar: Murthy's Cattage: a biographical dictionary of cats in literature; published by the author; Providence;

Bibliography

Rhode Island; 1911. With a portrait from a photograph of "Murthy." Pamphlet.

Euwer, Anthony Henderson: Christopher Cricket on Cats: with observations and deductions for the enlightment of the human race from infancy to maturity and even old age; introduction by Wallace Irwin; The Little Book Concern; New York; 1909. Illustrations by the author.

Hoffmann, E. T. A: Lebensansichten des Katers Murr: See collected works of Hoffmann.

Holbrook, Richard Thayer: Dante and the Animal Kingdom; Columbia University Press; New York; 1902.

Mangin, Arthur: L'Homme et la Bête; Firmin Didot frères, fils et cie.; Paris; 1872.

Pictet, Adolphe: Les origines Indo-Européennes ou les Aryas primitifs, essai de paléontologie linguistique; Joël Cherbuliez; Paris; 1859. Two Volumes. The cat, Vol. 1, P. 381.

XX

UNCLASSIFIED

The following books I have not seen, but as I have found references to them, I include them for the sake of the record.

A. W. B.: It was ever so long ago; the adventures of a cat-child; Headley Brothers; London; 1911. Ten plates in colour and small drawings in the text by Hugh Wallis.

Adeline, Jules: Le chat d'après les Japonais; Rouen; 1893.

Bennett, Charles: Nine Lives of a Cat.

Brentano: Die mehreren Wehmüller.

Dame Wiggins of Lee, and her seven wonderful cats. A humorous tale. Written principally by a lady of ninety; Newman and Co.; London; 1823. With eighteen coloured woodcuts. In 1885 the book was reissued by G. Allen of Orpington, for which John Ruskin added four stanzas, and Kate Greenaway made drawings.

Dick Whittington; the cat manual; London; 1902.

An Essaie on the Householde Cat; 1714.

Francois, Luise von: Katzenjunker.

356

Bibliography

Gardner, J. G.: The Cat, with hints for feeding, breeding, etc.; St. Mary Cray; 1892.

Gay, Jean: Les Chats; Gay; Paris and Brussels; 1866. (extraits de pièces rares et curieuses en vers et en prose . . . le tout concernant la gent féline)

Howitt, Mary: Household Pets: Cats and Parrots; Cassell, Petter, and Galpin; London; 1863. With three full-page woodcuts of cats engraved by Quartley after W. H. Freeman.

Hunt, Violet: The Cat; A. and C. Black; London; 1905. With twelve colour plates after paintings by Adolph Birkenruth.

Leopold, Svend: Goethe's Katze.

Maurogiannes: Chiens de Constantinople et chiens et chats de bonne maison; Paris; 1901.

Megede, J. R. zur: Ueberkater; 1904.

Minnett, Cora and Pellew Hawker: Lucky; F. V. White and Co.; London; 1911. Illustrated with eleven full-page drawings by A. MacNeill-Barbour.

Mitton, G. E.: Animal Autobiographies.

Pollock, W. Herries: Animals that have owned us; John Murray; London; 1904. Pages 66-136 devoted to cats.

Raton: Sur l'education du chat domestique; son histoire philosophique et politique; traitement de ses maladies.

Straus-Durckheim: Anatomie descriptive et comparative du chat; Paris; 1845.

Tales from Catland. Illustrated by Harrison Weir.

Vallé, I.: Epitaphs of Some Dear Dumb Animals; R. C. Badger, Boston; 1916.

Index

Index

Index

Index

Index

Index

Index

Index

366

Index

Wister, S. B., 14, 295, 341
Wolsey, Cardinal, 161
Wood, Rev. J. G., 4, 31, 45, 50, 62,
    125, 131, 325, 341
Wordsworth, William, 175, 256, 355
Wortley, Col. Stuart, 51

Wright, Cornelia, 80
Wynter, Andrew, 4, 5, 50, 341

Zola, Émile, 17, 240, 277, 333
Zucchero, Federigo, 216
Zut, Guy Wetmore Carryl's, 242, 243

A CATALOG OF SELECTED

DOVER BOOKS

IN ALL FIELDS OF INTEREST

A CATALOG OF SELECTED DOVER
BOOKS IN ALL FIELDS OF INTEREST

CONCERNING THE SPIRITUAL IN ART, Wassily Kandinsky. Pioneering work by father of abstract art. Thoughts on color theory, nature of art. Analysis of earlier masters. 12 illustrations. 80pp. of text. 5⅜ × 8½.				23411-8 Pa. $3.95

ANIMALS: 1,419 Copyright-Free Illustrations of Mammals, Birds, Fish, Insects, etc., Jim Harter (ed.). Clear wood engravings present, in extremely lifelike poses, over 1,000 species of animals. One of the most extensive pictorial sourcebooks of its kind. Captions. Index. 284pp. 9 × 12.				23766-4 Pa. $12.95

CELTIC ART: The Methods of Construction, George Bain. Simple geometric techniques for making Celtic interlacements, spirals, Kells-type initials, animals, humans, etc. Over 500 illustrations. 160pp. 9 × 12. (USO)		22923-8 Pa. $9.95

AN ATLAS OF ANATOMY FOR ARTISTS, Fritz Schider. Most thorough reference work on art anatomy in the world. Hundreds of illustrations, including selections from works by Vesalius, Leonardo, Goya, Ingres, Michelangelo, others. 593 illustrations. 192pp. 7⅛ × 10¼.				20241-0 Pa. $9.95

CELTIC HAND STROKE-BY-STROKE (Irish Half-Uncial from "The Book of Kells"): An Arthur Baker Calligraphy Manual, Arthur Baker. Complete guide to creating each letter of the alphabet in distinctive Celtic manner. Covers hand position, strokes, pens, inks, paper, more. Illustrated. 48pp. 8¼ × 11.
						24336-2 Pa. $3.95

EASY ORIGAMI, John Montroll. Charming collection of 32 projects (hat, cup, pelican, piano, swan, many more) specially designed for the novice origami hobbyist. Clearly illustrated easy-to-follow instructions insure that even beginning papercrafters will achieve successful results. 48pp. 8¼ × 11.		27298-2 Pa. $2.95

THE COMPLETE BOOK OF BIRDHOUSE CONSTRUCTION FOR WOOD-WORKERS, Scott D. Campbell. Detailed instructions, illustrations, tables. Also data on bird habitat and instinct patterns. Bibliography. 3 tables. 63 illustrations in 15 figures. 48pp. 5¼ × 8½.				24407-5 Pa. $1.95

BLOOMINGDALE'S ILLUSTRATED 1886 CATALOG: Fashions, Dry Goods and Housewares, Bloomingdale Brothers. Famed merchants' extremely rare catalog depicting about 1,700 products: clothing, housewares, firearms, dry goods, jewelry, more. Invaluable for dating, identifying vintage items. Also, copyright-free graphics for artists, designers. Co-published with Henry Ford Museum & Greenfield Village. 160pp. 8¼ × 11.				25780-0 Pa. $9.95

HISTORIC COSTUME IN PICTURES, Braun & Schneider. Over 1,450 costumed figures in clearly detailed engravings—from dawn of civilization to end of 19th century. Captions. Many folk costumes. 256pp. 8⅜ × 11¾.		23150-X Pa. $11.95

STICKLEY CRAFTSMAN FURNITURE CATALOGS, Gustav Stickley and L. & J. G. Stickley. Beautiful, functional furniture in two authentic catalogs from 1910. 594 illustrations, including 277 photos, show settles, rockers, armchairs, reclining chairs, bookcases, desks, tables. 183pp. 6½ × 9¼. 23838-5 Pa. $9.95

AMERICAN LOCOMOTIVES IN HISTORIC PHOTOGRAPHS: 1858 to 1949, Ron Ziel (ed.). A rare collection of 126 meticulously detailed official photographs, called "builder portraits," of American locomotives that majestically chronicle the rise of steam locomotive power in America. Introduction. Detailed captions. xi + 129pp. 9 × 12. 27393-8 Pa. $12.95

AMERICA'S LIGHTHOUSES: An Illustrated History, Francis Ross Holland, Jr. Delightfully written, profusely illustrated fact-filled survey of over 200 American lighthouses since 1716. History, anecdotes, technological advances, more. 240pp. 8 × 10¾. 25576-X Pa. $11.95

TOWARDS A NEW ARCHITECTURE, Le Corbusier. Pioneering manifesto by founder of "International School." Technical and aesthetic theories, views of industry, economics, relation of form to function, "mass-production split" and much more. Profusely illustrated. 320pp. 6⅛ × 9¼. (USO) 25023-7 Pa. $9.95

HOW THE OTHER HALF LIVES, Jacob Riis. Famous journalistic record, exposing poverty and degradation of New York slums around 1900, by major social reformer. 100 striking and influential photographs. 233pp. 10 × 7⅞.
22012-5 Pa $10.95

FRUIT KEY AND TWIG KEY TO TREES AND SHRUBS, William M. Harlow. One of the handiest and most widely used identification aids. Fruit key covers 120 deciduous and evergreen species; twig key 160 deciduous species. Easily used. Over 300 photographs. 126pp. 5⅜ × 8½. 20511-8 Pa. $3.95

COMMON BIRD SONGS, Dr. Donald J. Borror. Songs of 60 most common U.S. birds: robins, sparrows, cardinals, bluejays, finches, more—arranged in order of increasing complexity. Up to 9 variations of songs of each species.
Cassette and manual 99911-4 $8.95

ORCHIDS AS HOUSE PLANTS, Rebecca Tyson Northen. Grow cattleyas and many other kinds of orchids—in a window, in a case, or under artificial light. 63 illustrations. 148pp. 5⅜ × 8½. 23261-1 Pa. $4.95

MONSTER MAZES, Dave Phillips. Masterful mazes at four levels of difficulty. Avoid deadly perils and evil creatures to find magical treasures. Solutions for all 32 exciting illustrated puzzles. 48pp. 8¼ × 11. 26005-4 Pa. $2.95

MOZART'S DON GIOVANNI (DOVER OPERA LIBRETTO SERIES), Wolfgang Amadeus Mozart. Introduced and translated by Ellen H. Bleiler. Standard Italian libretto, with complete English translation. Convenient and thoroughly portable—an ideal companion for reading along with a recording or the performance itself. Introduction. List of characters. Plot summary. 121pp. 5¼ × 8½.
24944-1 Pa. $2.95

TECHNICAL MANUAL AND DICTIONARY OF CLASSICAL BALLET, Gail Grant. Defines, explains, comments on steps, movements, poses and concepts. 15-page pictorial section. Basic book for student, viewer. 127pp. 5⅜ × 8½.
21843-0 Pa. $4.95

BRASS INSTRUMENTS: Their History and Development, Anthony Baines. Authoritative, updated survey of the evolution of trumpets, trombones, bugles, cornets, French horns, tubas and other brass wind instruments. Over 140 illustrations and 48 music examples. Corrected and updated by author. New preface. Bibliography. 320pp. 5⅜ × 8½. 27574-4 Pa. $9.95

HOLLYWOOD GLAMOR PORTRAITS, John Kobal (ed.). 145 photos from 1926–49. Harlow, Gable, Bogart, Bacall; 94 stars in all. Full background on photographers, technical aspects. 160pp. 8⅜ × 11¼. 23352-9 Pa. $11.95

MAX AND MORITZ, Wilhelm Busch. Great humor classic in both German and English. Also 10 other works: "Cat and Mouse," "Plisch and Plumm," etc. 216pp. 5⅜ × 8½. 20181-3 Pa. $5.95

THE RAVEN AND OTHER FAVORITE POEMS, Edgar Allan Poe. Over 40 of the author's most memorable poems: "The Bells," "Ulalume," "Israfel," "To Helen," "The Conqueror Worm," "Eldorado," "Annabel Lee," many more. Alphabetic lists of titles and first lines. 64pp. 5³⁄₁₆ × 8¼. 26685-0 Pa. $1.00

SEVEN SCIENCE FICTION NOVELS, H. G. Wells. The standard collection of the great novels. Complete, unabridged. First Men in the Moon, Island of Dr. Moreau, War of the Worlds, Food of the Gods, Invisible Man, Time Machine, In the Days of the Comet. Total of 1,015pp. 5⅜ × 8½. (USO) 20264-X Clothbd. $29.95

AMULETS AND SUPERSTITIONS, E. A. Wallis Budge. Comprehensive discourse on origin, powers of amulets in many ancient cultures: Arab, Persian, Babylonian, Assyrian, Egyptian, Gnostic, Hebrew, Phoenician, Syriac, etc. Covers cross, swastika, crucifix, seals, rings, stones, etc. 584pp. 5⅜ × 8½. 23573-4 Pa. $12.95

RUSSIAN STORIES/PYCCKNE PACCKA3bl: A Dual-Language Book, edited by Gleb Struve. Twelve tales by such masters as Chekhov, Tolstoy, Dostoevsky, Pushkin, others. Excellent word-for-word English translations on facing pages, plus teaching and study aids, Russian/English vocabulary, biographical/critical introductions, more. 416pp. 5⅜ × 8½. 26244-8 Pa. $8.95

PHILADELPHIA THEN AND NOW: 60 Sites Photographed in the Past and Present, Kenneth Finkel and Susan Oyama. Rare photographs of City Hall, Logan Square, Independence Hall, Betsy Ross House, other landmarks juxtaposed with contemporary views. Captures changing face of historic city. Introduction. Captions. 128pp. 8¼ × 11. 25790-8 Pa. $9.95

AIA ARCHITECTURAL GUIDE TO NASSAU AND SUFFOLK COUNTIES, LONG ISLAND, The American Institute of Architects, Long Island Chapter, and the Society for the Preservation of Long Island Antiquities. Comprehensive, well-researched and generously illustrated volume brings to life over three centuries of Long Island's great architectural heritage. More than 240 photographs with authoritative, extensively detailed captions. 176pp. 8¼ × 11. 26946-9 Pa. $14.95

NORTH AMERICAN INDIAN LIFE: Customs and Traditions of 23 Tribes, Elsie Clews Parsons (ed.). 27 fictionalized essays by noted anthropologists examine religion, customs, government, additional facets of life among the Winnebago, Crow, Zuni, Eskimo, other tribes. 480pp. 6⅛ × 9¼. 27377-6 Pa. $10.95

FRANK LLOYD WRIGHT'S HOLLYHOCK HOUSE, Donald Hoffmann. Lavishly illustrated, carefully documented study of one of Wright's most controversial residential designs. Over 120 photographs, floor plans, elevations, etc. Detailed perceptive text by noted Wright scholar. Index. 128pp. 9¼ × 10¾.
27133-1 Pa. $11.95

THE MALE AND FEMALE FIGURE IN MOTION: 60 Classic Photographic Sequences, Eadweard Muybridge. 60 true-action photographs of men and women walking, running, climbing, bending, turning, etc., reproduced from rare 19th-century masterpiece. vi + 121pp. 9 × 12.
24745-7 Pa. $10.95

1001 QUESTIONS ANSWERED ABOUT THE SEASHORE, N. J. Berrill and Jacquelyn Berrill. Queries answered about dolphins, sea snails, sponges, starfish, fishes, shore birds, many others. Covers appearance, breeding, growth, feeding, much more. 305pp. 5¼ × 8¼.
23366-9 Pa. $7.95

GUIDE TO OWL WATCHING IN NORTH AMERICA, Donald S. Heintzelman. Superb guide offers complete data and descriptions of 19 species: barn owl, screech owl, snowy owl, many more. Expert coverage of owl-watching equipment, conservation, migrations and invasions, etc. Guide to observing sites. 84 illustrations. xiii + 193pp. 5⅜ × 8½.
27344-X Pa. $8.95

MEDICINAL AND OTHER USES OF NORTH AMERICAN PLANTS: A Historical Survey with Special Reference to the Eastern Indian Tribes, Charlotte Erichsen-Brown. Chronological historical citations document 500 years of usage of plants, trees, shrubs native to eastern Canada, northeastern U.S. Also complete identifying information. 343 illustrations. 544pp. 6½ × 9¼.
25951-X Pa. $12.95

STORYBOOK MAZES, Dave Phillips. 23 stories and mazes on two-page spreads: Wizard of Oz, Treasure Island, Robin Hood, etc. Solutions. 64pp. 8¼ × 11.
23628-5 Pa. $2.95

NEGRO FOLK MUSIC, U.S.A., Harold Courlander. Noted folklorist's scholarly yet readable analysis of rich and varied musical tradition. Includes authentic versions of over 40 folk songs. Valuable bibliography and discography. xi + 324pp. 5⅜ × 8½.
27350-4 Pa. $7.95

MOVIE-STAR PORTRAITS OF THE FORTIES, John Kobal (ed.). 163 glamor, studio photos of 106 stars of the 1940s: Rita Hayworth, Ava Gardner, Marlon Brando, Clark Gable, many more. 176pp. 8⅜ × 11¼.
23546-7 Pa. $11.95

BENCHLEY LOST AND FOUND, Robert Benchley. Finest humor from early 30s, about pet peeves, child psychologists, post office and others. Mostly unavailable elsewhere. 73 illustrations by Peter Arno and others. 183pp. 5⅜ × 8½.
22410-4 Pa. $5.95

YEKL and THE IMPORTED BRIDEGROOM AND OTHER STORIES OF YIDDISH NEW YORK, Abraham Cahan. Film Hester Street based on Yekl (1896). Novel, other stories among first about Jewish immigrants on N.Y.'s East Side. 240pp. 5⅜ × 8½.
22427-9 Pa. $6.95

SELECTED POEMS, Walt Whitman. Generous sampling from Leaves of Grass. Twenty-four poems include "I Hear America Singing," "Song of the Open Road," "I Sing the Body Electric," "When Lilacs Last in the Dooryard Bloom'd," "O Captain! My Captain!"—all reprinted from an authoritative edition. Lists of titles and first lines. 128pp. 5³/₁₆ × 8¼.
26878-0 Pa. $1.00

THE BEST TALES OF HOFFMANN, E. T. A. Hoffmann. 10 of Hoffmann's most important stories: "Nutcracker and the King of Mice," "The Golden Flowerpot," etc. 458pp. 5⅜ × 8½. 21793-0 Pa. $8.95

FROM FETISH TO GOD IN ANCIENT EGYPT, E. A. Wallis Budge. Rich detailed survey of Egyptian conception of "God" and gods, magic, cult of animals, Osiris, more. Also, superb English translations of hymns and legends. 240 illustrations. 545pp. 5⅜ × 8½. 25803-3 Pa. $11.95

FRENCH STORIES/CONTES FRANÇAIS: A Dual-Language Book, Wallace Fowlie. Ten stories by French masters, Voltaire to Camus: "Micromegas" by Voltaire; "The Atheist's Mass" by Balzac; "Minuet" by de Maupassant; "The Guest" by Camus, six more. Excellent English translations on facing pages. Also French-English vocabulary list, exercises, more. 352pp. 5⅜ × 8½. 26443-2 Pa. $8.95

CHICAGO AT THE TURN OF THE CENTURY IN PHOTOGRAPHS: 122 Historic Views from the Collections of the Chicago Historical Society, Larry A. Viskochil. Rare large-format prints offer detailed views of City Hall, State Street, the Loop, Hull House, Union Station, many other landmarks, circa 1904–1913. Introduction. Captions. Maps. 144pp. 9⅜ × 12¼. 24656-6 Pa. $12.95

OLD BROOKLYN IN EARLY PHOTOGRAPHS, 1865–1929, William Lee Younger. Luna Park, Gravesend race track, construction of Grand Army Plaza, moving of Hotel Brighton, etc. 157 previously unpublished photographs. 165pp. 8⅞ × 11¾. 23587-4 Pa. $13.95

THE MYTHS OF THE NORTH AMERICAN INDIANS, Lewis Spence. Rich anthology of the myths and legends of the Algonquins, Iroquois, Pawnees and Sioux, prefaced by an extensive historical and ethnological commentary. 36 illustrations. 480pp. 5⅜ × 8½. 25967-6 Pa. $8.95

AN ENCYCLOPEDIA OF BATTLES: Accounts of Over 1,560 Battles from 1479 B.C. to the Present, David Eggenberger. Essential details of every major battle in recorded history from the first battle of Megiddo in 1479 B.C. to Grenada in 1984. List of Battle Maps. New Appendix covering the years 1967–1984. Index. 99 illustrations. 544pp. 6½ × 9¼. 24913-1 Pa. $14.95

SAILING ALONE AROUND THE WORLD, Captain Joshua Slocum. First man to sail around the world, alone, in small boat. One of great feats of seamanship told in delightful manner. 67 illustrations. 294pp. 5⅜ × 8½. 20326-3 Pa. $5.95

ANARCHISM AND OTHER ESSAYS, Emma Goldman. Powerful, penetrating, prophetic essays on direct action, role of minorities, prison reform, puritan hypocrisy, violence, etc. 271pp. 5⅜ × 8½. 22484-8 Pa. $5.95

MYTHS OF THE HINDUS AND BUDDHISTS, Ananda K. Coomaraswamy and Sister Nivedita. Great stories of the epics; deeds of Krishna, Shiva, taken from puranas, Vedas, folk tales; etc. 32 illustrations. 400pp. 5⅜ × 8½. 21759-0 Pa. $9.95

BEYOND PSYCHOLOGY, Otto Rank. Fear of death, desire of immortality, nature of sexuality, social organization, creativity, according to Rankian system. 291pp. 5⅜ × 8½. 20485-5 Pa. $8.95

A THEOLOGICO-POLITICAL TREATISE, Benedict Spinoza. Also contains unfinished Political Treatise. Great classic on religious liberty, theory of government on common consent. R. Elwes translation. Total of 421pp. 5⅜ × 8½. 20249-6 Pa. $8.95

CATALOG OF DOVER BOOKS

MY BONDAGE AND MY FREEDOM, Frederick Douglass. Born a slave, Douglass became outspoken force in antislavery movement. The best of Douglass' autobiographies. Graphic description of slave life. 464pp. 5⅜ × 8½. 22457-0 Pa. $8.95

FOLLOWING THE EQUATOR: A Journey Around the World, Mark Twain. Fascinating humorous account of 1897 voyage to Hawaii, Australia, India, New Zealand, etc. Ironic, bemused reports on peoples, customs, climate, flora and fauna, politics, much more. 197 illustrations. 720pp. 5⅜ × 8½. 26113-1 Pa. $15.95

THE PEOPLE CALLED SHAKERS, Edward D. Andrews. Definitive study of Shakers: origins, beliefs, practices, dances, social organization, furniture and crafts, etc. 33 illustrations. 351pp. 5⅜ × 8½. 21081-2 Pa. $8.95

THE MYTHS OF GREECE AND ROME, H. A. Guerber. A classic of mythology, generously illustrated, long prized for its simple, graphic, accurate retelling of the principal myths of Greece and Rome, and for its commentary on their origins and significance. With 64 illustrations by Michelangelo, Raphael, Titian, Rubens, Canova, Bernini and others. 480pp. 5⅜ × 8½. 27584-1 Pa. $9.95

PSYCHOLOGY OF MUSIC, Carl E. Seashore. Classic work discusses music as a medium from psychological viewpoint. Clear treatment of physical acoustics, auditory apparatus, sound perception, development of musical skills, nature of musical feeling, host of other topics. 88 figures. 408pp. 5⅜ × 8½. 21851-1 Pa. $9.95

THE PHILOSOPHY OF HISTORY, Georg W. Hegel. Great classic of Western thought develops concept that history is not chance but rational process, the evolution of freedom. 457pp. 5⅜ × 8½. 20112-0 Pa. $9.95

THE BOOK OF TEA, Kakuzo Okakura. Minor classic of the Orient: entertaining, charming explanation, interpretation of traditional Japanese culture in terms of tea ceremony. 94pp. 5⅜ × 8½. 20070-1 Pa. $3.95

LIFE IN ANCIENT EGYPT, Adolf Erman. Fullest, most thorough, detailed older account with much not in more recent books, domestic life, religion, magic, medicine, commerce, much more. Many illustrations reproduce tomb paintings, carvings, hieroglyphs, etc. 597pp. 5⅜ × 8½. 22632-8 Pa. $10.95

SUNDIALS, Their Theory and Construction, Albert Waugh. Far and away the best, most thorough coverage of ideas, mathematics concerned, types, construction, adjusting anywhere. Simple, nontechnical treatment allows even children to build several of these dials. Over 100 illustrations. 230pp. 5⅜ × 8½. 22947-5 Pa. $7.95

DYNAMICS OF FLUIDS IN POROUS MEDIA, Jacob Bear. For advanced students of ground water hydrology, soil mechanics and physics, drainage and irrigation engineering, and more. 335 illustrations. Exercises, with answers. 784pp. 6⅛ × 9¼. 65675-6 Pa. $19.95

SONGS OF EXPERIENCE: Facsimile Reproduction with 26 Plates in Full Color, William Blake. 26 full-color plates from a rare 1826 edition. Includes "The Tyger," "London," "Holy Thursday," and other poems. Printed text of poems. 48pp. 5¼ × 7. 24636-1 Pa. $4.95

OLD-TIME VIGNETTES IN FULL COLOR, Carol Belanger Grafton (ed.). Over 390 charming, often sentimental illustrations, selected from archives of Victorian graphics—pretty women posing, children playing, food, flowers, kittens and puppies, smiling cherubs, birds and butterflies, much more. All copyright-free. 48pp. 9¼ × 12¼. 27269-9 Pa. $5.95

PERSPECTIVE FOR ARTISTS, Rex Vicat Cole. Depth, perspective of sky and sea, shadows, much more, not usually covered. 391 diagrams, 81 reproductions of drawings and paintings. 279pp. 5⅜ × 8½. 22487-2 Pa. $6.95

DRAWING THE LIVING FIGURE, Joseph Sheppard. Innovative approach to artistic anatomy focuses on specifics of surface anatomy, rather than muscles and bones. Over 170 drawings of live models in front, back and side views, and in widely varying poses. Accompanying diagrams. 177 illustrations. Introduction. Index. 144pp. 8⅜ × 11¼. 26723-7 Pa. $8.95

GOTHIC AND OLD ENGLISH ALPHABETS: 100 Complete Fonts, Dan X. Solo. Add power, elegance to posters, signs, other graphics with 100 stunning copyright-free alphabets: Blackstone, Dolbey, Germania, 97 more—including many lower-case, numerals, punctuation marks. 104pp. 8⅛ × 11. 24695-7 Pa. $8.95

HOW TO DO BEADWORK, Mary White. Fundamental book on craft from simple projects to five-bead chains and woven works. 106 illustrations. 142pp. 5⅜ × 8. 20697-1 Pa. $4.95

THE BOOK OF WOOD CARVING, Charles Marshall Sayers. Finest book for beginners discusses fundamentals and offers 34 designs. "Absolutely first rate . . . well thought out and well executed."—E. J. Tangerman. 118pp. 7¾ × 10⅝. 23654-4 Pa. $5.95

ILLUSTRATED CATALOG OF CIVIL WAR MILITARY GOODS: Union Army Weapons, Insignia, Uniform Accessories, and Other Equipment, Schuyler, Hartley, and Graham. Rare, profusely illustrated 1846 catalog includes Union Army uniform and dress regulations, arms and ammunition, coats, insignia, flags, swords, rifles, etc. 226 illustrations. 160pp. 9 × 12. 24939-5 Pa. $10.95

WOMEN'S FASHIONS OF THE EARLY 1900s: An Unabridged Republication of "New York Fashions, 1909," National Cloak & Suit Co. Rare catalog of mail-order fashions documents women's and children's clothing styles shortly after the turn of the century. Captions offer full descriptions, prices. Invaluable resource for fashion, costume historians. Approximately 725 illustrations. 128pp. 8⅜ × 11¼. 27276-1 Pa. $11.95

THE 1912 AND 1915 GUSTAV STICKLEY FURNITURE CATALOGS, Gustav Stickley. With over 200 detailed illustrations and descriptions, these two catalogs are essential reading and reference materials and identification guides for Stickley furniture. Captions cite materials, dimensions and prices. 112pp. 6½ × 9¼. 26676-1 Pa. $9.95

EARLY AMERICAN LOCOMOTIVES, John H. White, Jr. Finest locomotive engravings from early 19th century: historical (1804–74), main-line (after 1870), special, foreign, etc. 147 plates. 142pp. 11⅜ × 8¼. 22772-3 Pa. $10.95

THE TALL SHIPS OF TODAY IN PHOTOGRAPHS, Frank O. Braynard. Lavishly illustrated tribute to nearly 100 majestic contemporary sailing vessels: Amerigo Vespucci, Clearwater, Constitution, Eagle, Mayflower, Sea Cloud, Victory, many more. Authoritative captions provide statistics, background on each ship. 190 black-and-white photographs and illustrations. Introduction. 128pp. 8⅞ × 11¾. 27163-3 Pa. $13.95

EARLY NINETEENTH-CENTURY CRAFTS AND TRADES, Peter Stockham (ed.). Extremely rare 1807 volume describes to youngsters the crafts and trades of the day: brickmaker, weaver, dressmaker, bookbinder, ropemaker, saddler, many more. Quaint prose, charming illustrations for each craft. 20 black-and-white line illustrations. 192pp. 4⅜ × 6. 27293-1 Pa. $4.95

VICTORIAN FASHIONS AND COSTUMES FROM HARPER'S BAZAR, 1867–1898, Stella Blum (ed.). Day costumes, evening wear, sports clothes, shoes, hats, other accessories in over 1,000 detailed engravings. 320pp. 9⅜ × 12¼. 22990-4 Pa. $13.95

GUSTAV STICKLEY, THE CRAFTSMAN, Mary Ann Smith. Superb study surveys broad scope of Stickley's achievement, especially in architecture. Design philosophy, rise and fall of the Craftsman empire, descriptions and floor plans for many Craftsman houses, more. 86 black-and-white halftones. 31 line illustrations. Introduction. 208pp. 6½ × 9¼. 27210-9 Pa. $9.95

THE LONG ISLAND RAIL ROAD IN EARLY PHOTOGRAPHS, Ron Ziel. Over 220 rare photos, informative text document origin (1844) and development of rail service on Long Island. Vintage views of early trains, locomotives, stations, passengers, crews, much more. Captions. 8⅞ × 11¾. 26301-0 Pa. $13.95

THE BOOK OF OLD SHIPS: From Egyptian Galleys to Clipper Ships, Henry B. Culver. Superb, authoritative history of sailing vessels, with 80 magnificent line illustrations. Galley, bark, caravel, longship, whaler, many more. Detailed, informative text on each vessel by noted naval historian. Introduction. 256pp. 5⅜ × 8½. 27332-6 Pa. $6.95

TEN BOOKS ON ARCHITECTURE, Vitruvius. The most important book ever written on architecture. Early Roman aesthetics, technology, classical orders, site selection, all other aspects. Morgan translation. 331pp. 5⅜ × 8½. 20645-9 Pa. $8.95

THE HUMAN FIGURE IN MOTION, Eadweard Muybridge. More than 4,500 stopped-action photos, in action series, showing undraped men, women, children jumping, lying down, throwing, sitting, wrestling, carrying, etc. 390pp. 7⅞ × 10⅝. 20204-6 Clothbd. $24.95

TREES OF THE EASTERN AND CENTRAL UNITED STATES AND CANADA, William M. Harlow. Best one-volume guide to 140 trees. Full descriptions, woodlore, range, etc. Over 600 illustrations. Handy size. 288pp. 4½ × 6⅜. 20395-6 Pa. $5.95

SONGS OF WESTERN BIRDS, Dr. Donald J. Borror. Complete song and call repertoire of 60 western species, including flycatchers, juncoes, cactus wrens, many more—includes fully illustrated booklet. Cassette and manual 99913-0 $8.95

GROWING AND USING HERBS AND SPICES, Milo Miloradovich. Versatile handbook provides all the information needed for cultivation and use of all the herbs and spices available in North America. 4 illustrations. Index. Glossary. 236pp. 5⅜ × 8½. 25058-X Pa. $6.95

BIG BOOK OF MAZES AND LABYRINTHS, Walter Shepherd. 50 mazes and labyrinths in all—classical, solid, ripple, and more—in one great volume. Perfect inexpensive puzzler for clever youngsters. Full solutions. 112pp. 8⅛ × 11. 22951-3 Pa. $4.95

CATALOG OF DOVER BOOKS

PIANO TUNING, J. Cree Fischer. Clearest, best book for beginner, amateur. Simple repairs, raising dropped notes, tuning by easy method of flattened fifths. No previous skills needed. 4 illustrations. 201pp. 5⅜ × 8½. 23267-0 Pa. $5.95

A SOURCE BOOK IN THEATRICAL HISTORY, A. M. Nagler. Contemporary observers on acting, directing, make-up, costuming, stage props, machinery, scene design, from Ancient Greece to Chekhov. 611pp. 5⅜ × 8½. 20515-0 Pa. $11.95

THE COMPLETE NONSENSE OF EDWARD LEAR, Edward Lear. All nonsense limericks, zany alphabets, Owl and Pussycat, songs, nonsense botany, etc., illustrated by Lear. Total of 320pp. 5⅜ × 8½. (USO) 20167-8 Pa. $6.95

VICTORIAN PARLOUR POETRY: An Annotated Anthology, Michael R. Turner. 117 gems by Longfellow, Tennyson, Browning, many lesser-known poets. "The Village Blacksmith," "Curfew Must Not Ring Tonight," "Only a Baby Small," dozens more, often difficult to find elsewhere. Index of poets, titles, first lines. xxiii + 325pp. 5⅜ × 8¼. 27044-0 Pa. $8.95

DUBLINERS, James Joyce. Fifteen stories offer vivid, tightly focused observations of the lives of Dublin's poorer classes. At least one, "The Dead," is considered a masterpiece. Reprinted complete and unabridged from standard edition. 160pp. 5³⁄₁₆ × 8¼. 26870-5 Pa. $1.00

THE HAUNTED MONASTERY and THE CHINESE MAZE MURDERS, Robert van Gulik. Two full novels by van Gulik, set in 7th-century China, continue adventures of Judge Dee and his companions. An evil Taoist monastery, seemingly supernatural events; overgrown topiary maze hides strange crimes. 27 illustrations. 328pp. 5⅜ × 8½. 23502-5 Pa. $7.95

THE BOOK OF THE SACRED MAGIC OF ABRAMELIN THE MAGE, translated by S. MacGregor Mathers. Medieval manuscript of ceremonial magic. Basic document in Aleister Crowley, Golden Dawn groups. 268pp. 5⅜ × 8½. 23211-5 Pa. $8.95

NEW RUSSIAN-ENGLISH AND ENGLISH-RUSSIAN DICTIONARY, M. A. O'Brien. This is a remarkably handy Russian dictionary, containing a surprising amount of information, including over 70,000 entries. 366pp. 4½ × 6⅛. 20208-9 Pa. $9.95

HISTORIC HOMES OF THE AMERICAN PRESIDENTS, Second, Revised Edition, Irvin Haas. A traveler's guide to American Presidential homes, most open to the public, depicting and describing homes occupied by every American President from George Washington to George Bush. With visiting hours, admission charges, travel routes. 175 photographs. Index. 160pp. 8¼ × 11. 26751-2 Pa. $10.95

NEW YORK IN THE FORTIES, Andreas Feininger. 162 brilliant photographs by the well-known photographer, formerly with *Life* magazine. Commuters, shoppers, Times Square at night, much else from city at its peak. Captions by John von Hartz. 181pp. 9¼ × 10¾. 23585-8 Pa. $12.95

INDIAN SIGN LANGUAGE, William Tomkins. Over 525 signs developed by Sioux and other tribes. Written instructions and diagrams. Also 290 pictographs. 111pp. 6⅛ × 9¼. 22029-X Pa. $3.50

CATALOG OF DOVER BOOKS

ANATOMY: A Complete Guide for Artists, Joseph Sheppard. A master of figure drawing shows artists how to render human anatomy convincingly. Over 460 illustrations. 224pp. 8⅜ × 11¼. 27279-6 Pa. $10.95

MEDIEVAL CALLIGRAPHY: Its History and Technique, Marc Drogin. Spirited history, comprehensive instruction manual covers 13 styles (ca. 4th century thru 15th). Excellent photographs; directions for duplicating medieval techniques with modern tools. 224pp. 8⅜ × 11¼. 26142-5 Pa. $11.95

DRIED FLOWERS: How to Prepare Them, Sarah Whitlock and Martha Rankin. Complete instructions on how to use silica gel, meal and borax, perlite aggregate, sand and borax, glycerine and water to create attractive permanent flower arrangements. 12 illustrations. 32pp. 5⅜ × 8½. 21802-3 Pa. $1.00

EASY-TO-MAKE BIRD FEEDERS FOR WOODWORKERS, Scott D. Campbell. Detailed, simple-to-use guide for designing, constructing, caring for and using feeders. Text, illustrations for 12 classic and contemporary designs. 96pp. 5⅜ × 8½. 25847-5 Pa. $2.95

OLD-TIME CRAFTS AND TRADES, Peter Stockham. An 1807 book created to teach children about crafts and trades open to them as future careers. It describes in detailed, nontechnical terms 24 different occupations, among them coachmaker, gardener, hairdresser, lacemaker, shoemaker, wheelwright, copper-plate printer, milliner, trunkmaker, merchant and brewer. Finely detailed engravings illustrate each occupation. 192pp. 4⅝ × 6. 27398-9 Pa. $4.95

THE HISTORY OF UNDERCLOTHES, C. Willett Cunnington and Phyllis Cunnington. Fascinating, well-documented survey covering six centuries of English undergarments, enhanced with over 100 illustrations: 12th-century laced-up bodice, footed long drawers (1795), 19th-century bustles, 19th-century corsets for men, Victorian "bust improvers," much more. 272pp. 5⅜ × 8¼. 27124-2 Pa. $9.95

ARTS AND CRAFTS FURNITURE: The Complete Brooks Catalog of 1912, Brooks Manufacturing Co. Photos and detailed descriptions of more than 150 now very collectible furniture designs from the Arts and Crafts movement depict davenports, settees, buffets, desks, tables, chairs, bedsteads, dressers and more, all built of solid, quarter-sawed oak. Invaluable for students and enthusiasts of antiques, Americana and the decorative arts. 80pp. 6½ × 9¼. 27471-3 Pa. $7.95

HOW WE INVENTED THE AIRPLANE: An Illustrated History, Orville Wright. Fascinating firsthand account covers early experiments, construction of planes and motors, first flights, much more. Introduction and commentary by Fred C. Kelly. 76 photographs. 96pp. 8¼ × 11. 25662-6 Pa. $8.95

THE ARTS OF THE SAILOR: Knotting, Splicing and Ropework, Hervey Garrett Smith. Indispensable shipboard reference covers tools, basic knots and useful hitches; handsewing and canvas work, more. Over 100 illustrations. Delightful reading for sea lovers. 256pp. 5⅜ × 8½. 26440-8 Pa. $7.95

FRANK LLOYD WRIGHT'S FALLINGWATER: The House and Its History, Second, Revised Edition, Donald Hoffmann. A total revision—both in text and illustrations—of the standard document on Fallingwater, the boldest, most personal architectural statement of Wright's mature years, updated with valuable new material from the recently opened Frank Lloyd Wright Archives. "Fascinating"—*The New York Times.* 116 illustrations. 128pp. 9¼ × 10¾. 27430-6 Pa. $10.95

PHOTOGRAPHIC SKETCHBOOK OF THE CIVIL WAR, Alexander Gardner. 100 photos taken on field during the Civil War. Famous shots of Manassas, Harper's Ferry, Lincoln, Richmond, slave pens, etc. 244pp. 10⅝ × 8¼.
22731-6 Pa. $9.95

FIVE ACRES AND INDEPENDENCE, Maurice G. Kains. Great back-to-the-land classic explains basics of self-sufficient farming. The one book to get. 95 illustrations. 397pp. 5⅜ × 8½. 20974-1 Pa. $7.95

SONGS OF EASTERN BIRDS, Dr. Donald J. Borror. Songs and calls of 60 species most common to eastern U.S.: warblers, woodpeckers, flycatchers, thrushes, larks, many more in high-quality recording. Cassette and manual 99912-2 $8.95

A MODERN HERBAL, Margaret Grieve. Much the fullest, most exact, most useful compilation of herbal material. Gigantic alphabetical encyclopedia, from aconite to zedoary, gives botanical information, medical properties, folklore, economic uses, much else. Indispensable to serious reader. 161 illustrations. 888pp. 6½ × 9¼. 2-vol. set. (USO) Vol. I: 22798-7 Pa. $9.95
Vol. II: 22799-5 Pa. $9.95

HIDDEN TREASURE MAZE BOOK, Dave Phillips. Solve 34 challenging mazes accompanied by heroic tales of adventure. Evil dragons, people-eating plants, bloodthirsty giants, many more dangerous adversaries lurk at every twist and turn. 34 mazes, stories, solutions. 48pp. 8¼ × 11. 24566-7 Pa. $2.95

LETTERS OF W. A. MOZART, Wolfgang A. Mozart. Remarkable letters show bawdy wit, humor, imagination, musical insights, contemporary musical world; includes some letters from Leopold Mozart. 276pp. 5⅜ × 8½. 22859-2 Pa. $7.95

BASIC PRINCIPLES OF CLASSICAL BALLET, Agrippina Vaganova. Great Russian theoretician, teacher explains methods for teaching classical ballet. 118 illustrations. 175pp. 5⅜ × 8½. 22036-2 Pa. $4.95

THE JUMPING FROG, Mark Twain. Revenge edition. The original story of The Celebrated Jumping Frog of Calaveras County, a hapless French translation, and Twain's hilarious "retranslation" from the French. 12 illustrations. 66pp. 5⅜ × 8½. 22686-7 Pa. $3.95

BEST REMEMBERED POEMS, Martin Gardner (ed.). The 126 poems in this superb collection of 19th- and 20th-century British and American verse range from Shelley's "To a Skylark" to the impassioned "Renascence" of Edna St. Vincent Millay and to Edward Lear's whimsical "The Owl and the Pussycat." 224pp. 5⅜ × 8½. 27165-X Pa. $4.95

COMPLETE SONNETS, William Shakespeare. Over 150 exquisite poems deal with love, friendship, the tyranny of time, beauty's evanescence, death and other themes in language of remarkable power, precision and beauty. Glossary of archaic terms. 80pp. 5³⁄₁₆ × 8¼. 26686-9 Pa. $1.00

BODIES IN A BOOKSHOP, R. T. Campbell. Challenging mystery of blackmail and murder with ingenious plot and superbly drawn characters. In the best tradition of British suspense fiction. 192pp. 5⅜ × 8½. 24720-1 Pa. $5.95

THE WIT AND HUMOR OF OSCAR WILDE, Alvin Redman (ed.). More than 1,000 ripostes, paradoxes, wisecracks: Work is the curse of the drinking classes; I can resist everything except temptation; etc. 258pp. 5⅜ × 8½. **20602-5 Pa. $5.95**

SHAKESPEARE LEXICON AND QUOTATION DICTIONARY, Alexander Schmidt. Full definitions, locations, shades of meaning in every word in plays and poems. More than 50,000 exact quotations. 1,485pp. 6½ × 9¼. 2-vol. set.
Vol. I: **22726-X Pa. $16.95**
Vol. 2: 22727-8 Pa. $15.95

SELECTED POEMS, Emily Dickinson. Over 100 best-known, best-loved poems by one of America's foremost poets, reprinted from authoritative early editions. No comparable edition at this price. Index of first lines. 64pp. 5$^{3}/_{16}$ × 8¼. 26466-1 Pa. $1.00

CELEBRATED CASES OF JUDGE DEE (DEE GOONG AN), translated by Robert van Gulik. Authentic 18th-century Chinese detective novel; Dee and associates solve three interlocked cases. Led to van Gulik's own stories with same characters. Extensive introduction. 9 illustrations. 237pp. 5⅜ × 8½. **23337-5 Pa. $6.95**

THE MALLEUS MALEFICARUM OF KRAMER AND SPRENGER, translated by Montague Summers. Full text of most important witchhunter's "bible," used by both Catholics and Protestants. 278pp. 6⅝ × 10. **22802-9 Pa. $11.95**

SPANISH STORIES/CUENTOS ESPAÑOLES: A Dual-Language Book, Angel Flores (ed.). Unique format offers 13 great stories in Spanish by Cervantes, Borges, others. Faithful English translations on facing pages. 352pp. 5⅜ × 8½. **25399-6 Pa. $8.95**

THE CHICAGO WORLD'S FAIR OF 1893: A Photographic Record, Stanley Appelbaum (ed.). 128 rare photos show 200 buildings, Beaux-Arts architecture, Midway, original Ferris Wheel, Edison's kinetoscope, more. Architectural emphasis; full text. 116pp. 8¼ × 11. 23990-X Pa. $9.95

OLD QUEENS, N.Y., IN EARLY PHOTOGRAPHS, Vincent F. Seyfried and William Asadorian. Over 160 rare photographs of Maspeth, Jamaica, Jackson Heights, and other areas. Vintage views of DeWitt Clinton mansion, 1939 World's Fair and more. Captions. 192pp. 8⅞ × 11. 26358-4 Pa. $12.95

CAPTURED BY THE INDIANS: 15 Firsthand Accounts, 1750–1870, Frederick Drimmer. Astounding true historical accounts of grisly torture, bloody conflicts, relentless pursuits, miraculous escapes and more, by people who lived to tell the tale. 384pp. 5⅜ × 8½. **24901-8 Pa. $8.95**

THE WORLD'S GREAT SPEECHES, Lewis Copeland and Lawrence W. Lamm (eds.). Vast collection of 278 speeches of Greeks to 1970. Powerful and effective models; unique look at history. 842pp. 5⅜ × 8½. **20468-5 Pa. $14.95**

THE BOOK OF THE SWORD, Sir Richard F. Burton. Great Victorian scholar/adventurer's eloquent, erudite history of the "queen of weapons"—from prehistory to early Roman Empire. Evolution and development of early swords, variations (sabre, broadsword, cutlass, scimitar, etc.), much more. 336pp. 6⅛ × 9¼. **25434-8 Pa. $8.95**

CATALOG OF DOVER BOOKS

AUTOBIOGRAPHY: The Story of My Experiments with Truth, Mohandas K. Gandhi. Boyhood, legal studies, purification, the growth of the Satyagraha (nonviolent protest) movement. Critical, inspiring work of the man responsible for the freedom of India. 480pp. 5⅜ × 8½. (USO)　　　　24593-4 Pa. $8.95

CELTIC MYTHS AND LEGENDS, T. W. Rolleston. Masterful retelling of Irish and Welsh stories and tales. Cuchulain, King Arthur, Deirdre, the Grail, many more. First paperback edition. 58 full-page illustrations. 512pp. 5⅜ × 8½.
26507-2 Pa. $9.95

THE PRINCIPLES OF PSYCHOLOGY, William James. Famous long course complete, unabridged. Stream of thought, time perception, memory, experimental methods; great work decades ahead of its time. 94 figures. 1,391pp. 5⅜×8½. 2-vol. set.
Vol. I: 20381-6 Pa. $12.95
Vol. II: 20382-4 Pa. $12.95

THE WORLD AS WILL AND REPRESENTATION, Arthur Schopenhauer. Definitive English translation of Schopenhauer's life work, correcting more than 1,000 errors, omissions in earlier translations. Translated by E. F. J. Payne. Total of 1,269pp. 5⅜ × 8½. 2-vol. set.　　　Vol. 1: 21761-2 Pa. $11.95
Vol. 2: 21762-0 Pa. $11.95

MAGIC AND MYSTERY IN TIBET, Madame Alexandra David-Neel. Experiences among lamas, magicians, sages, sorcerers, Bonpa wizards. A true psychic discovery. 32 illustrations. 321pp. 5⅜ × 8½. (USO)　　　　22682-4 Pa. $8.95

THE EGYPTIAN BOOK OF THE DEAD, E. A. Wallis Budge. Complete reproduction of Ani's papyrus, finest ever found. Full hieroglyphic text, interlinear transliteration, word-for-word translation, smooth translation. 533pp. 6½ × 9¼.
21866-X Pa. $9.95

MATHEMATICS FOR THE NONMATHEMATICIAN, Morris Kline. Detailed, college-level treatment of mathematics in cultural and historical context, with numerous exercises. Recommended Reading Lists. Tables. Numerous figures. 641pp. 5⅜ × 8½.　　　　24823-2 Pa. $11.95

THEORY OF WING SECTIONS: Including a Summary of Airfoil Data, Ira H. Abbott and A. E. von Doenhoff. Concise compilation of subsonic aerodynamic characteristics of NACA wing sections, plus description of theory. 350pp. of tables. 693pp. 5⅜ × 8½.　　　　60586-8 Pa. $14.95

THE RIME OF THE ANCIENT MARINER, Gustave Doré, S. T. Coleridge. Doré's finest work; 34 plates capture moods, subtleties of poem. Flawless full-size reproductions printed on facing pages with authoritative text of poem. "Beautiful. Simply beautiful."—*Publisher's Weekly.* 77pp. 9¼ × 12.　　22305-1 Pa. $6.95

NORTH AMERICAN INDIAN DESIGNS FOR ARTISTS AND CRAFTS-PEOPLE, Eva Wilson. Over 360 authentic copyright-free designs adapted from Navajo blankets, Hopi pottery, Sioux buffalo hides, more. Geometrics, symbolic figures, plant and animal motifs, etc. 128pp. 8⅜ × 11. (EUK)　25341-4 Pa. $7.95

SCULPTURE: Principles and Practice, Louis Slobodkin. Step-by-step approach to clay, plaster, metals, stone; classical and modern. 253 drawings, photos. 255pp. 8⅛ × 11.　　　　22960-2 Pa. $10.95

CATALOG OF DOVER BOOKS

THE INFLUENCE OF SEA POWER UPON HISTORY, 1660-1783, A. T. Mahan. Influential classic of naval history and tactics still used as text in war colleges. First paperback edition. 4 maps. 24 battle plans. 640pp. 5⅜ × 8½.
25509-3 Pa. $12.95

THE STORY OF THE TITANIC AS TOLD BY ITS SURVIVORS, Jack Winocour (ed.). What it was really like. Panic, despair, shocking inefficiency, and a little heroism. More thrilling than any fictional account. 26 illustrations. 320pp. 5⅜ × 8½.
20610-6 Pa. $8.95

FAIRY AND FOLK TALES OF THE IRISH PEASANTRY, William Butler Yeats (ed.). Treasury of 64 tales from the twilight world of Celtic myth and legend: "The Soul Cages," "The Kildare Pooka," "King O'Toole and his Goose," many more. Introduction and Notes by W. B. Yeats. 352pp. 5⅜ × 8½.
26941-8 Pa. $8.95

BUDDHIST MAHAYANA TEXTS, E. B. Cowell and Others (eds.). Superb, accurate translations of basic documents in Mahayana Buddhism, highly important in history of religions. The Buddha-karita of Asvaghosha, Larger Sukhavativyuha, more. 448pp. 5⅜ × 8½. ,
25552-2 Pa. $9.95

ONE TWO THREE . . . INFINITY: Facts and Speculations of Science, George Gamow. Great physicist's fascinating, readable overview of contemporary science: number theory, relativity, fourth dimension, entropy, genes, atomic structure, much more. 128 illustrations. Index. 352pp. 5⅜ × 8½.
25664-2 Pa. $8.95

ENGINEERING IN HISTORY, Richard Shelton Kirby, et al. Broad, nontechnical survey of history's major technological advances: birth of Greek science, industrial revolution, electricity and applied science, 20th-century automation, much more. 181 illustrations. ". . . excellent . . ."—Isis. Bibliography. vii + 530pp. 5⅜ × 8¼.
26412-2 Pa. $14.95